Lord Carteret, a political biography, 1690-1763

Archibald Ballantyne

LORD CARTERET

PRINTED BY
SPOTTISWOODE AND CO., NEW STREET SQUARE
LONDON

LORD CARTER

A POLITICAL BIOGRAPHY

1690 — 1763

BY

ARCHIBALD BALLANTYNE

LONDON

RICHARD BENTLEY & SON, NEW BURLINGTO.

Publishers in Ordinary to Her Majesty the Queen

1887

'High above each in genius, lore, and fire,
With mind of muscles which no toil could tire,
With lips that seem'd like Homer's gods to quaff
From nectar urns the unextinguish'd laugh,
Frank with the mirth of souls divinely strong,
CARTERET's large presence floats from out the throng.'

LORD LYTTON: *St. Stephen's.*

PREFACE

———◆———

THE almost complete oblivion which covers the career of Lord Carteret is one of the curiosities of English political and historical literature. Few names were better known than his in the political world of his own day, no English statesman of his time had so wide a European reputation. Posterity has exacted an exaggerated revenge; for no first-rate statesman of the modern epoch has failed so completely to secure a place in its capricious memory. One still vaguely recollects that Dr Johnson disliked the word Carteret when used as a dactyl; one remembers a few paragraphs of Macaulay's characteristic rhetoric, or two or three of Horace Walpole's femininely exaggerated anecdotes But Carteret himself and his fifty years of public life are practically forgotten With one exception, the modern historians of the times in which he lived have not cared to make more than mere passing and second-hand allusion to him; and the one exception—Carlyle in his *Frederick the Great*—is concerned with only two or three years and one or two incidents of Carteret's career. The other writers, when Carteret comes in the way of their historical narrative, either dismiss him in a few lines of conventionally balanced epithets, or sketch a figure so full of distortions and contradictions as to be a mere fantastic impossibility

It is exceedingly easy to forget many of the men who played a political part in England under the first two Georges Wilmington, who was actually Prime Minister for a year or so, is now not even the shadow of a name No one willingly would remember Chancellor of the Exchequer Sandys, or Bubb Dodington, or Sir Thomas Robinson. Henry Pelham was a respectable but uninteresting mediocrity.   To his brother the Duke of Newcastle an amused posterity has indeed almost gratefully granted a unique fame as the most curiously ridiculous being who ever took a leading part in public affairs, the most foolish as well as the falsest of politicians, the most imbecile even of political Dukes. But it seems a pity that Carteret's name should be added to this dreary and uninviting list of extinct reputations. For Carteret was the most brilliant man of affairs of his time, equally conspicuous for bright genius and for homely, practical common-sense. He was an accomplished classical scholar ; an easy master of European languages ; completely at home in history, law, literature ; the friend of Berkeley, Bentley, Addison, Gay, Pope ; the chosen personal though not political friend of Swift ; a generous, competent patron of men of letters ; full of frankness and ease and good-nature, so that even his political enemies could not hate him ; yet always dignified and refined and commanding. 'I feel a pride,' the Earl of Chatham once said in the House of Lords, long after Carteret was dead, 'in declaring that to his patronage, to his friendship and instruction I owe whatever I am.' Horace Walpole reckoned that in all his life he had seen only five great men, and that the greatest genius of the five was Carteret. Chesterfield was by no means inclined to an indulgent estimate of Carteret; yet in the last days of Carteret's life Chesterfield wrote to his son: 'Lord Granville [Carteret] they say is dying. When he dies, the ablest head in England dies too, take it for all in all.' 'Since Granville was turned out,' wrote Smollett in *Humphrey Clinker*, 'there has been no minister in this nation worth the meal that whitened his periwig.' To Dr. Johnson doubtless Carteret was one of those vile Whigs of whom the Devil was the first; yet Johnson's recognitions of Carteret are generous enough; while Swift, also removed from Carteret in political opinion, was his intimate personal friend, and repeatedly expresses his admiration for his character, learning, and genius. Among later writers, Carlyle, though always very reserved in his estimates of eighteenth-century men, is quite unstinted in his appreciation of Carteret. He groups him among the Fredericks, the Voltaires, the Chathams, as one of the not too numerous men of his time in whom there was 'an effective stroke of work, a fine fire of heroic pride;' and in the impersonal way in which he reveals his own opinions, Carlyle speaks of Carteret as 'thought by some to be, with the one exception of Lord Chatham, the wisest Foreign Secretary we ever had.' Yet the statesman who is thus praised by men who do not praise lightly is now unremembered; the very books of reference are in a conspiracy of silence about him; and

the present is the first attempt which has been made
to give any complete and connected account of his
career

It therefore seems desirable to make some slight
reference to the chief printed and manuscript authorities on which the following pages are mainly based. To
draw up a list which should include the many ephemer-
ral and obsolete productions which have been consulted
would be absurd   Of special value are the Works of
Horace Walpole, particularly his Correspondence and
his Last Ten Years of the Reign of George II ; but
Horace Walpole, especially when he is dealing with
personal questions, must always be used with care.   In
the Works of Swift, Carteret's intimate friend, there are
some few letters from and to Carteret ; but most of the
correspondence between the two men must be either
unprinted or lost.   Carteret is, however, the subject of
one of Swift's ironically humorous pamphlets.   Arch-
deacon Coxe's voluminous and chaotic Memoirs of Sir
Robert Walpole and of the Pelhams are absolutely
valueless from the literary point of view ; but they are
essential to a knowledge of Carteret's time because of
the original material to which Coxe had access   The
same distressing writer's Memoirs of Sir Robert's less-
known brother Horatio (*old* Horace as he is generally
called, to distinguish him from his nephew Horace
the letter-writer) have some slight concern with Carteret
and his fortunes   Lord Shelburne's Autobiography (in
Lord Edmond Fitzmaurice's Life of Shelburne) contains
some curious and interesting particulars , and Lord
Hervey's Memoirs of the Reign of George II. are of

course indispensable, though Hervey can seldom spare a good word for any opponent of Walpole. Earl Waldegrave's Memoirs, the Earl of Marchmont's Diary, and the Marchmont Papers are also useful. And further may be mentioned: The Parliamentary History; the Works of Chesterfield; Sir R. J. Phillimore's Memoirs of Lord Lyttelton; Harris's Life of Lord Chancellor Hardwicke; J. M. Graham's Annals and Correspondence of the Earls of Stair; Sheridan's Life of Swift; the Letters of the Irish Primate, Hugh Boulter; and Mrs. Delany's Autobiography and Correspondence.

Of unpublished materials, the Carteret Papers in the British Museum are essential for a real knowledge of Carteret's political life. These Papers consist of thirty-four volumes, and are numbered Additional MSS. 22,511–22,545. They contain Carteret's official correspondence during the various periods for which he held office between 1719 and 1744. They are full on all points of his public policy, but have hardly any private or personal details. The voluminous set of manuscripts known as Coxe's Collections offers a good deal of welcome assistance, and is specially useful for part of the time during which Carteret was Lord-Lieutenant of Ireland. The Manuscripts at the Record Office supply some of the defects of the British Museum Collections for this special period. Scattered letters from and to Carteret, and letters containing facts and criticisms concerning him, are to be found in almost countless volumes of the Museum's Additional and Egerton Manuscripts. References to the more important of these are given in

It only remains to add that the chief object of the present biography is not to throw any fresh light on the general history of the times in which Carteret lived, but, so far as it is possible now to do so, to recover from a really undeserved forgetfulness some idea of Carteret himself, and of a character and a career which only a few names in modern English politics exceed in interest and in varied attractiveness

A. B

CONTENTS

LORD CARTERET.

CHAPTER I.

EARLY LIFE AND WORK IN PARLIAMENT.

1690–1716.

JOHN, LORD CARTERET, EARL GRANVILLE, was descended
from two noble and ancient families, each of which had
on various occasions risen to high distinction in the
political history of England. The Carterets and the
Granvilles were both Norman houses; the towns of
Granville and Carteret still commemorate their names
in Normandy. The Carterets, some of them accompanying their Norman duke into England, and all of
them, in the troubled times that followed, remaining
faithful to the newly established line of kings in England, gradually lost their Norman possessions on the
mainland, and settled chiefly in the largest of the
Channel Islands, almost within sight of their old home.
They became the commanding family in Jersey, where
part of their principal seat, the manor house of St.
Ouen, may still be seen; and many romantic as well as
historical tales are told of their life and exploits there.
Romance, perhaps, has played its accustomed part in
giving picturesque embellishment to some of the family
annal

actual history have nothing prosaic about them. Their
loyalty was very conspicuous. George III. was not
using the language of exaggerated compliment when he
once said of a member of the Carteret house: 'This
young man belongs to one of the most ancient and
most loyal families in my dominions.' The never-falsi-
fied motto of the Carterets was *Loyal devoir* They
kept Jersey out of the hands of Constable Bertrand du
Guesclin; and eight Carterets, Reginald de Carteret
and his seven sons, were knighted in one day by
Edward III. for this feat Over and over again they
foiled French attempts on the Channel Islands, and
received many royal recognitions of their bravery and
loyalty. Queen Elizabeth gave them the island of
Sark, and the practical governorship of Jersey was
frequently in their family. One of them was governor
there when Prynne, who had attacked plays and
masques in his puritanical *Histrio-mastix*, was imprisoned from 1637 to 1640 in Mont Orgueil Castle,
one of the two chief fortresses of Jersey A terribly
gloomy cell in Mont Orgueil is still shown as the apartment in which Prynne was confined; but the dreariness
of his imprisonment was considerably lessened by the
kindness of Sir Philip Carteret and his family, whom
Prynne is never weary of thanking 'for all your love
and courtesy' They often invited him to pass his time
with them, and it seems that Lady Carteret's irresistible
goodness occasionally seduced the stern pamphleteer to
an unpuritanical game of cards Prynne wrote, in a
distressingly unpoetical manner, a metrical description
of the very picturesque fortress where his confinement
was thus pleasantly tempered, and dedicated his wonderful rhymes to his 'ever honoured worthy friend, Sir
Philip Carteret,' and to Sir Philip's wife, Prynne's 'most

highly honoured, special kind friend, the truly virtuous and religious Lady Anne Carteret.' Others of Prynne's astonishing metrical productions were dedicated to the daughters of his kindly custodians; one of them to

> Sweet mistress Douce, fair Margaret,
> Prime flower of the house of Carteret.

General history, however, has dropped from its memory the story of the career of the Carterets in the Channel Islands; and the very faint surviving recollection even of the name of the family is mainly due to two such very dissimilar books as Pepys' *Diary* and Lord Clarendon's *History of the Rebellion* In these two books the name of a Sir George Carteret is of very frequent recurrence. This Sir George Carteret, almost more royalist than the King, was prominently connected with the two unhappy Charleses who were successive Stuart sovereigns of England When the civil war broke out, the parliament desired to give to Carteret, who was controller of the navy, the position of vice-admiral. He thought it his duty first to ask the King's consent, and Charles, who reckoned his fleet as good as lost to him, ordered Carteret to decline. A mistake on the King's part, thought Clarendon and many others; for, if Carteret had been permitted to accept the appointment, it was commonly believed that he would have kept the greater part of the fleet true to the King, —'his interest and reputation in the navy was so great, and his diligence and dexterity in command so eminent.'[1] Carteret retired to his Jersey home to raise forces for his master; and his energetic proceedings there and in the Channel so exasperated the parliamentary authorities that in all the fruitless peace

[1] Clarendon *History of the Rebellion* III 116 Ch O edition 1826

negotiations Carteret's name was in the list of those
for whom there could be no pardon   When in April
1646 the boy Prince of Wales, insecure even in the
Scilly Islands, wandered as far as Jersey for safety,
Sir George Carteret gladly entertained him in Elizabeth
Castle, where Charles, hardly yet sixteen years old, held
levées and dined in state, proving himself already a
proficient in the art of obtaining popularity; for, says
the old Jersey chronicler, *c'etoit un prince grandement
benin*.   Sir George Carteret got him a pleasure-boat
from St. Malo, and the Prince spent hours in steering
about the island-bays, but never venturing beyond
range of the Castle guns   He stayed more than two
months in Elizabeth Castle, and before taking leave of
his host created him a baronet , having already personally confirmed the knighthood which Charles I. had
only been able to bestow on Carteret by patent.   Some
of the Prince's exceedingly numerous retinue remained
behind in Jersey when Charles himself left to go to his
mother in Paris; among these being the Chancellor of
the Exchequer, Edward Hyde, who stayed in the island
for two years longer.   While Charles had been living
in the fortress with Sir George Carteret, Hyde's quarters
had been in the town of St. Helier's, from which at
high water Elizabeth Castle was entirely cut off   In
the evenings, when the tide was low, Hyde and the two
or three English friends who were with him walked
regularly upon the sands instead of supping, and often
found their way to the Castle and Sir George Carteret,
who received them always with unbounded kindness
When the departure of his friends left the Chancellor
somewhat solitary, Sir George Carteret invited Hyde to
leave the town altogether, and come to him in Elizabeth
Castle   Hyde gladly agreed, and stayed in the Castle

for two years ; quietly busy, seldom for less than ten hours in the day, with his books and his history ; amusing himself in spare moments with the cultivation of a minute garden of his own creation, and enjoying, as he himself used to say, the greatest tranquillity of mind imaginable In his own words, he 'remained there, to his wonderful contentment, in the very cheerful society of Sir George Carteret and his lady, in whose house he received all the liberty and entertainment he could have expected from his own family ; of which he always entertained so just a memory, that there was never any intermission or decay of that friendship he then made.'[1]

When Charles I. was executed, Sir George Carteret at once proclaimed King Charles II. in the Channel Islands, and the new nominal King, greatly perplexed where to find a safe refuge, remembered Carteret and his former quiet security in Jersey Accompanied this time by his brother, the Duke of York, Charles once more arrived in the island in September 1649 ; and in that same year made to Carteret one of his too facile promises, though in this instance his word was very fairly kept. He wrote to Carteret ——

'I will add this to you under my own hand, that I can never forget the good services you have done to my father and to me, and if God bless me [*which He did not*] you shall find I do remember them to the advantage of you and yours , and for this you have the word of your very loving friend,

'CHARLES R'[2]

This six months' residence with Carteret in Jersey

---

[1] Clarendon's *Life*, I. 207–208 Ed. Oxford, 1857.
[2] Brit. Museum, Add. MSS. 27,402. fol 124.

seems to have been one of the pleasanter episodes of
Charles's futile existence. Carteret managed affairs,
while the prince-king devoted himself to amusements.
He yachted round about the island, rambled with dogs
and guns after wild fowl, enjoying such quiet hospitality
as the families of the island could offer, and making
himself very popular among the people by his easy affa-
bility. Banquets and other entertainments were frequent at Elizabeth Castle, and Charles spent his time in
busy idleness, solaced by the talk and ways of his French
dwarf, and encouraging that mischievous little jester in
the congenial performance of practical jokes. The only
royal duty which the islanders exacted from their King
was to touch them for the king's evil. Before leaving
in February 1650, to start on his ten years' wanderings,
Charles made Sir George Carteret treasurer of his navy;
a rather barren honour at that time, for such navy as
Charles had consisted mainly of the fleet of privateers
which Carteret himself had got together. But ten
years later this distinction, and many others, became
real enough for Carteret

If his royal navy was rather phantasmal to Charles,
Carteret's frigates were exceedingly real to Cromwell.
The Protector now interfered in earnest, resolved to end
these spirited royalist proceedings in the Channel
Islands. In the closing months of 1651 a parliamentary
army was landed in Jersey, and one by one the island
fortresses were compelled to yield Still Sir George
Carteret was undaunted and shut himself up in Elizabeth Castle with a garrison of 340 men. He hoped that
of all the royal strongholds in the kingdom Elizabeth
Castle might be the last to surrender to the Parliament
For three months he was besieged, the enemy making
little or no impression upon him, till they brought

artillery far more powerful than anything that had yet been seen there, and from a neighbouring height poured down into the castle what Clarendon calls ' granadoes of a vast bigness,' and forced Carteret to submit. His little garrison surrendered in December 1651, but his ambition had been realised. He and his men were allowed honourable departure, and Carteret set out on European travels, to find his way at last to his roaming King in Holland.

The Restoration ended the wanderings of these two, and established Carteret's fortunes. He rode into London on Restoration Day with the King, and honours and official appointments were abundantly awarded him. Politically the most important of the various posts which he held was the Treasurership of the Navy ; and thus Pepys, a young subordinate at the Admiralty, was brought into very frequent intercourse with Carteret and received much personal kindness from him. Many pleasant allusions to the Carteret family occur in the garrulous gossiping of the *Diary*. Sir George and his wife, who also was his cousin and a Carteret, were both very good to the young Clerk of the Acts, and Pepys was not ungrateful, while he also was shrewd enough to put a high value on so desirable a friendship. 'I find,' Pepys writes of Sir George Carteret, ' that he do single me out to join with me apart from the rest, which I am much glad of.' Lady Carteret, thought Pepys, was ' the most kind lady in the world,' and her daughters' friendly cheerfulness often delighted him and made him ' mighty merry.' Enthusiastic Pepys was really sorry when at times his most kind lady in the world looked around her with a somewhat dejected anxiety, ' and I do comfort her as much as I can, for she is a noble lady.' But things were generally bright in that household, and Pepys enjoyed its unstinted hospitality. The conversation current in the house of one who, like Sir George Carteret, after very varied experience of men and manners, was now in the centre of English political life, was also much to Pepys' taste ; and perhaps the Carterets themselves at times found a passing amusement in slightly mystifying the innocent credulity of their frequent guest. But this was rare, and Pepys heartily congratulated himself on what he thought the really extraordinary goodwill and kindness with which the influential family treated him. 'Most extraordinary people they are,' he wrote, 'to continue friendship with, for goodness, virtue, and nobleness, and interest.

Pepys too introduces the next in the family line, Sir George Carteret's eldest son, Philip ; but is only particular over one episode in his career. This Sir Philip Carteret had, like his father, fought bravely in the Civil War, and had been knighted by Charles II in Jersey. With all that Pepys had nothing to do ; but when Sir Philip came to be married to the daughter of the Earl of Sandwich, the bustling importance of the diarist was quite in its element. To Sir Philip Carteret the necessary preliminaries of marriage were a much more difficult business than fighting, and he was glad to have Pepys to advise and instruct him in the usual formalities. Pepys found him a very modest man, 'of mighty good nature and pretty understanding ;' but he was far readier to give Pepys an account of the sea fights with the Dutch than to be conversationally enthusiastic over his own private prospects. But if Sir Philip was somewhat backward, the other members of the two families chiefly concerned were extremely interested in the affair. Lady Carteret could

not do enough for Lady Jemima Montagu 'But Lord!'
says Pepys, with his usual exclamation, 'to see how
kind my Lady Carteret is to her! Sends her most
rich jewels, and provides bedding and things of all
sorts most richly for her; which makes my Lady
[Sandwich] and me out of our wits almost to see the
kindness she treats us all with, as if they would buy the
young lady.' Pepys accompanied Sir Philip Carteret
on his first formal visit to Lady Jemima, and was
considerably surprised by his friend's unromantic proceedings. 'But Lord! what silly discourse we had as
to love-matters, he being the most awkward man ever
I met with in my life as to that business!' Neither
before nor after supper had the gentleman a word for
the lady, whom indeed he afterwards told Pepys that he
liked mightily; 'but Lord! in the dullest insipid manner that ever lover did.' The second day of their visit
was a Sunday, and Sir Philip was to take Lady Jemima
to church Pepys was minute in his previous instructions; told Sir Philip what compliments he was to pay,
how he was to lead the lady by the hand, and generally
make the best use of his happy opportunities Still the
terribly timid wooer was not very successful; but did
better in the afternoon, when the company considerately
left the two by themselves, 'and a little pretty daughter
of my Lady Wright's most innocently came out afterwards, and shut the door to. as if she had done it, poor
child, by inspiration: which made us without have
good sport to laugh at.' Before the two days' visit was
over, Pepys, who was himself distantly connected with
the Sandwich family, took Lady Jemima apart, and tried
to discover her feelings 'She blushed, and hid her face
awhile, but at last I forced her to tell me She answered that she could readily obey what her father and

mother had done; which was all she could say, or I
expect. So anon took leave, and for London In our
way Mr Carteret did give me mighty thanks for my
care and pains for him, and is mightily pleased.' Thus
with the minimum of demonstration, at least before third
parties, Sir Philip Carteret got a wife, who also seems to
have been of a pleasant gravity by nature, and the
sober and refined merriment of their wedding entertainment struck Pepys, who was present in his finest clothes,
as the most delightful thing in the world.

Sir Philip Carteret's career was honourably cut short
Fighting against the Dutch in Southwold Bay in 1672,
he was drowned, along with his father-in-law. He
might, like many others, have left the ship; but he
refused to desert the Earl of Sandwich. Of the short
life of his eldest son, almost nothing can be told. He
was born in 1667, and when only fifteen years old
was made a peer, with the style of Baron Carteret of
Hawnes, in Bedfordshire. Charles had intended a
similar honour for Sir George Carteret, but death had
interfered; and now this early peerage was granted to
Sir Philip's son as some acknowledgment of the distinguished services of his father and his grandfather
But George, this first Lord Carteret, did not live long
enough to take any part in public affairs or to associate
his name with history He died at the age of twenty-
six, having by his marriage united his family with that
of the Granvilles, and leaving behind him an eldest son,
John, the famous English statesman of the eighteenth
century.

The Granvilles, like the Carterets, were an ancient
Norman family, and traced their origin, in unbroken
line of honourable descent, back to Duke Rollo of Normandy Like the Carterets, also, the Granvilles had

been conspicuous for bravery and patriotism, and had written their names on many pages of English history. One of the heroes of their house was the famous Sir Richard Grenville, whose single-handed battle in the little *Revenge* against a Spanish fleet of fifty-three vessels was the most wonderful fighting exploit of the Elizabethan seamen 'At Flores, in the Azores,' with a little squadron of only six or seven ships, Lord Thomas Howard and Sir Richard Grenville found that the Spanish fleet was close upon them. Howard, unable to fight, put to sea Grenville, who had many of his Devonshire men sick on shore, waited to take them on board, and so was left alone, separated from the rest of the small squadron The Spaniards soon surrounded him From three o'clock in the afternoon of the last day of August, 1591, till next day's dawn, he fifteen times repulsed the whole Spanish fleet :—

And the sun went down, and the stars came out far over the
    summer sea,
But never a moment ceased the fight of the one and the fifty-
    three
Ship after ship, the whole night long, their high-built galleons
    came
Ship after ship, the whole night long, with her battle thunder
    and flame ,
Ship after ship, the whole night long, drew back with her dead
    and her shame
For some were sunk and many were shatter'd, and so could
    fight us no more——
God of battles, was ever a battle like this in the world before ?[1]

Grenville fought on, covered with wounds, till the little *Revenge* was a helpless rolling hulk Rather than yield to Spain, he wished to send himself, men, and ship to

[1] Tennyson: *The Revenge.*

the bottom; but the crew would not, and the one English ship struck to the Spanish fifty-three. Grenville died on board the Spanish fleet three days after his wonderful fight; and his dying words are his best memorial: 'Here die I, Richard Grenville, with a joyful and quiet mind; for that I have ended my life as a true soldier ought to do, fighting for his country, queen, religion and honour: my soul willingly departing from this body, leaving behind the lasting fame of having behaved as every valiant soldier is in duty bound to do.'

Grandson of this far-famed Sir Richard was the almost equally renowned Sir Bevil Granville, whose death in the battle of Lansdowne deprived the Royalists of all rejoicing in their victory. Where, asked exaggerative eulogy on the death of Sir Bevil—

Where shall the next famed Granville's ashes stand ?
Thy grandsire's fill the sea, and thine the land

Like all his family, Sir Bevil Granville was a devoted royalist; and, had he lived, he would have enjoyed such honours as his King could have given him A letter of thanks from Charles I was in Granville's pocket when he fell, and with it the patent which appointed him Earl of Bath The honour passed to Sir Bevil's son, who indeed was loaded with dignities ; being by birth Sir John Granville, and by position in the peerage the first Earl of Bath, Viscount Lansdowne, and Baron Granville. If it had been possible, this Sir John Granville would have excelled his father in devotion to the cause of the Stuarts He was commanding in the Scilly Islands when he heard of the execution of the King. With passionate indignation he immediately proclaimed King Charles II , as Sir George Carteret did in Jersey. He could not find words hard enough for Cromwell and the regicides. He wrote violently from Scilly when he heard the astonishing news :—

'The extraordinary ill news I have heard since my being here concerning the horrid murder and treason committed on the person of his most sacred majesty has transported me with grief . . . I hope God will revenge it on the heads of the damned authors and contrivers of it. . . . As soon as I was assured of this sad truth, and had solemnly paid here our abundant griefs in infinite tears, having commanded throughout these islands a day of mourning and humiliation for our most fatal and incomparable loss, I thought it my particular duty to proclaim his majesty that now is King.' [1]

In the negotiations which changed Charles II.'s titular majesty into as real a one as so merely titular a being as Charles could ever make it, Sir John Granville had a prominent part. Through all the details of the Restoration he was deep in the confidence of Charles and General Monk. He brought from Breda the royal letter of easy promises, easy to make and easy to forget ; and he received the public thanks of the House of Commons on what naturally, but too deceptively, seemed the happiest May-day that England had lately seen. He obtained the peerage which death had denied to his father, and his sisters were allowed to rank as Earl's daughters. From children of his there are still living many highly distinguished descendants; and his youngest daughter, Grace, was mother of John Lord Carteret.

George, first Lord Carteret, husband of Grace Granville, died at an early age in 1695. Their son John was born on April 22, 1690 : and he thus succeeded to the

---

[1] Brit. Mus. Egerton MSS 2,533, fol 474, v°.

barony of Carteret when less than five years old His school
life was passed at Westminster, a far more famous establishment then than in more recent times   Many of the
most distinguished Englishmen of the eighteenth century
had their earliest education at Westminster The school
was especially prolific in bishops and statesmen. Sprat,
bishop of Rochester, used to thank God that he was a
bishop, though he had *not* been educated at Westminster.
Many of those who in later life were closely connected
with Carteret's political fortunes had been boys at the
same school as himself Pulteney, who afterwards led
in the House of Commons the great opposition to Walpole, of which in the House of Lords Carteret was himself the head; the Duke of Newcastle, as false as he was
foolish, whose treachery and imbecility were equally
disturbing factors in Carteret's political career : Murray,
more famous as Lord Mansfield , Hervey, famous or infamous as 'Sporus' ; Prior and Atterbury, who touched
Carteret's life more lightly than these others. were all
Westminster boys   'Pray, don't you think Westminster
School to be the best school in England ? bookseller
Lintot once asked Pope in 1714. 'Most of the late
Ministry came out of it ; so did many of this Ministry.'
Bentley, who was to be Carteret's intimate friend, became
Master of Trinity when Carteret was ten years old ; and
Bentley says that in the earlier years of his mastership
the Westminster scholars gained the greater number of
the fellowships   In Carteret's school-days the head
master was Thomas Knipe; the second master, who soon
himself became the head, was the better known Dr.
Robert Friend, celebrated chiefly for his skill in classical
verse His Sapphics, written on Carteret's younger
brother, a Westminster scholar who died when only
nineteen. were reckoned the most favourable specimen

of his workmanship in elegant trifling, and have been approved by later authorities

The connection of Westminster was specially close with Christ Church and with Trinity College, Cambridge Carteret went to Christ Church No details of his university life are recoverable; but it is possible dimly to trace his friendship at ' the House' with Lord Hatton and with Edward Harley, only son of Queen Anne's statesman Carteret was at Oxford in 1709, the year of the terrible Malplaquet battle; and it was perhaps in the long vacation of that or the following year, when Anne dismissed the Whigs, and when Robert Harley and St. John became rival colleagues in power, that he wrote from Longleat ' to Mr. Harley at Christ Church in Oxford':—

'I now write at a venture, for I am not sure this will find you. I can never think that you are got privately again to Christ Church whilst the affairs of state are in such agitation; and if you are not, I won't advise you to go I rather could wish that as you imitate Apollo in some things, you would also imitate his tree:—

Parnassia laurus
Parva sub ingenti matris se subjicit umbra

I need put no comment to enable you to decypher my meaning. You'll pardon my making use of so rural an image. Sometimes one may compare great things to little without diminution.'[1]

There are no details of Carteret's Oxford life; but

---

[1] Harleian MSS 7,523, fol. 173. The only date is August 16. This letter is printed in the *Gentleman's Magazine* for 1779, p 283, and the date 1732 is there added This is impossible, for in 1732 'Mr Harley' had for eight years been Earl of Oxford He had become Lord Harley in 1711, and the letter must have been written before that The right date is probably August 16, 1710, the year and month of the change of government

he evidently did not make his residence the sinecure which his patrician position would have allowed and even encouraged. A nobleman at an English university in the eighteenth century could practically do what he liked, and many liked to do nothing. But Carteret must have worked hard. When he was Lord-Lieutenant of Ireland, his friend Swift, in a humorous vindication of Carteret's political conduct, wrote of him that from Oxford, 'with a singularity scarce to be justified, he carried away more Greek, Latin, and philosophy, than properly became a person of his rank; indeed much more of each than most of those who are forced to live by their learning will be at the unnecessary pains to load their heads with.'[1] In a letter to Carteret himself, recommending Berkeley, who was about to publish a little tract containing his whole scheme of a life 'academico-philosophical,' Swift adds in a parenthesis after these two words: 'I shall make you remember what you were.' No political enemy or anonymous libeller ever ventured to dispute Carteret's learning; and the foundation of his lasting delight in the poetry, oratory, and philosophy of the great classical authors was firmly laid at Oxford.

From Oxford Carteret seems to have come at once to London, and to have been received in the very best circles which London in Queen Anne's days could offer. With Swift, then in London on church business from Ireland, Carteret commenced an intimate and life-long friendship. Swift himself gives one or two glimpses of this early period of Carteret's London life. Gravely continuing his ironical vindication, Swift has to admit that Carteret, on his first appearance in the great world, split upon the rock of learning. 'For, as soon as he

[1] Swift's *Works*, VII. 281.

came to town, some bishops and clergymen, and other
persons most eminent for learning and parts, got him
among them' From these distinguished friends, however, and from London itself, Carteret vanished for a
little time ; for, young as he was. he at once settled down
in life, marrying at Longleat on October 17, 1710, Lady
Frances Worsley, granddaughter of the first Viscount
Weymouth. Then he returned to town and to politics.
A few slight references to him in 1711 and 1712 occur
in Swift's Journal to Stella. Carteret sets down Prior
in his chariot ; and Prior, who could pun and not be
ashamed, thanks him for his 'charioty.' Twice Carteret
dines with the Secretary, St. John, when the very small
circle of guests was on each occasion entirely selected
by Swift. Swift himself jestingly expresses his high
opinion of Carteret, who was still a young man under
age. ' I will tell you,' writes Swift to Stella, ' a good
thing I said to my Lord Carteret. " So," says he, " my
Lord ——— came up to me, and asked me, etc." " No,"
said I, " my Lord ——— never did, nor ever can *come up* to
you." We all pun here sometimes ' [1] For Lady Carteret
also, who was married before she was seventeen, Swift,
the intimate friend of her mother, had great respect
and admiration. A curious glimpse of social manners
in high life in the closing years of Queen Anne's reign
accidentally introduces Lady Carteret's name Swift
was dining with Lady Betty Germaine, and among the
company were the young Earl of Berkeley and his
Countess. ' Lady Berkeley after dinner clapped my hat
on another lady's head, and she in roguery put it upon

---

[1] To Stella, Jan. 4, 1710–11 The best of all puns is connected with
Carteret and Swift When Carteret was Lord-Lieutenant of Ireland, and was
entertaining once at the Castle, a lady's impetuous mantle overset a Cremona
fiddle. Swift repeated to himself Virgil's line —
    Mantua vae miserae nimium vicina Cremonae.

the rails. I minded them not, but in two minutes they
called me to the window, and Lady Carteret showed me
my hat out of her window five doors off, where I was
forced to walk to it, and pay her and old Lady Weymouth a visit.'[1]

Carteret took his seat in the House of Lords on May
25, 1711, a few weeks after he had attained his majority.
The previous year had produced a dramatically sudden
change in the state of English political affairs. From the
beginning of Anne's reign, and through the years made
eventful by Marlborough's victories, the fortunes of
the Whigs were aided by the success of Marlborough's
career. Marlborough was nominally, as Godolphin was
really, a Tory; the first of Queen Anne's parliaments
had a Tory majority. Yet the Tory ministers found
themselves gradually looking for their chief support
to the Whigs Godolphin and Marlborough practically
cared little about the differences of the Whig and Tory
party politics of their time. They put one question to
all political persons: Do you support the war or not?
The High Tories frigidly answered, No; the moderate
Tories did not profess any enthusiasm in the business.
It was a Whig war, King William's war; the Tories had
little relish for a war against the chief supporter of the
House of Stuart. Naturally the extreme Tories began
to drop away from the ministry Those of a milder
type still supported the Government; and in 1704 Harley and St. John joined it But the Whigs were becoming its main defence. In 1705 Cowper, the finest
Whig orator in the Commons, was made Lord Chancellor,
and in 1706 the Whig Sunderland, Carteret's special
friend, became Secretary of State But this union of
real Whigs and real and nominal Tories did not work

[1] Swift to Stella, June 6, 1711

very well. Harley's cautiously intriguing nature very soon proved dangerous The Whigs commonly called him the Trickster; he was a master of backstairs caballing; solemn, reserved, and mysterious. He carefully worked on the one subject which most touched the sluggishly feeble nature of the Queen. His measures, privately supported by his relation, Abigail Hill, Sarah of Marlborough's needy dependant and successful rival, confirmed Anne's natural inclination to the Tories by convincing her that under the Whigs the Church was in danger. Gradually Anne withdrew her confidence from her Whig ministers; and Harley, thinking his complete triumph sure, soon allowed himself to intrigue and manœuvre with very little attempt at concealment. But an accident for a short time interrupted his plans In spite of his solemn seriousness and assumption of mysterious profundity, he was incredibly careless in the performance of business, and managed his office so negligently that unscrupulous clerks found an opportunity of conveying secret information to the enemy No crime of this sort was proved against Harley personally; but Marlborough and Godolphin refused any longer to act with him Early in 1708 he was thus forced to resign, and St John resigned with him, being succeeded as Secretary at War by his life-long opponent Walpole. The general election of 1708 gave again a large Whig majority, and the fortunes of the party seemed firmly established

But a dramatic change soon followed Towards the close of 1709, Sacheverell, an extremely insignificant High Church clergyman, preached two foolishly ultra-Tory sermons, and, borrowing a nickname from Ben Jonson's famous play, alluded to Godolphin as Volpone. Sacheverell was an unimportant, ignorant man, whose fatal stupidity was probably at times amusing ; though it is hardly worth while to read his obsolete dis- courses for the sole satisfaction of finding the simile ' Like parallel lines meeting in a common centre ' To have treated him and his noisy Jacobitism with in- different contempt would have been the wiser way , but Godolphin was irritated by the nickname, and in oppo- sition to prudent advice resolved to prosecute him. Sacheverell was convicted ; but the very light sentence was reckoned as his practical victory, and a strong Tory reaction followed the ill-advised trial An impetus was thus given to the desires and plans of the Queen, Harley, and Mrs Masham. Anne dismissed Sunderland, and, though the Whigs remained for some months in office, they were no longer in power In August 1710 the Government fell ; Harley and St. John became the leaders of the new Tory administration ; and the general election of the same year gave to the Tory party an ascendency as complete as it was ephemeral

The new Government seemed to have a very firm seat in power when Carteret entered the House of Lords in May 1711 Carteret might naturally have been ex- pected to join the Tories His not very remote ancestors had been almost passionate in their Stuart loyalty. He had himself just come from the Tory and Jacobitical influences of Christ Church and Oxford. His relative George Granville, Lord Lansdown—Pope's ' Granville the polite '—was extreme in his devotion to the Tories, and was actually Secretary at War in the new Govern- ment. Swift was Carteret's personal friend, and was definitely relinquishing the Whigs ; and friendship with Swift had led to at least some intimacy with St. John. But Carteret throughout his career never allowed politi- cal considerations to interfere with his private friendships, and he was not now inclined to the Tory party because he was privately intimate with the Tory leaders. He did not perhaps at the very first definitely attach himself to either of the political parties. On some questions of minor importance he seems to have voted with the Court. But on the one domestic question of overpowering interest in the closing years of Queen Anne's reign, the question of the Protestant succession, Carteret unhesitatingly took his place among the Whigs.

The Whig party, when Carteret entered parliament, was divided, though the dividing-line did not appear very distinctly till George I. was on the throne. One Whig section was then clearly seen to be headed by Sunderland and Stanhope; another, by Walpole and his brother-in-law, Townshend. The rivalries of these four leaders were destined to end in open quarrels and political changes; but in 1711, when the Tories were in overwhelming force, the Whigs could not very well afford to quarrel among themselves. The more advanced and enlightened section was that to which Stanhope and Sunderland belonged, and these were the two statesmen with whom Carteret, in his earlier political career, was most closely connected. Charles, Earl of Sunderland, had proved the decisive triumph of the Whig element in the Government by his appointment as Secretary of State in 1706; and he was the first of the Whigs whom Anne, after Sacheverell's trial, ventured to dismiss. A man of strong temper and restlessly vehement, he was considered in those days as being even violent in Whiggism. Lord Shelburne wrote of him :—

'Lord Sunderland was not only the most intriguing, but the most passionate man of his time . . . Lord Holland, speaking of those times, said he once asked

Sir Robert Walpole why he never came to an understanding with Lord Sunderland. He answered, "You little know Lord Sunderland. If I had so much as hinted at it, his temper was so violent, that he would have done his best to throw me out of the window." [1]

Stanhope's early reputation had been made in war, the capture of Minorca in 1708 being his most notable performance. He had no special fitness for parliamentary management. The eager boldness which characterised him on the military side became, when applied to parliamentary affairs, a passionate impetuosity not too safely suitable even for quiet times, and in every way dangerous in the sudden storms of politics. He was brave and incorrupt: his knowledge of foreign affairs was large; but his chief distinction with posterity rests on his advocacy of religious toleration. Here he was much in advance of his time. He brought about the repeal of the educational persecution known as the Schism Act; he would have liked, if he could, to have modified the Test and Corporation Acts, and to have offered some tolerance to Roman Catholics and Dissenters. That proved impossible, but the fault was not Stanhope's.

Stanhope and Sunderland were leaders in the cause of the House of Hanover and the Protestant Succession. On this matter Carteret fully shared their views, and his first parliamentary work was concerned with this much and angrily debated subject. In the last years of Anne's reign, the political arrangement which had been devised to secure the succession of a Protestant sovereign seemed in considerable danger. In the very year in which Carteret took his seat, a Jacobite

[1] Shelburne's *Autobiography*; Lord E. Fitzmaurice's *Shelburne*, I., 34-35.

agent wrote that if the Pretender would only land with 10,000 men, not a sword would be drawn against him. The Roman Catholics, the landowners, the High Churchmen were to a large extent Jacobite. Anne herself was more than suspected of no particular devotion to the Act of Settlement and its favoured Hanoverians. With hardly an exception, the leading statesmen of her reign had been or were intriguers, or at least correspondents, with St. Germains. On St. John, most of all, Jacobite hopes were now confidently inclining to rest; St. John, who from the very formation of the Tory ministry had been in eager rivalry with Harley, and as Anne's reign drew towards its close was clearly getting the better of him. It does not seem open to doubt that if the Pretender could only have renounced his Catholic religion, the immense majority of the people would have declared for his succession. The ministry of course insisted that there was no danger; parliament and the Government, in wearisomely repeated debates, asserted their attachment to the Protestant cause; but there was a great air of unreality and insincerity about these formal periodical proceedings. One moment the House of Commons declared its devotion to the Hanoverian family; the next, it ordered Sacheverell to preach before it on Restoration Day. Royal speeches made the most satisfactory professions; but royal manners and actions did not care to correspond too closely with the royal words. When in 1713 the House of Lords, a far more liberal assembly than the House of Commons, wished Anne to urge friendly governments altogether to discountenance the Pretender, the Queen, not altogether untruly, but not at all reassuringly, replied that the best way to secure the Protestant succession would be to cease from animosities at home. The Lords were

told in language of conventional politeness to mind their
own affairs.   In such quarrelsome and contradictory circumstances, the general excitement increased daily, for
the question was highly interesting then, though it is
extremely dull now   Steele in 1713 produced the *Crisis*,
a now unreadable pamphlet, in support of the House
of Hanover   Swift anonymously replied in his *Public
Spirit of the Whigs*, and severely attacked the Scotch
Union, which was reckoned a great security against
the schemes of the Jacobites   When the new parliament met in March 1714, the addresses of both Houses
expressed entire confidence that the Protestant cause
was not in the slightest danger ; and having thus satisfied the demands of formality, parliament settled down
to furious debates on the subject.   The Lords attacked
Swift for his pamphlet against the Whigs ; the Commons
kept the balance even by falling foul of Steele and ex-
pelling him from the House

In 1714, in one of the numberless debates on this
interminable question, Carteret definitely took his place
with the Whigs.   He was in the minority, for the Lords
at last voted that the Protestant succession was in no
danger ; but the majority was only twelve, the exact
number of the batch of recently created Tory peers,
whom Wharton on their appearance in the House unkindly asked if they meant to vote by their foreman
The victory of the Government was a very poor one,
and the attack of the opposition was soon renewed.
Oxford put his hand on his heart and protested his
devotion to the Protestant cause , but the general feeling
was so strong that Wharton barbarously proposed to offer
a reward for the apprehension of the Pretender alive or
dead.   This encouragement to murder was indeed rejected : one peer, while protesting his affection to the

House of Hanover, declining to venture damnation for them. The milder and reasonable proposal that a reward should be offered for the arrest of James II. if he should land or attempt to land in Great Britain or Ireland was supported by Carteret. Anne at first refused her consent, but the Government found itself forced to yield, and issued the proclamation.

The angry debating and real danger were ended in a dramatically sudden way Three weeks after Anne had prorogued this parliament, she died, in August 1714, her illness aggravated by the bitter disputes between her two rival ministers. Bolingbroke had already triumphed so far as to obtain the dismissal of Oxford, and was planning a cabinet of his own which would really have been a Jacobite one; but the Queen's sudden death ruined all his plots Two days before she died, Anne appointed the Duke of Shrewsbury to Oxford's vacant place, and the whole tendency of political affairs was silently but decisively reversed. The all-powerful Bolingbroke, bantered by the amused malice of fortune, was almost insultingly hurried out of office, and all despatches addressed to him passed into the novice hands of Addison. Not a Tory or Jacobite was ready to move, and the Whigs quietly entered upon a period of political power which lasted uninterruptedly for almost half a century.

With the new reign came distinctions for Carteret. Before the coronation of George I. he was appointed one of the lords of the bedchamber; in 1715 his mother was created Viscountess Carteret and Countess Granville in her own right, with limitation of these honours to her son, and in 1716 Carteret was made Lord-Lieutenant of Devonshire, one of the western counties with which the Granville family had been much connected In the troubled year of 1715 Carteret, a young man of twenty-five, was in the West, doing all he could in support of the new Hanoverian establishment. While the Jacobite rebellion was at its height in the North, Carteret was writing from Stowe to Robethon, French secretary of George I :—

'I am now two hundred long miles from you, situated on a cliff overlooking the sea, and every tide have fresh prospects in viewing ships coming home. In this corner of the earth have I received your letter, and without that I should have heard nothing since I came.

'Most of the neighbouring gentlemen have been with me, and I am satisfied that the king will have no reason to expect any disturbance from the west. I did not think there was so good a company amongst [them]. I will do all I can to improve their thoughts of the ministry, and discountenance all the little seeds of faction that have been sown here '[1]

Carteret's first parliamentary work had been in support of the legal Hanoverian claim to the English throne, and his first parliamentary distinction was gained in defence of the newly established line. Though George had been received in England with a languidly peaceful indifference, a good deal of disturbance and discontent was early evidence of a dangerous temper in various parts of the country. Serious outbreaks had led to the passing of the Riot Act, and a rebellion had broken out in Scotland and England. Many of the Tories were Jacobites, and the Tories who were not Jacobites were discontented, for they were totally excluded from the Government. In these rather disquieting circumstances, and in accordance with the Triennial Act, a general election was nearly due. Riots

---

[1] Sept. 25, 1715. Brit Mus Sloane MSS. 4,107 ; fol. 171, v°

and confusion were even in untroubled times a matter of course ; but on the present occasion there was the further fear of the election of an increased number of Jacobites. Rather than risk a general election, and probably weaken the new and not very popular establishment, the ministry resolved to repeal the Triennial Act.

Though the matter chiefly affected the House of Commons, the Bill was introduced in the Lords. Every one knew the real reason for the repeal, but formality required that ministerial speakers should indulge in much declamation against the ruinous expense and shameful corruption and dangerous party passions which were the inevitable attendants of the frequent general elections throughout the country. Carteret supported the measure, and this first reported fragment of a speech of his is interesting as showing that at the very beginning of his career his attention was already directed to foreign affairs and European politics. He mainly urged that the increase in the average duration of each English parliament would strengthen the hands of the King and the Government in their dealings with the statesmen of Europe The sudden changes produced by very frequent general elections perplexed foreign countries, and relatively weakened England in her foreign policy; for continental statesmen did not care to show more complaisance than was necessary to ministers whose hold on power was exposed to such frequent and capricious interruptions. Carteret's point was an important one; though the fine old English feeling of satisfaction with everything that is English, and of condescending indifference to the pursuits and proceedings of mere foreigners, of course found a rather confused expression in demands to know why English-

men and English ministers should pay any attention
to the convenience of European statesmen. The Sep-
tennial Bill, however, was carried easily enough, and
the question does not in itself require any consideration
in an account of Carteret's life ; but the fact that
Carteret's first recorded parliamentary utterance concerned itself with the foreign politics of England and of
Europe gives an artistic symmetry and singleness to the
story of his political career. For throughout his very
varied public life this was the one question which interested him most. It formed the argument of this first
youthful speech, and it was the subject of the last
recorded words which he uttered on his death-bed.

CHAPTER II.

DIPLOMACY.

1717–1719.

DURING the first half of the eighteenth century the great Whig party in England was divided into two main sections, definable, with sufficient accuracy, as Whigs in place, and Whigs out of place In the earlier years of the reign of George I. one of these rival sections was headed by Walpole and Townshend, the other by Stanhope and Sunderland. The four statesmen had all, on the accession of the King, been fellow-members of the same united Whig Government, Townshend, practically Prime Minister ; Stanhope, chief director of foreign affairs ; Walpole, Paymaster ; and Sunderland, considerably to his own disgust, Lord-Lieutenant of Ireland. But this union, never very cordial, did not last long. Differences and disputes were increased by underhand caballing and unedifying intriguing, and Walpole and Townshend fell. Their colleague-rivals came into undivided power, and by them admission into official life was gladly offered to Lord Carteret.

The schism between the four ministers had reached its crisis over the question of foreign politics. The position of George on his accession was not a reassuring one European enemies were many, allies few and unsatisfactory France had recognised George as King, and was perfectly willing to recognise his rival Spain

was a mere province of France   The German Emperor,
Charles VI., had been full of irritated contempt for
England ever since Harley and St John had made their
Treaty of Utrecht, and had astonished him by refusing
to fight for his Spanish succession any longer   Peter
of Russia was sulkily jealous, for George stood in the
way of certain Russian schemes in Germany   Charles
XII. of Sweden, though his country was now in a
disastrous condition, and he himself an exile in Turkey,
was enraged when he heard that George was joining
the alliance against him, and preparing to take possession of Bremen and Verden.   To balance all this
opposition of Kings, and Czars, and Emperors, England
could only boast of the friendship of the States-General,
and, in a fitful sort of way, of the attachment of the
King's son-in-law, Frederick William of Prussia. Neither
of these alliances was very satisfactory   Holland was
now very different from the Holland of Cromwell's time ;
the value of its alliance, even when the Dutch sluggish
officialism could be got to act practically at all, was
painfully slight, as Carteret himself in later years more
than once experienced to his cost. And assistance
procurable from Prussia was mainly of the shadowy,
problematic kind, its King quite new on his own
throne, and his famous army still a thing of the future,
even if the domestic relations of the English and
Prussian sovereigns had not generally been acrid
enough   For England the European outlook was decidedly gloomy, and George had many troubles of his
own to vex and bewilder him. His new kingdom had
not the slightest enthusiasm or admiration for him ; his
desirable Bremen and Verden, bought as the cheapest
of bargains from the ruins of the empire of Charles
XII hung very loosely and undecidedly to him, and

his Hanover, which seems to have been his singular synonym for heaven, lay open to the attacks of enraged Swedes or intriguing Russians His condition was unenviable.

In such circumstances, the question of making a real ally of France, of detaching France from the party of the Pretender, soon seemed one of much importance to George. The state of affairs in France at the time offered fortunate encouragement to this rather startling change in English diplomacy. Louis XIV had died a year after the accession of the English King The Duke of Orleans was regent; if his ward, the delicate child Louis XV, should die, Orleans himself, according to the Treaty of Utrecht, would be King; for though the Spanish King was a nearer Bourbon in blood, that treaty forbade one sovereign to wear together the crowns of Spain and of France. Yet in spite of the renunciation which he had duly made, Philip V. of Spain, inspired by Alberoni, might attempt to secure the French throne, and make no more of his pledged word than Louis XIV. had done before him. Such a claim, if made, would lead to war; to the Regent, therefore, an alliance with England was a question of direct material advantage The two countries being thus personally interested, England and France began to draw together. A quite new line of European policy was opened up, and George, chiefly from Hanoverian anxieties, became eager to conclude a definite engagement without loss of time

The negotiations were troublesome and tedious. Commenced at Paris by the ambassador Lord Stair (best remembered now as English commander at the battle of Dettingen, if there was any commander at all in that singular engagement) they were continued at

the Hague by Horatio Walpole, Sir Robert's younger
diplomatic brother.   For the union was not to be between England and France alone ; Holland was to be
included ; if there was strong desire to secure a new
ally. there was no wish to offend or alarm an old one
Horatio Walpole gave his word to the States-General
that no treaty should be made without them, and he
quite sincerely meant it   But as Marlborough had
found in the days of Queen Anne. and as Carteret, and
Stair, and Chesterfield were to find in the days of
George II , the Dutch were very slow and exceedingly
formal.   George became very impatient.   Let the
treaty with France get signed at once, he earnestly
urged ; let the Dutch come in to it when they like,
whenever their slow formality is ready.   Dubois himself therefore took the affair in hand ; the Limousin
apothecary's son, who had risen so high by base, brutish
methods   He went to the Hague, pretending to be
merely buying pictures and rare books in which a dissolute abbé, of some culture, might decently affect interest.   From the Hague to Hanover, under mysterious
incognito, though all the English newspapers knew of it,
and there in August 1716, after the due diplomatic
wrangling and haggling, Stanhope and he came to
terms ; England renewing her assurance of support to
the French Regent, and France promising to dismiss the
Stuart Pretender beyond the Alps.

George had thus secured his desired French alliance,
though without the concurrence of the Dutch as yet ; but
he had involved himself in ministerial disputes at home.
It was mainly this French treaty and the negotiations
which accompanied it that brought the rival parties
in the Whig government to a decisive rupture

The King, who had shown no particular hurry to

come to England when its crown became his, showed a
very particular hurry to get back to his German home
again as soon as he possibly could   Accompanied by
Secretary Stanhope, and leaving Walpole and Townshend to manage affairs in England, he went to Hanover
in the summer of 1716, while this French treaty was
still in the doubtful hands of diplomacy , and to Hanover soon wandered Lord Sunderland in a more or less
discontented condition   He had received royal permission to leave England on the plea of ill-health, and
had gone to Aix-la-Chapelle to drink the waters there
From Aix he easily found his way to Hanover. The
two ministers in London knew perfectly well that their
colleague was inclined to intrigue against them; they
seriously suspected that nothing but the hurry of the
royal escape to Hanover had hindered a decisive ministerial change already.   Sunderland had, of course, protested.   'Lord Sunderland,' writes Lady Cowper, ' took
leave of Lord Townshend with a thousand protestations
that he would do nothing to hurt any of them, and that
his main intention in going was to persuade the King
to come back soon '[1]   Walpole seems partly to have
believed these protestations ; but Sunderland was only
veiling falsehood under formality.   He was exceedingly
discontented : dissatisfied that he was merely Lord-
Lieutenant of Ireland and not Secretary of State ; disgusted with the superiority of Townshend and the ascendency of Walpole.   At Hanover, therefore, he found
his passionate pleasure in strengthening the King's suspicions of the leading ministers in England.

These suspicions in the King's dull though honest
mind rested chiefly on the seemingly unnecessary slowness in signing the treaty with France   Townshend,

[1] Lady Cowper's *Diary*, 124-125

remembering the formal promise to the Dutch, was cautious. Horatio Walpole, whose private word was emphatically pledged, felt that he could not honourably sign the agreement which Stanhope and Dubois had made. After many pressing entreaties on each side, he was allowed to extricate himself from the negotiation altogether, and returned to London. There he found things in the greatest confusion. Letters had come from the King, from Stanhope, from Sunderland, full of reproaches against Walpole and Townshend, charging them with needless slowness, with opposing the King's continental policy, and with favouring the party of the Prince of Wales, who was Regent in England and on the usual bad terms with his father. 'It is a family,' said Carteret on another occasion, 'that has quarrelled from generation to generation, and always will quarrel.' George was disgusted that his son was Regent at all, and was annoyed with the ministers who had compelled him to consent. All these causes of pique and discontent were carefully cherished and anxiously magnified by the Hanoverian ministers and favourites who naturally enough surrounded the King. A hungry, slightly vulgar crew, these Germans looked upon the good things of England as plunder providentially supplied for persons of mere limited Hanoverian ways and means; and Walpole and Townshend, who took a different view of the subject, stood in their way with annoying effectiveness. Of Bothmar, one of the chief of these objectionable foreigners, Townshend said that he had every day some infamous project or other on foot for getting money. Robethon, another of them, whom Swift in one of his political tracts calls 'a very inconsiderable French vagrant,' was publicly spoken of by Walpole in the House of Commons as a mean fellow, an impertinent busybody ; and the Government took it as a matter of course that he would do them all the harm he could. Bernsdorf, as interested and corrupt as any, seems to have been considerably a fool in addition, a mischievous, stupid old creature, poking about with solemn stupidity in whatever dirt offered the possibility of an acceptable shilling, puzzling in negotiations 'with the adroitness of a cow,' said Secretary Craggs, who was always uncomplimentary to the bovine Hanoverian. To one of these grasping vagrants, detected in some mendacity in the King's presence, Walpole once exclaimed, in the only dialect in which he could communicate with Germans, *Mentiris impudentissime : You are a most impudent liar*; but George only laughed. All these vulgar, hungry persons were working with the implacability of disappointed greed, upon the King's annoyance with Walpole and Townshend, and the rapacious German women who reigned in a queenless court were equally bitter against the ministers who excluded them from the glory and the profit of the English peerage. The discontents and misrepresentations grew so unbearable that Townshend resolved to resign when the King returned, and Walpole spoke of his brother-in-law and himself as chained to the oar and toiling like slaves.

It was almost in despair that the two statesmen decided to send Horatio Walpole to Hanover, that they might have at least one friend in the crowd of schemers who surrounded the King For the moment, Walpole's presence seemed to interrupt the intrigues. Stanhope reasserted his protestations of attachment to the ministers in England; the King regretted that he himself had formed misconceptions, and, after receiving from Townshend a justification of his conduct, declared that his confidence was restored. Thinking that now all was

well, Horatio Walpole returned to England towards the
close of 1716 ; but his arrival in London was almost
instantly followed by a despatch from Stanhope, announcing that Townshend was dismissed from his office
of Secretary of State.   Walpole, never afraid of using
frank language, remonstrated earnestly with Stanhope,
and said in his plain, direct way that all those who had
spread reports against his brother-in-law and himself
were ' confounded liars from the beginning to the end '
Expostulation was useless   Even the Lord-Lieutenancy
of Ireland, which Townshend had accepted after first
indignantly refusing it, was, early in 1717, taken from
him   Walpole immediately threw up his own employment, and Stanhope and Sunderland rose to unrestricted
power.

Carteret himself had no share in this political
quarrel; but the two statesmen who thus gained undivided influence were his willing introducers into the
high places of diplomacy and politics   Stanhope made
him ambassador to Sweden in 1719 ; Sunderland made
him Secretary of State in the early months of 1721

It was noticed with considerable disgust that the
first foreign complication which entangled England
under George I. was the direct result of the Hanoverian
connection   For twenty years, ever since 1697 and the
accession of the boy-king Charles XII. to the throne of
Sweden, all the north of Europe had been in a state
of confused quarrel   The northern rulers, August the
Strong, Elector of Saxony and King of Poland, Frederick
IV. of Denmark, and the Czar Peter, anxious to tear
back from Sweden the possessions gained by Gustavus
Adolphus and the Thirty Years' War, thought their
opportunity had come when the new Swedish King was
little more than a child; and they were filled with

alarmed astonishment when the opportunity proved to
be the young King's, and not theirs at all. Hurrying
from victory to victory, Charles would not listen to
anxious proposals for peace, and the war dragged on
till the battle of Pultowa sent him, a fugitive, to
Turkey. Doggedly and uselessly he spent five years
at Bender or Demotica, while the northern allies were
busily attacking his possessions in Germany. Frederick
William of Prussia joined the league and took firm
possession of Stettin; while Denmark, by occupying
Bremen and Verden, was indirectly drawing England
into the quarrel. Suddenly in the dead of a November
night of 1714, Charles, who had ridden through Europe
in disguise, appeared all covered with snow at the gates
of Stralsund, his own town in Pomerania. Frederick
of Denmark, alarmed for the Swedish territories which
he had gained, and anxiously afraid that Charles might
be too much for him after all, sacrificed some of his
conquests that he might make quite sure of the others,
and sold Bremen and Verden, on the cheapest of terms,
to George as Elector of Hanover. Thus England, too,
was drawn into the coalition against Sweden, and an
English squadron, under Admiral Norris, sailed to the
Baltic to protect what interests England might have
there. With prompt retaliation, Charles, exasperated
with the Elector who was also a King, joined the councils
of the Jacobites, and a probable Swedish invasion of
England became a serious political consideration.

Sweden by herself, in her very broken condition,
need not have caused England very great anxiety; but
the unscrupulously adventurous policy of a new Swedish
minister made her proceedings too formidable for contempt. This minister was Baron Goltz, a Franconian,
who had entered the service of Charles XII. A man

of no high birth,' said Carteret of him in the House of
Lords many years after, ' nor any supereminent qualities ; yet by his cunning he got such a power over his
master that nothing was done without him , no post,
civil or military, was bestowed but according to his
direction.' The policy of Gortz aimed at a reconcilement between Sweden and Russia, and reckoned confidently that Spanish money would then support the
union of Charles and the Czar with the Jacobites Peter
and Charles were both poor monarchs ; but they had a
rich friend eagerly ready to help them in Alberoni, the
Italian working-gardener's son, once servant to a parish
clerk, now practically King of Spain Gortz, abundantly
supplied with Alberoni's gold, began to work his Jacobite plots in Sweden, in Holland, and in England itself ;
but he could not keep his doings secret from the English ministers, whose instant activity quickly sent the
schemer and his schemes together to irrecoverable ruin
In January 1717 the Government took the strong step
of arresting the Swedish ambassador to England, and
gave no heed to the shocked and sorrowful anger of Spain
at so frightful an incident in international deportment.
The ambassador's letters and papers sufficiently revealed
a Swedish-Jacobite plot, of which Carteret afterwards
discovered the full details in Sweden. Gortz also,
hitherto unknown in England, was arrested by England's ally, Holland, and an English fleet appeared in
the Sound. In close succession followed two fatal blows,
which cut short the plans and plots of Charles and
Alberoni in a very decisive manner. On the 10th of
August. 1718, Admiral Byng destroyed the Spanish fleet
in the roads of Messina, and England shortly afterwards
declared war against Spain ; and a second, far severer
blow to the Spanish Cardinal was the death of Charles

XII, near the close of the same year. The political condition of the North was at once completely changed. The projected reconciliation between Russia and Sweden was laid aside; Gortz was tried and executed; and, not very much later, his fantastic scheme finally vanished in the sudden and complete disgrace of Alberoni.

Before this last event had taken place, Carteret and diplomacy had appeared conspicuously on the scene. The new young Queen of Sweden, Ulrique Eleanora, Charles's younger sister, was very anxious for peace with England. To exhausted Sweden, impoverished in men and money, and menaced on all sides by the fleets and armies of four hostile powers, peace and friendship with one at least of them was almost a necessary condition of existence. That it should be England with which peace should first be made was the notion and wish of Ulrique and George alike; first with England, and then England would willingly offer her general mediation to obtain for Sweden the best possible terms from her three remaining enemies. The diplomatic task would be complicated, perhaps difficult, Carteret found it far more difficult than he had imagined; but it was the plan which seemed best and most likely to succeed. It was entrusted to Carteret. His political abilities had already excited attention; and now in the early months of 1719 his friend Stanhope, the chief manager of foreign affairs, appointed him ambassador extraordinary and minister plenipotentiary to the Queen of Sweden.

When the parliamentary session ended, and the early summer came round (parliament generally meeting in January or February and ending in April or May, in those days), the King and Stanhope left for Hanover, and Carteret in June sailed for Sweden.[1] A fortnight afterwards he landed at Gothenburg, thence to make his way as speedily as possible overland to Stockholm. Every day was precious to Sweden in its disastrous condition, and Carteret personally was always prompt and indefatigable in public business. A week, he hoped, would take him from Gothenburg to Stockholm, though he was slightly disappointed in that. There were unusually great difficulties in travelling in Norway and Sweden at the time; a hostile Danish fleet sailing to Norway, a Swedish army marching to meet it, and in such circumstances few horses to be procured except for military purposes. In spite of his anxiety to hurry on, Carteret was detained three days at Gothenburg, and could not in any way find horses till the governor of the town had requisitioned the peasants to bring them in. It was July 11 before he reached Stockholm, accompanied by a young Swedish nobleman whom the Queen had sent to attend him

Queen Ulrique very gladly and kindly, as she well might, received the English plenipotentiary, appointed ministers to come to terms with him, and cheerfully saw the peace negotiations begun Her husband, too, the Prince of Hessen-Cassel, showed Carteret great favour, and a strong personal liking arose among all three. These and other private friendships made in Sweden were personally pleasant enough, but the negotiations were capricious and intricate. Carteret had four dis-

---

[1] Everything that is contained in the rest of this chapter is based upon Carteret's own unprinted despatches from Stockholm and elsewhere to the ministers in London. The story of the embassy, so far as it concerns Carteret himself, has never before been told, and even on the strictly impersonal, political side, the events of 1719 and 1720 are passed over very lightly in the general histories of that period Carteret's despatches are in Brit Mus. Add. MSS 22 511 22 511

tinct pieces of work to bring, if possible, to a successful issue ; and there was a fifth, to which also he was to lend a helping hand. Sweden's peace was to be made with England, with Prussia, with Russia, and with Denmark ; and, as a preliminary to all this, peace was also to be made with George as Elector of Hanover, and the tiresome business of Bremen and Verden to be so settled. George's own Hanoverian minister, Bassewitz, was already at Stockholm, working at this last arrangement, and had made considerable progress in it when Carteret arrived. But Carteret saw at once that there could be no satisfactory settlement except on one preliminary condition. The most pressing want of Sweden was effectual assistance against the Czar, who was keeping the whole country in constant dread of invasion and destruction If no help came, Sweden would be simply compelled to make peace with Peter on his own terms There was a Swedish party which desired this ; though the more influential leaders were in favour of the agreement with England. But if England gave no sign of practical as well as of diplomatic good-will, this patriotic party might be unable to prevail. Sir John Norris and his fleet were anchored at the Skaw Could they not come nearer to Stockholm ? Carteret, who saw that this would be the best of all possible aids to his negotiations, himself anxiously desired it He had been less than a week at Stockholm when this question of the fleet became the one point on which all turned. News suddenly arrived that the Czar's troops were embarking, designing to land close by Stockholm The Swedish negotiators hurried to Carteret. Nothing now, they urged, could save them but the English fleet. In the name of the Queen and Prince, let Norris come ; and within eight days George's treaty as Elector should be settled as satisfactorily as he could wish. And George's interests as King of Great Britain? asked Carteret, requiring the Queen's own word for satisfactory performances. The Queen readily gave it, and Carteret undertook to write to the admiral as soon as the preliminary promises were formally fulfilled. 'The alarm changes every thing in our favour,' he wrote to his friend Secretary Craggs; 'I shall make all the use of it I can, and if the fleet sails, I believe we shall do our business with honour.'

Diplomatic matters were thus pleasantly hurried, and negotiations became very active Bassewitz's preliminary treaty, by which Bremen and Verden were formally handed over to the Elector of Hanover, was signed and ratified; and on the very same day (July 22, 1719) Carteret, though only with great difficulty, obtained the Swedish signatures to a preliminary convention with George as King of England Never, says Carteret, were people more unwilling to set their hands to a paper than were the Swedes to sign this preliminary treaty. It was the hope of the fleet, and that alone, which carried the day; for Carteret on his side promised to write by express urging Norris to advance. He waited only till the Swedish senate should ratify this convention which the Swedish negotiators had accepted; the letter then should go to Norris at once.

Yet Carteret was still harassed by further difficulty and delay The Secretary of State soon came to him, bringing, Carteret supposed, the desired ratification; but it proved to be otherwise The plenipotentiaries were already frightened at what they had done They now asserted that Carteret's terms had been too hard on them; that his promises were too vague; that the Senate would never ratify such an agreement The

Secretary argued with Carteret for three hours, and, not making any impression, declared that the whole thing must be looked upon as broken off. Carteret was not the man easily to agree to that. Late at night, at his request, the plenipotentiaries were summoned to meet him again. They were very emphatic; the states, they said, would pull them to pieces for such a treaty as they had signed, and any ratification of it was impossible. Carteret simply refused to accept another agreement which they had prepared for him; but in order that the failure of the negotiation might not in any degree rest upon himself, he patiently sat down to draw up a third paper which might be sufficiently acceptable to the Swedes. It was a hopeless attempt, and at three o'clock in the morning the negotiators separated, no agreement having been concluded Carteret, however, would not even yet despair. He told the statesmen that he would not go to bed, but would wait for them three hours more. If no ratification was obtainable by six o'clock, he would go down from Stockholm to the army, to see whether the Prince approved these proceedings of Swedish diplomacy.

Six o'clock came, but no ratification; and Carteret indefatigably started on a six hours' journey to find Queen Ulrique's husband in his quarters with the army His business there was successfully accomplished, the Prince and the Field-marshal (who was also one of the leading Swedish statesmen) giving him a letter which might materially assist him if the temper of the negotiators should be still the same Late in the evening Carteret returned to Stockholm; the bright lights which he saw as he rode that hot July night from the camp to the capital were the fires with which the Czar and his Muscovites were burning the islands on the Swedish

coast. 'He burns all upon the islands, and takes the
men prisoners. I saw his fires as I came back,' writes
Carteret, who, however, did not stop to look at them,
for his negotiation had become more pressing than ever.
While he himself had been with the Prince that afternoon, the Czar's minister · had been actually in the
Swedish camp with propositions of peace from Russia.
Here was news likely to make the more patriotic
Swedish statesmen less obstinate in their dealings with
England , for if the English negotiation failed, Sweden,
in her almost defenceless condition, would be forced to
accept what terms it might please Russia to offer. In
these circumstances, without the slightest loss of time
(though Carteret must have been very weary), a new
agreement was devised to the contentment of each side,
and Carteret very gladly got his ratification safe at last
—so near, as he said himself, had he been losing all in
the very port. At midnight that same night, the affair
being now happily settled, Carteret wrote to Norris
urging him, if his instructions were sufficient, to join
with his fleet the Swedish ships in the Baltic, and complete the deliverance of Sweden

But the days passed on, and Norris did not come.
As Carteret had partly conjectured, Norris would not
venture to take so decisive a step without express
orders from the King, and Stanhope had already written
to the admiral that the King was resolved to send no
further instructions till he knew that the negotiation
in Sweden had been successful. Carteret's situation,
therefore, became very difficult It was only the
promise of the fleet that had gained the much-desired
signature, and after all there was not the slightest sign
of the fleet's arrival. The Swedish Senate, which does
not impress one as having been an unusually wise

assembly, began to turn again to thoughts of peace
with Russia. The Queen anxiously implored Carteret's
presence at the palace of Carleberg, where the Senate
was, and as he walked in the royal gardens with the
Prince there, senators were sent out to converse with
him, eager to know if anything might still be hoped for
from Admiral Norris. Carteret gave them the best
hopes he could, but all his assertions must have seemed
far too problematical; for that same day, early in
August 1719, the Senate decided for peace with the
Czar on what terms he pleased. Slightly ashamed of
their tame resolution, and abashed by the courage of
the Queen (true sister of Charles XII.), they did indeed
next day venture to mention that some conditions on
their side would be necessary, but their vacillating
conduct was endangering all the negotiations, and
throwing everything loose again If only the fleet
would come! longed Carteret, and he eagerly awaited a
reply to the despatches which he sent to Stanhope at
Hanover. 'The moment a courier arrives,' he writes
to Stanhope, 'my house is full of senators, inquiring
about the fleet;' and Carteret had to listen, with uncomplaining patience, to their exceedingly unpleasant
remarks. He himself could do nothing but wait and
hope, really sorry for the actual condition of Sweden,
and for the worse things that would come upon it if
the Czar should be able to impose his own terms of
peace Sweden 'as yet does not feel all her wounds,'
Carteret rather eloquently wrote; 'they are warm.
The late King put a spirit and a courage, and left a
motion in this nation which is not yet expired, but it
abates daily, and will soon cease.'

Carteret's situation was sufficiently unpleasant, yet
just at this point his difficulties were suddenly and

seriously increased   While he had been busy at Stockholm, George and Stanhope at Hanover had been carrying on negotiations with Frederick William of Prussia, anxious to induce him to accept English mediation, and so secure his peace with Sweden   Stanhope had succeeded, though much plagued by the usual self-interested interference of the sordid Hanoverians, and he now despatched instructions to Carteret informing him that a fair acceptance by Sweden of Prussia's reasonable terms must be the essential condition of any English reconciliation with Sweden. George's own arrangement with Sweden as Elector of Hanover was already practically safe, and with infinite difficulty Carteret had brought the settlement between England and Sweden into a fair way of success; but here was likely to be a fatal blow to the whole negotiation which had painfully advanced so far. Carteret hastened to the Prince, who was very cold and disappointed when he heard the news; but Carteret, speaking with frank sincerity, told him that he was positively ordered to break off his negotiation altogether if this point were not granted   The Prince at length was personally gained over to consent by Carteret's arguments and frankness, but he declared that it was hopeless to fancy that the Senate would ever accept such a plan   In no case whatever would there be the slightest chance of success for any such scheme without the actual junction of the English and Swedish fleets, and the guarantee by England that Sweden should recover Revel and Livonia from the Czar

Having succeeded so far with the Prince, Carteret had next to deal with the Swedish plenipotentiaries. The cessions which Frederick William required from Sweden were principally Stettin and its dependent towns, which were included in that part of Pomerania obtained by Sweden at the end of the Thirty Years' War, though Brandenburg had had long previous legal claims on them. By joining the alliance against Charles XII, Frederick William had made himself master of Stettin and Stralsund. He surrendered all claims on Stralsund, but Stettin he was resolved to keep, and the English Government supported him. When Carteret informed the Swedish statesmen of the Prussian and English requirements, he found them perfectly firm. England, they said, must absolutely guarantee the recovery of Revel and Livonia, or the cessions to Prussia would not be listened to for a moment. It was in vain that Carteret, with his usual recognition of realities, urged upon the Swedes that in no case could they ever regain the possessions which Frederick William now held; that it would be better for them to accept the friendly mediation of England and to grant Prussia's moderate demands, than to break off the whole negotiation, and possibly throw Frederick William into the arms of the Czar. Arguments were useless; neither side would give way, and Carteret, looking upon the case as desperate, gave up all hope of success. But he met the negotiators once more, and this time an exceedingly fortunate incident secured what diplomacy seemed unable to reach. On August 30, 1719, Carteret writes from Stockholm to Stanhope at Hanover :—

'Yesterday we met again. The whole matter was talked over in the same terms. They told me the Senate would never consent to it; and just as I was leaving them, giving all for gone, I had the good luck to receive a letter from Sir John Norris, so prudently and discreetly writ, that I could show it them, in which he said, he waited only for the first fair wind to come to Hanoe This prevailed infinitely more than anything I could say; turned the balance in my favour. They immediately, while I stayed in the Chancery, went and communicated that letter to the Senate. Count Sparre, who had all along opposed this matter, said I had acted frankly and honourably; that he saw, by the letter of the admiral, that the King of Great Britain and his ministers were in earnest; therefore he would not be ashamed to change his opinion, and be for concluding the treaty with me, if I would admit of some alterations The plenipotentiaries returned, and told me the Senate was inclined to advise the Queen to conclude with me, making some amendments, which they would acquaint me with the next day '

Here was the negotiation rescued from the fire once more: the proposed alterations were agreed to, and the fleet was coming, not to stop at Hanoe, but to sail on to Stockholm itself Carteret, in his usual generous way, ignoring his own hard work and persistent energy, gave to Norris the credit for whatever might be the consequent success, reserving only for himself the blame of possible mistakes and misadventures. The third of his five pieces of work, Sweden's peace with Prussia, was thus successfully started; and on September 1, 1719, he gladly wrote to Norris on the news of his approach .—

'I received your letters of the 15th and 17th [August 26 and 28, N.S.] about eleven o'clock this night, with inexpressible joy and satisfaction. I went immediately to Court; but her Majesty was abed I called up his royal highness, who received the news with the utmost pleasure; and to him I delivered your letter to the Queen You have now a very glorious scene of action open to you, in which you will show to the whole world what the English nation can do 'Tis the honestest cause that ever man was engaged in The great business is to intercept the Czar, that he may not get to Revel Cut off his retreat, and we are sure of him I am afraid those two frigates that hovered about our fleet will have carried him advice of your dispositions to sail, and he will run away [*This turned out to be the case.*] There is not an honest man in Sweden that would not now lay down his life for our King. I must do the good Queen the justice to say, that she always trusted to the King's word, and has shown a certain courage and greatness of soul in her distress, which is hardly to be met with out of this country and our own God bless you, Sir John Norris. All honest and good men will give you just applause Many persons will envy you ; but nobody will dare say a word against you.'

Carteret adds in a postscript —

'I now thank God that I have prevented their making peace with the Czar. It lay heavy upon my conscience, whilst I saw their misery, and heard of no succours coming.'

Queen and Prince, too, were very glad and grateful. '*Mon ami!*' said the Prince to Carteret, '*ne me regardez pas comme prince, mais comme gentilhomme et officier anglais*' The actual arrival of the fleet, and the splendid entertainments given on board by the admiral, increased the good feeling. Carteret was personally much relieved, for his situation had been very embarrassing He speaks of it in a note to Secretary Craggs in September —

'No public minister was ever, for a month together, upon so bad, nor upon so dangerous a situation I

have been. The common people looked upon me as
the author of their misery, by preventing the peace
with the Czar, while no succours came.   . However, I still went on in the same strain, and have
worked through with some success ; so that at present
no ambassador was ever upon a better footing in a
country than I am   I hope not to stay long ; though
the Court, when I hint at going, are in concern   I say
I will return in spring, if the King will let me, with
the fleet.   I don't doubt but you will continue to me
your friendship · for I shall be, dear Craggs, yours for
ever.'

So high was the reputation of England in Sweden
at this particular moment, that Carteret thought he
might hopefully venture upon the fourth part of his
work : the arrangement of peace between Sweden and
Denmark.   From the very first, this had seemed likely
to be the most difficult of all his tasks   More than
against all the other enemies that had attacked them,
the feelings of the Swedes were bitter against the
Danes   When Carteret, soon after his arrival, had
hinted at some cessions to Denmark, the Swedish negotiators had flamed out at once, declaring that they
would rather give everything to the Czar than anything
to Denmark.   Rügen and Stralsund were already in
possession of the Danes, but when Carteret alluded to
the Danish retention of those places, and peace between
Sweden and Denmark on such terms, the Prince desired
him, as a personal friend, never more to mention such
a thing to him.   The animosity against the Danes was
almost incredible, wrote Carteret ; and he had felt
obliged to be mainly silent on that point ; all the more,
perhaps, because it was the Danes who, by the bait of
Bremen and Verden, had drawn George and England

into the quarrel But now when England was high in
favour—for on the first news of the approach of Norris
the Czar had withdrawn his fleet and galleys—Carteret
thought he might venture to reopen the question.
He began by offering the King's mediation to obtain for
Sweden peace with Denmark, and was glad, perhaps
a little surprised, to find that accepted He even prevailed on Sweden, though with difficulty, to agree to
a cessation of arms for six months. After all the re-
pulses he had met with in this delicate affair, this
seemed to Carteret a fair and hopeful beginning; it
might be possible to get actual peace agreed to before
the six months were out But Carteret knew that the
question of Rugen and Stralsund would be an almost
insuperable difficulty; it would be the hardest thing
possible to persuade Denmark to restore what it had
conquered from Sweden. That the question had been
actually opened was the most hopeful thing that could
yet be said about it, its settlement would be at least
a matter of time; and meanwhile Carteret, who had
now four separate negotiations on hand at once, was
very anxious to get some of them definitely decided,
and removed beyond the reach of often-threatening
accidents

Of George's treaty as Elector of Hanover, the main
point, the transfer of Bremen and Verden, was already
completely settled Only some little, trifling disputes,
in which George's Hanoverian ministers, greatly to
Carteret's disgust, were constantly interfering, still remained open These German ministers, with their
miserable little chicanery and the interrupting pettiness
of their letters to Bassewitz, were a mere nuisance and
hindrance Ever since the negotiations had begun,
their trickery and knavery had been meddling and

thwarting; and their continued interference, in such complicated circumstances, was becoming dangerous. On some of the endless little diplomatic differences they sent orders to Bassewitz to answer *dilatorie*; 'for which I don't know an English word,' writes Carteret sarcastically. 'What can a minister do under such orders? These people desire a plain and positive answer.' Bernsdorf, one of the chief of these heavy Hanoverian functionaries, ventured, not knowing his man, to send some of what Carteret called his 'trifling stuff' to Carteret himself. 'I regarded that advice,' Carteret wrote to Stanhope, 'as an honest man should do, with great contempt.' If the treaty had been in Carteret's province, he plainly says that he would have ventured to sign and accept it at once. As it was, he could do little more than stand aside and disdainfully wait till rapacious Hanoverians unwillingly concluded that the field of possible plunder was exhausted. When even Hanoverian hopes found it useless to struggle for a single shilling more, the treaty was at last absolutely signed on November 20, 1719, and so one at least of the diplomatic arrangements was made as safe as such things commonly are.

So far the ground was cleared; the Electoral rubbish was out of the way, and room was made for royal negotiations. Carteret now took up his character of ambassador extraordinary, and though, in consideration of the suffering condition of Sweden, his audience was private, he had yet, as his good friends the Queen and Prince assured him, made the best possible entry, for he had approached the Queen with a friendly fleet. Carteret at once earnestly turned to the completion of Sweden's treaties of peace with England and with Prussia. He was quite willing to let these two treaties run hand in hand, if Prussia would act harmoniously in such an arrangement; and at first it seemed that Prussia would do so. When the Prussian minister, Cnyphausen, arrived at Stockholm in October 1719, Carteret had worked so well and successfully that the final treaty was really ready for signature. Cnyphausen, though privately he had very extensive views, showed himself quite inclined to act on the basis which Carteret had prepared for him, and there were hopes that all would soon be finished. Difficulties did not seem at all insurmountable. Cnyphausen himself presented a project of arrangement; the Swedish ministers on their side did the same, and out of these two plans Carteret, assisted by the French minister Campredon, formed a third, apparently to the satisfaction of all parties Two or three meetings would be sufficient, thought Carteret, to finish matters; and he kept back his own treaty with Sweden out of consideration for the King of Prussia.

Things had gone so well and so far, that before the end of 1719 Carteret was able to assure the Queen that the arrangement was practically ready But suddenly Cnyphausen declared that he could not stand to his agreement. Contrary to his promise to Carteret and to Campredon, Cnyphausen had sent home to Berlin the project which the Swedish ministers had presented to him. The French and the English ministers had both assured him that this proposed plan should be altered entirely to his satisfaction, and that what he found objectionable in it was entirely due to the very roundabout manner in which Sweden performed its official business. Yet Cnyphausen sent it home, and the King of Prussia was thrown into one of his fits of petulant bad temper A 'little start of passion. Carteret called it' and was greatly perplexed by it. Cnyphausen would not sign, and it seemed that the negotiation must be lost. Early in January 1720, Carteret wrote to the English minister Whitworth, at Berlin, unfolding his perplexities:—

'I know but one way that is to be taken, in which I see great hazards and difficulties too: which is for me to accept the treaty, as we have settled it, signed by the plenipotentiaries, and finish my own. If I finish my own without the King of Prussia's, his treaty is lost. If I don't finish mine, the Queen and Prince and our friends will have strange difficulties in the Assembly of the States, which will certainly bring new difficulties upon the King our master's treaty already signed. If Mr. Cnyphausen will sign the treaty, I am sure the States will approve every step that has been taken. If they have not my treaty to be laid before them, they will approve none. What can I do? 'Tis in vain to ask. The States assemble in fifteen days, before which time I can have no answer from anybody. I would give a good sum of money out of my own pocket to be well out of these circumstances. I don't care for bold strokes, and yet I have lived by nothing else here. Since I must venture. I will do that which is honestest, finish my treaty, and keep my word to the Queen and Prince, who will suffer extremely (especially the Prince, to whom our master has great obligations) if I don't keep my word. This is what I can best answer to myself, and I hope everybody, especially our master and his ministers, will likewise think it the wisest thing I can do in these difficult circumstances, since it is the honestest.'

Carteret, who had thought all his risks were over, thus found himself in as intricate a case as ever. The English treaty must be signed before the meeting of the Estates, or there would be endless fault finding and re-

proaches from the Assembly. The Prussian treaty, if
not signed at the same time, would be referred to a
Congress, which was planned to meet (though happily
it never did) at Brunswick, and possibly would be lost
altogether. In such circumstances, Carteret thought
that it would be his wisest, though somewhat venture-
some, plan to accept on his own responsibility the
Prussian treaty as it stood, though only Swedish, and no
Prussian, signatures were attached to it, and so to give
Frederick William at least the chance of finally accepting or rejecting it as he pleased. Cnyphausen, personally,
had no real fault to find with the treaty, though his
hands were so vexatiously tied up; and privately he
acknowledged that Carteret could not do otherwise than
he proposed On the first day of February 1720 Carteret accordingly signed the two treaties; his own complete in all points , the King of Prussia's still unfixed,
and to be restored by Carteret to the Swedes as cancelled,
if Frederick William should not ratify it within six
weeks England undertook to subsidise Sweden so long
as the Northern war might last, and to assist her against
Russia by the presence of an English fleet in the Baltic.
The pith of the Prussian treaty was the surrender of
Stettin and its dependent towns by Sweden, while
Prussia, in its turn, agreed to pay a sum of two
million florins. A curious little instance of Frederick
William's economics came out in the course of the
negotiations He stipulated that the waggons and
horses which brought the Prussian money should be
precisely paid for. ' So minute a particular,' wrote
Carteret, ' has hardly ever been inserted in a treaty to
be made between two crowns '

The day after the signing of these two treaties, the
Swedish session began Carteret was home already sent

of the opening, at which he was present. The formal ministerial speakers were followed by the spokesmen for the different orders; one each for the nobility, the clergy, and the burghers :—

'And then the Peasant, who was chosen speaker by that Estate, who did very well, and made a compliment to the Prince for the care he had taken last campaign in the defence of the country. . . . Every one of the Estates sat apart in divisions prepared for them They were in number not above six hundred. They were near two thousand together the last year There are fifteen hundred families of the nobility. The chief of the family only sits in the House, and they give their proxies as we do There is not one in ten of them that has not served his country as a soldier'

Much to Carteret's satisfaction, there were soon signs that Frederick William would accept the treaty for which Carteret had laboured so hard. Well within the prescribed six weeks the ratification arrived, and Carteret's bold move had turned out perfectly successful After further diplomatic formalities, the ratifications were exchanged and the thing ended, a fact which Carteret after all the interminable proceedings declared he could hardly have believed had he not seen it with his own eyes. On March 20, 1720, heralds proclaimed in the streets of Stockholm that peace was made between Sweden, Hanover, and Prussia. 'It was the new queen of Sweden, Ulrique Eleanora (Charles's younger sister, wedded to the young Landgraf of Hessen-Cassel),—much aided by an English Envoy,—who made this peace with Friedrich Wilhelm. A young English envoy, called Lord Carteret, was very helpful in this matter, one of his first feats in the diplomatic world' [1]

 ¹ Carlyle, *Frederick*, Book IV., Chap. VI.

So three of the five pieces of work which Carteret had come to do were successfully finished. A fourth, the reconciliation between Sweden and Russia, he never had the chance of attempting, for the Czar had at once refused the mediation which Carteret in England's name had offered him. The fifth, the peace with Denmark, the most wearisome and obstinate of all, had been languidly dragging on its slightly tiresome existence during these slow months of Prussian negotiating. Carteret had managed in October 1719 to arrange a six months' armistice between Denmark and Sweden, but that was practically about all that had been accomplished. The Danes had taken Malstrand, and claimed to keep it. Rugen and Stralsund they also held, handed over to them by Frederick William, who had captured them. These too the Danes would keep, or, on lowest terms, Sweden should give an equivalent in land elsewhere for their restoration. And they had possession of Sleswick, from which they had driven Charles the Twelfth's friend, the Duke of Holstein. Further the Danes demanded that Sweden should resign a long-enjoyed privilege, and should pay toll for her ships that passed the Sound as other nations did. Such were Denmark's chief requirements, and they seemed to Sweden altogether intolerable. Exorbitant and absurd demands, Carteret called them; and for a considerable time he saw small likelihood of a satisfactory arrangement. Sweden might possibly surrender Sleswick, might consent to pay toll at the Sound, and might even offer money to make Rugen and Stralsund her own again, but little more than that seemed practicable. Yet the Danish Court was very obstinate, thinking it had but to insist strongly and could not fail to obtain; and though Lord Polwarth (afterwards Earl of Marchmont, English

ambassador at Copenhagen while Carteret was in
Sweden) was able in some degree to reduce the Danish
demands, the prospects of a settlement were not encouraging 'I shall do my best to bring all to a happy
conclusion.' wrote Carteret to Stanhope in the course of
these Danish negotiations, 'and though I foresee great
difficulties in the way, I have gone through worse and
will not despair.' Months however passed on, and even
Carteret began seriously to think of leaving Sweden and
wasting no more time on what appeared a hopeless
undertaking

A slight impulse was given to the languid proceedings by the appointment of a Danish minister to treat
at the Swedish Court. Carteret worked most indefatigably now, to obtain, before the Danish negotiator should
arrive, a definite and final settlement of what Sweden
would and would not grant, hoping that the Danes too
would draw up their plan in a similarly serious spirit.
With great difficulty he persuaded Sweden to grant one
pressing demand of Denmark, and to pay toll at the
Sound. Sweden also consented that France and
England should decide the fate of Sleswick, and that
the Danes might reckon Malstrand theirs till the signing of a definite treaty ; but the Swedes could not agree
to part with Rugen and Stralsund. These concessions
were practically the Swedish preliminary for peace, and
were only obtained by Carteret's ceaseless efforts. It
soon became clear that if they were to have any definite
result, the remainder of these negotiations must be
managed and adjusted at Copenhagen itself The Danish
ambassador, Major-General Lewenohr, did indeed
arrive at Stockholm in March 1720 ; but it was
shrewdly suspected that he had no intention of concluding an arrangement. The Danes indeed plainly

hinted that he had been sent only out of complaisance
to the King of England 'They have a very pleasant
manner of showing their respect,' wrote Carteret rather
annoyedly; and he resolved that, unless the ambassador
clearly showed from the very first a sincere desire to
come to terms, he would himself quit Stockholm at
once If however he found any real evidence of Danish
sincerity, Carteret, though heartily tired of the whole
business, was resolute to leave nothing untouched that
might contribute to a settlement.

In accordance with his resolution, Carteret had
early interviews with Lewenohr at Stockholm, and finding that the ambassador's instructions were impracticable,
he prepared to leave Sweden Lewenohr at once declared that if Carteret went, he himself would also go.
This once more made Carteret's situation an anxious
one If they both left, the whole negotiation would be
thrown into the air. There remained now but a very
few weeks of the six months' armistice, and if no treaty
were made the war must break out again. Rather
than risk such a possibility by any precipitate action of
his own, Carteret gave Denmark one chance more.
Lewenohr (whom Carteret personally liked, and whose
own private intentions were good) promised to write
decisively to his Court at once, and Carteret undertook
to await the Danish reply Meanwhile, urged Lewenohr
on Carteret, could not Sweden, besides the promises in
its preliminary arrangement, be induced to give Denmark a consideration in money? · He said that the
King of Denmark would never make his peace without
a sum of money, unless he was forced to it He asked
me frankly if we intended to force him into the preliminary I answered that we would persuade him. He
said t'   os-

sibly mean the same thing. I added, that he was too jealous.'

Carteret and Lewenohr both awaited anxiously, and somewhat hopefully, the letter from Denmark But within the reasonable time no letter came, and Carteret, as he had said he would do, began to make his preparations for departing. Once more however he was delayed Lord Polwarth at Copenhagen sent hopes that though the armistice was now so nearly over, all might yet go well; and Carteret, who was exceedingly desirous to do nothing to endanger even the faintest possibility of success, was induced on this information still to prolong his stay He even persuaded the Swedes to accept a compromise on the chief point which remained in dispute, and to agree to pay a sum of money to Denmark Not enough, said Lewenohr; but Carteret declined to do anything more; and, having brought matters so far, decided to take a definite and final step on his own responsibility, as he had once already done with success. The armistice had been informally prolonged, and Carteret now thought he saw peace within reach at last, ' of which once I very much doubted ; but yet would never despair, nor quit the station, while there was the least light to carry us through' If Lewenohr would not join Carteret in drawing up and signing a treaty of peace, then Carteret said that he would enter into a conference with the Swedes by himself; and, having done all he possibly could for Denmark, would venture to do what he had already done in the case of Prussia and, accepting the treaty himself on behalf of the two countries, would leave to the King of Denmark the responsibility of rejecting the terms which the mediation of England had procured for him. Lewenohr, in his heart thinking that Carteret was right as minister

found himself compelled to object, taking all the proposals of the Swedes merely *ad referendum*, 'which
cursed word,' says Carteret, 'has kept me here these
four months.' Carteret therefore vigorously commenced single action, and on June 14, 1720, just a year
after he had left England, signed the treaty between
Sweden and Denmark. As in the case of Prussia, he
had some anxiety about the step he was taking, but
pretty confidently hoped for success. Indeed the King
of Denmark himself seemed already to approve what
Carteret had done, and invited him to come direct to
himself at Fredericksburg, without passing through
Copenhagen.

Carteret had now accomplished all that he could do
in Sweden, and was ready to leave at last   He took the
kindest farewells of his friends—the Queen, for whom
he had clearly a chivalrous regard, and the Prince, who
by this time had become the King, and on June 24,
1720, left Stockholm at night for Fredericksburg, arriving there before the end of the month   He was received
at the palace with every possible mark of distinction,
and lost no time in attempting to put the finishing
touch to his protracted and intricate business. On the
day after his arrival he explained to the King what he
had ventured to do, and reasoned with him upon the
general condition of affairs. The King seemed not dissatisfied with Carteret's conduct ; but the Danish ministers had many objections to make   Two conferences
with them led to nothing ; but, suddenly, on the fourth
day after Carteret's arrival at Fredericksburg, the treaty
was accepted almost in the exact terms which he had
settled at Stockholm. The manner in which this was
brought about was, as Carteret said, singular. After
Carteret's second conference with the ministers he mind

with the King, and. in reply to questions, informed him
of the great difficulties which the Danish statesmen were
putting in the way The dinner over, Carteret rode out
with the King to see his stud, and during that little
excursion he found several opportunities of discussing
these points of difficulty with Frederick himself.
Returning to the palace, the King took Carteret up with
him to his private apartment, and seriously urged one
point upon him Would the King of England definitely
guarantee to him the peaceable possession of Sleswick?
Would George procure for him an absolute cession of
it, and so protect him against possible disturbance from
the ousted Duke of Holstein? Carteret answered as
carefully as he could, but had no authority to make such
an engagement, and, indeed, dwelt on the comparative
needlessness of it, seeing that the King already held
Sleswick by right of conquest, a fairly satisfactory
method, added Carteret, 'whatever the lawyers and
pedants may say to it'

Frederick did not press the matter further upon
Carteret as ambassador, but was content to urge him to
use his influence privately with George in regard to it.
This Carteret readily undertook to do, and the King
then immediately replied that he accepted the treaty.
The ministers were at once called in, and in Carteret's
presence, to their complete surprise, were informed that
the whole thing was finished

Little more now remained for Carteret to do. The
very trifling alterations which had been made in the
treaty were readily agreed to by the Court of Sweden;
Stanhope, at Hanover, and the ministers in London were
full of congratulations on the state of affairs, and Carteret's personal credit rose high At Copenhagen, where
he ne. . . . . . . the Kin. . t w notic d that no foreign

minister had ever been so well treated as Carteret
'*Milord*,' said Frederick to him one day, '*comme par
votre entremise j'ai fait la paix, et qu'à cette heure mes
armes me sont inutiles, permettez-moi que je vous fasse
présent de mon épée*', handing to him a sword valued at
20,000 crowns, specially made for the occasion He
went on hunting expeditions with the King at Fredericksburg; made a military tour with him in Zealand,
and in every way was treated with most unusual kindness. But he was desirous to get away from it all His
private affairs. after so long an absence, required his
examination He was also not quite sure what his exact
public situation might be. While he was still at Stockholm he had had the offer of the English embassy at Paris ;
while he was at Copenhagen he was appointed to go
with Stanhope to the Congress of Cambrai. Neither of
the projects was to take effect, but Carteret could not foresee that, and was anxious to be able to begin his necessary preparations. One thing only detained him at
Copenhagen . France, which through all these northern
negotiations had been working as fellow-mediator with
England, was somewhat slow in ratifying this last treaty
between Denmark and Sweden. Till this was done. the
affair was not absolutely and technically settled, and
Carteret, therefore, waited on. The waiting proved so
unexpectedly wearisome that, on the announcement in
September 1720 of his appointment to Cambrai, Carteret desired to take leave of the King of Denmark ; but
Frederick would not part with him till all was actually
finished, and politely waved the leave-taking aside.
Weeks passed, and still France delayed Frederick began
to lose his good-humour, and Sweden to fear that all
might yet be broken off At last. but not until Denmark has actually intervened and threatened to withdraw ry

preparations, near the end of October, Carteret received the desired ratification The very next day Denmark formally accepted, and Carteret's seventeen months' negotiating was at a successful end He had his farewell audience of the King, and at once left to make his way, over bad roads, by Osnabrück and the Hague to England. The Hague was reached by the end of November, but stormy, contrary winds kept him waiting there many days At last the fair wind came, and on December 13 he sailed from Helvoetsluys for home

CHAPTER III

SECRETARY OF STATE.

1721—1724.

ENGLISH domestic affairs were in a very excited condition when Carteret arrived in London Two sentences from Copenhagen letters of his own are concerned with the cause of the public confusion In August, 1720 he wrote to a friend : 'My mother and wife have also got something in the South Sea ; but they don't tell me how much. I have had no letters from them this month, but at that time their good fortune had been considerable.' And again, two months later : 'I don't know exactly how the fall of South Sea has affected my family ; but they have lost considerably of what they had once gained' By the time that Carteret returned, the decisive crash of the South Sea Company had come. The big bubble burst like the thousand smaller ones, and caused hardly less political than social ruin. The nation, with a rage almost equal to its credulous infatuation, abused the King, demanded the blood of the directors, and fiercely turned against those members of the Government who could be made to feel the weight of its passionate, self-inflicted disappointment. Against Aislabie, the Chancellor of the Exchequer, the outcry was particularly keen. He was expelled and sent to the Tower, amid the bonfires of the bitterly rejoicing city Sunderland was head of the Government Craggs was Secretary

of State   The secret committee of the Commons reported against each of them. Fortunately, perhaps, for
himself, Craggs died on the very day on which the
report was presented ; and Sunderland, though cleared
by a large majority, yielded to the popular clamour and
resigned. Stanhope, the other Secretary, defended the
ministry in the House of Lords so eagerly that he made
himself ill, and next day died.

The ministry was practically destroyed   Two
Secretaries of State had died within little more than a
week of each other   Walpole, having found himself
unable to weaken Stanhope's Government, had, with
unembarrassed inconsistency, rejoined it as an inferior ;
and the unanimous voice of the nation now demanded
that he should return to power to repair the ruined
finances. With him came back his brother-in-law,
Townshend, to take Stanhope's empty place   Thus
Walpole and Townshend had almost dramatically
complete revenge for the intrigues of Stanhope and
Sunderland at Hanover, some two or three years
before. In the now remodelled Government room was
made for Carteret. Sunderland, though practically
driven from office, kept with no diminution at all his
influence and reputation with the King ; and it was
through Sunderland that Carteret was appointed to the
office vacant by the death of Craggs. In March 1721
Carteret received the seals as Secretary of State for
the Southern department. He was only thirty-one,
and ought, as Swift said, to have been busily losing
his money at a chocolate-house ; but he had already
had ten years' parliamentary and political experience.
Another office had been destined for him   He had
actually been appointed ambassador extraordinary to
France, and was on the point of starting, when the

collapse of the ministry altered that and many other arrangements of the English political world. As Carteret himself wrote, the sudden death of his two best friends changed his destiny. It is not probable that a life of diplomacy would have been pleasing to him. He had already had brilliant success in that department; but he had also had sufficient experience of its vexations and difficulties, especially annoying to a man of an actively practical mind, with a genius for work. To be a member of the Government in London was doubtless preferable to Carteret, and his selection for one of the leading posts in the Cabinet is a proof of the high estimate which had already been formed of his ability. Needless to say that the selection was not made by Walpole, who dreaded nothing so much as talents in those with whom he had to share his rule. In Walpole's Government to be a mediocrity was to be safe But Carteret could not be a political nonentity or a mere clerk to do Walpole's unquestioned bidding Walpole's frightened jealousy would tolerate nothing else; and after three years Carteret accordingly had to go, as Pulteney was to go, and Townshend, and Chesterfield, and many less distinguished men than these Men of genius and Walpole could not long work harmoniously together; a ridiculous Duke of Newcastle, a middling Harrington or Hardwicke, suited Walpole's purposes, as no abler man might hope to do

The management of foreign affairs was at this period entrusted—subject to the direct personal interference of the King—to two Secretaries of State, who divided Europe between them. To the Secretary for the North fell the Scandinavian kingdoms, with Russia, Prussia, Hanover; to the Secretary for the South, mainly the other and more important parts of Europe Newcastle was Northern Secretary, and, in his absurd way, believed that Hanover, included in his department, must therefore be north of England. Carteret, as Southern Secretary, had the direction of the negotiations with France, Spain, Austria, and the various princes in Italy; and as affairs between England and all these powers were in a most complicated condition when he entered office, it seemed likely that Carteret would have hardly a less leading part in pacifying the South than he had already had in arranging the North. At the same time he had to take a leading part in support of the Government at home, for his abilities as a speaker caused much of the work in the House of Lords to fall upon him. But his main business was with foreign affairs.

The Emperor of Germany was Charles VI He had been one of the claimants for the Spanish crown in the war of the Spanish Succession As a lad of eighteen, on his way to Spain to call himself King there, he had been received with all pomp by Queen Anne at Windsor, and had stayed there three days, grave, modest, silent. England and Marlborough had fought for him; Peterborough had done knight-errantry for him in Spain, and it had all resulted in nothing. He had become Emperor while the Succession war was still unfinished; King of Spain he never became And when England, in a somewhat singular manner, and with very base treatment of Marlborough, discovered that she had had enough of the war and made the Peace of Utrecht with Louis XIV., Charles took it almost as a personal affront. He would have nothing whatever to do with the peace; would go on with the war alone; and even tried to do so for a time, till he saw it was hopeless He found himself compelled to make his peace with Spain; but though he lost all chance of its throne, he still clung

desperately to the title Here was one leading trouble
of his ; and another question, still more important to
him, was just at this time forcing itself upon his notice.
He had no son ; who was to succeed him ? Very privately, in this same year of the Utrecht peace, he had
drawn up the document afterwards too well known as
the Pragmatic Sanction, declaring fixedly that if sons
altogether failed him, daughters should be equally good
to succeed to his hereditary possessions. When Carteret
became English Secretary of State, the existence of this
Pragmatic Sanction was already pretty generally known,
and it was the great toil of the Emperor's life to persuade Europe to accept it.

In Spain the nominal Sovereign was Louis XIV 's
grandson, the Bourbon Philip V , crazy in brain and
broken in constitution, desiring nothing, said Alberoni,
but a wife and a prayer-book. The real Sovereign was
Philip s second wife, Elizabeth Farnese, a very fiery
Italian woman, who singularly falsified gently patronis-
ing predictions concerning her A good girl she had
been called when it became necessary to find a second
wife for Spain—fat with the butter and the milk of the
Picentine. addicted to nothing more emphatic than
needlework and embroidery Things proved very
different. For years she kept Europe in a state of
delirious agitation. She had an infant son, Don Carlos
by name, a child who was not the heir to the Spanish
throne. For years too wearisome to think of this
entirely superfluous infant was the greatest nuisance in
Europe. Nothing would satisfy his mother till certain
Italian Duchies—Tuscany, Parma, Piacenza—should be
handed over to him : but the Emperor was feudal
superior of the Duchies, and to gain his consent to
Elizabeth's desired arrangement proved difficult almost

to impossibility Demands and refusals caused a con-
tinual bickering between the two potentates, who kept
Europe in a state of constant alarm, and terribly
agitated the interestingly delicate balance of power.
Even when the Emperor was forced to agree, in a
sullen sort of way, to the Treaty of Utrecht, and so to
peace with Spain, the quarrel was by no means settled
Charles did not even acknowledge Philip as King of
Spain—far less would he permit Spanish troops to
garrison the Italian Duchies, and keep them warm for
the infant till his time should come Charles would
not hear of such a thing ; and Elizabeth, backed by
Alberoni, began to make serious preparations for war

The Emperor took alarm at Elizabeth's doings, and
a series of treaties and counter-treaties followed, designed
to give, if possible, some feeling of security to Europe
in its state of agitated uncertainty The first of these
arrangements was a reconciliation between Charles and
England, signed at Westminster Next came the agreement between England and France, which busied Dubois
and Stanhope at Hanover and the Hague Third followed
the Triple Alliance between England, France, and Holland, settled in January 1717, mainly intended to arrange
the points in dispute between Charles and Elizabeth.
Charles, mortified by this alliance—for it guaranteed
the peace of Utrecht, which secured Spain to Philip—
refused at first to come into it, but alarm at Elizabeth's
Spanish preparations soon brought him to terms. Thus
the Triple Alliance was, in the summer of 1718, made
quadruple, and if now Spain could be induced to join,
and the arrangement so become quintuple, the thing
might be looked upon as satisfactorily settled. But
this was the point where the real difficulty began.
The terms of the Quadruple Alliance seemed altogether
unendurable to Spain Don Carlos was indeed to be

recognised as eventual heir to the desired Italian Duchies, and the Emperor agreed to grant that Philip was King of Spain. But on the other hand no Spanish troops were to be admitted into Italy, and Charles was expressly allowed to appropriate Sicily—King Victor of Sicily by way of compensation receiving Sardinia, which a Spanish fleet had recently taken from the Emperor himself Other points of dispute were left over to be settled at a Congress at Cambrai, where France and England were to mediate between the two quarrelling powers.

Three months were granted to Spain in which to accept this treaty. Stanhope went to Paris and to Madrid to try to secure a settlement; an English fleet was fitted out for the Mediterranean; strong arguments for peace were brought to bear on Alberoni But Spain would not listen, and, rather than accept the terms which had been sorted out for her, impetuously ventured into something very like war. Here was the first slight outbreak of a war—always confused and complicated, sometimes almost meaningless, which in very varying forms and circumstances was the plague of Europe for thirty years to come A Spanish fleet sailed from Barcelona, made for Sicily, and attacked and took Messina. But Byng was there with his English ships ready to help the Emperor to recover his island. On the 10th of August, 1718, in the roads of Messina, Byng fell upon the Spanish fleet, and practically annihilated it, the Spaniards themselves being now besieged in the town of which they had hardly yet got complete possession. This was a very severe and quite unexpected blow to Spain; the beginning of the end of Cardinal Alberoni, and a mortifying check to his fiery mistress. In England the news was received with great satisfaction, and it was Carteret

who, when parliament met in November, moved in the
Lords the address of thanks to the King, congratulating
him on the alliance with the French Regent, and on the
success of Admiral Byng.   Other events rapidly followed, all of an unfortunate nature for Spain   England
declared war before the year was over, and made a
successful descent on Vigo.   The Spaniards were forced
to evacuate Sicily   France discovered a Spanish plot
against the Regent, and at once declared war.   A
Spanish invasion of England in favour of the Pretender
had been projected, and an expedition actually sailed
from Cadiz, but it was scattered and ruined by a storm.
These accumulated misfortunes, and the sudden death
of Charles XII of Sweden, compelled Spain, threatened
on all sides by the united hostility of England, France,
and the Emperor, to yield to the terms which Europe
offered.   Alberoni was dismissed at the end of 1719,
and in February 1720 Spain joined the Quadruple
Alliance   The war, such as it had been, was over for
the time, and a Congress at Cambrai hoped to bring
things to a final settlement.   Such was the state of
European affairs when Carteret became Secretary of
State for the Southern Department.

At the Cambrai congress England and France were
to be mediators between the Emperor and Spain, but
before the pacific proceedings could begin there were
many difficulties to remove, and these difficulties were
sometimes seemingly insuperable.   At the very outset
there was considerable doubt if France was perfectly
sincere in its alliance with England.   Carteret's foreign
policy was a continuation and development of his late
friend Earl Stanhope's, and he was anxious, as he himself wrote to the Archbishop of Cambrai, to strengthen
between the two countries the alliance which Stanhope

had done so much to bring about. But at the same time Carteret's letters to his friend Schaub, the English ambassador at Paris, show that his confidence in Archbishop Dubois was very far from perfect. Carteret, writing to Dubois, promised from himself fairness and candour in his dealings, and hoped for the same in return; but smooth words alone from France would go but a moderate length with him. Proof of sincerity by action was what Carteret wanted, and it happened that there was a pressing question in agitation at this time between England and Spain which might very fairly test the reality of French professions. This was the question of Gibraltar—a question which must be satisfactorily solved before England and Spain could harmoniously enter the Congress together.

Earl Stanhope had been of opinion that Gibraltar might, on reasonable terms, be restored to Spain, and as an inducement to Spain to join the Quadruple Alliance the French Government had promised to use what influence it had with England on this matter. But when the plan had been mentioned in England, both parliament and the nation had opposed it with excited determination, and by the time that Carteret entered office the English Government had firmly decided that the fortress must be kept. Yet Spain, whose hopes had been raised high, seemed equally resolved; and here for Carteret was a preliminary difficulty which must be removed before there could be anything like reconciliation between the two countries. A proof of the reality of French friendship was fortunately given when the Regent was brought to agree that England might fairly insist on the renewal of her treaties with Spain—which had been broken off by the war—without touching on the Gibraltar question at all. Yet it

seemed very doubtful if Spain would yield its point.
Spain harped on the promise of restoration which she
insisted that Earl Stanhope had given, and ventured to
demand a definite and formal assurance that Gibraltar
should be surrendered before she would settle any other
point whatever with England   But even the Court of
Spain soon discovered that it was worse than useless to
adopt a tone of this kind. The English ambassador
at Madrid, Mr. Stanhope (better known afterwards as
the Earl of Harrington), plainly declared that England
would rather carry on the war for ten years longer
than either give up Gibraltar now or definitely promise
to do so in the future. Spain therefore made another
proposal   Let the King of England make a conditional
promise of the restoration, the conditions being that
Spain should offer an equivalent to England, and the
English parliament give its consent. George, who
himself was personally indifferent about the thing, did
write such a conditional letter to the King of Spain—
his ministers knowing well that it was a mere empty
form, for parliament would never sanction the surrender   If such a letter, utterly meaningless on the
English side, would materially assist the negotiations
on hand, there was no reason why it should not be sent.
England even went further; for when the irritable
Court of Spain, having obtained this letter, querulously
insisted that the equivalent should be left out, George
wrote again in June 1721, yielding to their pettish irritation. So long as the consent of parliament was
insisted upon, what else might or might not be mentioned was to England a matter of complete indifference.
Carteret saw that Spain would not yield with a good
grace; let her yield with a bad one, then, since her
notions of deportment were of no practical significance.

The signing of the treaty between England and Spain followed, and the ground was cleared somewhat for the approaching Congress. Stanhope, who was cordially assisted by Carteret, had great difficulties to overcome before the signatures were actually affixed The Spanish Court was almost unendurably dilatory in its manner of transacting public business ; and when the English ambassador opposed its impossible pretensions, the fiery Queen herself burst out upon him that he was an enemy of peace, and anxious, because he was a soldier himself, to obtain a continuance of the war [1] But Stanhope took it all patiently, and Carteret was glad to see the firmness and prudence of the relative of his own late friend. The treaty was successfully signed at Madrid (June 13, 1721), and on that same day another piece of preparation for the Congress was also made. This was an alliance between England, France, and Spain, to be kept, if possible, a secret from the Emperor till the Cambrai Congress was well over. It was hoped that this arrangement might be something of a guarantee for the preservation of peace, and that if all remonstrances and reasonings with the Emperor at Cambrai should fail, the discovery that he had an alliance of the three crowns to contend with might be more effectual with him than any other argument could be. These two treaties were settled together, and so far things seemed to promise fairly well.

But there were hardly fewer preliminary difficulties to overcome on the Austrian side . difficulties so great that the advisability of doing without the Congress altogether was seriously discussed. The petty points which were painfully magnified till they overshadowed

---

[1] Stanhope to Carteret, May 29, 1721. Brit. Mus , Add. MSS. 22,520 , fol 105.

things of real importance, the ponderous stolidity with
which disappointed persons insisted on clinging to the
shadow of the substance which they had lost, must have
vividly reminded Carteret of many of his experiences in
Sweden and in Denmark. The Emperor's ambassador
in London was an old man, and at times of a very bad
humour; and his petulant outbursts, though they received no practical attention from Carteret, who took
them simply as things which must be put up with, were
a hindrance and a danger to the negotiations. Instead
of plain honesty and prudent discretion, there were
diplomatic mystifications and so-called fine political
strokes which, much as the contrary has been stated,
Carteret both hated and despised. His real political
genius, accompanied by calm and complete knowledge,
turned instinctively from the mock-mysteries which
appeal in a singularly similar way to the flightily clever
and to the solemnly stupid. Carteret was simply
annoyed when diplomatic persons insisted on treating
the excrescences of a subject as if they were the essential point itself. The excrescences of the dispute between Austria and Spain, though small, were intricate
and obstinately troublesome; and besides these there
were two or three preliminary questions on which the
diplomatic arguing and despatching was almost endless
One of these points was the so-called question of the
titles. The Emperor obstinately clung to the title of
King of Spain, and even, by distributing the Order of the
Golden Fleece, seemed resolved to make the title somewhat more than nominal only   On the other hand, the
King of Spain insisted on calling himself Archduke of
Austria and Count of Hapsburg   Nominal only, for the
mere honour of the thing, the Spanish minister at
Madrid assured Stanhope, just as the King of England

still called himself King of France, the minister insinuat-
ing, in a slightly malicious way, that that also was
a title the reality of which was not perfectly plain to
everybody   Then there was the question of the letters
of investiture, the Emperor's formal pledge of the re-
version of the Italian Duchies to Don Carlos.   Austria
was exceedingly slow over this matter; the Emperor,
indeed, for whom Byng's sea-fight had secured Sicily,
had in that way acquired all that he himself could gain,
and was in no hurry to redeem the promises which
he had given when he joined the Quadruple Alliance
The Austrian minister in London continually assured
Carteret that these investitures were being prepared, but
nothing more convincing than this reiterated formality
was forthcoming.   And, as a third point, Spain especially desired that Don Carlos and a sufficient number
of Spanish troops might at once enter Italy.   The Duke
of Tuscany was old, his son was in bad health; the
actual presence of the Spanish infant in Italy would be
better than any other guarantee of the Emperor's sincerity   But here again the Austrian reply was merely
dilatory and evasive.   To add to all these tedious difficulties, there were even hints that Spain, in spite of
the treaty so lately made with England, was anxious to
moot again the question of Gibraltar.   Carteret so firmly
put his foot down on this that nothing more was heard
of it; but the various questions in vexed dispute seemed
so unlikely to be settled before the meeting of the
Congress, and so dangerous to touch at the Congress
itself, that to do without that assemblage altogether
began to seem to some by far the safer plan   This
was the hint and proposal of Archbishop, now Cardinal,
Dubois, a hint which might be acted on, thought and
hoped Carteret   Spain itself showed no anxiety to meet

Europe in Council, for Spain had no sincere desire
for peace ; and the Emperor could not hope to come
out of a Congress practically any better off than when
he had entered it Carteret, writing to Schaub, declared the conviction of the English ministers that, in
the complete absence of any even elementary understanding between the two powers, a Congress, instead of
procuring a peace, would be only the signal for the
beginning of a new war.

Unfortunately, it was found impossible to do without the Congress. The Emperor, though as yet he
knew nothing of the secret treaty between England,
France, and Spain, had already become suspiciously
sensitive, and vaguely feared the completion of some
arrangement contrary to his own interests By the end
of 1721, nearly two years after Spain had joined the
Quadruple Alliance and the Congress had been proposed, Charles resolved at once to send his ministers to
Cambrai, and then to call them home again if the Congress did not open. English ministers were also therefore
appointed, that no blame for delay might rest on
England Lord Whitworth, ambassador at Berlin, and
Lord Polwarth, minister at Copenhagen, were chosen
for the dreary work. But Carteret had not much
hope of any satisfactory result. He foresaw that it
would be impossible to satisfy both the Emperor and
Spain : he doubted—and his doubts were realised—if it
would be possible to satisfy either of them England,
however, had accepted the part of mediator, and would
do what she could to sustain it ; the union between
England and France might prove of some effectiveness,
and at least one could try To hurry nothing, to watch
events carefully from day to day, to discountenance all
ambitious desire for elaborate and perhaps only artifi-

cial decisions, and to keep close to the alliance with
France, was all that Carteret's policy could at present
propose To give any definite instructions to the plenipotentiaries was impossible; for though through many
long months official persons of all kinds were crowding
into Cambrai, then meetings and discussions were as
yet all of the informal kind. No full powers could
be assumed, no definite Congress could be formally
constituted, till some preliminary arrangement between
Spain and Austria gave the negotiators firm ground to
go upon; and it seemed as if this first arrangement
would never be made. It was actually nearly three
years before the Courts and diplomatists ended their
pedantic discussions and wearisome delays It was the
beginning of 1723 before the Emperor sent to
England the plan of the letters of investiture for Don
Carlos; it was April before Carteret could write to
Polwarth and Whitworth that hopes of some conclusion
of this matter were coming after all Six months more
passed before the slight necessary changes made in the
Austrian plan were agreed to at Vienna, and then at
length, the Congress being now ready to begin, in November 1723 Carteret signed the full powers for the
English plenipotentiaries at Cambrai. After all its
weary waiting the Congress was ready to open at last,
and here for the present we may gladly leave it.

Meanwhile, for the last six months, George had been
in Hanover. The Jacobite conspiracy known indifferently as Layer's, or as Atterbury's plot, had deprived
him of his usual visit to Germany the year before; but
this summer things were quiet in England, and as soon
as parliament had risen, the King embarked, accompanied
by Carteret and Townshend This seemingly commonplace visit to Hanover had very important results for

Carteret. It gave Walpole an opportunity of which
he was not slow to avail himself; for jealousy of colleagues of ability marked all Walpole's political life,
and he had felt jealous of Carteret almost from the
moment of the formation of his ministry. Walpole,
son of a hard-drinking, sporting, cattle-breeding Norfolk
squire, had had originally no intention in the parliamentary way. He was only a third son, destined, in
those little-scrupulous times, to find his way to fortune
by preferment in the Church. 'If I had not been
Prime Minister, I should have been Archbishop of
Canterbury,' he used to say in later days. But he
became heir; followed his father's illiterate, drinking,
hard-living ways, and got into Parliament for one of
the family seats   A coarse, noisy man; no orator, no
scholar; with no nearer approach to even a tincture of
literature than the conventional possession of a few stale
tags from Horace   In his own library at Houghton he
once found Henry Fox reading, and said to him: 'You
can read   It is a great happiness   I totally neglected
it while I was in business, which has been the whole of
my life, and to such a degree that I cannot now read a
page—a warning to all ministers. [1] He opened his
gamekeeper's letters before all official or other correspondence [2]   But he was exceedingly industrious and
clear-headed; a man of business and direct common
sense; of great physical endurance and power of work;
thoroughly understanding Parliament and his own aims
and intentions there. His aims were low and were
reached by low means; yet the cynical frankness of his

[1] Lord Shelburne's *Autobiography*, in Lord E. Fitzmaurice's *Shelburne*
I. 37

[2] A very different man from Walpole, Viscount Althorp, 3rd Earl
Spencer, did something of the same kind. See Sir D. Le Marchant's *Earl
Spencer*, p 543.

parliamentary corruption escapes much of its deserved
censure by its almost brutal freedom from hypocrisy
Since that was the way the Government was carried on,
why pretend that it was not? Walpole giving bribes
is a far less unpleasant sight than many high-professing
politicians receiving them.

What, in twenty years, did Walpole really do? He
kept himself at the top of English political affairs.
Touching nothing that he could possibly leave alone,
giving way always rather than run the risk of any
serious parliamentary danger, he clung doggedly to the
power which he allowed no others to share with him
Personally mild, good-natured, and in other matters even
carelessly indifferent, he worked for his own individual
predominance in politics with a terribly intense determination He spared no one who stood, as he thought,
in his way; no one whose abilities, of a higher stamp
than his own, might possibly venture to dispute with
him the position which he had fixedly arrogated to himself. Thus from the very first he had felt a dread of
Carteret. Carteret had become Secretary of State in
Walpole's Government in March 1721. In June of that
same year, Walpole opposed the election of a particular
member to the House of Commons, simply because
Carteret favoured it [1] One cause of Walpole's jealousy,
doubtless, was the fact that Carteret belonged to the
Sunderland and Stanhope section of the Whigs. A person of a comparative turn of mind, who one day saw
Sunderland and Carteret, Walpole and Townshend, come
out of a coach together at Kensington, found himself
thinking of two duellists arriving on the ground with
their seconds [2] Carteret could not be ignorant that

---

[1] Coxe's *Walpole*, II. 217
[2] Brit. Mus Sloane MSS. 4,163; fol 269, v°.

G

Walpole was rather his political enemy than his colleague.
A curious entry in Lord Marchmont's diary proves that
when Sunderland died, in April 1722, Carteret already
thoroughly understood his position 'Lord Chesterfield
told me,' writes Marchmont, 'that on the death of Lord
Sunderland, Lord Carteret had applied to the late King'
(George I) 'to support him, as he was then surrounded
by his enemies · that the King promised it him, but told
him the necessity of the time forced him to temporise;
that hereupon Lord Carteret spoke to the Duchess of
Kendal, who bid him have patience, and told him the
King hated his other ministers'[1] But even if Carteret
had not, as it were, innocently succeeded to the grudge
which Walpole felt against Sunderland and Stanhope,
Walpole's jealousy would have soon found occasion for
quarrelling with him, as he quarrelled with his own
brother-in-law Townshend, with Pulteney, and with
many others.   It was enough that Carteret was a man
of unquestioned ability, who would not agree to forfeit
all reality of power, if only he might keep its outside
dignities and ceremonious distinctions.   From the very
first, therefore, Walpole, true to his constant theory,
felt that he must free himself from Carteret. An opportunity seemed to fall to Walpole's hands when, in 1723,
Carteret went with the King to Hanover. A political
intrigue, carefully worked by Walpole and Townshend
in the usual underground fashion, was set in full play,
and the statesman whose abilities and influence Walpole
forebodingly dreaded was before long sent into political
exile   Walpole had, indeed, great difficulty in getting
rid of Carteret; for Carteret's weight was quite dis-
proportioned to his years, and the King, who knew his
worth, was very unwilling to part with him.   But Wal-

[1] *Marchmont Papers*, I 3 Aug 2, 1711.

pole's dogged determination to be freed from a dangerous rival had its way in the end ; and when Carteret returned to England in the beginning of 1724, the brother-ministers felt sure that he would not be able long to escape them. But before noticing the details of Walpole's plot against his colleague, we may follow Carteret from Hanover to Berlin.

Visits between Berlin and Hanover when George was on the continent were, in the course of things, natural enough. Queen Sophia Dorothea of Prussia was the King of England's daughter, and often when her father was at his Hanoverian palace of Herrenhausen, she left her own capital to visit him, her husband, Frederick William, sometimes accompanying her. Queen Sophia, in these Hanoverian visits of hers, was mainly intent on the famous double-marriage scheme between Prussia and England. George's grandson, Frederick, would be Prince of Wales when his grandfather died, and presumably one day—though it turned out not so—King of England. Let him, thought his aunt, Queen Sophia Dorothea, marry a Prussian princess-cousin of his ; and let her own son Frederick, Prince-Royal of Prussia, afterwards Frederick the Great, choose an English princess to be the third Prussian Queen. This was Queen Sophia's plan, which she had much at heart ; but the two Kings, her husband and her father, were by no means so anxious about it as Sophia herself. So the proposal had dragged considerably, but now in the year 1723 it seemed easily possible to infuse a little more life into the somewhat languid negotiations. George had successfully ended his Jacobite and South Sea troubles, and European affairs, it was vaguely hoped, might after all be tending to a satisfactory settlement at Cambrai. In this somewhat serene interval, the marriage scheme was

accordingly more attentively looked at; the Queen of
Prussia was more diligent than ever, and visiting between
the two friendly continental Courts became decidedly
brisk   It was near the end of June 1723 when George
arrived at Hanover, closely followed by his two ministers; and before the month was over Frederick William
was there too   'The King of Prussia is just arrived,'
writes Carteret to Walpole.   'The cannon of the town
are now firing, six o'clock in the evening'[1]   Carteret
had a long private audience with Frederick William,
and found him full of expressions of friendship for his
father-in-law the King of England.   In less than a month
after, the Queen—Frederick William having returned to
Berlin after a visit of a few days—arrived at Herrenhausen to make a longer stay, and, for the sake of her
matrimonial plans, was very anxious, as Carteret and
Townshend also were for more pressing political reasons,
to persuade George to return the visit at Berlin.   To
leave Hanover, unless it were to go to his shooting-seat
not very far away, was never a thing which seemed desirable to George; and it was somewhat difficult, even on
this occasion, to get him to agree.   But he was at this
moment greatly agitated by certain disturbing movements of the Czar and his fleet; and to be on good
terms with the King of Prussia was to have for a friend
the absolute master of a standing army of 80,000 men
The English King's slightly lethargic delight in the trim
charms of Hanover was actually sacrificed for reasons
of politeness and policy; Queen Sophia hoped her
maternal plans were about to be sealed by a formal
treaty, and English statesmen saw pleasant visions of an
enviable political alliance

George, accompanied by Carteret and Townshend,

[1] Brit Mus. Add MSS. 22,523. fol. 3, v°   June 29, 1723.

left Herrenhausen on October the 7th, 1723, and next evening arrived at Charlottenburg, one of the Prussian palaces a mile or so south of Berlin; a palace built by George's own sister, Sophie Charlotte, first Queen of Prussia, made immortal by a pinch of snuff. The Royal Prussian family were all at Charlottenburg ready to receive their heavy relative from Hanover; and though George terribly alarmed the whole household, and especially his own ministers, by his sudden illness that night, all was well again next morning when the sight-seeing and entertainments began. Carteret gives Walpole a slight programme of the proceedings:—

'All this Court is at the height of joy to see his majesty so full of health, as well as of goodness and graciousness You will easily imagine that the time is spent in variety of entertainments, in which the King of Prussia strives to show his utmost satisfaction at his majesty's presence. I shall not enter into a description of all that passes, but his Prussian majesty's favourite pleasure, his troops, appear in their exercise and in everything exact and perfect beyond imagination The Queen entertained his majesty yesterday at dinner at a very pretty garden-house her majesty has just out of the gates of Berlin, called *Mon Bijou*, and in the evening there was a fine ball and supper at the Castle To-morrow we shall attend the King to Potsdam, where his majesty will see the great grenadiers, and after dinner go onwards as far as Fehrbellin, in order to reach the Gohr[1] with ease on Thursday '[2]

Frederick William's favourite hobby, his regiment of the tallest men to be bought, pressed, or kidnapped in Europe, was duly paraded before his royal visitor

---

[1] George's Hanoverian hunting-seat
[2] Brit Mus. Add. MSS. 22,524, fol. 10-11.

'Nothing could make a finer appearance,' reports a *feuillet* which Carteret sent to Polwarth and Whitworth to amuse them in their dreary work at Cambrai. 'They marched before the King and then drew up and performed the exercise of advancing and retreating, and firing by platoons, which they did with that order and dexterity that they fired upwards of 10,000 shot in about fifteen minutes, each man firing fourteen times.' But far the most notable sight which George saw at Berlin was of a different, though also military, order; the Crown-Prince Cadets, some three hundred boys of good family, performing their exercise, headed by a boy of some thirteen or fourteen years old, George's own grandson, one day to be Frederick the Great. The English King, who was probably a good deal bored by Court dinners and the painful necessity of being generally polite, was especially pleased with the behaviour of the young prince. But doubtless what pleased him most of all was his safe return to his own Hanover once more.

And the double marriage, and the Prussian alliance? In spite of all the hopes and desires, not very much was done to secure the one, and absolutely nothing to secure the other. No double-marriage agreement was signed now, or ever was; Queen Sophia's unending toil on this point soon went all to ruin. A political alliance, perhaps not of a very definite kind, was indeed arranged; a promise between the two crowns of mutual friendship and help in dangers that might arise, signed at Charlottenburg by Carteret and Townshend on the English side. But that was all. Assurances of good-will were profuse on both sides; Frederick William, who had a good heart under his exceedingly rough exterior, showed really great cordiality to his somewhat inarticulate

father-in-law.   But for practical purposes this visit,
from which great things had been expected, proved to
be only a more or less enjoyable episode, which left
high political affairs very much where it had found
them

George had chiefly been reconciled to this visit to
Berlin by his alarm at certain threatening proceedings
of the Czar, and it was in argument over English policy
towards Peter the Great that it first became indisputably
evident that Walpole and Townshend were in reality the
rivals of their colleague Carteret   Well-founded information came to Hanover that Peter was fitting out a
powerful expedition; there could be little doubt that its
object was an attack on Sweden.   In Sweden there
was a considerable faction anxious to produce a change
in the Government; and if this party should unite with
the Czar, the result might be to place upon the Swedish
throne a nominee of Russia; a disastrous result for the
commercial and political interests of England   George
was exceedingly concerned at such a prospect, and discussed with Carteret and Townshend the necessary
counter-measures.   Townshend, quite as much as Carteret, recognised the serious condition of affairs and the
dangers which might throw all the north of Europe into
confusion again, and he pressed Walpole to consider
some financial plan by which money might be forthcoming in case of an emergency.   But Carteret was inclined to go further.   He urged that some English men-of-
war should at least be put into a state of readiness, that
they might join the Danish fleet without loss of time if
the Czar's action should force England to oppose him.
Townshend objected to this, and the result was a struggle
between the two Secretaries; the first actual glimpse of
their real opposition to each other   They went together

to the King, and argued the point before him, and
greatly to Townshend's delight, the royal opinion sided
with his view Carteret, says Townshend, was much
mortified ; he went out shooting for a few days in a perplexed condition.   Townshend solaced himself with
very flattering reflections, and effusively communicated
his joy to Walpole.

For by this time Walpole and Townshend had begun
to consider Carteret a serious danger in their way.
Carteret's personal charm, his great attention to business, his perfect knowledge of European politics—a
subject on which Walpole did not profess to be any
special authority—had gained him the complete favour
of the King It was much in his favour, too, that he could
speak German, while Walpole in all his conversations
with George, who had no English and spoke no French,
was restricted to an unsatisfactory, and perhaps sometimes unintelligible, dog-Latin It is curious to notice how
little progress German made in England under its first
two German Kings In 1736, when the Princess Augusta
of Saxe-Gotha was about to be married to Frederick,
Prince of Wales, it was suggested that she might ad-
visedly be taught either French or English.   Her
mother, however, with a ludicrous misconception of the
Teutonic enthusiasm of the English nation, replied that
knowledge of English or French must be quite unnecessary ; for the Hanover family had been on the English
throne for more than twenty years, and to be sure most
people in England, and especially at Court, must speak
German as well and as often as they spoke English.
Yet Lord Hervey bluntly declares that there were probably not three people in the kingdom who spoke a word
of it better than they had done in the reign of Queen
Anne.   Of German, however, Carteret was an easy

master; and amusing accounts tell with what jealous, suspicious wonder the other ministers heard Carteret conversing with the sovereign in that unknown tongue. Carteret's weight at the same time was great for another reason The influence which Earl Stanhope had possessed over Cardinal Dubois, and so over the French Court, had passed to Carteret, who thus was the chief guarantee in the Government for the continuance of the French alliance. The English ambassador at Paris had been appointed by Carteret, and was his attached personal friend. And while Carteret had these striking political and personal advantages, he decidedly had political ambition, though it was ambition of the sort which despised the labyrinthine littlenesses of the party politics of the day, and was utterly above money and ribbons and gaiters A man of this kind and Walpole could not possibly long work together, and the crisis of their disagreement came during this visit to Hanover.

No English statesman of the first half of the eighteenth century, however high his personal character and unquestionable his abilities, could keep his head above water without a firm hold of Court favour, and in the reign of George I. this favour was only to be obtained through channels of a somewhat unsavoury kind. A minister was obliged to use self-interested agents whom, if he were a man like Carteret, he thoroughly despised, and could hardly be got to endure in his presence. A man like Walpole handled such tools with a sort of cynical good-humour, as if there were a kind of unmentioned but half-understood *camaraderie* between them while a creature of the Bubb Dodington stamp would soil himself among them with a genial familiarity, accepting it as a first principle that dirt was matter in the *right* place. No English states-

man of the day kept his hands so clean as Carteret ; no
one suffered so much for having despised dirty effrontery
and back-stairs bribery   But, under the first Hanoverian sovereign of England, to have a friend at Court was
for a minister almost a necessity of political existence ;
and, so far, Carteret had to follow the fashion or deform-
ity of the time

From Hanover, George brought with him to England
two leading favourites who are inextricably entangled in
the political life of his reign   One of these Teutonic
women is best remembered by the title of Countess
of Darlington ; a fierce-eyed, red-faced, intolerably fat
woman—a really great character if size is to be the
criterion. She was so ponderous that the amused English
people compared her to an elephant and castle ; but
George could stand a very large quantity of fat   Some
of the English ladies of larger bulk, seeing the royal
predilection that way, did what they could to increase
the magnitude of their attractions   ' Some succeeded
and others burst,' sneers Chesterfield, less unjustifiably
than usual   They say that this overpowering Countess
had been beautiful once, though now she had got into
this mere giantess condition, finding all warm weather
oppressive   The world has forgotten her in spite of her
imperious influence in the Court of George I. How
much did she weigh ? posterity asks with languid interest, and learns with the completest indifference that the
amount is unknown.

The other favourite. a woman of various German and
English titles, still vaguely hangs on to memory as
Duchess of Kendal. Physically, she was a great contrast
to the Countess of Darlington   Not at all beautiful ;
' a very tall, lean, ill-favoured old lady,' was Horace
Walpole's boyish reminiscence of her   She was so tall,

gaunt, and scraggy that she was familiarly known as
the 'Maypole' Except for her insatiable appetite for
money, in which the Darlington fully equalled her,
there was no particular harm in this simple old creature Her abilities were too trifling to require any
mention. Chesterfield plainly says that she was very
little above an idiot. She was so complacently foolish
that her society was very attractive and soothing to
George I.; and, in spite of her deficiency in fat, her
influence with him was considerably greater than her
rival's She was a Lutheran, with a reputation for piety
of a sort; painfully going seven times every Sunday to
Lutheran chapels in London More curious was the
tinge of superstition in the Countess, who piously cherished a black raven which had flown in at her window
soon after the King's death, and firmly believed that here
was the soul of his departed majesty whom she was
never more to see 'Quoth the raven, Never more'

So exceedingly influential with the King were these
ludicrously unprofitable German women, that statesmen had to take the chances of their support or ill-
will into their best and most serious consideration
In addition, therefore, to the politicians who were
inclined to follow Carteret's lead, when the deaths of
Sunderland and Stanhope left him as the chief representative of that section of the Whigs, it became
necessary for Carteret to secure, if possible, the good-
will of one of the two feminine favourites who swayed
the King very much as they pleased. Carteret so far
succeeded that he might reckon on the support of the
Countess of Darlington, so long as it should not be her
interest to favour any one else. But, on the other hand,
the Duchess of Kendal was in a thorough understanding
with Walpole and Townshend; and the Duchess was

more influential with the King than the Countess.
Townshend, in view of the coming contest with Carteret,
was particularly well satisfied with the state of this
feminine question. In his letters to Walpole, the
Duchess of Kendal was the 'Good Duchess,' their fast
friend; and he exultantly wrote from Hanover in October 1723: 'I believe I may venture to say she reposes
a more entire confidence in me at present than in any
other person about the King.' So far, the brother-
ministers might fairly congratulate themselves on their
probabilities of success, with all the more malicious
certainty when they remembered that the Duchess of
Kendal, quite apart from her Court rivalry, had a private jealousy against the family to which the Countess of
Darlington belonged.

It was over a rather contemptible affair, more or less
connected with these uninteresting denizens of a Court
where there was no Queen, that the quarrel in the
English ministry came to its crisis

A Swiss, Sir Luke Schaub, who had been the Earl of
Stanhope's private secretary, and was Carteret's intimate
friend, was at this period English ambassador at Paris
He had been appointed by Carteret, and was, therefore,
suspiciously regarded by Walpole and Townshend. The
want of harmony among the English ministers was, of
course, known to Schaub; and Dubois, who had become
Prime Minister of France through English influence,
was also perfectly aware of it   The three ministers—
Walpole, Townshend, and Carteret—had, indeed, unitedly signed a letter to Dubois, after the death of Sunderland, and had formally announced their union and their
desire to continue towards France the policy of Sunderland and Stanhope; but Carteret, writing to Schaub
at the same time, had spoken plainly of the probability

of disagreements   He told Schaub that he felt his
position strong ; but he also declared himself resolved
not to remain long united with his colleagues, if he were
not fully persuaded of their good intentions.[1]   He
refused, however, to believe that Walpole and Townshend meant to deal dishonestly with him.[2]   Schaub,
on his side, naturally upheld at Paris the interest and
influence of Carteret ; and Schaub's own weight with
Dubois, which was a considerable guarantee for the continuance of good relations between England and France,
no doubt seemed to Carteret a guarantee also for his
own safe position in the ministry   If, then, Walpole
could weaken Carteret's influence here—could give a
blow to Carteret's reputation at Paris, that would be to
damage Carteret where he seemed to be most strong,
and to injure him in the place where he would feel it
the most   Walpole resolved to try.

One of the schemes which Schaub at Paris was anxious to carry out was a marriage between a niece of the
Countess of Darlington and a young French nobleman,
son of the Marquis de la Vrilhère   The King of England
was eager for this match; but one condition the
Darlington family imperatively desired   They insisted
that the Marquis de la Vrillière must be made a Duke.
There was likely to be some difficulty in gaining the
assent of the French Court   George, who could not
with dignity make such an application to Louis XV.
unless he knew that it would be at once granted, did
actually himself write a letter requesting the promotion;
the letter only to be presented if success was certain
The negotiation was thrown into the hands of Schaub,

[1] Carteret to Schaub May 4, 1722 Brit Mus Sloane MSS 4,204,
fol 66, v°.

[2] *Id.* to *id* Sloane MSS 4,204, fol 67, v°

and, necessarily, of Carteret, to whom, deep in the affairs of the Congress of Cambrai, the thing was doubtless as insignificant as it deserved to be. Yet this merely vulgar affair, a question concerning nothing more important than the lumbering etiquette of a handful of objectionable Teutonic people, served as well as anything else to overthrow an English statesman of genius, and firmly to secure Walpole in a position which he was to hold for nearly twenty years to come.

The first check which Carteret received was the death of Cardinal Dubois in August 1723. Rumours of the disagreements between Carteret and Townshend at Hanover had already been floating in London and giving rise to various inconsistent conjectures. Some said that Carteret would soon be back in England to form, along with Walpole, a reorganised ministry; others, that he was returning in disgrace. The death of Dubois, opening to the brother-ministers the possibility of procuring the recall of Schaub from Paris, gave them also a chance to make it clear to every one that it was Carteret who was in the weak position and whose political power was declining. If the ambassador who practically was Carteret's nominee, who was devoted to Carteret's interests, could be removed, a blow would be struck which every one would be able to appreciate, and all rumours of Carteret's superior influence with the King would be effectually contradicted. Walpole and Townshend accordingly began to make disparaging representations of Schaub, to assert that any influence which he might have had at Paris had been destroyed by the death of Dubois, and that to retain him in his embassy there would be damaging to the King's affairs. They did not dare flatly to ask Schaub's recall, but went about the thing in an intriguing way, which they thought was

certain, sooner or later, to produce the desired result.
A special incident helped them. On the death of
Dubois, the Regent Orleans recalled to Paris one Count
Nocé who had been banished by the influence of the
Cardinal, but now returned to renewed perfect intimacy
with the Regent. Carteret himself was rather anxious
when he heard of this, for Nocé was on bad terms
with Schaub, whose influence with Dubois he considered
to have been the real cause of his disgrace Walpole
and Townshend gladly took advantage of this convenient
occurrence. Townshend, at Hanover, suggested to the
King that it would be well to send to Paris an envoy
who with all discreetness, and concealing as far as he
possibly could the real intention of his journey, should
ascertain what Schaub's influence with the French Government really was. But how could this be done without disgusting Carteret? France was in his department;
any appointment to Paris was Carteret's affair To avoid
the chance of an open and premature quarrel, Townshend suggested that the thing should be managed as
informally as possible. The envoy should not adopt a
diplomatic character; should not even go direct from
Hanover to Paris, but should start from London with a
supposed intention to make his way to Hanover, taking
Paris only on his road, as if with merely private curiosity
to see it. To explain a somewhat prolonged stay there,
he should make pretence of visiting the neighbouring
palaces and other objects of reasonable interest, in which
an intelligent foreigner might naturally profess to find
excusable attraction. And for this slightly ambiguous
enterprise, Townshend very quietly proposed Horatio
Walpole, Robert Walpole's younger brother

This appointment, brought about without any previous information to Carteret, was the second check

which he received, and Townshend was very triumphant.
A spy was about to be sent into Carteret's own department, and Carteret had not even been consulted in the matter. Other little incidents, trifling in themselves, pointed
towards the same zealous undermining of Carteret's
position. On various small occasions Townshend did
all he could to thwart Carteret at Hanover, opposing
his recommendations, and endeavouring to weaken his
influence Yet Carteret seems to have taken it all good-
humouredly enough, and probably did not think the
state of affairs too serious. Townshend, after one of
his little successes over his colleague, wrote home to
Walpole—'Perhaps you may have some curiosity to
know what my good colleague's behaviour was upon
this victory We came home very lovingly together,
and he was lavish on his old topic, how well he intended
to live with you and me' At the same time, Townshend
evidently did not care to appear too confident; for he
begged Walpole to mention these particulars to Newcastle alone. 'Nothing would give his majesty greater
offence than our making any such affair a matter of
triumph, and the less we boast, the more we shall certainly have to boast of Townshend was determined
to have a great deal more to boast of Hardly had
Horatio Walpole started on his ambiguous mission when
Townshend, having succeeded so far, thought he might
with cheerful confidence go further He suggested that
Walpole's position at Paris would be much improved if
he had some credentials from the King There was an
easy excuse to make for this. The King of Portugal
was about to join the Quadruple Alliance, let Horatio
Walpole, then, have full powers to manage from Paris
the various formalities which such an occasion required
The King agreed, spoke of it to Carteret as if it had been

a thought of his own, and Carteret could not venture to oppose. But Townshend says that Carteret was extremely mortified, and a duller man than he could easily have foreseen the end of all these little slights and irritations Yet Townshend seems, with wishful eagerness, to have exaggerated the effect which the appointment of Horatio Walpole had on Carteret He declared to the minister in London that Carteret had been perfectly astonished by the stroke. 'I never observed in him on any occasion such visible marks of despair' In ascribing despair to Carteret, Townshend was doubtless wrong Carteret might easily enough have been disgusted, and may very probably not have cared to conceal it—suspicious of his colleagues he had only too good reason to be; but despair, even in far more serious circumstances than these, was altogether out of Carteret's way. His own language shows that he knew well enough the plots which were being laid against him, but that he did not take them at all in the tragic manner which Townshend fancied he had perceived. Writing of Horatio Walpole's appointment, Carteret said: '*Cette affaire ne me cause point de peine, quoique mes collègues aient certainement quelque chose en tête en cet égard qu'ils ne m'ont point expliqué, et peut-être pas même au roi Vous serez fort attentif à voir si Horatio Walpole tache me mettre mal dans l'esprit du Duc d'Orleans et du Comte du Morville. Mais vous vous garderez bien de lui laisser entrevoir mes soupçons ou les vôtres, si vôtres*'[1] Carteret was suspicious, but practically not much disturbed It is almost amusing to see the precisely opposite views which he and Townshend took of their political circumstances. The very day after Carteret had written

[1] Carteret to Schaub, Oct 24, 1723 Brit Mus Sloane MSS 4,204, fol 93-94

as above to Schaub, Townshend cheerfully told Walpole
that his own interest with the King was daily rising,
while that of Carteret was daily sinking [1] Before the
year 1723 was ended Townshend wrote to his brother-in-
law: 'I will venture to assure the Duke of Newcastle
and you, that we have all reason to be satisfied with
our Hanover expedition.' [2] A month later, Carteret,
referring to rumours which represented his decline in
influence, says to Schaub: 'All the reports to which
you allude are false I have mentioned them to the
King, who expressed as much kindness as ever, and the
same approbation of my conduct, and of my zealous
though feeble services . . . My colleagues instead of
attacking have courted me for some time past' [3]

Quite apart from the personal relations of Carteret
and Townshend at Hanover, the position of Schaub and
Horatio Walpole at Paris soon became embarrassing
and ridiculous It was impossible to keep up the pretence that Walpole was there out of mere private
curiosity A diplomatic person sniffing about the
sights of Paris, and doing mere innocent dilettantism,
was something more than absurd, and could impose on
no one. Every one understood that it was a trial of
strength between the two men Schaub, on his side,
was naturally mortified that any one should have been
sent at all, especially one of Walpole's social position
and ministerial connections His letters to Carteret are
full of the disgust he not unnaturally felt. On the
other hand, Walpole wrote that Schaub had lost all
influence with the Duke of Orleans, that to get the

[1] MSS of Earl of Ashburnham, Hist MSS Commission. Rep. VIII
part III., p 4.
[2] Coxe *Walpole* II 295 Dec 5, 1723
[3] Carteret to Schaub, Jan 8 1724 Brit Mus Add MSS 9,151,
fol 23.

desired dukedom was impossible; that the ambassador was in no way fitted for his post. Yet the brother-ministers could not get Schaub recalled. Horatio Walpole soon began to feel his position intolerable. Whenever he and Schaub appeared in public together people laughed in an amused, half-puzzled fashion, hardly knowing which was ambassador and which was not. That Walpole had actually come was presumptive evidence in his favour, but that Schaub did not go was actual evidence in his. People were perplexed. Walpole was annoyed, and even beginning to feel angry. Carteret, according to the King's commands, had sent him credentials, but Walpole declared that he would not use them. He even took offence at the harmless letter with which Carteret accompanied the documents. 'His letter, by-the-bye, was the most dry, not to say the most impertinent, I ever received from a Secretary of State to a minister,' wrote Walpole to his brother in a slightly ungrammatical manner, 'but that don't trouble me at all.' Surely official Horatio could hardly have expected lyrical congratulations from Carteret, and as a matter of fact the letter, which was a formal one only, had nothing in it with which Walpole, if he had not been in a state of querulous irritation, could have found any fault. But Walpole, who had a very considerable estimation of his own diplomatic abilities and self-importance, was annoyed to find that the simple fact of his appearance on the scene did not at once bring about the result which he desired.

Yet even second-rate diplomatists of an irritable turn of mind get what they want if they will only wait long enough for it. To Walpole, wanting to drop easily into a desirable appointment, the delay was undoubtedly

provokingly long   Carteret's influence was so great
that impetuous action was out of the question.   There
was even a rumour that Carteret himself would take
the post of ambassador at Paris—a possible removal of
Schaub which to Walpole must have seemed nothing
short of tragic   But the end of Walpole's anxieties
came at last.   The Regent Orleans had died in December, and had been succeeded by the Duke of Bourbon
The new Regent, who at first spoke vaguely, at length
definitely declared that to grant the dukedom to the
Marquis de la Vrilhère was absolutely impossible.   Yet
so powerful was Carteret's influence that even this was
not enough to procure the recall of Schaub.   Townshend therefore resolved on a decisive step   He instructed Horatio Walpole to write home a despatch
asserting that Schaub was an obstacle to the efficient
performance of the King's business, and urging his immediate recall   This letter was written by Walpole in
March 1724, and brought the long contest to an end
Schaub was recalled in April, and the fall of Carteret
was the necessary consequence

The brother-ministers had carried their point, but
their success. though very considerable, was far from
complete.   They were not able to remove Carteret's
political adherents from their official posts, and they
were not able to get rid of Carteret himself altogether
He ceased to be Secretary of State, and, as if it were
desired to emphasise the fact that it was a man of
genius who had been removed, the Duke of Newcastle
was appointed to succeed him.   But to dismiss Carteret
altogether was what his rivals could not venture to do.
Townshend wrote to the Duke of Grafton, at that time
Lord-Lieutenant of Ireland, that to remove Carteret
with   was

simply impossible, and he politely informed Grafton that he must make way for the fallen Secretary   In Dublin, Carteret would give Walpole less cause for alarm than anywhere else   He would be, for half the year at least, removed from the Court and from London political life; and this was a great consideration to ministers who dreaded Carteret's remarkable personal influence, and the special friendship and approbation with which the King treated him. Carteret's forced resignation was by no means to the satisfaction of the King, and when, a few days afterwards, he was appointed Lord-Lieutenant of Ireland, George told him that if he had had anything better to offer him he should have had it.[1] The night after the ministerial changes were announced, the King spoke for half an hour to Carteret in the drawing-room, and had hardly a word for any other person[2] Considerable doubt was soon current whether Carteret, though named Lord-Lieutenant, would ever go to Ireland at all   It did not seem at all unlikely that he might soon be restored to office with even more power than he had had before. Even the limited amount of self-congratulation with which Walpole and Townshend might perhaps cheer themselves was reckoned by many political onlookers as decidedly premature   Carteret's friends were sanguine. 'His enemies would be very glad to see his back turned, and they begin to find they have gained no strength by the late change. He is certainly as well if not better than ever with the King; constant in his attendance at Court, and supported by almost all the foreign powers.'[3] Carteret's

---

[1] Papers of W King, Archbishop of Dublin   Hist MSS Commission, Report II 235.

[2] St John Brodrick to Lord Chancellor Midleton, April 14, 1724 Coxe, *Walpole*, II 389

[3] Brodrick to Midleton   April 20, 1724   Add MSS 9245, fol 13 14

own disposition was always hopefully sanguine, but it
does not seem that on this occasion he shared the too
confident expectations of some of his political adherents.
The only remaining fragment of personal evidence
rather shows that he judged the situation quite im-
partially, and recognised the facts as they were. He
did not pretend to deny that Walpole and Townshend
had played the political game ungenerously and unfairly; he complained much of the way in which
Townshend had treated him at Hanover, and especially
of the unjust and intriguing interposition of Horatio
Walpole at Paris, but he recognised that though the
fair rules of the game had been broken the play was
over, and he had lost. He took his defeat with his
usual good-humour, simply saying that as he had no
political obligations to Townshend he would never, as
Secretary of State, have consented to be Townshend's
mere subordinate, and, for the rest, that he had no
quarrel with the ministers who had beaten him, and
would do nothing to oppose their measures [1] In this
good-natured frame of mind, relieved from the annoy-
ances as well as from the responsibilities of an office in
which he had been very badly treated, he remained
in England for six months more, till the seriously
threatening condition of Irish public affairs called him
to new duties and difficulties in Dublin.

[1] Stephen Poyntz to Horatio Walpole, April 5, 1724. Add. MSS.
9,151, fol. 156

CHAPTER IV.

LORD-LIEUTENANT OF IRELAND

1724—1730.

WHILE Walpole and Townshend had thus in 1723 and 1724 devoted themselves to intrigue against Carteret in London and at Hanover, Walpole's own Government in Ireland had involved itself in serious difficulties. True to his constant practice of sacrificing men, policy, and principles to his own personal hold on power, Walpole, fearful of offending the Duchess of Kendal, was now pushing forward an Irish scheme in which he himself had no particular interest. He, probably, even disapproved it; but the favourite Duchess was especially solicitous, and Walpole was not inclined to irritate or alienate her For two years the relations between England and Ireland were strained almost to the breaking point, because the Duchess of Kendal was ravenously fond of money, and Walpole could not personally afford to annoy her.

For some time there had been a great want of copper coin in Ireland. There was no doubt about this; Swift in his *Drapier's Letters* admits it While Lord Sunderland was still minister, the coinage question was under consideration; and as Ireland had no mint of its own, various proposals were made in England for remedying the Irish want Nothing was agreed upon

during Sunderland's life-time; but in 1723, when
Walpole was at the head of affairs, a Wolverhampton
iron-founder, named Wood, obtained a patent to coin
copper money for Ireland to the value of 108,000*l.*
Perhaps there was nothing unusual about such a proceeding, but on this particular occasion everything was
mismanaged, and went wrong from the first The
scheme was not clearly explained to the Irish people;
the leading men in Ireland were not even consulted
about it   Before the coin could be got into circulation,
murmurs of discontent came from Ireland. Wood was
disliked as a foreigner; he was vain, impudent, bragging   He was a rich man of business; but Swift never
wearied in contemptuously insulting him   In the profuse
vocabulary of Swift's *Drapier's Letters* Wood was a
vile fellow, a mean ordinary man, a hardware dealer, a
sorry fellow, a little impudent hardwareman, a diminu-
tive insignificant mechanic   In the title of one of his
broadside poems, Swift called him 'brazier, tinker,
hardwareman, coiner, founder, and esquire' The angry
feelings roused by this unlucky scheme were further
excited by the rumour that this unknown Englishman
owed his patent to mere corruption, and that the
condition of his contract implied a substantial bribe
to one of the Hanoverians, the insatiable Duchess of
Kendal. Soon the general cry insisted that the coin
was bad, and would ruin the shop keepers and poor
people who would be forced to accept it; while from
better-instructed persons came the more weighty
objection that the amount of the proposed coinage was
absurdly large, and out of all proportion to the currency
of gold and silver in Ireland   Passion and argument
were very strangely mixed throughout the course of the
whole affair.

The agitation in Ireland had become very general and embittered, when the Lord-Lieutenant, the Duke of Grafton, landed at Dublin in August 1723, after his usual yearly visit to England He found that the question of the coinage was the universal subject of conversation and complaint Irishmen who in all other matters were very well affected to the English Government had not a word to say in defence of the patent, or if they had, they dared not open their lips to hint approval. Grafton instantly took alarm, and foresaw an inevitably troubled parliamentary session. From the very first he predicted to Walpole that the affair would end in a manner disagreeable to both of them [1] When the Irish Houses met in September, the temper of the members was so evident that Grafton, fearing bad results if he should refer to the matter in the terms of his instructions from England, made no mention of it at all in his opening speech to parliament But when he attempted to hinder parliament itself from inquiring into the patent which the English Government had granted, he found his task hopeless He could not prevail upon a single member to support the Government view of the question, or to oppose parliamentary examination of it. He could get no better promise from any one than that members would discuss the matter in a decent and respectful way. From some he could not get even so little satisfaction as this He told Walpole that while the Irish Lord Chancellor, Midleton, was giving daily assurances of mildness and moderation, his son, Mr. Brodrick, was moving or supporting the most peevish resolutions, and making the most inflaming speeches —

'The son was yesterday overheard to say (after

[1] Grafton to Walpole, Aug 22, 1723 MSS Record Office.

he had used some very odd expressions in a debate about addressing for some papers) that nobody was too great in another kingdom to be reached for what he had done in prejudice to this, for that a first minister in England had been impeached upon grievances complained of by this nation. You see what an unhappy situation I am in here. I am labouring from morning to night under the greatest difficulties and uneasiness, and fear at last that the event will be very far from being agreeable either to you or myself."[1]

Far from leaving the matter without parliamentary notice, the Irish Houses took it up with cheerful anger. A call of the House of Commons was ordered, and in Committee resolutions were adopted which declared that the patent was unjust and ruinous, and had been obtained by misrepresentation and fraud. Grafton announced this unpleasant proceeding in a letter which was too much for Walpole's usually unruffled good-humour. It was well that things were no worse, Grafton rather meekly said. What might not have happened if Brodrick and the more violent spirits had had their way! They would have insisted upon resolutions full of bitterness; perhaps, even, have demanded a vote of censure on those ministers who had advised the King to grant this patent. But all that had been over-ruled. Walpole was exceedingly annoyed by what he reckoned Grafton's indifferent and cowardly excuse for so serious an attack upon the Government. As Secretary of State, Walpole refused to write a word to the Lord-Lieutenant on his conduct and management; but in a private letter he told him that the difference of their views on this matter could not possibly be greater. A vote of censure, murmured Grafton, had been avoided.

[1] Grafton to Walpole, Sept. 14, 1723. MSS. Record Office.

'A notable performance! I know very well what these things mean in an English parliament, but I suppose you talk another language in Ireland. But let that pass. I have weathered great storms before now, and shall not be lost in an Irish hurricane. And when I am lost [I hope] that those who are insensible of such unjust scandal heaped upon me will not know the want of me And I give your Grace my word, when this comes to be retorted upon you, as much as I am hurt, I will not be indifferent. . If Brodnick attacked, nobody defended And what is still more, you seem to think that we must here give in to it too Where is then the great crime to start a question in parliament, so very popular that nobody there dared to oppose, and when it comes to be considered here again, the ministry who passed the grant must confess that there was just cause of complaint' . Pray don't do in this. as you have in every other step, stay till all is over and then speak '[1]

Walpole was thoroughly angry; and many other letters, reproachfully complaining on Walpole's side, apologising and explanatory on Grafton's, passed between the two. Grafton defended himself against the charge of indifference to Walpole's friendship, and lukewarmness in support of the administration At great length he justified all he had done at every stage of the coinage question, but ended by declaring that he did not know what to advise. 'I wish to God I was able to advise what is proper to be done in the present situation of affairs It is above my reach . . In the English storms you have weathered, I never endeavoured or desired to get first to shore, nor could I imagine that in an Irish hurricane I could have any view of safety

' Walpole to Grafton Oct 3, 1723 MSS Record Office

where you are in danger.'[1]   But Walpole was not much
mollified by Grafton's elaborate defence; and in an
earlier private letter, he had been exceedingly severe :—

  ' Forgive me . . . . if I tell you I do not wonder at all
that nobody appears in defence of the King's patent
when you think it advisable to write and express yourself in the manner you do . . I shall wonder at nothing
that shall happen upon this occasion . . . The parliament under your administration is attacking a patent already passed in favour of whom and for whose sake alone
you know very well. Will it be for the service to suffer
an indignity in that vein ? The patent was passed by
those that you have been hitherto looked upon as pretty
nearly engaged with in that public capacity, are they
no longer worth your care or trouble ? It was passed
under the particular care and direction of one upon
whom the first reflection must fall, that never yet was
indifferent where you was concerned. . . . Does your
Grace think you will be thought to make a glorious
campaign, if by compounding for this you should be
able to carry all the other business through without
much difficulty? . . . I never knew more care taken
upon any occasion than in passing this patent. I am
still satisfied it is very well to be supported   What
remedy the wisdom of Ireland will find out for this supposed grievance I am at a loss to guess, and upon whom
the consequence of this Irish storm will fall most heavily
I will not say   I shall have my share, but if I am not
mistaken there are others that will not escape. I hope
your Grace is not mistaken when you are persuaded to
be thus indifferent   There are some people that think
they are ever to fatten at the expense of other men's
labours and characters, and be themselves the most

1 Grafton to Walpole, Oct. 19, 1724. MSS. Record Office.

righteous fine gentlemen. It is a species of mankind that I own I detest. But I'll say no more, and if your Grace thinks I have said too much I am sorry for it; but mark the end.'[1]

Grafton no doubt thought that Walpole had said too much by far; and further letters, following this sufficiently emphatic one, thoroughly annoyed the Duke. Townshend wrote to Grafton a letter of remonstrance so passionately expressed that Walpole judged it imprudent to send it, but he hardly took the sting out of Townshend's angry rebuke when he told Grafton that though he had burnt the letter he perfectly agreed with it   Walpole was always merciless in crushing anything like insubordination in members of his Government, and on this particular occasion his business instinct was offended by the rather limp procedure of one whom he plainly called a mere fair-weather pilot.   He was further embittered by the belief that the Irish opposition to the patent rested very considerably on the knowledge that there were divisions in the Government in England, and on the belief that Carteret must prevail over the ministers who were plotting against him.   Walpole was not at all disposed to yield, but felt himself in embarrassing difficulties   For while he was scolding the Lord-Lieutenant and fretting against the Secretary of State, the resolutions and addresses of the Irish parliament were on their way to Carteret at Hanover, to be presented to the King   Grafton had implored that the answers might not be of a kind to further irritate the nation. It was indispensable for Walpole to get the Irish Money Bill through the Irish parliament, yet that parliament had declared that till the patent was disposed of it would touch no other business whatever.   Walpole was determined not to

[1] Walpole to Grafton, Sept 24, 1723 MSS Record Office.

admit either that the patent in itself was what the Irish
represented it to be, or that the King in granting it had
in any way overstepped his authority and prerogative
Yet if the King's reply should fail to satisfy the Irish
nation, the whole Irish Government would probably be
thrown into confusion.　Walpole was doubtless much
disgusted, but in the circumstances he could do nothing
but recommend a conciliatory answer.　By his advice
the King's reply expressed regret for the uneasiness
which had been caused in Ireland, and promised that if
any abuses had been committed by the patentee Wood
they should be inquired into and punished　From
Hanover, in November 1723, Carteret sent royal answers
in this sense to Grafton, and the Irish parliament,
thanking the King, and assuming that the whole thing
was practically at an end, voted the supplies for the
customary two years, and broke up, not to meet again
till the autumn of 1725

The royal promise was kept, with a result very
different from the expectations of the Irish parliament.
A committee of the Privy Council investigated the Irish
complaints　Sir Isaac Newton, Master of the Mint, examined specimens of Wood's coinage, and in July 1724
the committee produced its report, drawn up by Walpole
himself　The committee found that the conditions of
the patent had been observed, that the coin was good,
and was needed in Ireland, but recommended that the
proposed amount should be much reduced, and that
40,000*l* should be the utmost value which the patentee
should be allowed to coin.

This report was sent to Dublin, but it only exasperated
a strife which had seemed about to die away.　The
unwise patentee boasted over his seeming success　He
declared, or it suited Swift to assert that he declared,

that his coin should be swallowed in fire-balls, and that Walpole would cram his money-bags down the throats of the people   But far more fatal for Walpole and the Duchess of Kendal than Wood's noisy bragging was the terrible appearance of Swift   With a personal grudge against Walpole, and a detestation of everything Whiggish, Swift seized an opportunity ready-made to his hand   As a Dublin tradesman quietly writing his simple *Drapier's Letters* to his fellow-shopkeepers of Ireland, he produced a storm before which England was forced unwillingly to yield.   And it was when this storm was at its very highest and angriest that Carteret landed in Ireland as Lord-Lieutenant

The position which Carteret now held was not in any case a very attractive one, and the special circumstances in which he accepted it did not gift it with any unusual charm.   Carteret was about to undertake a difficult and rather thankless piece of work, and some at least of his colleagues positively hoped that his work might fail   When Walpole and Townshend began to understand that the Irish opposition to the English patent was really serious, then jealous suspicion readily convinced itself that Carteret in some way or other must be connected with this   Carteret was on terms of private friendship with the Brodricks, a leading Whig family in Ireland, but firmly opposed to the Whig Walpole on the coinage question   While Townshend and Carteret were with the King on the continent, one of the Brodrick family arrived at Hanover in the autumn of 1723   Walpole and Townshend both assumed that his object was to intrigue with Carteret against them. 'Lord Carteret, in this attack, has different views,' Walpole wrote to Townshend : 'he shuns the Duke of Grafton, he flings dirt upon me, who passed the patent, and makes

somebody [the Duchess of Kendal] uneasy, for whose
sake it was done; and this is one of the instances wherein
those that think themselves in danger begin to be upon
the offensive.'[1] Yet beyond the fact that Carteret knew
the Brodricks and that the Brodricks were against the
patent, there is positively no evidence to justify Walpole's
suspicion. Such evidence as there is points rather the
other way, and goes to prove that Carteret held himself
quite apart from a thing which as yet did not especially
concern him. When the addresses of the Irish parliament were forwarded to him at Hanover, he wrote in
reply to Grafton that he had placed them before the
King 'in the most effectual manner that I was able, considering that I had no knowledge of this affair, until it
was taken up by each House of Parliament.'[2] When
Carteret and Townshend spoke on the question together,
Carteret said that as the coinage was an inherent prerogative of the Crown, he did not see what either House
could have to object to it. Six months later than this,
when Carteret, already officially Lord-Lieutenant of
Ireland, was still in London, the very Brodrick family
with whom he was supposed to be intriguing are witnesses that he was holding himself quite apart from
interference on either side. St. John Brodrick, writing
to Lord Chancellor Midleton in April 1724, and acknowledging Carteret's very great personal kindness, says of
the coinage dispute: 'Our friend seems resolved to be
perfectly passive in this affair.'[3] Carteret, indeed, far
from caballing with Midleton and his relations, had four
months before the date of this letter privately informed
Grafton that the King was so displeased with the Lord

[1] Coxe *Walpole* II 276, 277. Oct. 12, 1723
[2] Brit. Mus. Add. MSS 22,524, fol. 30
[3] Brit. Mus. Add. MSS 9,245. fol. 13 14. April 29, 1724

Chancellor's conduct that he intended to deprive him of the seals

Carteret became Lord-Lieutenant of Ireland in April 1724 ; and though, as Brodrick wrote, he was personally passive in the matter of the patent, it then became his official duty to attempt a solution of this much-vexed question   It is interesting to note that the proposal which he made, though it was disapproved by the other ministers and objected to by the King, was precisely the one which in the end was adopted, to the complete justification of Carteret's common-sense statesmanship.   Carteret always looked upon facts as they really were   So late as August 1724, after the affair had been in serious agitation for more than a year, Newcastle wrote that the King and his ministers were at a great loss what to do.   They were full of querulous insistence that the patent must be maintained, while at the same time they were distressed and irritated to see that the government officials in Ireland entirely failed to win the consent of the Irish people or parliament. But Carteret saw clearly and proposed boldly.   It was already plain to him that the patent must be surrendered, and he expressed his views to Townshend and Newcastle. Ireland, he said in his homely idiomatic style, might very well pay the fiddler, and, in return for the complete cancelling of the formally sanctioned scheme might award Wood some fair compensation for his pecuniary loss.   This is exactly what was afterwards done ; but Newcastle and Townshend considered such a proposal sheer absurdity   The affair, they said, was no longer a mere question of coinage and patents ; it concerned the honour of the King and of the nation.   They would not listen to Carteret's proposal ; neither did the King approve it   But one practical measure the King did desire. Little as it was to his taste to sacrifice Carteret, he now wished that Carteret should go to Ireland as soon as possible This was also Walpole's view Walpole firmly believed that the Irish officials, Lords-Justices, and others, had been plotting against the scheme which it was their official duty to promote, and he thought it worse than hopeless to trust to their conduct any longer. He therefore wished that the new Lord-Lieutenant should go over at once, since everything must now depend on what Carteret might do or advise Carteret promptly agreed, and arrived in Dublin on October 23, 1724

Newcastle, of course, professed friendship, and of course professed it perfidiously On the 8th of September he wrote to Carteret, repeating his facile and frequent assurances of support and assistance. In the same month Newcastle wrote also to Horatio Walpole, exulting over Carteret's departure from England, and maliciously anticipating his possible failure 'Lord Carteret,' wrote Newcastle in an early specimen of the duplicity with which he constantly treated Carteret, 'is contrary to his wish sent to Ireland, to quell the disturbances he has himself fomented This you may imagine is no easy task for him, and possibly may end in——'[1] There is nothing mysterious in the blank left in Newcastle's treacherous letter Failure, disgrace, ruin, the strongest of these words would have filled up the gap to Newcastle's complete satisfaction Townshend's feelings were very much the same. If a letter supposed to be his is really so, Townshend was capable of believing that Carteret had condescended to deliberate lying about his connection with Ireland.[2] Carteret cannot have

[1] Brit Mus Add MSS 9,152; fol 136 Sept 26, 1724
[2] Brit Mus Add. MSS 9,243, fol 38. Aug 23, 1724.

deceived himself, it was too clear that though he was the nominal colleague of Walpole and Townshend and Newcastle, he must expect support only from himself. But he undertook his task with his usual courage. Before starting, he wrote to Newcastle with a frank openness, which the most treacherous of politicians by no means deserved :—

'I give your Grace a thousand thanks for the comfort of your letter in your own hand, in which you assure me of your Grace's protection and also of my Lord Townshend's. I will endeavour to deserve it, and I am sure your Grace is too just to measure services only by the success of them. In full confidence that you will set my good intentions and zeal for his majesty's service from time to time in a true light, I shall cheerfully proceed. . . We drank your health, as well as that of all the Pelhams in the world.'[1]

On the same date Carteret wrote to a subordinate official friend —

'Certainty of success is in nobody's power; however, I'll do my best, and it is not the first difficult commission that I have been employed in. Often goes the pitcher, &c , says the old proverb, but it frightens me not ; and if I am to have the fate of the pitcher, people shall lament me, and say I deserved better luck There are some people in Ireland who say they are my friends. I shall now see what they will do, or can do To both their *telle* and their *posse* I am as yet a stranger.'[2]

Carteret's arrival was anxiously expected by the leading men in Dublin It was universally hoped that the new Lord-Lieutenant would at once declare the

---

[1] Sept 10, 1721. MSS. Record Office
[2] *Idem.*

patent cancelled Already in April, the month of Carteret's appointment, his old friend Swift, at the request
of many influential persons in Ireland, had written
hoping that Carteret would do what he could for their
relief; and Carteret had replied, unable to say anything
very definite, but recognising the unanimous feeling of
the Irish people 'I hope the nation will not suffer by
my being in this great station ; and if I can contribute
to its prosperity, I shall think it the honour and happiness of my life.' When the date of Carteret's arrival
was drawing near, Swift wrote again .—

'We are here preparing for your reception, and for
a quiet session under your government; but whether
you approve the manner, I can only guess It is by
universal declarations against Wood's coin. One thing
I am confident of, that your Excellency will find and
leave us under dispositions very different, towards your
person and high station, from what have appeared towards others.'

Carteret landed on October 23, 1724 ; and by bringing Lady Carteret and his daughter with him was
thought to meditate a long stay 'He looks well and
pleased.' wrote one who saw him that first day . 'but
how long he may continue so I know not. We seem
here bent upon our own ruin '[1] The first few days of
Carteret's residence in Ireland were mainly occupied
with the usual complimentary ceremonials He was
exceedingly well received, and especially delighted the
University and the citizens of Dublin by his replies
to their congratulations But what would he say
about the coinage? That was the one question which
every one was asking 'Master Wood's brass money '

[1] Downes, Bishop of Meath, to Nicolson, Bishop of Derry Nicolson's
Corres, *June* II 556

was the sole subject of universal interest. The day
after Carteret's arrival, the Dublin bankers published a
declaration that they would neither receive nor utter
any of Wood's coin. Carteret would make himself the
darling of the nation, wrote an Irish Judge to the Irish
Secretary of State, if he would rid the people of the
patent.[1] Carteret himself, to whom Ireland was a new
field, intended to say nothing on either side till he had
made his own investigations on the spot. He seems at
once to have repeated the assurance that the Government had never thought to force the coin upon any
persons who might be unwilling to accept it, but
whether the patent was to be maintained or cancelled
was a question on which at present he had absolutely
nothing to say. His first business was to examine the
situation and find out for himself the temper of the
people and their leaders; till he had done this, he
intended to make no mention of the views of the
ministers in London, or of his own private and personal
opinions. Unfortunately, however, on his very arrival
he found himself compelled to a special proceeding
which the excitedly anxious people interpreted as evidence that Carteret was against them. Carteret had
been in Dublin a very few hours, when what he himself called an 'unforeseen accident' forced unwelcome
business into his hands. Three of the too well known
Drapier's Letters had appeared before Carteret arrived
in Ireland. The fourth and most famous of the series
was published on the day of his landing, and was
being cried through the streets and even sold within
the gates of the Castle, while Carteret was on his way
to take the oaths as Lord-Lieutenant. His first greeting

---

[1] Dr Coghill to Rt Hon. E. Southwell, Oct. 31, 1724. Add MSS.
21,122; fol 20, 21.

in Ireland was the jingling of Wood's half-pence; a fact upon which Swift congratulated himself with metrical satisfaction. Carteret perhaps did not on his first day in Ireland see his old friend's manifesto, but it was brought to him on the following day, and, whether he liked the duty or not, his official position compelled him to take serious notice of it. Carteret of course knew that Swift was the author of the *Drapier's Letters*: it was equally of course that political differences could not interrupt the private friendship of Swift and Carteret. In this fourth Letter itself, which practically was an indictment of the English Government in Ireland, Swift took occasion to speak highly of the new Lord-Lieutenant:—

'I speak with the utmost respect to the person and dignity of his Excellency the Lord Carteret, whose character was lately given me by a gentleman [Swift himself in disguise] that has known him from his first appearance in the world. That gentleman describes him as a young nobleman of great accomplishments, excellent learning, regular in his life, and of much spirit and vivacity. He has since, as I have heard, been employed abroad, was principal Secretary of State; and is now, about the thirty-seventh year of his age [Carteret was really only thirty-four], appointed Lord-Lieutenant of Ireland. From such a governor this kingdom may reasonably hope for as much prosperity as, under so many discouragements, it can be capable of receiving.'[1]

But Carteret was a member of the English Government as well as Swift's friend. Whatever might be his own personal opinion in this particular dispute between England and Ireland, his first official duty was to preserve order and promote loyalty; and as soon as Carteret had read the Drapier's fourth Letter, he told Lord Chancellor Midleton that it struck at the dependency of Ireland on the throne of Great Britain. Midleton, who had not cared to conceal from Walpole his objections to the patent, though he declined to make himself responsible for his son's violent proceedings against it in Parliament, had not yet seen the Letter, but when Carteret spoke so seriously of it, he at once carefully read it, and frankly confessed that he thought it highly seditious. He agreed with Carteret that it could not be passed over unnoticed. Carteret, who was anxious to discover the real temper and disposition of the leading officials in Ireland, resolved to summon the Privy Council and discuss the whole question with them.

Carteret had not yet been a week in Ireland when he met the Privy Council, the late Lords Justices, and the Judges on this important matter. He delivered his thoughts to them, as he himself says, very freely. But the unquestionable legality of the patent, a point on which he insisted, was not his main point. The popular outcry against the coinage scheme was now being artfully employed to weaken Irish feelings of allegiance, and to encourage Irish rebellion against English rule. The Drapier's fourth Letter was a concrete instance of this. Carteret, therefore, proposed that its author, printer, and publisher should be prosecuted.

After some debate this proposal was accepted; and Carteret, anxious not to run the risk of fresh difficulties in a second Council, insisted that the necessary proclamation should be drawn up at once. One or two of the members, among them William King, Archbishop of Dublin, doubted the expediency of these measures. They feared that the people disregarding

legal and constitutional subtleties, would insist on seeing in the prosecution of the Drapier a proof that the
hateful coinage was to be forced upon the country.
They even feared that it might be impossible to keep
the public peace. Carteret answered quietly and cha-
racteristically: 'As long as I have the honour to be
chief governor here, the peace of the kingdom shall be
kept.' King was not convinced, and said publicly that
he feared Carteret would have reason to repent what
had been done in Council that day. But Carteret was
fully persuaded that his action was necessary, and
the majority of the Council, and even the reluctant
minority, accepted his opinion. For they were all
loyal to England, though all firmly opposed to the
patent The Privy Council therefore agreed that a
proclamation should at once be issued, offering a reward of 300*l* for the discovery of the author of the
Drapier's fourth Letter.

Swift himself allows that Carteret's official position
compelled him to this action. 'What I did for this
country,' Swift wrote nearly ten years later, 'was from
perfect hatred of tyranny and oppression, for which I
had a proclamation against me of 300*l. which my old
friend, my Lord Carteret, was forced to consent to,* the
very first or second night of his arrival hither' No
such act of necessary formality could interrupt the
friendship between two such men, but their personal
intercourse in Ireland was renewed in a rather extraordinary way, springing directly from this incident.
The day after the issue of the proclamation, Carteret
held a levée at the Castle. While the official polite-
nesses were proceeding, Swift entered the drawing-
room, and made his way through the crowd to the

circle. He wasted no time on ceremony, but directly and emphatically addressed himself to Carteret : ' So, my Lord-Lieutenant, this is a glorious exploit that you performed yesterday, in issuing a proclamation against a poor shop-keeper, whose only crime is an honest endeavour to save his country from ruin. You have given a noble specimen of what this devoted nation is to hope for from your government I suppose you expect a statue of copper will be erected to you for this service done to Wood ' The crowd of courtiers were struck dumb at such a scene and such a profanation of their sacred mysteries Carteret alone was not in the least disconcerted. He listened to Swift's speech with quiet composure, and instantly replied to his friend in Virgil's line :—

> Res dura et regni novitas me talia cogunt
> Moliri

' The whole assembly was struck with the beauty of this quotation, and the levée broke up in good-humour, some extolling the magnanimity of Swift to the skies, and all delighted with the ingenuity of the Lord-Lieutenant's answer ' [1]

Two days after the Privy Council had sanctioned the proclamation, Archbishop King came to Carteret, and after speaking of the affairs of Ireland in what Carteret reckoned a ' very extraordinary manner,' told the Lord-Lieutenant that the Drapier had some thought of declaring his name, and acknowledging the author-ship of the Letters Carteret knew who the writer was as well as King or the Drapier himself, but he had no official knowledge or formal proof of the fact. King believed that in a legal trial the Drapier would be in no

[1] Sheridan's Swift, 213 214

danger whatever. His crime was popularly assumed
to be his attack on Wood's half-pence, and on that issue
no jury would convict him.   Carteret could not listen
to arguments of this kind   He noticeably left the
question of the coinage quite alone, but the other
question he could not pass over even if he had wished
to do so. 'I told him,' wrote Carteret in his account
of his interview with King, 'that the libel contained
such seditious, and in my opinion treasonable matter,
as called upon a chief governor here to exert his utmost power in bringing the author of it to justice'[1]
Not that Carteret thought this would be a very easy
proceeding.   The event, he also acknowledged, was
uncertain.   But he was resolved to go on vigorously.
'If the boldness of this author should be so great as
the Archbishop intimates, I am fully determined to
summon him before the Council, and though I should
not be supported by them as I could wish, yet I shall
think it my duty to order his being taken into custody,
and to detain him, if I can by law, till his majesty's
pleasure shall be further signified to me ; for if his offer
of bail should be immediately accepted, and he forthwith set at liberty, after so daring an insult upon his
majesty's Government, it is to be apprehended that riots
and tumults will ensue, and that ill-disposed persons
will run after this author and represent him to be the
defender of their liberties, which the people are falsely
made to believe are attacked in this affair of the half-
pence   . . It is the general opinion here that Dr.
Swift is author of the pamphlet, and yet nobody thinks
it can be proved upon him, though many believe he
will be spirited up to own it   Your Grace by this may
see what opinion the Archbishop of Dublin and Swift

[1] (   )

have of the humour of the people, whose affections they
have exceedingly gained of late by inveighing against
the half-pence [1]

Archbishop King's hints proved of no real value.
The Drapier did not come forward, and it was impossible
to compel him to confess himself His printer was
arrested, but the general suspicion that the grand jury
would find no true bill against this insignificant man
was fully justified On the evening before the presentation of the bill, one of Swift's numberless manifestoes,
Seasonable Advice to the Grand Jury, was widely distributed, with such telling effect that the bill was
unanimously rejected. One of the jury ventured to
treat Swift's paper with some coldness. He was a
banker, and immediately so violent a run was made
upon his bank that it was feared he would be compelled
to stop payment The Lord Chief Justice discharged
the grand jury, and summoned another; but the second
was more obstinately resolute than the first. Its first
act was to make a presentment (of course by Swift) declaring Wood's half-pence a nuisance, and the temper
of the jurymen was so evident that the Government
found it prudent to make no mention to them of the
scheme or of anything whatever connected with it
However much Carteret might be thinking of the
strictly political side of the question, the people
would see nothing in the affair but Wood and his
coinage. Carteret noticed that since the Government
had shown some vigour, writers also had shown
more caution; but there was no diminution at all in
the agitation Town and country were both perfectly
unanimous Carteret, himself quite lukewarm about
the coinage, was astonished at the passionate and

[1] Carte

universal excitement. The copper money then current in Ireland was, says Carteret, the worst that ever was seen, and much of it had been lying by—a mere loss to its owners; yet now, with perverse patriotism, this base coinage was put into currency again as an answer to the argument that more copper coin was needed in Ireland. One of the leading men in Ireland told Carteret that this question of Wood's patent was the only affair he remembered in which he could make no friends or find any one to listen to reason. Though England had already so considerably yielded, there was still a common suspicion that the currency would be forced on the nation. Trade was suffering through imaginary fears which thus became real evils. Carteret, reporting home, when he had been only three weeks in Dublin, modestly declined after so very short a time to offer any deliberate opinion, but he did not minimise the situation :—

'This rage, for I can call it no otherwise, is now working up to such a height that the best of his majesty's subjects here, who do not agree in the popular clamour, but condemn the late heat of their parliament, and dread the consequences that such another session may bring upon Ireland, say it is to be wished that his majesty, who has always made the law the rule and measure of his government, would now be . . pleased to recede from that rule in this one instance.'[1] A few days later Carteret expressed his fear that an Irish jury would find treason itself not to be treason, if it were coloured over with the popular invectives against Wood's half-pence.

Carteret had not ventured, after three weeks' experience of Ireland, to state definitely what must be done.

[1] . . . . 17 . . . . 16–48.

But a second three weeks left him without a doubt
In December 1724, the Government in London wrote
anxiously to him. The King, concerned that Carteret's
endeavours had as yet produced so little effect, wished
his advice, the King and the ministers wished to know
how to uphold the law, and at the same time satisfy
the Irish people. Carteret, who had actively gleaned
information from every source of value, could come to
only one conclusion. The patent must be given up.
No other advice, he said, could be given by any one who
had examined the condition of Ireland. If once the
'terror' of the half-pence were withdrawn, the Irish
parliament would cause no further trouble; would vote
some compensation to Wood, and so close the incident.
No counsel could have been clearer and more direct
than Carteret's on this matter.

The Government had asked Carteret's advice; but
did not particularly like it when it was given. It had
taken a long time to convince Walpole and Townshend
that the Irish discontent was really serious. When
Walpole was once convinced, he was statesman enough
to decline to match his personal views against the feelings
of a whole nation But Townshend, always passionate,
wrote angrily to Carteret. Was the English King to
make private bargains with the Irish parliament? With
impotent indignation Townshend was still informing
Carteret, in December 1724, that the search for some
'expedient' to quiet the minds of the Irish people was
yet going on. Carteret, speaking on this subject with
more authority than all the other ministers taken together, had plainly told them that there was only one
expedient Boulter, the newly appointed Primate of
Ireland, an Englishman, and a man not likely to advise
measures of the good of the Irish people,

was also strongly urging upon the Government the view
which Carteret was expressing.   Like Carteret, Boulter
took pains to discover for himself the opinions of the
leading men in Ireland, and of the various sections of
the people   He found Protestants and Catholics, Whigs,
Tories, and Jacobites, disagreeing in all things else, at
one in their views on the coinage ; and Boulter's voluminous letters to the ministers in England insist with
much emphasis upon the solution which Carteret had
urged months before he had even left England : the
abandonment of the patent, and some fair compensation
to Wood.   'Without doing something like this, there is
no prospect of any end of our present heats and animosities'[1]   A few days before the date of this letter
Carteret had reiterated his advice, and had told Townshend that the ferment among the people, only in part
allayed, was ready to break out again on the slightest
occasion ; while a private letter from Dublin, written
on the same day as Carteret's, shows how the popular
dread of the currency stood in the way of Carteret's
already great personal popularity.   ·My Lord-Lieutenant
does all that can be thought on, to obtain upon the
minds of the people, and with great applause ; but
then, it is curious with 'em to say that *all he does is
with design to introduce the half-pence, but that shall not
do ; neither eating and drinking, civility nor good words,
shall alter their minds as to that*'[2]

In spite of the pressing appeals of Carteret and
Boulter, the spring and summer of 1725 passed by, and
the ministers in London made no sign.   The time for
the meeting of the Irish parliament was drawing near,
and on all sides there was prophecy of parliamentary

[1] To Newcastle, Jan 19, 1725   Boulter's *Letters*, I 13.

trouble if the patent were not disposed of to the satisfaction of members at the very beginning of their
deliberations. Would Carteret be authorised to say in
his speech that the whole scheme was cancelled?
Midleton, no longer Lord Chancellor of Ireland, and
not able to boast of any special favour from Carteret,
was inclined to think that the ministers in England
were anxious to ruin Carteret's chance of success in
Ireland and to make him appear unable to do the
King service there; and that, therefore, they would
refuse to do anything which might assist Carteret to
hold a successful session.[1] Parliament was to meet
in September; in August nothing was yet settled
The absurd Duke of Newcastle was continuing to write to
Carteret in an irritatingly placid manner, mildly asking
if Carteret had yet found any way to end this unhappy
business. As if Carteret had not months before told
the absurd Duke what must be done! And not only had
he told the ministers what they must do; he had also
urged upon them the necessity of doing it at once. But
the Government had not acted upon his advice, and
parliament was now about to meet while all was still in
suspense Carteret wrote once more in August, and
plainly told the ministers that no viceroy could carry
on the affairs of the session till this question was once
for all settled They had disregarded the warnings
which for nine months he had been giving them, and
now there was only one effectual way of freeing themselves from their embarrassment He desired to be
authorised to declare in his speech at the opening of the
session that the patent was entirely cancelled

It was impossible for the ministers any longer to

---

[1] Midleton to Thos Brodrick, July 4, 1725. Add. MSS 9,243, fol.
59–63

neglect Carteret's advice   The inevitable resolution, which might have been taken so much more gracefully at a far earlier date, was adopted only some two or three weeks before the parliament met   On September 21, 1725, Carteret delivered the speech from the throne with an eloquent emphasis which much delighted those who heard it ; but it needed none of the charms of rhetoric to make his very first words palatable :—

'I have his majesty's commands at the opening of this session to acquaint you that an entire end is put to the patent'

The end had come at last.   A little unavoidable parliamentary wrangling followed, and Wood and his patent became extinct for ever.   The House of Commons dutifully thanked the King for his goodness, and in very warm terms thanked Carteret also for what he had done for them, but the discontented spirits in the Lords, and especially Archbishop King and ex-Chancellor Midleton, hoped to make what mischief they could. Carteret had appointed Primate Boulter to prepare and move the address of the Lords to the King, and Boulter proposed gratefully to acknowledge the King's favour and condescension in cancelling the patent which he had granted, but King maliciously moved that they should thank the royal *wisdom* too, clearly hinting that if the King had been wise in ending the patent, his ministers had been exceedingly foolish in accepting it. The Lords agreed to King's sarcastic gratitude, but, thanks to Carteret's earnest endeavours, the addition was flung out again on a later stage of the proceedings, and the address restored to its original wording.   So Carteret's first Irish session opened auspiciously, and ran through its course with all the quiet that could be exp

Carteret was Lord-Lieutenant of Ireland for six years; but after the coinage incident was concluded, these years offer—with one exception—little or nothing of any personal interest or of any real connection with the biography of Carteret. The details of the official speeches which he delivered, and of the various sessions which he held, belong to parliamentary history, and only very formally to Carteret's life. It is very incidentally that anything beyond the barren official traces of Carteret's political connection with Ireland can now be recovered. But he took real interest in Ireland, and the testimony of both friends and enemies of the English government of Ireland agrees that he was a good viceroy. His position was by no means an easy one. To say that the two most prominent men in Dublin during Carteret's Lord-Lieutenancy were Dean Swift and Archbishop Boulter, is almost to write in short the Irish political history of the time. Swift and Boulter were radically opposed to each other in their political views; one of them the adored delight of the Irish people, the other the embodiment of that English policy towards Ireland which found favour in the first half of the eighteenth century. Boulter, an Englishman, and practically the ruler of Ireland, outdid even the Whig ministers in England in his disregard of Irish interests and Irish national feeling. Ireland in his view existed simply and solely for the advantage of England. The 'English interest,' as it was called, was the object of his unceasing solicitude. His copious letters are full of agitated watchfulness on behalf of the 'English party,' the 'friends of England,' the 'English interest.' Whenever an official post of any kind fell vacant, Boulter was in a condition of fluttered anxiety till an Englishman was safely deposited in it. Even when he did anything

that was politically or socially good for Ireland, he did
it only because it was for the benefit of England also.
On the other side stood Swift, also an Englishman,
though, as he bitterly phrased it, he had been 'dropped'
in Ireland ; with no affection for Ireland, and cursing
the exile's life which he was forced to pass there.
He despised the Irish people, but he could oppose a
tyranny which neglected the elements of natural justice ;
and even before his memorable appearance as the
Dublin Drapier, he had decisively joined the Irish
party, and had denounced with all the force of his indignant irony the wrongs done by the strong country
to the weak one. He allowed even the play of his
casual conversation to illustrate his contempt of the
English method of ruling Ireland. Lady Carteret once
remarked to him on the pleasantness of the Irish air.
Swift fell down on his knees and said, 'For God's sake,
madam, don't say so in England, they will certainly tax
it.'[1] Even if better reasons for indignation had failed
him, Swift had wrongs of his own to avenge, for he
had been neglected by Walpole, and he hated the
Whigs. The Whig Carteret was indeed his personal
friend, but that did not blunt Swift's opposition to the
political system of which Carteret was the official representative. Swift never forgot anything in the nature
of a personal affront, and he never forgot that the
Whigs had managed to do without him.

Between the rival policies personified in Boulter and
in Swift, the position of a Lord-Lieutenant who was a
member of the English Cabinet, and yet, like Carteret,
without prejudice and prepossession in his dealings with
Ireland, was not free from embarrassment. He could

---

[1] Anecdote told by Voltaire at Ferney in 1778 Sherlock's *Letters of
an E.*

not be anti-Irish enough to satisfy Boulter, or anti-English enough to please Swift. And there was not much assistance to be hoped for from the Irish parliament ; an assemblage indeed which, considering its total want of legislative independence, could not be a very striking political body. Very many years after his own connection with Ireland was over, Carteret expressed what could not help being a very contemptuous opinion of the Irish Houses. In 1758 the Duke of Bedford was Lord-Lieutenant, and found his parliament very difficult to deal with. Carteret and Fox had some conversation on the subject, and Fox reported to Bedford what Carteret had said :—

'His Lordship says your Grace has nothing to do but to let them dash their loggerheads together, and to transmit whatever nonsense they may cook up to England to be rejected, remaining quietly and coolly at the Castle, till with the last transmiss of bills your Grace desires leave to come away' [1]

English policy towards Ireland in the reigns of the first two Georges was preparing the mischief which did not fail to follow. One political fact is as eloquent as a hundred. The Irish parliament which met in 1727 continued to sit till 1760. But things were very tranquil during Carteret's Irish rule. The people had triumphed over the English Government, Walpole had been forced to humble himself before Swift, and the Irish were satisfied. Carteret had his little administrative troubles of the usual sort ; but the factious and the disaffected found that he had a mind and will of his own, and that, while he was governor, impudent meddlesomeness was not the road to very brilliant success. A fussily

---

[1] Lord J. Russell's *Correspondence of the 4th Duke of Bedford*, II 316. Jan 7

h

important section of members, elated by their victory
over Wood and his patent, with gratuitous condescension offered to manage all public affairs to Carteret's
complete satisfaction if only the Lord-Lieutenant would
throw himself entirely into their hands   Carteret plainly
replied that he had not come to Ireland to be put into
leading-strings, and completely extinguished the insolent
hopes of these ambitious busy-bodies.   Of course they
afterwards gave him all the trouble they could.   But
Carteret had a perfect temper, and was not at all disturbed by the excited extravagances of petulant passion.
Absolutely refusing to make himself the tool of any
faction, he endeavoured, as far as the fettered position
of a Lord-Lieutenant would allow, to act with equal
friendliness towards the representatives of both the
English and the Irish parties.   Swift and Boulter
both recognise his good-will towards them.   Carteret
of course could not always do what Swift would have
wished ; Swift complains that he sometimes had to speak
surdis auribus   Yet Carteret, not thinking that Tory
and traitor were necessarily synonymous, listened when
he could to Swift's recommendations, and gained Swift's
thanks for doing so   The very little which Carteret
ventured to do for the so-called patriotic party in Ireland
produced loud and persistent outcry from disappointed
partisans ; with one excellent result so far as Carteret
was personally concerned, for it drew from Swift his
humorously serious *Vindication of Lord Carteret from
the charge of favouring none but Tories, High Churchmen,
and Jacobites.*   To be praised by both Boulter and
Swift was at least a proof of impartiality, and Boulter's
words are·—

' We are obliged to your Lordship for the early care
you t   ?   I   ,   I   h ?   l   l   l   is

sensible of what advantage it will be to his majesty's service that we have had a governor of your Excellency's abilities long enough amongst us to know as much of this country as any native.'[1]

When Carteret's Lord-Lieutenantship was closing, Boulter congratulated himself that in Carteret Ireland had a friend who on all occasions would be able to serve her.

Carteret's Irish rule ended in 1730 His personal success had been unbounded, and his political management characterised by great dexterity and unwearied industry. His careful inquiry into financial and other details which were commonly let alone with contented indifference, disturbed the sluggish routine of easily satisfied officials, but gained for the Lord-Lieutenant great popularity with all other classes of the people; while his affable manners, his wit, and his courteous hospitality made him the favourite in Ireland which an English governor too seldom was Newcastle's malicious hope that Carteret's viceroyalty might prove a ruinous failure was falsified as completely as it deserved to be. Swift had prophesied differently, and Swift's anticipations were realised

A pleasant incident of Carteret's Lord-Lieutenancy was the renewal of his personal intercourse with Swift. A gap of ten years had interrupted it. The death of Queen Anne and the consequent fall of Bolingbroke had made Swift's political situation hopeless, and he withdrew to the dreary exile of his Dublin deanery. After ten years' experience of that unwelcome retirement, the announcement of his friend Carteret's appointment to Ireland was no doubt welcome to Swift In that year he wrote a poem which is a panegyric on Carteret's

character and conduct at the University, at Court, and
in foreign negotiations; and closed his verses with a
reference to Carteret's expected arrival at Dublin :—

> Fame now reports, the Western Isle
> Is made his mansion for a while,
> Whose anxious natives night and day,
> (Happy beneath his righteous sway,)
> Weary the gods with ceaseless prayer,
> To bless him and to keep him there ;
> And claim it as a debt from Fate,
> Too lately found, to lose him late.

But the renewal of the friendship of the two men
was prefaced by a slight misunderstanding. Swift, as
soon as he heard that Carteret was to be the new Lord-
Lieutenant, had written to him, expressing his pleased
expectation of seeing him, and promising to be neither a
too frequent guest nor a troublesome solicitor. Carteret,
who was making various excursions in the country at
the time that Swift's letter reached him, was a little slow
in replying ; and Swift, fancying himself slighted, wrote
testily :—

'I have been long out of the world, but have not
forgotten what used to pass among those I lived with
while I was in it ; and I can say that during the experience of many years, your Excellency, and one more,
who is not worthy to be compared to you, are the only
great persons that ever refused to answer a letter from
me, without regard to business, party, or greatness ; and
if I had not a peculiar esteem for your personal qualities,
I should think myself to be acting a very inferior part in
making this complaint. . . . I know not how your conceptions of myself may alter, by every new high station ;
but mine must continue the same or alter for the worse.
I often told a great minister whom you well know, that

I valued him for being the same man through all the progress of power and place I expected the like in your Lordship, and still hope that I shall be the only person who will ever find it otherwise. I pray God to direct your Excellency in all your good undertakings, and especially in your government of this kingdom.'[1]

This letter, in spite of its hasty assumption that Carteret was neglecting him, is ample evidence of Swift's very high estimation of Carteret The compliment that Swift's opinion of Carteret, if it changed at all, could only change for the worse, is a very fine one Carteret's letter of reply, with just a touch of light sarcasm where he speaks of the 'agreeable freedom with which you express yourself,' is proof on his side of his affectionate regard for Swift, and of the admirable temper with which he received Swift's unfounded suspicions :—

'To begin by confessing myself in the wrong will, I hope, be some proof to you that none of the stations which I have gone through have hitherto had the effects upon me which you apprehend. If a month's silence has been turned to my disadvantage in your esteem, it has at least had this good effect, that I am convinced by the kindness of your reproaches, as well as by the goodness of your advice, that you still retain some part of your former friendship for me, of which I am the more confident from the agreeable freedom with which you express yourself, and I shall not forfeit my pretensions to the continuance of it by doing anything that shall give you occasion to think that I am insensible of it. . . . I hope the nation will not suffer by my being in this great station, and if I can contribute to its prosperity, I shall think it the honour and happiness of my life. I desire you to believe what I say, and particularly

[1] Swift to Carteret, June 9, 1724. Works XVI, 122-123.

when I profess myself to be with great truth, Sir, your most faithful and affectionate humble servant.'[1]

This kind reply—the omitted sentences explain the cause of Carteret's delay in writing—made Swift ashamed of himself and his testy assumptions; and he wrote again to Carteret :—

'I humbly claim the privilege of an inferior, to be the last writer, yet, with great acknowledgments for your condescension in answering my letters, I cannot but complain of you for putting me in the wrong I am in the circumstances of a waiting-woman, who told her lady that nothing vexed her more than to be caught in a lie. But what is worse, I have discovered in myself somewhat of the bully, and, after all my rattling, you have brought me down to be as humble as the most distant attender at your levée It is well your Excellency's talents are in few hands; for, if it were otherwise, we who pretend to be free speakers in quality of philosophers should be utterly cured of our forwardness; at least I am afraid there will be an end of mine, with regard to your Excellency. Yet, my lord, I am ten years older than I was when I had the honour to see you last, and consequently ten times more testy Therefore I foretell that you, who could conquer so captious a person, and of so little consequence, will quickly subdue this whole kingdom to love and reverence you.'[2]

Carteret gracefully refused to let Swift be the last writer.—

'Your claim to be the last writer is what I can never allow, that is the privilege of ill writers, and I am resolved to give you complete satisfaction by leaving it with you, whether I shall be the last writer or not. Methinks I see you throw this letter upon your table in

[1] Carteret to Swift June 20 1724 Swift, *Works*, XVI 454 154
[2] Swift *Works* XVI 454 455 July 9, 1724

the height of spleen, because it may have interrupted some of your more agreeable thoughts. But then, in return, you may have the comfort of not answering it, and so convince my Lord-Lieutenant that you value him less now than you did ten years ago. I do not know but this might become a free speaker and a philosopher. Whatever you may think of it I shall not be testy, but endeavour to show that I am not altogether insensible of the force of that genius which has outshone most of this age, and, when you will display it again, can convince us that its lustre and strength are still the same.

'Once more I commit myself to your censure, and am, Sir, with great respect,

your most affectionate humble servant,

' CARTERET.' [1]

Swift managed to have the last word, and soon after this last letter the two correspondents met each other again in Dublin The extraordinary scene at the Castle levée probably first reintroduced Carteret and Swift; and their acquaintance was soon renewed with the old private pleasantness. Lady Carteret, who from her window thirteen years before had pointed out to Swift his hat flung upon the railings by the wild boisterousness of ladies of title, was also glad to meet again her own and her mother's friend Lady Carteret was a special favourite with Swift, and in his intercourse with her there was no trace of the domineering roughness which he so commonly adopted towards ladies of rank. With her mother, Lady Worsley, Swift had been specially intimate in the Queen Anne and Bolingbroke days; and now that he was far away from nearly all his old friends he had hoped that Lady Worsley would have accompanied her daughter to Ireland She did not do so but the presence of Lady Carteret was for Swift a pleasant renewal of the friendship in the second generation They were on terms of affectionate and, on each side, respectful intimacy Lady Carteret bids him come to dine with her at the Castle. He goes, but his spirits fail him at the thought of Viceregal state, and he escapes home Lady Carteret forgives him; and as he had not dined with her she instead visits him, and Swift, as a condition of forgiveness, turns the little incident into easy rhyme in his pleasant *Apology to Lady Carteret*:—

> Can it be strange, if I eschew
> A scene so glorious and so new ?
> Or is he criminal that flies
> The living lustre of your eyes ?

Swift's poor health, the deafness and giddiness which repeatedly distressed him and sometimes drove him from Dublin in search of country air, prevented him from being so much with his friends at the Castle as he felt inclined to be ; for it was only in verse that he feared the living lustre of Lady Carteret's eyes. The intimate terms of his friendship with her and with her mother, Lady Worsley, are well illustrated by three letters, two of which are not printed in the Works of Swift. In April 1730, the month in which Carteret's Lord-Lieutenancy ended, Swift wrote to Lady Worsley:—

' My Lady Carteret (if you know such a lady) commands me to pursue my own inclination, which is, to honour myself with writing you a letter ; and thereby endeavouring to preserve myself in your memory, in spite of an acquaintance of more years than, in regard to my own reputation as a young gentleman, I care to recollect. I forget whether I had not some reasons to be angry with your ladyship when I was last in England. I hope   ·   nd mother in Europe; and fifteen years hence (which I shall have nothing to do with) you will be at the amusement of—" Rise up, daughter," &c. You are to answer this letter, and to inform me of your health and humour; and whether you like your daughter better or worse, after having so long conversed with the Irish world, and so little with me. Tell me what are your amusements at present; cards, Court, books, visiting, or fondling (I humbly beg your ladyship's pardon, but it is between ourselves) your grand-children? My Lady Carteret has been the best Queen we have known in Ireland these many years; yet is she mortally hated by all the young girls, because (and it is your fault) she is handsomer than all of them together Pray do not insult poor Ireland on this occasion, for it would have been exactly the same thing in London And therefore I shall advise the King, when I go next to England, to send no more of her sort, (if such another can be found) for fear of turning all his loyal female subjects here against him . . . My Lady Carteret has made me a present, which I take to be malicious, with a design to stand in your place Therefore I would have you to provide against it by another, and something of your own work, as hers is; for you know I always expect advances and presents from ladies ' [1]

In reply, Lady Worsley promised Swift a writing-box, and he wrote in response:—

'I am in some doubt whether envy had not a great share in your work, for you were, I suppose, informed that my Lady Carteret had made for me with her own hands the finest box in Ireland; upon which you grew jealous, and resolved to outdo her by making for me the finest box in England . . . In short, I am quite

Swift, IV. XVII.

overloaden with favours from your ladyship and your daughter, and, what is worse, those loads will lie upon my shoulders as long as I live But I confess myself a little ungrateful, because I cannot deny your ladyship to have been the most constant of all my goddesses, as I am the most constant of all your worshippers. I hope the Carterets and the Worsleys are all happy and in health. .
I beg your ladyship will prevail on Sir Robert Worsley to give me a vicarage in the Isle of Wight; for I am weary of living at such a distance from you. It need not be above forty pounds a year ' [1]

The present arrived, and Swift acknowledged it What a contrast between the easy familiarity and light banter of his first sentences, and the *sæva indignatio* of the last !

' The work itself does not delight me more than the little cares you were pleased to descend to in contriving ways to have it conveyed so far without damage, whereof it received not the least from without : what there was came from within : for one of the little rings that lifts a drawer for wax hath touched a part of one of the pictures, and made a mark as large as the head of a small pin ; but it touches only an end of a cloud ; and yet I have been careful to twist a small thread of silk round that wicked ring. who promiseth to do so no more

' I beg you, madam, that there may be no quarrels of jealousy between your ladyship and my Lady Carteret : I set her at work by the authority I claimed over her as your daughter The young woman showed her readiness, and performed very well for a new beginner, and deserves encouragement Besides, she filled the

---

[1] This and the following letter of Swift, not printed in Scott's Edition of Swift's *Works*, are given in *Notes and Queries*, series I vol. IV. pp 218-220. Th ' '· M 1 1733 ·, 1 N··· 1 173?

chest with tea, whereas you did not send me a single pen, a stick of wax, or a drop of ink; for all of which I must bear the charge out of my own pocket. And, after all, if your ladyship were not by, I would say that my Lady Carteret's box (as you disdainfully call it, instead of a tea-chest) is a most beautiful piece of work, and is oftener used than yours, because it is brought down for tea after dinner among ladies, whereas my escritoire never stirs out of my closet, but when it is brought for a sight. Therefore, I again desire there may be no family quarrels upon my account. . . .

'Are you not weary, madam? Have you patience to read all this? I am bringing back past times; I imagine myself talking with you as I used to do; but on a sudden I recollect where I am sitting, banished to a country of slaves and beggars; my blood soured, my spirits sunk, fighting with beasts like St. Paul, not at Ephesus, but in Ireland'

'In Ireland', that was half of Swift's wretchedness Was he, in his own words, to die there in a rage, like a poisoned rat in a hole? The presence of the Carterets, recalling to him old scenes and old friends in England, was doubtless a very acceptable relief to Swift; and Carteret found his renewed intimacy with the Dean one of the not too numerous attractions of his residence in Dublin. Swift and the friends of Swift were the society in which he delighted. One of these most intimate friends was the well-known schoolmaster, Dr. Sheridan, whose scholarship Carteret could well appreciate. Carteret delighted to lay aside the tedious formalities of his position, to slip quietly from the Castle in a hackney-chair, and pass private evenings at Sheridan's with Swift Sheridan was a learned, absent-minded, simple-hearted man and, in a very particular degree, a in the kingdom ; perhaps, the best in Europe. He was one of the first whom Swift recommended to Carteret in Ireland, and Carteret, attracted by Sheridan's scholarship, gladly gave him such small preferment in the Church as was at his disposal, and privately treated him on terms of much friendship Sheridan's pupils delighted Carteret by the performance of a Greek play, while Carteret astonished Sheridan by his intimate knowledge of the original The play happened to be one of Sophocles'; and Sophocles was one of the few books which Carteret had had with him during his wearisome negotiations in the North While in Denmark, and confined to his house partly by illness, partly by severe weather, he had read his author so repeatedly that he had learnt the plays almost line for line, and his naturally very strong memory did not let them go. Carteret modestly read over with Sheridan the selected play before the public representation ; but Sheridan found that his new pupil needed no assistance. Being, as Swift says, very learned himself, Carteret delighted to encourage learning in others ; and it was after this classical performance that he did all that he could for Sheridan Unfortunately, Sheridan did not keep his Church appointments long, but ruined his clerical outlook by his own innocent absent-mindedness. Preaching on the anniversary of the Hanoverian accession, he selected for his unfortunate text : ' Sufficient unto the day is the evil thereof' Disappointed and spiteful busy-bodies chose to represent this as an intentional insult and profession of Jacobitism ; and the outcry of the Whigs compelled Carteret to cancel the small official favour which he had gladly shown to a learned man who happened to be also a Tory

Otl ' ' will on hin them

Sheridan, for Carteret attended to Swift's recommendations whenever he could possibly do so. It was not
always possible Carteret was the representative of a
Whig Government, and considerably fettered by the
traditions of the political relations between England
and Ireland ; while Swift hated things Whiggish and
the Whig party which had ventured to neglect him,
and especially disliked the principles that regulated the
English rule in Dublin. The policy which Swift desired
and the policy which Carteret's position compelled
him to carry out were often very widely separated.
But Swift always recognised the necessities under
which Carteret acted ; and when they had to differ on
political matters, they differed always in the friend-
liest manner Swift summarised their relations by saying that in Carteret he hated the viceroy, but loved
the man

For Swift himself there was of course nothing that
Carteret could do politically. A rather vague authority
asserts that Swift would have been willing to accept
some not very leading official appointment in Ireland, as,
for instance, trustee of the linen manufacture, or justice
of the peace, but that he never could prevail upon
Carteret to consent Carteret's reply always was: 'I
am sure, Mr Dean, you despise those feathers, and
would not accept of them. [1] Swift quite understood
Carteret's position and the meaning of this polite
refusal. The Lord-Lieutenant must appoint to official
posts supporters of the official Government The last
person in Ireland likely to support the Irish administration of a Whig ministry was the Dean of St Patrick's,
and he frankly told Carteret that he knew that was why

---

[1] Scott, *Life of Swift*, Swift's *Works*, I 362n. Founded on
Swiftiai

he was passed over. With equal frankness Carteret
replied · 'What you say is literally true, and, therefore, you must excuse me.' This open sincerity
always characterised their relations. In January 1728
Swift wrote to Carteret : 'As long as you are governor
here. I shall always expect the liberty of telling you
my thoughts ; and I hope you will consider them, until
you find I grow impertinent, or have some bias of my
own' Swift's fairness could not refuse to confess that
Carteret had always been willing to listen to him, and
that he had done in deference to Swift's views all that
his position would allow him to do. Writing to his old
friend Gay shortly after Carteret's Lord-Lieutenancy
ended, Swift said of Carteret : 'I have told him often
that I only hated him as Lieutenant   I confess he had
a genteeler manner of binding the chains of this kingdom than most of his predecessors' In granting to
natives of Ireland such small appointments as he was able
to offer them, Swift thought that Carteret acted a more
popular part than his successor, the Duke of Dorset.
But if, on the official side, Carteret could not always do
what Swift desired, their private relations were very
close and intimate. Here is Swift writing to the
Lord-Lieutenant : 'I told your Excellency that you
were to run on my errands .   . I, therefore, command your Excellency to,' etc.   . . 'And I desire
that I, who have done with Courts, may not be used
like a courtier ; for, as I was a courtier when you were
a school-boy, I know all your arts   And so, God
bless you, and all your family, my old friends ; and
remember, I expect you shall not dare to be a courtier to me.' Carteret and Swift never played the
courtier with each other. Swift, kept waiting once at
the C o while the presentation of the *Drapier's*

Letters was still a question of public policy, wrote down the complaining lines :—

> My very good Lord, 'tis a very hard task
> For a man to wait here, who has nothing to ask.

Carteret wrote in reply :—

> My very good Dean, there are few who come here
> But have something to ask, or something to fear.

Carteret was always able to hold his own with Swift. Conversing with him once on a political action disapproved by Swift, Carteret replied to Swift's objections with such power that Swift broke out into passionate abuse which conveyed high praise: ·What the vengeance brought *you* among us? Get you back —get you back; pray God Almighty send us our boobies again!' On another occasion, Swift, whose estimate of the Irish people was a very contemptuous one, wrote that Carteret ought to be the governor of a wiser nation than Ireland; for a fool would be the fit manager of fools Thus the two men always thoroughly understood each other, and acted with very characteristic frankness 'When people ask me,' wrote Carteret to the Dean, 'how I governed Ireland, I say that I pleased Dr. Swift *Quæsitam meritis sume superbiam.*'[1]

---

[1] Carteret to Swift, March 24, 1727. Swift, *Works*, XIX. 50, 51.

CHAPTER V

OPPOSITION TO WALPOLE : HOME AFFAIRS.

1730–1737

BEFORE noticing Carteret's further connection with Walpole and with English domestic politics, a word is due to the curious history and miraculous disappearance of the Congress which after long struggles had managed to meet at Cambrai. Carteret himself had not been neglectful of European affairs because he had ceased to be Secretary of State During the seven years of his Lord-Lieutenancy he had frequently visited England. The Irish Viceroy was expected to reside in Dublin only during the months in which the Irish parliament was sitting ; the rest of the year he usually spent in England. And as the date of the Irish session did not exactly correspond with the sitting of the English Houses, it was open to a Lord-Lieutenant, who had not had enough of parliamentary proceedings in Dublin, to take active part in the performances at Westminster. Carteret was thus able to take his share in the discussion of the one absorbing topic of the time. Domestic affairs were almost at a standstill A languid interest, chiefly of a personal kind, might be taken in the impeachment of a late Lord Chancellor for corruption, or in debating the dangers of Bolingbroke's possible reappearance in England ; otherwise, home politics were duller than the dul   ,   ,   ,   ,   ,   affairs

it was different   The vivacity on this side was almost
excessive; treaties and counter-treaties succeeding one
another in bewildering variety; war always threatening,
and once breaking out in what might have been a very
serious manner; while England, as was usual in those
times, was inextricably involved in all the shiftings of
continental politics

At the end of 1723 the Congress of Cambrai was
ready to begin business at last, after all its wearisome
delays. Early in 1724 it accomplished its formal opening
Never was so utterly futile a Congress.   A whole host
of diplomatic personages filled the little town, dazzling
the eyes of the quiet Flanders people, but doing nothing
of any practical value.   All their diplomatic discussions
and formalities were mere beating of the air; for it had
already become clear enough that in the very highest
quarters there was no sincere desire for the success of
diplomatic efforts.   When diplomacy asked the Emperor
Charles if he would definitely give up his fantastic
title as King of Spain, if he would once for all settle the
eternal dispute about the Italian Duchies, the Emperor
would give no satisfactory reply   So the futile Congress
dragged on in a very magnificent and useless manner.
In its first year at Cambrai, young Voltaire had seen it
there, eating, drinking, playing, and had reported its
proceedings in those directions to dissolute old goat-faced
Dubois, who was Archbishop of the place   As Voltaire
had seen it, so it continued; dragging out the years in
shining entertainments and fruitless diplomatic solemni-
ties, until the King and Queen of Spain, and especially
the Queen, grew impatient of the futility of so magnificent a Congress, and turned to a different line of
action

To c......... ....

had at the head of affairs another vagabond foreigner,
Ripperda, a Dutchman, who rose very high indeed for a
time, and had astonishing adventures in the end.   He
had been a Protestant, but had not found it too hard to
change his religion, when the change seemed well worth
his while.   A man full of projects and speculations,
with views very much larger than his abilities ; rash,
hot-headed, loud tongued ; very blustering indeed, when
he seemingly sat at the head of the universe for the
time being   His big, grandiose way of planning and
talking had completely gained Elizabeth's attention ; and
now when the wearisomely futile Congress had passed
through nearly three years of its useless existence,
Ripperda suggested to the irritated Queen a political
plan of his own.   Let the Congress continue to
demonstrate its unrivalled capacity for doing nothing,
was in effect Ripperda's advice, send me to Vienna,
I will settle terms with the Emperor, and Cambrai may
still diplomatise and dine at peace   Elizabeth resolved
at least to try ; and near the end of 1724 Ripperda,
with full powers from Spain, in secrecy left Madrid

The secrecy was maintained at Vienna.   Mysterious
conferences of carefully disguised negotiators were held
at night.   Ripperda, well supplied also with persuasive
money arguments, was confident of success, and sent
cheering reports home to Spain   Yet his efforts might
possibly have been useless, and at least would certainly
have been prolonged, had not a sudden action on the
part of France excited all Spain's eagerness for peace
with the Emperor   The little Spanish Infanta, betrothed
when a child of four years old to Louis XV., the boy-
King of France, was now, at the beginning of 1725, un-
ceremoniously sent home again to Spain by the new
French Regent Bourbon, and the match peremptorily

declined Philip and Elizabeth flamed out in violent
passion. 'All the Bourbons are a race of devils!' exclaimed the fiery Queen to the unfortunate French
ambassador, with a hastily apologetic 'except your
majesty,' to the King, when she remembered that he too
was one of that diabolical family. Spain naturally had
no further relish for French mediation at Cambrai.
That was at once declined, and when England could
not undertake to persuade the Emperor without the co-
operation of France, Spain's one remaining hope rested
on Ripperda's secret negotiations He was ordered to
agree to terms of peace without delay, and in this
altered state of things a settlement was easily arranged
On April 30, 1725, a Treaty of Vienna was unexpectedly announced—Austria and Spain suddenly reconciled, and the plenipotentiaries at Cambrai left gazing at
one another in a state of astonished collapse.

The excitement among official persons all over
Europe at the news of this sudden stroke was unbounded.
Kings and statesmen did not know what to make of it.
The treaty as it was published seemed innocent enough.
Spain guaranteed the Emperor's Pragmatic Sanction, and
recognised his rights to the Milanese. Naples, and Sicily.
The Emperor on his side surrendered his pretensions to
the crown of Spain. But a treaty of this kind was all
in favour of the Emperor, whose claims on Spain had
long been of the merely shadowy kind. Spain would
never, men argued, have made a peace with Austria if
this were all; and rumours of secret articles immediately
spread Rumour spoke of large engagements under-
taken by the Emperor for Don Carlos, of unbounded
subsidies to be paid to Austria by Spain; above all, of
a surprising marriage-scheme by which the two Austrian
Arch-duchesses should be wedded to Spanish Elizabeth's

two sons.   Thus Don Carlos, in addition to all else his
mother could get for him, would gain Maria Theresa as
his wife; Italy and the Empire would be united; and if
Don Carlos should, as was not impossible, himself become
King of Spain, the Empire, Spain, and Italy would be
all in the hands of one man, and the European balance
in a condition painful to think of.   England, too, conceived that she had special cause for alarm.   It was more
or less vaguely asserted that the restoration of the Pretender was one of the conditions of this unintelligible
treaty · blustering Ripperda, made more windy than usual
by his seemingly admirable success, was not shy of admitting it   And Spain's demand for Gibraltar might in such
circumstances be a more serious affair than formerly.

The one thing clear to the King of England was that
in some way or other this Treaty of Vienna must be
counteracted   George lost no time   The parliamentary
session of 1725 being happily over, he left England as
usual for his summer and autumn abroad, arriving at
Hanover at the end of June   There, while England, if
it thought about him at all, thought that he was busy
merely with hunting and other not unquestionable
amusements, painful diplomacy was again at work,
eager to set up an equivalent for the Vienna Treaty, and
to render it as harmless as possible   Secretary Townshend was with the King, anxious to do his best   The
question of Prussia was the real centre of the business.
Could England and France persuade Prussia to join them
against the designs of Spain and Austria?   This was
successfully accomplished.   Frederick William himself
came to Herrenhausen, to do diplomacy as well as
hunting, and in September a sudden counter-treaty,
the Treaty of Hanover, was produced; England,
France, and Prussia agreeing to stand by one another

and to induce the Protestant powers of the North to join
their alliance.

Thus Europe was divided into two great parties, and
war might come at any moment. The Emperor gained
over the Czarina Catherine, widow of Peter the Great ;
money poured in to him from Spain ; Ripperda continued to bluster in the noisiest manner, and Charles
felt quite contemptuous of all that his enemies might do.
But England also took her measures Fleets were sent
out ; one to the Baltic, to guard against mischief from
Russia ; one to the Spanish coasts, to keep an eye
on Gibraltar ; one to the West Indies, to blockade
the galleons in Porto-Bello and check the supplies of
Spanish gold. All through 1726 this strained condition
of affairs lasted without any actual outbreak of war.
But in the early weeks of 1727 hostilities really began.
In the angry state of feeling between England and Spain,
there were various pretexts which would do well enough
to excuse this last decisive step ; there was always one
convenient argument for convenient quarrel in the long-
standing question of Gibraltar. Spain, now backed up
by the Emperor, renewed her demand for the fortress ;
and as England's only answer was flat refusal, Elizabeth
resolved to try what force could do. So began in
February a siege of Gibraltar ; in which siege Laurence
Sterne's father, the veritable Uncle Toby, was a lieutenant
of foot.

But though the angry Queen of Spain had thrown
diplomacy to the winds, England was not rash in declaring war. Walpole was anxious for a peaceful settlement. So was Fleury, now in power in France after
the fall of the Duke of Bourbon :—

Peace is my dear delight—not Fleury's more [1]

[1] Pope's *Satires*, I.

And Prussia had fallen away from the Treaty of Hanover; gained over to the Emperor by the Treaty of Wusterhausen in October 1726 This was a heavy blow to England and her allies; for Frederick William had a standing army of 60,000 men But, on the other hand, the Emperor soon lost Russia, for the Czarina Catherine died, and the Hanoverian allies had already been joined by Holland, Sweden, and Denmark. It began to be clear to the Emperor that there was not much help for him in his alliance with Spain; that the combination against him was too strong Negotiations were accordingly opened; and Charles, seeing nothing but disappointment on all sides, threw Spain over, and came to terms. Preliminaries of peace were signed in May 1727, an armistice was to exist for seven years, and all further disputes between the allies of Vienna and the allies of Hanover were once more to be referred to a general Congress ' Quick, a Congress, two, three Congresses; four, five, six Congresses,' as Béranger sings.

Thus Spain was left standing quite alone, and there seemed little likelihood that she could long maintain a solitary refusal of reconcilement Negotiations with Spain did begin, of which George, though nothing positive could be said, informed his parliament in the last speech he ever made to it Within less than a month he was dead at Osnabruck, the home of his Bishop-brother This interrupted the negotiations. The Spanish ambassador at Vienna had already, in the early part of June, signed preliminaries of peace; the preliminary articles for opening the Congress, which had been appointed to meet at Soissons, were brought to London on the same day on which the King's death became known there. But the death of George raised

Spanish hopes   Spain hoped that with the accession of George II. there might be a break in the alliance between England and France, and she also counted on the probability of Jacobite troubles.   In spite, there fore, of the negotiations that had advanced so far, Spain now began to make formal objections, and went on with the Gibraltar siege for about another year. But her hopes of quarrel between France and England were disappointed ; and it proved impossible to take Gibraltar. Elizabeth at last gave up the useless, single-handed contest, and at the Pardo, a royal palace near Madrid, agreed to accept the peace and join the approaching Congress.

The Congress duly met at Soissons in June 1728 ; Walpole's brother Horatio, Stanhope (soon to become Lord Harrington), and Stephen Poyntz being the English plenipotentiaries   But in spite of the profuse presence of diplomatists, and the seeming easiness of the work they had to do, the Congress could not manage to accomplish anything   Though the Emperor had come to terms on the points of his disputes with England and France, and though he had settled his quarrel with Spain by admitting Don Carlos' claim to inheritances in Italy, the Congress could really never so much as begin business. For before any other matters should be touched, Charles insisted that his Pragmatic Sanction must be ratified ; and France would not hear of such a thing   Charles would do nothing without his Pragmatic Sanction ; Fleury would do nothing with it In such circumstances, the Congress did absolutely nothing   It sat on for some eighteen months, chiefly engaged in dining ; acting out as great a farce as had been played at Cambrai. Once more the diplomatic futility was ended by a private arrangement. Spain, which had been left in isolation at the close of the war, was alarmed lest too close a union should arise between the Emperor and the other powers   Elizabeth accordingly required from him an explicit consent to the marriages of the Austrian Arch-duchesses with the two Infants of Spain.   Charles refused to make any definite statement, and Elizabeth at once turned to private negotiation.   The result was announced in November 1729, when a new treaty, the Treaty of Seville, was produced; England, France, Holland, Spain, all now in agreement, while the Emperor was left to look out on Europe alone.   The treaty was not made at Soissons at all, but at Seville, where the Spanish Court then was, Stanhope having left the futile Congress and returned to Spain to complete the business   Absolute peace, said diplomacy with its never-failing humour, should exist between England, France, and Spain, a pleasant arrangement to which Holland soon afterwards became a fourth party, while Spain was specially gratified by the agreement that the 6,000 neutral troops garrisoning towns in the Italian Duchies for which Don Carlos was waiting, should be changed for Spanish soldiers, to make assurance doubly sure.   This was the one thing which brought Spain to agree, for it made Don Carlos seemingly safe at last   The treaty was fairly advantageous for England too, for it said not a word about Gibraltar, but tacitly dropped the Spanish claim; and on the commercial side a real peace with Spain was much to be desired.   Stanhope was immediately made Earl of Harrington for his share in this business, and Walpole politically felt the good effects of it, and was considerably helped in his next session of parliament by its happy accomplishment.

Thus in his turn the Emperor was left standing alone,

he and his Pragmatic Sanction in an unhappy condition
He had managed to displease everybody   He had made
France and England angry by his secret Treaty of
Vienna   He had made Spain angry by not fulfilling that
treaty.   And now he was made angry himself by the
union of France, England, and Spain against him   He
was so angry that he prepared for war, declared that if
Spanish troops ventured to enter Tuscany he would
himself drive them out, broke away altogether from his
understanding with Spain, and seized Parma on the
death of its Duke.   But Walpole was anxious that
Charles should not be driven to extremities.   Very
cautiously Walpole was already attempting to gain him
over, and was in the midst of a secret negotiation with
him, when in January 1731 the English parliament met.
Of this private negotiation the opposition, which now
reckoned Carteret among its numbers, knew nothing.
On the contrary, they naturally supposed that the English war preparations were directed solely against the
Emperor ; that the force which the royal speech plainly
told parliament it might be necessary to use would be
employed to compel Charles to accept the Treaty of
Seville   Such a line of action opened the way for a
European danger which was very real in those days,
and against which Carteret was always carefully on
guard.   Territorial increase of France at the expense of
Germany was an ever-present object with French statesmen, and in Carteret such a policy had a determined
and unwavering opponent.   If in the present instance
France, joined by England, should attack the Emperor,
the Rhine or the Netherlands, or both, would probably
be the important scenes of action ; and any decisive
success there would almost infallibly throw part of
Germany into the hands of the French.   If then there

must be war, urged Carteret, let all necessary measures
be taken to save the Netherlands and the Rhine from
such a danger; a motion which, under these polite parliamentary forms, really meant: Do not, in company
with so dangerous and interested an ally as France,
make war upon the Emperor at all. Pulteney in the
House of Commons supported the same view, and
wished that he could reduce to zero and burn publicly
in Palace Yard the innumerable treaties and counter-
treaties that England and all Europe had with such
infinite futility been making; a desire which the modern
reader notes with abundant sympathy, and with sorrow
that Pulteney could not do so. Walpole, saying not a
word about his secret negotiation, opposed and defeated
Carteret and Pulteney; but, if they had known it, his
own wish and policy were in this instance the same as
theirs. And in spite of all the gloomy appearances, war
was not coming after all. It was true that nothing but
delays and excuses had taken the place of the one
undertaking which had brought Spain into the peace:
the admission of the Spanish garrisons into the Italian
Duchies. Instead of compelling the Emperor by force
to agree to this, there were, especially on the part of
France and Fleury, mere postponements, and words
leading to nothing. Spain's angry irritability would
have flashed out into war against Charles But Walpole's private negotiation proved happily successful.
After the most tedious diplomatic difficulties, he reconciled the Emperor with England and Holland; and one
more treaty, hoping to be final this time, was at last
accomplished This was the second Treaty of Vienna,
signed in March 1731; a kind of ratification and completion of the Treaty of Seville. The Emperor, gratified
by England's guarantee of his Pragmatic Sanction, fully

yielded Spain's Italian requirements. Spain formally
accepted this Treaty in July, and before the year was
out Spanish troops and Don Carlos himself in person
had firm possession of the Duchies. Spain actually had
the Duchies; the Emperor seemingly had his Pragmatic
Sanction; Europe vaguely hoped that she had peace.

In English domestic politics not very much of real
interest had happened during the seven years of Carteret's Viceroyalty. Steadily and stolidly, during all these
years, Walpole had been consolidating his power, and
at the same time had been compelling into more or less
united action the heterogeneous forces of the opposition
which in the end ruined him. Once, for a moment, his
downfall had to all observers seemed certain, and even
to himself a temporary retirement had appeared inevitable. From the hot-tempered Prince of Wales, who
now so suddenly, after the fatal night at Osnabruck,
had become King George II., the chief minister of
George I. could expect nothing but disgrace and dismissal. The new King had been at no pains to conceal
his likes and dislikes. In the language of the political
gutter, in the lumbering epithetic abuse of a vulgarly
spoken age, George easily had a vulgar pre-eminence.
When he relieved his feelings in personal criticism of
the English ministers, Walpole was a great rogue, a
rascal; Townshend, a choleric blockhead; Newcastle, an
impertinent fool; Horatio Walpole, a fool, a scoundrel,
a dirty buffoon. Walpole did not for a moment deceive
himself by fancying that a great rogue and rascal could
uninterruptedly continue Prime Minister of England, as
if there were no fussily important, apoplectically passionate little King now on the throne. The minister
went to Richmond, to announce to the new sovereign
the sudden death of George I. George, roused from

sleep—he not only slept, but actually went to bed every afternoon—came hurriedly out, 'his breeches in his hand,' probably in a half-awake, irritable condition; and having sulkily said to Walpole : 'Go to Chiswick and take your directions from Sir Spencer Compton,' retired, presumably to put the royal breeches on. Walpole did as he was ordered For a very few hours, Compton, a respectable cypher and excessively formal person, seemed destined to find himself in the high places of politics At Court for a moment Walpole was slighted as a fallen favourite. low bows were lavished on Compton, who took snuff and looked as wise as possible, while Newcastle was trembling like an aspen.[1] But Walpole soon found that he had little to fear. Compton's ludicrous incapacity for the leadership was clear from the very beginning; and if George was a very foolish King, his wife Caroline was one of the wisest and most remarkable of Queens. She knew, and had always recognised, Walpole's political value ; and she was far too politically sagacious to allow personal incompatibilities or the remembrance of objectionable epithets which Walpole, in his usual coarse way, had applied to herself, to stand in the way of the advantageous settlement of public business The ' wee, wee German lairdie ' of the Jacobite songs firmly believed himself absolute master of every one about him, and especially of his wife. But Caroline, a strangely wise wife for so foolish a husband, in her prudent and seemingly deferential way managed George as she pleased ; and the first illustration of her carefully veiled influence was the almost immediate re-establishment of Walpole in all his former power.

Three years later, Walpole still further strengthened

---

[1] Brit Mus Add MSS. 18,558, fol 20

his personal position His jealousy of colleagues who were too able and independent for his purpose had already succeeded in banishing the ablest of them to Dublin, and Walpole's next victim was his own brother-in-law, Townshend. Townshend, rough, passionate, impatient, but thoroughly honest and well-meaning, would not consent to be a mere government clerk and ministerial lay-figure : Walpole was determined that he should be nothing else. The firm, said Walpole in city metaphor, should be Walpole and Townshend, not Townshend and Walpole, but it proved impossible to carry on the business under either designation. Sullen jealousies rose to angry words. Gossiping writers, with a turn for the picturesque in anecdote, dwell almost tragically upon a personal scuffle in a lady's drawing-room, where swords were near flashing out among the patches and the tea-cups, these picturesque details being perhaps mythical mainly. In any case, things had gone too far for further co-operation, especially now that Dorothy Walpole, Townshend's wife, Walpole's sister, was dead, and Townshend resigned. This strengthened Walpole ; for Townshend, fearing lest his own impetuosity might, in opposition, lead him too far and produce results which he himself would regret, very honourably withdrew from political life altogether, and retired to the cultivation of turnips in Norfolk

But that was not the way with all the statesmen whom Walpole's jealous engrossment of power repulsed and alienated. Walpole had himself very much to thank for the fact that, while he was the acknowledged leader of the Whig party, a considerable section of that party was banded together in direct personal, rather than political, opposition to him. This knot of Whigs out of place, who called themselves the 'Patriots,' and so distinguished themselves from the Whigs in place who were commonly known as the 'Courtiers,' was constantly increasing in numbers during all the earlier years of George II.'s reign, and Walpole himself gave them their great leader in the House of Commons, the Whig Pulteney In an indirect way, this had been connected with the dismissal of Carteret. Pulteney, who had always belonged to the Walpole section of the Whigs, had resigned along with Walpole in 1717 When, after the South Sea crash, Walpole and Townshend came back to power, Pulteney returned to office with them, but received only an inferior appointment. Three years later, Carteret went to Dublin, and Pulteney then aspired to the vacant Secretaryship of State. Lord Hervey, always partial to Walpole, and always specially prejudiced against Walpole's two greatest rivals, says that Pulteney suggested this arrangement to Carteret while it was still uncertain whether Carteret himself might not get the upper hand over Townshend and Walpole ; and that Walpole, hearing of this, determined not to forgive it. The simpler reason is probably the true one. Walpole dreaded Pulteney's great abilities, and for that reason refused to appoint him. The Duke of Newcastle, with the maximum of parliamentary patronage and the minimum of ability of any kind except for treachery, was a far more suitable man for Walpole's purpose, and became the new Secretary. Carteret was sent into Ireland, Pulteney was sent into opposition. In the coming years, these two men, Carteret in the Lords, Pulteney in the Commons, were the great leaders of opposition to the statesman who had treated them both so badly

Opposition, however, beginning with the very

beginning of the new reign, was for some few years
very feeble and ineffective. The regular opposition of
the Tories was not very formidable, that party was not
itself at one; 'downright' Shippen heading its Jacobites,
Wyndham leading the so-called Hanoverian Tories;
while Bolingbroke, whose overtures for restoration to
parliamentary privileges Walpole had not unreasonably
refused, worked and wrote behind the scenes. The
spirits of the Patriots, too, were considerably dashed
when Walpole, after Sir Spencer Compton's few hours
of impotent authority, appeared more firmly seated in
his place than ever, and though the minister's colleagues were ridiculously weak, it was not possible to
make any impression upon his majority. For two or
three years, therefore, practically nothing was done
against him; but in 1730, the year in which Carteret
returned from Ireland, the long struggle between
Government and Opposition may fairly be said to have
begun.

What line would Carteret himself take? Early in
his Lord-Lieutenancy Carteret had clearly seen that
there were only two possible policies open to his choice;
he must side definitely with Walpole, or go definitely
against him. He had, accordingly, through a common
friend, endeavoured to come to a clear understanding.
He frankly declared his willingness and wish to be on
terms of sincere friendship with Walpole, and left it to
Walpole to decide whether that should be so or not.
'If that friendship can be obtained,' Carteret wrote to
his friend, Richard (afterwards Lord) Edgecumbe, 'I
shall think myself happy, and be for ever faithful to it,
if not, you will bear me witness that I endeavoured it.'
Walpole himself described Carteret's proposal as 'the
most ample tender and offer of services that words

M

could express,' and wrote what he himself called a
civil, but only general, reply to it.   But when Carteret
formally pressed the matter, it became necessary for
Walpole to speak a little more definitely; and it is worth
while to let Walpole himself, in his own terrible literary
style, show how he dealt with Carteret's proposal.   He
wrote to Townshend :—

'Upon this, I was of opinion that I should encourage him to hope for our friendship. . . . I now explained
that upon condition he would enter cordially and
sincerely into the King's measures in conjunction with
us at present in the administration, and without any
reserves, I was ready to agree with him, and as he
knew with whom I was so far engaged as to do nothing
but in concert, this must be understood to extend
equally to those with whom I was engaged, and that to
render this reconciliation more perfect, I would by the
first opportunity acquaint your lordship with it, and
did not doubt of your concurrence upon the same conditions.   By this means, my lord, we shall hinder him
from entering into any engagements with Roxburgh,
Pulteney, etc.; we shall have the use of him and his
assistance in the House of Lords next winter, where his
behaviour may make him so desperate with them that
he may have no resource.   I say nothing of his sincerity, so as to answer for it, but we know him enough to
watch him, and be upon our guard.   . . If we keep
him and Berkeley. . . . I think we have all that are
worth having of that clan.'[1]

Walpole's literary style is very distressing; but he
could hardly have asserted more clearly that he was
willing enough to receive from Carteret all he could

---

[1] Carteret's letter to Edgecumbe and Walpole's to Townshend are in
Coxe's *Walpole* II 188–190   The dates are Sept and Oct. 1725.

get, and had no intention of giving anything in return
Carteret cannot have mistaken the spirit of Walpole's
reply; and as the years of his Irish government passed
on must have more and more clearly seen that any
real union was impossible. In December 1727 his
friend Schaub wrote from Versailles that the ministers
in London were doing all they could to undermine Carteret's influence at Paris, and to represent him as
uninfluential and on the point of falling. Walpole, in
short, was determined to get rid of Carteret, and that
was made perfectly evident when Carteret returned
from Dublin to London. The only attempt to keep
him in some slight relation to the Government was the
offer of a ceremonial position at Court, with a stick of
some colour or other attached to it. Carteret immediately declined this ornamental absurdity, which Walpole
cannot have supposed he would accept. It was the
year of Townshend's resignation; the year in which
Walpole's supremacy became absolute. Carteret was
only one political enemy the more, and Walpole felt
himself very firm.

The long struggle against Walpole, the great Wal-
polean battle as it got to be called, faint at first, but
growing strong and stronger year by year, till it became
almost dramatic in its intensity, may be said to have
begun in earnest in the year of Carteret's return from
Ireland. It was not difficult to find many points for
plausible and justifiable attacks on Walpole. His policy
could not rouse much enthusiasm even among his own
supporters. He was content to let things alone; to
touch no abuses which were not too scandalous and
importunate; to give way on all occasions rather than
face any parliamentary trouble or risk any parliamentary
defeat. Cynical political proceedings of this sort might

be well adapted for securing a long hold of office; but
they were terribly uninteresting. Still, so long as seriously exciting questions did not arise, it was difficult
for the opposition to do very much. It was not, on
many occasions, the want of a good cause that hampered Carteret and Pulteney, Chesterfield and Argyle,
it was rather the want of much political interest in the
nation at large; the general rather heavy and dull
satisfaction with a minister who was trusted in money
matters, and who kept the nation fairly at peace. If
the long period of the struggle is divided into two
parts, the death of Queen Caroline in 1737 being taken
as the dividing mark, it will be clear that in the first of
these periods Walpole was practically master of the
situation, and that the performances of the opposition
were trifling. But in the second a change is manifest
at once. The Queen, Walpole's firm friend at Court,
was gone; long-continued exclusion from office had
heightened the energies of his political adversaries,
and, most important of all, a number of foreign questions
were arising for solution on which both Court and
nation were opposed to Walpole's views. His authority,
therefore, gradually waned, becoming weaker and
weaker with each succeeding session, till at last the
great majority which had so long registered his decrees
failed him, and he fell from the power to which, till
the very last moment, he clung with a sort of fanati-
cal desperation.

The first of these two periods, not in many ways
very interesting, and not requiring very detailed treatment even in a general history of the time, may, in a
biography of Carteret, be passed over with comparative
lightness. From 1730 to 1733, the parliamentary sessions were very quiet. But in 1733 there was a decided

storm, and although Carteret had nothing personally
or politically to do with it, it served to produce some
curiously absurd criticism of his character by Queen
Caroline. Walpole had proposed his celebrated Excise
scheme, a scheme which, in his own words, would have
tended to make London a free port, and the market of
the world. But there was a general outcry against it
The very name of Excise was hateful, and though Walpole's plan was of the most moderate and restricted
kind, unscrupulous writers and speakers did not hesitate
to ruin it by the most falsely exaggerated alarms It
would have merely altered the method of collecting
the duties on wine and tobacco, but it was persistently
represented and everywhere spoken of as a scheme for
taxing everything, down to the most necessary articles
of food and dress The unscrupulous agitation caused
great excitement in the country; and parliamentary
circles eagerly discussed the important question · What
will Walpole do?

To the interesting companion question. What will
the Opposition do? a partial answer was soon given by
a considerable section of the House of Lords Nothing
was so powerful a support to Walpole as the steady
favour of the Queen. This Excise incident which had
roused such ignorant passion and universal alarm might,
thought some of the peers, well be used to weaken
Walpole's influence in that quarter, and to frighten
Caroline by convincing her that the Prime Minister
whom she supported was the most unpopular man in
the country. This rather amateurish plan was adopted;
and the Earl of Stair (of later Dettingen renown) was
chosen to approach the Queen with argument and with
oratory. Unwilling to spoil the effect of his harangue
by the mildness of his language, Stair asserted that

never was a minister so universally hated as Walpole, and that his obstinate insistence on his Excise scheme was endangering the crown   Stair became almost tragic in remonstrances, in a seemingly superfluous way hinted that Englishmen never would be slaves, and, forgetting that he was in the Court of George II, solemnly spoke about his conscience 'Ah! my lord!' burst out the Queen, '*ne me parlez point de conscience; vous me faites évanouir.*'

Caroline, who had a very sharp tongue, and was quite well aware of that fact, castigated Lord Stair in a very outspoken fashion. She frankly told him that his professions of patriotism only made her laugh; and she let him understand that she reckoned him merely a puppet in the hands of two worthless men of genius. The interesting fact here is that Carteret was one of the two men whom the Queen had in her mind   Lord Bolingbroke was the other, and Caroline bracketed them together in this ungrammatically vigorous sentence. 'My Lord Bolingbroke and my Lord Carteret, whom you may tell, if you think fit, that I have long known to be two as worthless men of parts as any in this country, and whom I have not only been often told are two of the greatest liars and knaves in any country, but whom my own observation and experience have found so '[1] From the point of view of ungrammatical vigour nothing could be finer, but as far as Carteret is concerned there is not a word of truth in this impetuous accusation.   Queen Caroline had no right to bracket Carteret and Bolingbroke as working together in political life; for beyond the fact that they were both in opposition, they had no political connection of

[1] Lord Hervey, *Memoirs*, I 171, 172 who had his account of the interview from the Queen herself.

any kind whatever. The other charge of lying and knavery is with regard to Carteret simply and supremely ridiculous. Caroline's sharp sayings were never particularly refined, but noisy bombast of this kind brings her literary style down almost to the level of her tyrannical little lord's outbursts of passionate and personal abuse.

There is no evidence that Carteret had any share in this rather weak and quite ineffective attempt to shake the Queen's confidence in Walpole. Carteret spoke out his opposition to the minister frankly and uncompromisingly from his seat in parliament; but on this subject he had nothing to say, for the Excise Bill never reached the House of Lords. So powerful was the opposition in parliament, and so excited the feeling in the country, that though Walpole was firmly convinced of the excellence of his plan, and though the King and Queen gave him all the support in their power, the Excise scheme had to be dropped. This was a check which Walpole felt very much. His usual gay indifference momentarily forsook him. Yet, after all, he managed. as he always did in such cases to gain some temporary advantage from what was undeniably a defeat. He at once dismissed from their official positions those who had either actually opposed him on the question, or had not effectively enough supported him. In this way Chesterfield was dismissed. Unfortunately for Walpole personally, such temporary advantages unfailingly brought their revenges. Every dismissed official surely found his way into the ranks of the opposition. The jealously imperious minister was left more and more to surround himself with mediocrities only, whose support, satisfactory enough for the moment, could not be any long-lasting strength. Long as Walpole's Govern-

ment existed after this incident, holding hard to office
and practically doing nothing else, the beginning of the
end may fairly be dated from 1733 and the Excise
scheme The opposition, especially in the House of
Lords, where Carteret was already clearly becoming its
leader, began to be more definite, vigorous, and important Walpole himself increased its numbers next year
by dismissing the Earls of Marchmont, Bolton, and Cobham, whose conduct had failed to satisfy him. Carteret,
Chesterfield, Argyle, Bedford, and Stair were far too
strong for a fussily ridiculous Duke of Newcastle and
for such other official supporters as Walpole could
muster in the House of Lords, and his position in that
House at least was far from satisfactory

The years immediately following Walpole's Excise
defeat, occupied almost exclusively with domestic
politics, are chiefly interesting, so far as Carteret is
concerned. for their evidence of his decisive pre-eminence in opposition. Some observers, with a turn for
the small gossip of political accommodations, professed
to believe that Carteret was already secretly anxious
for a reconciliation with Walpole Lord Hervey, who
might easily have spared himself the trouble, thought
it worth while to ask Walpole if there was any truth
in these rumours. Walpole's answer had at least the
merit of clearness 'He asked me,' reports Hervey,
'if I thought him mad enough ever to trust such a
fellow as that on any consideration, or on any promises
or professions, within the walls of St James's.' 'I had
some difficulty,' added he, 'to get him out; but he
shall find much more to get in again '[1] From Walpole's personal point of view, it was decidedly a wise
thing to put a strong barrier between Carteret and

----

[1] Lord Hervey, *Memoirs*, I 461, 462.

Court favour. Carteret, on the other hand, had an unquestioned right to further, by all fair methods, his own
and his party's political interests. Walpole could not
appropriate quite all the political field to himself and
to the insignificant officials who were allowed to call
themselves his colleagues. That Carteret should desire,
after all that had passed, to take office in Walpole's
Government, was too ridiculous to be believingly asserted; but he was a practical statesman of large and
seriously considered views, and naturally and necessarily desired to be able to give effect to his political
opinions. There was none of the hypocritical humility
in Carteret which professes, when out of office, to be
entirely indifferent to the possession of political power.
But just for this very reason, Walpole could not have
desired a fairer, more straightforward political adver-
sary. The practical certainty that he himself must soon
be high in power made opposition in Carteret's case
only a little less responsible than government itself. A
fair instance of his parliamentary conduct in opposition
occurred in the session of 1736. The Quakers were
anxious for relief in a small matter which pressed hard
on their conscientious scruples. Walpole was desirous
to meet their views; but the bishops would not hear of
it. The bishops had their way, and threw out the
small measure of relief. George and Caroline—the
Queen was never very orthodox—were both exceedingly angry. 'Scoundrels, black, canting, hypocritical
rascals,' George called the bishops in his passionate
style; and hard words fell thick on them in parliament
and in the country. The Duke of Argyle abused them;
Lord Chief Justice Hardwicke dwelt bitterly on their
rich pluralities, and Carteret, while declaring that
every one knew his extreme hostility to the existing

Government. asserted that he would never join in attacking any minister who was ecclesiastically insulted

More serious annoyance than the bigoted opposition of the bishops soon interrupted the placid security of the Government This same year 1736 was one of considerable disturbance throughout the country generally , but none of the more or less riotous outbreaks attracted such general attention as the so-called Porteous riots at Edinburgh. A well-known smuggler had been arrested and sentenced to death There was always a lurking feeling of sympathy with offences of the smuggling kind , and, in this particular case, the rather romantic way in which the imprisoned smuggler had assisted the escape of a fellow-prisoner had quite turned popular sentiment in his favour To avoid, if possible, a riot and a probable attempted rescue of the prisoner, the Edinburgh Town Guard, under Captain Porteous, was drawn up at the place of execution The sentence, however, was carried out quietly enough ; but immediately afterwards all was in confusion. The mob was very large ; stones began to fly at Porteous and his Guard, who still stood under arms round about the gallows. 'Fire!' said Captain Porteous to his men ; and some half-dozen of the crowd fell. Porteous was at once put upon his trial for this order, and to the fierce delight of the infuriated people was sentenced to death.

The case of Porteous seemed, however, somewhat too hard ; and, in response to an influential petition from Scotland, Queen Caroline—for George had already escaped to Hanover—sent down a reprieve But the Edinburgh mob was in no mood to surrender its victim It seized the city gates ; broke into the prison ; dragged Porteous to the Grassmarket, and there formally carried out the sentence to its own complete satisfaction, meeting its own views of legal requirements by punctually paying for the necessary rope. Then it quietly dispersed.

Something of the sort had been expected, but no precautions had been taken. General Moyle, who commanded the King's troops in Scotland, was in the suburbs of Edinburgh; and late at night, while the riot that preceded the execution of Porteous was still taking its course, Lindsay, Member for Edinburgh, slipped out of the city by a small wicket-gate which was not in the hands of the rioters, and went in search of Moyle. But Moyle would not move, declining to act against the rioters unless ordered to do so by the civil magistrates. So the hours passed by, and absolutely nothing was done. And when, later on, the Edinburgh magistrates undertook a judicial investigation of the affair, it proved impossible to produce condemning evidence that had any legal weight. The Queen was very angry. She was very angry with Moyle, and declared that if the rioters deserved to be hanged he deserved to be shot. She was indignant with the magistrates who had done nothing to hinder or to punish the riot, and with the people of Edinburgh generally, whose zeal against Porteous made it impossible to procure either prisoners or witnesses. And she felt considerable personal pique that this outbreak against authority had occurred while the government of the country was in her hands.

Parliament accordingly turned to the matter. Parliament had been waiting long for the return of the King, whom bad weather was detaining abroad; but at last could wait no longer, and opened itself without him in the beginning of February 1737. The absent King's speech was eloquent in condemnation of the riotous insults which had been offered to the Government, and it was impossible to avoid parliamentary inquiry yet the question somewhat annoyed and embarrassed Walpole. He was anxious not to irritate the Scotch, and feared any possible unpleasantness in the proceedings which might alienate them from his Government Ill-natured observers like Lord Hervey. who always go out of their way to find mean, spiteful reasons when plain common-sense ones are staring them in the face, assert that this difficulty of Walpole's was Carteret's chief inducement to take a leading part in the parliamentary investigation Here was Carteret's chance, says in effect Hervey; why should he not turn Scotland against Walpole. and make a grand electoral move of it? Simpler persons, looking without prejudice, see things differently The support of the Government of the country against lawless outbreaks was as important to Carteret, who had been a minister and might at any moment be one again, as it was to Walpole himself. Walpole's enthusiastic but inextricably chaotic biographer distinctly states that Carteret's action was a relief to Walpole. and helped him out of his embarrassment

In opening the question, Carteret, while severely condemning the lawless doings of the Edinburgh mob, declared his own view that the condemnation of Porteous had been illegal, and hoped that the conduct of the magistrates, as well as the action of the rioters, would be taken into consideration All this is now of no consequence or interest to any one, but there are glimpses of Carteret's personality, and evidence of the reasoned seriousness of his political principles, in the remaining records of this quite temporary episode. 'In the body politic,' said Carteret in one of his

speeches, 'as in the body natural, while the cause
remains, it is impossible to remove the distemper. . . .
I shall never be for sacrificing the liberties of the
people, in order to prevent their engaging in any riotous
proceedings; because I am sure it may be done by a
much more gentle and less expensive method A wise
and a prudent conduct, and a constant pursuit of
upright and just measures, will establish the authority
as well as the power of the Government' Carteret had
already explained what he meant by the distinction
between authority and power 'Power and authority
we must always look on as two things of a very
different nature Power, the legislature may give, but
authority it can give no man. Authority may be
acquired by wisdom, by prudence, by good conduct
and a virtuous behaviour; but it can be granted by no
King, by no potentate upon earth. A man's power
depends upon the post or station he is in; but his
authority can depend upon nothing but the character
he acquires among mankind' And then in one short
decisive sentence he clenched his definition by applying
it to the Government of the day 'I must observe, and
I do it without a design of offending any person, that
ever since I came into the world, I never saw an administration that had, in my opinion, so much power
or so little authority.'

Carteret's proposal that the Provost and magistrates
of Edinburgh should be summoned to the bar of the
House of Lords was agreed to On the appointed day,
these officials were duly in attendance, and Carteret,
to help the House in its management of the business,
sketched the lines which the examination should follow.
But having done so much, he very justly thought that
the arrangement of further and decisive action was

work for the Government itself. Carteret had done, as
he said, his duty so far; it was now time that responsible Government should take its responsible place
Yet no sooner were the ministers thus compelled to act
for themselves than the conduct of the affair fell into
almost complete confusion The examination of the
magistrates by the House of Lords showed clearly that
the Edinburgh people had set their hearts on the death
of Porteous, and that the magistrates, though certainly
forewarned by common rumour, had taken no precau-
tionary measures of any kind. Thus neither of the
political parties could deny that punishment was deserved and necessary; there was only one question in
dispute: What shall the punishment be? On this
question the contests were frequent and violent Those
of the peers who held more closely to Walpole, and
naturally such Scotch peers as the Duke of Argyle
and his brother Lord Isla, were opposed to any severe
measures But Newcastle, who was not at present on
very good terms with Walpole, and the Lord Chancellor
opposed these milder arguments; and they were joined
by Carteret's friend Sherlock, Bishop of Salisbury, who
took this opportunity of repaying Argyle for the attacks
which he had lately made on the bishops generally.
The views of this stronger party seemed likely to prevail, and Walpole was induced by the remonstrances of
Newcastle and the Chancellor to show a little more
severity, and especially to agree that the chief of the
judges at the trial of Porteous should be immediately
summoned to London But here Walpole's friend
Hervey, a leading supporter of the more moderate
party, struck into the argument. He went to the
Queen, with whom he was on the most intimate terms,
and urged his views upon her with very considerable

success. Caroline sent for Newcastle and bullied him 'What the devil,' she said in her strong way, ' signifies all this bustle about the Scotch judges? Will worrying the Scotch judges be any satisfaction to the King for the insult offered to the Government in the murder of Porteous?' Newcastle, who was as timid as he was ridiculous, was terribly frightened by the Queen's attack; and from that moment the whole affair went forward in a half-hearted fashion. The many debates on the punishment which should be dealt out to Edinburgh ended in the gentle resolution that its Provost should be for ever disgraced, and that one of its city gates should be pulled down And even this mild sentence was in the end made milder still.

The action taken in regard to the conduct of the judges and the legality of the sentence on Porteous was even more feeble and inconsequent Carteret moved to declare that the condemnation of Porteous was erroneous, and discussed the question thoroughly from the legal point of view. But practically nothing was done The Lord Chancellor, in spite of all his warm talk, was now for caution and delay Newcastle, thoroughly frightened, did indeed help Carteret by not speaking in support of him; but helped in no other way The thing became almost farcical. The Scotch judges had been got up to London, after debates of passionate excitement The Lords could not agree what to do with them. Should they be examined at the bar, or at the table, or on the wool-sacks? Seat them on the wool-sacks, urged one party What right have Scotch judges to sit on English wool-sacks? cried another To get rid of them altogether, and as soon as possible, remained the only common-sense escape from a situation which was becoming ridiculous merely, and a most lame conclusion ended the whole business. Edinburgh was to pay a fine of 2,000*l.* to Porteous' widow.

The combined influence of Court and Government had been too strong for Carteret, and he had been compelled to give way. Hervey repeats a conversation which he had with Carteret after Parliament had decided that the Scotch judges should be allowed to go home again. 'You saw,' said Carteret, 'I found how it went, and made my retreat. Whilst Lord Chancellor and the Duke of Newcastle went along with me, I thought I could deal with you . . . but I found my Lord Isla and you had got the better of him and the Duke of Newcastle at St. James's; and when I felt how matters stood, I retired too.' 'But,' said Hervey, 'if this was your opinion, how came you not to let your friend Sherlock into the secret?'—for the bishop had been anxious to detain the judges in London. 'Why did you not tell him that half the pack of those hounds on whom you most depended were drawn off, and the game escaped and safe, instead of leaving his lordship there to bark and yelp by himself, and make the silly he has done?' Carteret's reply was very keen. 'Oh! he talks like a parson; and consequently is so used to talk to people that don't mind him, that I left him to find it out at his leisure, and shall have him again for all this whenever I want him.'[1]

Only one other incident in this terribly barren and uninteresting period of English domestic history—it would be hard to find a more completely barren decade in home politics than the period from 1727 to 1737—requires some notice as bearing on Carteret's political life. As the King himself had quarrelled with George I.,

[1] Lord Hervey's *Memoirs*, II. 323, 324.

so his own son Frederick, Prince of Wales, was on exceedingly bad terms with George II. What the particular cause of disagreement was, whether even there was any one definite cause or not, is not very clear or at all important Perhaps as much as anything else, the unfortunate double-marriage scheme, in the neighbourhood of which Carteret had found himself for a moment, may have been at the bottom of it. George I., the grandfather, had never been very eager for this arrangement, and in the end had quite ceased to favour it; while George II. and Frederick William of Prussia were never on cordial terms. 'My cousin the corporal' had very limited admiration for 'my cousin the dancing-master.' But the third party, Prince Frederick himself, held very decided views on the question. The marriage with Wilhelmina of Prussia was a thing he was resolved on, and idle rumour soon formed a complete myth about it and him. Rumour was shocked to assert that as all other methods seemed hopeless Frederick had impetuously decided on a secret match, and that George, hearing of the terrible piece of insubordination, had imperatively ordered the discomfited Prince to show himself in London at once All of which is mythical; and fact notes only that Frederick came to London in December 1729. Till now the King had very gladly done without his son's presence, had very willingly left him to his own idle, lounging ways at Hanover. But it was hardly possible to overlook the heir to the crown any longer, and in obedience to orders, Frederick, aged twenty-two, arrived in England He was coolly received, and for some two or three years did no particular harm to anybody except himself He held aloof from politics doing feeble performances in the French madrigal department

and mild patronage of literature in a slightly imbecile
manner. But he gradually, also in an imbecile manner,
turned towards political affairs and especially towards
the opposition party in politics, gathered its leading
men about him, and thought to find his own advantage
out of them. Men whose reputation was already made,
Carteret, Pulteney, Chesterfield; younger men whose
reputation was still to come, Pitt, Lyttelton, the Grenvilles, the 'boy patriots,' as Walpole called them, the
'Cobham cousins,' as others nicknamed them, were more
or less closely mixed up with the foolish Prince. They
were the most brilliant set of public men in London,
and were backed up by the leading men of letters, by
Carteret's friend Swift, Pope, Thomson, Gay, Arbuthnot;
all disregarded by Walpole, who thought that any Grub-
street scribbler would do as well. These opposition
leaders all despised the Prince, they could not do
otherwise; but they accepted what aid he could give
them, and the countenance they showed him filled the
King and Queen with vexation and anger. When
Caroline occasionally indulges in venomous abuse of
Carteret and other opposition statesmen, it is well to
remember that the Queen had a personal reason for
regarding them with bitter ill-will.

In these circumstances, the original estrangement
of the Prince from his parents went on widening in
a rather rapid way. Further causes of dispute arose
from time to time. Frederick quarrelled with his sister
because she ventured to be married before him. He
set himself at the head of the Lincoln's Inn Fields'
opera because the rest of the royal family patronised
the Haymarket and Handel. His conduct was so generally foolish that for some considerable time the King
and Queen could afford to treat him with contemptuous

indifference. But at last, in 1734, he took a decisive step. He requested an audience with the King, and Walpole with some difficulty persuaded George to grant it. When admitted, the Prince made three definite requests. He was in debt: he asked an increased and regularly paid income. He had been disappointed of Wilhelmina; he wished that some other suitable match should be arranged for him. And he had nothing particular to do; he wished to go to the wars. To the first and last of these demands George had nothing whatever to say; but he agreed that the marriage was a point which should be settled. This one cause of the Prince's discontent was soon removed. In 1735, at Hanover, the King's choice fell upon the young Princess Augusta of Saxe-Gotha; Frederick, with good enough grace, assented; and early in 1736 the marriage took place.

But, as things turned out, this settlement proved only the starting-point of a more embittered controversy than ever. The conduct of the opposition on the occasion of the marriage was very displeasing to the King; for their congratulations to the son were so turned as to be tolerably plain reflections on the father. Pitt made his maiden speech on this affair, and at the end of the session Walpole dismissed him from his cornetcy for it. But far more annoying to George was the action of the Prince himself. Frederick's not very large allowance of 24,000*l* a year had been, on his marriage, increased by his father to 50,000*l*. In Frederick's view, this was merely robbing him. George himself, when Prince of Wales, had had 100,000*l*. a year; parliament, when it settled the Civil List on the King at his accession, had meant that Frederick should have the same; to give him an income of 50,000*l* was therefore,

Frederick argued, really nothing else than to rob him of half his due.   But it was useless to attempt to move George   The King would not yield, and the Prince of Wales, insisting that common justice was denied him, at last resolved to lay his grievances before parliament.

The Queen would not for some time believe that Frederick's resolution was really taken, and through all the stages of the question she showed great concern and anxiety   Her language about the Prince was terribly strong, while Princess Caroline called her brother a 'nauseous beast,' and, like her mother, fervently longed for his death   The King on no occasion minced his words, but he took this particular affair with a good deal more coolness than might have been expected. The Prince himself was all expectant of the result ; Lord Chesterfield and some of the younger discontented Whigs inciting and encouraging him.   Political quid-nuncs devoted themselves to busy speculation on the number of his probable majority, and Walpole began to feel some little alarm.   But Carteret disapproved of the Prince's action ; so also did Pulteney.   The Prince's success would weaken the influence of the royal family ; it would be a blow to the Whig party, the chief supporters of the House of Hanover   Frederick, however, was resolved to go on ; private arguments brought to bear upon him were decisively rejected.   The day for the parliamentary discussion was fixed, and Walpole, now fairly frightened by the possible dangers of the position, as a last resource attempted to secure a compromise. He urged the King to send a message to the Prince, promising that a yearly sum should be settled on the Princess of Wales, and that Frederick's own income, which he received simply at the King's pleasure, should be formally settled on him. The message was sent, but King and Queen were both exceedingly enraged at its reception Frederick's reply, quite respectful, but perfectly decisive, simply stated that the whole affair had now passed from his hands, and that he could not receive any proposition in regard to it

The two opposition statesmen who blamed Frederick for forcing this discussion on parliament were the two who, as leaders, found themselves compelled to introduce the subject early in 1737 Pulteney in the Commons, and, on the following day, Carteret in the Lords, urged that Frederick should be treated as his father had been before him, chiefly supporting their contention by arguments of historical precedent Walpole, to the extreme delight of the Court, managed to defeat Pulteney by a fair, if not very large, majority; a victory gained by the abstention of a considerable number of Tories. Carteret's speech was, on the express evidence of Hervey, a cold performance; it is probable that, after the defeat in the Commons, Carteret renewed his objections to touch this question in the Lords, but was overruled It is certain that Carteret despised the Prince, certain also that he had no wish needlessly and uselessly to offend the Court But the resolution to press the thing had been taken, and Carteret, with hardly concealed dislike, had to comply. The victory of the Court party in the Upper House was of course easy.

The whole course of this miserable affair had rather weakened Walpole with the King and Queen It was Walpole who had advised the message to the Prince; and the message had been a complete failure A victory had indeed been won in the House of Commons, but could not, in the circumstances, be much boasted of The Queen, too, was entering into communications with Carteret, and listening to his advice and arguments This filled Walpole with alarm at once ; and in his dogged, common-sense fashion he spoke very plainly to Caroline about it, introducing Carteret at the very outset of his expostulations. The Queen told Walpole that Carteret had given her explanations of his conduct ; that he had been driven against his will to support the Prince of Wales. ' He says,' continued the Queen, ' that he found you were too well established in my favour for him to hope to supplant you ; and, upon finding he could not be first, that he had mortified his pride so far as to take the resolution of submitting to be second ; but if you would not permit him even to serve under you, who is there that could blame him if he continued to fight against you ? ' Which seems a reasonable question But Walpole had the inevitable answer ready : in no circumstances could he and Carteret continue to work together. The Prime Minister plainly told the Queen that she must choose between them. " ' I know, Madam,' continued Sir Robert, ' how indecent it is generally for a minister and servant of the Crown to talk in this style, and to say there is anybody with whom he will not serve I therefore ask your pardon ; but I thought I should be still more in the wrong if I suffered your Majesty to make any agreement with Carteret, and afterwards quitted your service on that event without having previously told you I would do so ' " [1] The same unwavering resolve that in no case would he accept Carteret as a colleague was about this same date announced by Walpole to Newcastle also Carteret and Newcastle had both been Westminster boys, and returned together one night from a

[1] Lord Hervey's *Memoirs* II. 294-296

Westminster School dinner. Newcastle, who, says Hervey, was half-intoxicated, went that same night to Walpole's, and, probably in a state of maudlin imbecility, offered himself as surety for Carteret's good behaviour, if only Walpole would accept him. Walpole's brother, Horatio, and Newcastle's brother, Henry Pelham, alone were present There was no ambiguity about Walpole's reply. 'I am glad, my lord, you have given me this opportunity once for all to let you know my determined sentiments on this matter . . Your Grace must take your choice between me and him, and if you are angry at my saying this, I care not; I have said it to your betters, and I'll stick to it.'[1]

To Walpole's asseverations and arguments the Queen replied with assurances of her confidence; and, the parliamentary session of 1737 being now over, the Premier left London for his usual hunting and riotous joviality at Houghton. He was hardly back again when he was renewing his complaints at the Court, and tortured by his anxious jealousy of Carteret He thought that Mrs. Clayton—better known as Lady Sundon, one of Voltaire's friends during his English sojourn—was urging Carteret's claims on the Queen, and in language of his habitual brutality called her a 'damned inveterate bitch' for her pains. Caroline herself told Walpole that Carteret was writing the history of his own times, and vague rumours spread of mysterious meetings between Carteret and Lady Sundon, 'on the Queen's gravel walk in St. James's Park,' where the conversation turned on this literary performance; and where, if Lady Sundon and Hervey are to be literally trusted, this one definite sentence was spoken by Carteret : 'Madam, if you dare own at Court you talk to so obnoxious a man as I am, you may tell the Queen I have been giving her fame this morning;' a remark which, in that precise form, it is tolerably safe to say was never made by Carteret. Caroline once exchanged a few words with Hervey on this history of Carteret's, when the irascible little King—who did not yet know how valuable Carteret was to be to him—broke out: 'Yes, I dare say he will paint you in fine colours, *that dirty liar!*' 'Why not?' said the Queen. 'Good things come out of dirt sometimes; I have eat very good asparagus raised out of dung.' What a charming Court![1]

George's passionate outbursts against a statesman of whom, so far, he knew only this, that he was in opposition, are, of course, of no real significance. Caroline, though her language lost little of its coarse vigour, was distinctly inclining towards Carteret. But it was just at this period that the quarrel in the royal family took an exceedingly aggravated turn; and this aggravation brings with it distinct proof that the King and Queen judged and spoke of Carteret not as a statesman—they had practically had no experience of him in office—but entirely from a personal point of view. He was more or less mixed up in a bitter family quarrel. It was little to his taste to be concerned in it at all; and some few years later, when he was himself practically Prime Minister, he was doubtless thinking of the vexation caused to every one who had anything to do with this miserable squabble, when he wrote to one of the English ambassadors abroad· 'The family affairs of Princes are of such delicacy, that ministers in their wits will never interfere if they can possibly help it'[2] It was,

[1] At this period, Carteret, Chesterfield, and Bolingbroke were all assumed to be writing Memoirs of their time. Nothing is known of Carteret's work.

[2] Add MSS 22,534, fol. 55

however, impossible for Carteret as a political leader to stand entirely apart from the dispute; and nothing is clearer than the fact that the language used by the King and Queen about him depended entirely on the fluctuations of this domestic quarrel, and on nothing else whatever. If Carteret was thought to be encouraging the Prince in what his parents regarded as outrageous behaviour, then at Court endless variations were played on the one theme—'liar.' But when it was rumoured that Carteret disapproved of Frederick's conduct, the language of the Court veered round; the 'liar' was followed by an explanatory mitigating 'but.' In this way the temporary personal judgments of a very clever woman and a very foolish man found adequate expression; but the language, either of praise or blame, is from no other point of view of even the slightest importance.

A vague sort of reconciliation had been brought about in the royal family at the close of the quarrelsome session of 1737; and in the summer recess King, Queen, Prince, and Princess were all staying together at Hampton Court. This idyllic state of things did not last. Very suddenly, without a syllable of information to the King or Queen, the Prince hurried his wife away to St James's Palace, in order that her child might not be born in the house where his parents were. Feeble excuses were made by the Prince in attempted justification of his conduct, but there was practically no defence. The anger which George and Caroline had previously felt against their son was trifling compared with the passion which now consumed them. Caroline, indeed, in common decency could do no less than visit her daughter-in-law on this interesting occasion; no one had any fault to find with the Princess, who simply had to do what her husband told her. But after that one visit, all intercourse with the Prince was instantly broken off. The King and Queen sent him a message, expressing their extreme anger, and bluntly declining to see him. It was all that Walpole could do to prevent them from declaring open war against him. George refused to allow Frederick to remain in his house, and sent him a peremptory order to quit St. James's. 'Thank God, to-morrow night the puppy will be out of my house,' the King exclaimed after despatching this order; and Caroline over and over again repeated, 'I hope in God I shall never see him again.' His guard was taken from him; foreign ministers were requested not to visit him, and exclusion from the King's Court was the inevitable penalty for attendance at the Prince's.

On Frederick's arrival at St. James's with his wife, he had summoned Carteret, Pulteney, and Chesterfield to meet him. They all not only privately disapproved of his conduct, but plainly told him so. Instantly the King and Queen began to speak well of Carteret. He might be a great knave, said Caroline, but she would not believe that he had had anything to do with her son's conduct on this occasion. The King said to Walpole: 'I know Carteret disapproves this whole affair.' Such royal sentiments were too dangerous; and Walpole at once proceeded to check them. He was far more afraid of Carteret at Court than in the House of Lords, and thought him the most likely person to supplant him in the favour of the King and Queen, who both, on the express evidence of Speaker Onslow, disliked Carteret less than any other member of the opposition.[1] Walpole therefore went again to Court and attacked Carteret. Carteret was a very lucky man, insinuated Walpole,

[1] Onslow's *Remarks*, in Coxe, *Walpole*, II 569.

to be high in favour in the two hostile Courts Carteret
asserted that his visits to the Prince were only formal ;
and indeed, while the royal quarrel was at its very
height he had been at his own seat in Bedfordshire ;
but Walpole dwelt so alarmingly on the subject to the
King and Queen that these exceedingly fickle royal personages once more changed their tone The old ' liar '
theme was once again produced ; the Princess Caroline
on this occasion performing a remarkable variation.   If
the Queen were actually to meet Carteret at the Prince's
house, said this vivacious performer, Carteret was
capable of endeavouring to persuade her that the devil
had put on his figure, *seulement pour lui rendre un
mauvais office auprès d'elle.*   The Princess's conceptions
of Carteret's persuasive powers, and of the devil's undeniable interest in the personalities of party politics,
are wanting in moderation ; but there are excuses for
the erratic vivacity of a young girl. For Sir Robert
Walpole there is no excuse   He did not disdain in his
jealous dread of Carteret to injure his rival by direct
falsehood and deception. It is his own devoted follower
and Carteret's opponent who tells the tale.   The Prince
of Wales, at his house in Pall Mall, received the congratulations of the London Corporation on the birth of
his daughter   Printed copies of the King's message to
the Prince were distributed on this occasion and moving
comments relieved the feelings of those present on the
conduct of a father who had turned his son and his
daughter-in-law out of his house The proceedings at
this meeting were reported by Walpole to the King and
Queen, and he informed them that it was Carteret who
had had the message printed for this occasion. The
King and Queen doubtless took Walpole's word , but
posterity knows better More than a week before,

Walpole himself had informed Hervey that he designed
to let the message slip into print as if by accident.
Hervey adds his own mild comment: 'I am apt to
imagine that he put that upon Lord Carteret which
was entirely his own doing.'[1]

Walpole might well have avoided such despicable
trickery as this, and on this particular occasion it does
not seem to have done Carteret very much harm. The
Court was once more veering round, and definitely inclining towards belief in Carteret and conviction that
he was no real adherent of the Prince of Wales. He
never had been, he despised him while he used him.
Frederick, who was a very imbecile creature, no doubt
thought that Carteret and Pulteney were his very
obedient servants, and that he could do with them
as he chose. 'He had a notion,' says Lord Shelburne,
'that he could get round anybody by talking nonsense
to them, and after playing a dirty trick, or being caught
in some infamous lie by such a man as Lord Granville
[Carteret], he would take them into a corner, and say
he had "raccomodé" all that.'[2] Such a man as Carteret
thought otherwise 'What the devil else can you think
I ever went to the Prince for?' asked Carteret, when
Lyttelton reproached him for using Frederick and flinging him away. Caroline at length began definitely to
see that this was the real state of the case; and Walpole found her language once more tending towards
justification of Carteret's action As Prime Minister,
Walpole's opportunities for expostulation and argument
were unlimited. He knew the Queen's heart was set on
getting the better of her son The question, therefore,

[1] Hervey, *Memoirs*, II. 462.
[2] Shelburne's *Autobiography*, in Lord E Fitzmaurice's *Shelburne*, I
62. 63

which it was Walpole's interest to press upon the Queen, narrowed itself down to this: Which of the two men, Walpole or Carteret, did she think could better help her to defeat the Prince? 'Is your son to be bought? Walpole asked the Queen. 'If you will buy him, I will get him cheaper than Carteret And yet, after all I have said, if your majesty thinks he can serve you better than me [*sic*] in this contest with the Prince, I own it is of such consequence to you to conquer in this strife, that I advise you to discard me and take Carteret to-morrow.'

Fortunately, the royal quarrel need not be followed any further Its crowning bitterness had been in August and September 1737 ; before the year was over Queen Caroline was dead. On her death-bed she recommended her husband to Walpole's care ; and even if she had lived, no change in the Government was likely to have taken place She had received Walpole's arguments against Carteret with what the minister himself called a flood of professions of favour; and while Walpole remained in the Government there was no chance of admission for Carteret in any capacity whatever. '*I am a rock*,' said Walpole at this time to two or three of his political friends ; 'I am determined in no shape will I ever act with that man.'

CHAPTER VI.

OPPOSITION TO WALPOLE: FOREIGN AFFAIRS.

1738–1742.

So far, on the side of domestic politics at least, the opposition could hardly be said to have had much practical effect   Walpole was sitting even more firmly in power in 1737 than in 1730.   But side by side with these debates on the Excise, on Porteous, on the Prince of Wales, the political affairs of Europe had repeatedly called for discussion ; and it was precisely in this year 1737 that foreign complications began to threaten very serious disturbances.   This, too, was always the ground on which Walpole was most open to attack   His foreign policy had not only to defend itself against the parliamentary assaults of the opposition, but it was, on personal and political grounds, distinctly repugnant to the King himself   Even Caroline warmly objected to the peace policy of her favoured minister   When one looks back, at the safe distance of a century and a half, on the first ten years of the reign of George II., it is undeniable that Walpole's dogged determination to keep England out of Polish election wars and the unending confusions and complications of the Empire was absolutely right.   But in 1737 a question was arising with regard to which it is quite possible to believe that Walpole's view was wrong.   In any case, the feeling of the nation was with the opposition on this point; and Walpole's action regarding it was the prelude to his fall

The second Treaty of Vienna, which had more or less satisfied Spain about its Duchies and the Emperor about his Pragmatic Sanction, was not allowed to keep Europe at peace for very long. Soon after the beginning of 1733, August, King of Poland and Elector of Saxony, died. August the Strong, who, deposed by Charles the Twelfth, had in turn managed to depose his rival, and had been King of Poland ever since His death was the signal for a continental quarrel which involved Europe from Spain to Russia The sole question at issue: Who shall be the new King of Poland? might have seemed simple enough; but it really meant a war in which all the leading powers of the Continent took part; and to keep even England out of it was a very hardly won triumph for Walpole.

Stanislaus Leczinski, ex-King of Poland, whom Charles XII. had set up in 1704. and August the Strong had in turn deposed in 1709, had, after visiting Charles at Bender, been living quietly and comfortably on the borders of France, where his daughter, married to Louis XV., was now Queen It would be suitable to the dignity of France that its Queen's father, who had once been King of Poland, should be so again; and his candidature was naturally supported by Fleury On the other hand. the Empire and Russia favoured Frederick Augustus, son of August the Strong, for Russia feared that if Stanislaus were once again on his old throne he might help Sweden to recover what she had lost to Russia, and the Emperor, otherwise disinclined to the presence of a powerful French influence so near his own doors, had still his inevitable Pragmatic Sanction to secure in every European change. He was anxious to

get a King of Poland who would guarantee that;
and young August, eager for the Emperor's help in an
election which otherwise would probably be unsuccessful for him, had already thoroughly promised to do so.
But the first steps taken were in favour of Stanislaus
and France. The kingship of Poland was elective,
and the question therefore necessarily involved bribery;
the Polish Primate, into whose hands during an inter-
regnum sovereign rights fell, had already been secured
to the French view in the usual way. By his advice
the Polish electors swore to choose no foreigner for
their King; Augustus, a Saxon, thus seemed to be effectively excluded. But hereupon the Emperor and the
Czarina struck in with their armies, and from their two
respective sides, the Czarina from Lithuania, the Emperor
from Silesia, prepared to march on Poland. France
instantly delivered a counter-stroke, sending 60,000 men
under Marshal Berwick to the Rhine, ready to cross
over and fall upon the Emperor if he should venture to
interfere against the French candidate. Yet Fleury did
not wish war; and most certainly Charles, poor in men
and in money, in an almost defenceless condition, neither
wished nor was ready for it. He was so eager to avoid
any attack from France that he hoped to leave Berwick
without any excuse for falling upon him; and, counter-
manding the order to his troops, he stopped their march
towards Poland. This first French success was soon
followed by another. The actual election began in
Poland in August 1733, and according to law must be
completed within six weeks. Dressed in disguise as a
merchant, Stanislaus arrived at Warsaw, and before the
middle of September was actually chosen King there.
The success of France seemed complete.

But this was by no means the end of the thing.
Th . . . . advance

of his troops, the Russians had marched on and were joined by the Polish party in opposition to Stanislaus. After exactly ten days of kingship, Stanislaus found himself obliged to flee from Warsaw. Another election was held, the Russian soldiers being now actually in the Warsaw suburbs; and just a single day within the legal time the crown, by the vote of a handful, was given to Augustus.

France was indignant at the insult to its Queen's father, and immediately declared war on the Emperor. It was useless for Charles to assert that he had taken no active steps against Stanislaus; that he had marched no troops into Poland. The presence of his army on the frontier was essentially the same thing, argued France; and without further waste of time seized Lorraine and crossed the Rhine into Germany. On the Italian side also France was prepared; had gained over Spain by large promises for Don Carlos in Italy; and had secured the King of Sardinia by holding out to him too a share of the spoil. All thus being in order here, Marshal Villars passed the Alps; and the Emperor, unready everywhere, was on all sides beaten upon and almost reduced to despair. Before the year was out Villars and the King of Sardinia, on the one side, had already got Lombardy and the Milanese; and on the other, Lorraine was lost, and Berwick was preparing for the siege of Philipsburg, to gain himself a bridge across the Rhine, and by it penetrate well into Germany next season.

When, therefore, the English parliament met in January 1734, the Emperor's affairs were in a very bad way. The royal speech could make the satisfactory announcement that England was standing entirely apart from the war; but how long this happy isolation might

last was altogether problematical. Every hour the
Emperor's condition was becoming worse and worse.
A trifling accident might at any moment embroil
England and Spain, and then the Gibraltar question
would once more demand painful attention. The future
was full of possible risks and dangers; yet the Government did nothing more than slightly increase the forces.
It was not till the very short parliamentary session was
about to close that a royal message was sent down asking
for a vote of confidence. Let the King, said this message,
have power during the recess to increase the forces if
necessary, and let parliament promise to make good
any action which the existing state of affairs might induce the King to take. The proposal caused very warm
debates. It was not a vote of confidence at all, said
those who opposed it; it was a vote of credit, unconstitutional, a danger to the liberties of the nation, making parliament a farce. Government, on the other side, argued
that in the circumstances it was essential. Money and
men had not been asked for at the beginning of the
session, when the utter breakdown of the Emperor could
not have been foreseen; but now this misfortune had
actually happened, and the King and Cabinet must have
increased powers. Carteret, on constitutional grounds,
took the lead in opposing this message. It was not
factious opposition; Carteret by no means found
fault with the policy of vigorous defence. His only
objection on this side was that measures for the
national security had not been taken long before.
But now that the Government were at length doing
something, why, asked Carteret, were they doing it in
this unconstitutional way? Why were practically unlimited powers to be granted to the King, and why was
parliament to bind itself beforehand to approval of his

action, whatever it might be? Do the thing in a strictly constitutional way, was Carteret's point, or leave it alone altogether. Then, if during the recess imminent danger should arise, the King had power at once to increase his forces and borrow money, and parliament should immediately be assembled

After long debates, the Government had its way easily enough But it does not seem that Walpole was personally very eager in the matter He wished more to humour and quiet the King than anything else For the unfortunate condition of the Emperor alarmed George. He was anxious to give the help which for a long time back the Emperor had been eagerly demanding; the money to fight the French, which was due to him by the last Treaty of Vienna. If George could have had his own way, Charles would have had no occasion to complain The King of England was completely German; here was the Emperor, his official head, reduced to a desperate condition by the House of Bourbon And George was fond of war, in heart a soldier; he seems to have held the curious conviction that he possessed really unusual military genius. In a pleasantly metaphorical style during these early months of 1734, the small martial King daily rhapsodised to Walpole on the laurels of war, and their extreme suitability to his own person Walpole, entering the royal presence full of business and papers, with a multitude of claims to satisfy, appointments to make, instructions to receive, found it hopeless to get himself so much as listened to, nothing but military harangues, battles, sieges, fortunes, dwelt lingeringly upon by a royal Othello to a listener who was *not* seriously inclined to hear these things The martial enthusiasm over, George would give the ... the minister of the

cabinet, his business was no further advanced than when
he had entered it. Still, in his really difficult task,
Walpole clung firmly to his dogged resolution to keep
out of the war. On the eve of a general election to
plunge England into a war to give a King to Poland!
Wait at least, urged the minister to his master, till the
new parliament is chosen; and meanwhile he himself
kept on his own way in spite of all opposition; returned
vague answers to the imploring, and finally indignant,
Emperor; bore all the abuse from Vienna; held out
against King, Queen, and even his own fellow-ministers;
and carried his point successfully. 'I told the Queen
this morning,' he said one day in 1734, ' " Madam, there
are 50,000 men slain this year in Europe, and not one
Englishman." '

But though Walpole would take no active part in
the European quarrel, he was willing enough to try what
peaceful intervention could do. In July 1734 he sent
his diplomatic brother Horatio over to the Hague, to
gain Holland's assistance in an offer of mediation.
Horatio was successful; but the Emperor would not
hear of such a thing, and even did all he could to
bring about the fall of Walpole. In the end, however,
his misfortunes compelled him to listen to the policy of
peace. The war had continued to go hopelessly against
him. Don Carlos, leaving his Duchies, had marched
south, and had been declared King of Naples and Sicily
as Charles the Third. On the German side, though
Berwick had been killed in the siege of Philipsburg,
Prince Eugene had not attacked his army, and the
French had taken the town. In such circumstances,
very reluctantly the Emperor agreed to accept the
mediation of the sea powers; and the English royal
speech in January 1735 announced that England

and Holland had made ready a plan of reconciliation

The parliament to which this speech was made was
a new one. The opposition had hoped, though not
too confidently, that the result of the general election
might improve their prospects. Carteret, writing to
the Earl of Marchmont in June 1734, had said : ' We
do not despair, nor are too sanguine We shall find
ourselves much weakened in the House of Lords ; we
have at present reasonable hopes of a very strong party
in the House of Commons.'[1] These hopes were not
very strikingly fulfilled ; for though Walpole's majority
was smaller than it had been, it still remained quite
large enough for the minister's purpose. The opposition
felt slightly depressed. Yet there were some successes
and encouragements. Young men of ability were
entering parliament, and were naturally opposed to
Walpole's policy. This year 1735 first saw Pitt in parliament as member for Old Sarum. It was Lyttelton's
first session, too ; his, and Richard Grenville's, afterwards Earl Temple, Pitt's intimate friends. On the
whole, the progress of the opposition, if not very
remarkable, was distinctly appreciable, and its parliamentary activity was very decided

The noteworthy point of the royal speech was its
reference to the war England and Holland had
concerted plans for attempting to restore peace and
for preventing, if possible, another campaign on the
continent The powers at war had agreed to listen to
the mediation. Therefore, urged the Government, let
parliament now play its due part, express its satisfaction with the condition of affairs ; and, above all, vote
abundant supplies But the opposition was by no

[1] *Marchmont Papers,* ll 28

means inclined to such a complacent view of the situation. Carteret, leading the opposition in the Lords, and backed by Chesterfield, pierced through the various rose water declarations of the official speech. One more treaty was to be added to the endless number of recent agreements, all of them intended to preserve the peace of Europe, and not one of them doing it. As for English concert with the States General, what was the real meaning of that? While England was spending money and increasing her forces, Holland did not add a man or a ship. The concert seemed chiefly to consist in telling Holland from time to time how much we were spending. Then, when he came to the real heart of the question, Carteret pointed out that the acceptance of the mediation really meant nothing. France and the Emperor had given a general assent to mediation; but they had not given any assent at all to the particular plan which had been devised. Any one with a smattering of grammar and mastery of pot-hooks could draw up a plan, but what after all was the use of that? Carteret was far too shrewd to fancy that any mere plan, however beautiful in itself, could be of much real value; well-meaning mediators might produce harmonious arrangements on paper, but the side that had been stronger in war would have very much its own way in negotiations. Considering, therefore, that matters were still in an altogether doubtful condition, Carteret was not inclined to express any blind approval of the action of the Government. He desired simply to assure the King of a general support, and of a readiness for action if that should be necessary; but he would have no compliments over what was past, and no premature exultation over a very uncertain future.

The opposition was numerically too feeble to make

much impression, and the Commons soon voted the
desired increase of the forces. Carteret spoke with
very great distinction against this augmentation. Even
Lord Hervey, usually so sparing of a good word for an
opponent of Walpole, writes on this occasion of Carteret's 'strength, knowledge, and eloquence,' and even
wishes that he could give a report of Carteret's speech—
a wish at every date hopelessly impossible to gratify.
But Carteret's eloquence and strength, supported by
Chesterfield's wit and satire, had of course no chance
against the Government majority; though again Walpole
himself was perhaps not very enthusiastic in support of
his own policy, while he yielded so far to George's
military notions, and allowed him at least the pleasure
of possessing an army which he might not use.

Carteret's shrewd suspicion that the proposed
mediation would fail was soon fully justified. France
rejected it, and everything was thrown loose again.
Once more the Emperor made a last and most imploring
appeal to England. He was in a state of almost complete collapse, and was reduced to despair, almost to
mental insanity, when England decisively refused him
assistance. This refusal was almost entirely due to
Walpole's dogged determination. He was ready enough
to exhaust all the resources of diplomacy in favour of
the Emperor, but venture men or money in the business he would not. Though his first pacific effort had
failed, Walpole undertook to try again; attempting,
this time, to secure a preliminary agreement with
France. It was now well enough known that Fleury's
real design in the whole affair was Lorraine, that he
was resolved to quit the war with Lorraine in his
possession. Accepting this inevitable basis, Walpole
came to an understanding with France; it remained his

difficult task to gain over the Emperor to the settlement
The negotiations were very intricate, but preliminaries
of peace were at length drawn up, and a suspension of
arms on the Rhine was the result, in October 1735.
As for Stanislaus, in favour of whose Polish claims
France had simulated such tragic indignation, nothing
was required for him but an acknowledgment of titular
royal dignity, the solid article being left in possession of
Augustus. But France for herself (nominally for her
Queen's father as long as he should live) got definite
possession of Lorraine; its Duke Francis, soon to be
Maria Theresa's husband, receiving Tuscany in exchange.
Don Carlos, already in possession of Naples and Sicily,
kept them; lost Lombardy was restored to the Emperor,
and France undertook to guarantee his Pragmatic
Sanction. Spain was quite overlooked by France, and
left out remorselessly in the cold, much to Spain's angry
disgust. though she was forced to accept the European
arrangement. So one more Treaty of Vienna was added
to the already considerable number of such articles,
securing peace to Europe for at least two or three
years Once again Walpole, though never pretending
to any mastery of foreign politics, had been successful;
and, however the more insignificant of his opponents
might cavil and deride, the leading men in opposition
did not attempt to withhold their approval. Bolingbroke, in his acrid way, declared that if the Government
had had any hand in procuring this peace, there was
more sense in them than he thought there had been; and
that if they had not, they had far better fortune than
they deserved. Pulteney was glad of the happy event,
whoever might have had the honour of accomplishing
it; and Carteret in his homely fashion called Walpole
the luckiest dog that ever meddled with public affairs

Walpole's peace policy had succeeded, but it was for the last time   All events were already steadily and irresistibly gravitating towards war between England and Spain, and Walpole, in struggling against such a conclusion, was striving uselessly against fate. War was inevitable, and, unless war is never justifiable, England's war against Spain in 1739 was a just one. Cleared of all diplomatic chicanery and technicalities, and of the various petty questions which always accompany a great crisis, and often for a time loom larger than the essential point at issue, the question for decision really was: Has Spain the right to appropriate the New World to herself, and to shut England out from half the globe? Spain, through her not very magnificent patronage of Columbus, had undoubtedly the external credit, if Columbus had all the real glory, of the re-discovery of America   But because the little boats in which Columbus and his comrades touched one or two minute specks of the new hemisphere were Spanish, Spain had set up a monstrous and altogether inadmissible claim. All America was Spanish; a Bull of the Pope had satisfactorily sanctioned that , the highest of clerical persons had by his Bull made all America a part of Spain   To the other European nations the divinity of the Pope's proceeding in this matter was by no means apparent; and as occasion offered, and especially after Spain's naval power was broken and the Armada had gone to ignominious ruin, England, Holland, and France planted themselves here and there on the coasts and islands of America, and did such trade and commerce as were possible   Spain still held to the divinity of her Bull, and looked with jealous anger on the violation of her sacred property; but in the circumstances could not effectually stop it, and only by various treaties and agreements tried to limit it to the minimum. In order to cripple the trade of the Old World with the New, commerce might not act at all without a licence, and its dealings were restricted to certain well-defined articles; all else was contraband, to be seized by the Spanish officials in the exercise of their Right of Search. The English South Sea Company was only permitted to send once a year one ship of fixed burthen to trade at Vera Cruz under these limited conditions.

Treaty arrangements of this very conditional kind are only definable as treaties for the production of contraband trade. That was their inevitable result, with the connivance even of Spain herself when England happened to be on good terms with her. The one South Sea ship was attended at a respectful distance by various others, which refilled her when her one legal cargo was exhausted. Smuggling traders sent off their long-boats to the shore, and obtained American gold and silver for their Old World wares. Accidents of a slightly fabulous kind would often compel a vessel to put into a Spanish port; and opportunities for trade were not wanting while the mythical repairs were being done. So that the notion of confining the trade to the one annual ship began to seem a meaningless condition to the English merchants. But when, as under the first two Georges was too often the case, the relations between England and Spain were the reverse of friendly, things were altogether different. Then the Spanish guarda-costas were exceedingly vigilant; boats were boarded under just suspicions or not; cutlasses flashed, and very angry feelings were roused on each side. They were thousands of miles and months of time distant from Spain and England; very hot things, just and

unjust, were done in those years on those otherwise
silent seas

Ominous mutterings began to be heard in England.
The journalists and pamphleteers, the loungers in the
coffee houses, the merchants in the city, gave signs of
unmistakable and angry excitement. Wherever one
went, stories of the Spanish cruelty were on every hand.
At length, towards the close of 1737, the merchants
took a decisive step. Many hundreds of them signed a
petition, imploring the King's redress for the wrongs
which they had already suffered, and begging his
efficient protection for the future. The King handed
the petition to the Cabinet; the Cabinet heard the merchants; and Newcastle drew up a memorial to be despatched to Spain The memorial was sent, demanding
satisfaction for the cruelties and injustices of the Spanish
officers and guarda-costas. No answer had been received when parliament met at the beginning of
February 1738, and a session which was the decisive
beginning of the end of Walpole's power commenced.

The session was practically monopolised by the
Spanish question, and it is worth while to mention a
debate which took place near the beginning of it; for
partisan and partial writers have repeatedly misrepresented the conduct and views of some at least of the
opposition on this particular occasion. It was a question of the numbers of the army for the year. Reduce
the army by some five thousand men, urged Pitt and
Pulteney and Lyttelton in the Commons, and Carteret
in the Lords Yet, scornfully and exultingly the partisan writers urge, it was precisely these statesmen who
were loudest in reproach of the behaviour of Spain,
and were doing all they could to bring about a war.
What inconsistency, petulance, factious opposition;

with one breath they threaten war; with the next they
weaken the army! Whether or not there were factiously
inconsistent members of the opposition is a question of
little interest and no profit; but that Carteret was not
one of them is certain. Reviewing on this occasion the
general condition of Europe, he admitted that as far as
England was concerned Spain was the one threatening
spot upon the map. He spoke of the guarda-costas
and their insults : and, though using statesmanlike reserve, did not allow his meaning to be mistaken. 'Peace,
my lords, is a desirable thing for any nation, especially
a trading nation; but whoever thinks that a peace
ought to be purchased at the expense of the honour
of his country, will at last find himself egregiously
mistaken.' How then could Carteret, recognising the
possibility of war, urge a reduction of the numbers of
the army? The answer is very simple. 'In such a
war, what can we have to do with a *land* army? . . . .
It is by means of our navy only that we can pretend to
force Spain to a compliance with our just demands;
and, therefore, if we are in danger of being involved in
a war with that nation, we ought to reduce our army,
that we may with the more ease augment our navy.'
The Government, of course, objected to Carteret's proposal : the Duke of Newcastle, with well-grounded
expressions of diffidence, attempted to answer him.
'Always extremely sorry when I differ from him,' said
the apologetic Duke; though Carteret must generally
have been glad. Carteret's views were defeated, but
it is only a wilful misreading of the facts which can
call his conduct factious or inconsistent.

A few days before this speech of Carteret's the discussion on the Spanish question had begun in earnest.
The West Indian merchants presented to parliament a

petition which covered all the ground of the dispute by
relating how Spanish promises were broken, treaties
disregarded, and English subjects plundered and imprisoned. Let the House consider all this, implored
the merchants, and see how to put an end to it. The
flame broke out at once. 'Seventy of our brave sailors
are now in chains in Spain!' exclaimed one patriotic
member; ' our countrymen in chains and slaves to
Spain!' As the days passed on petitions on petitions
poured in, painfully reciting the Spanish cruelties and
the Government's neglect. Can these things be proved?
asked Pulteney. If so, ' I think our ministry have been
guilty of a scandalous breach of duty, and the most
infamous pusillanimity ' Walpole, anxious not to offend
Spain, tried to smooth things down Redress by negotiation was not hopeless yet, he soothingly argued,
await the result of the representations that have already
been made, and do not, by passionate violence, rouse
the pride of Spain and make a peaceful solution of the
difficulty impossible In spite of inflammatory speeches,
Walpole's moderating arguments were heard with acceptance; and parliament and people stood aside to let
diplomacy continue her efforts

The efforts of diplomacy proved of little worth.
Spain paid no heed to the English expostulations; and
Walpole, on his part, was in no way energetic in urging
Spain to heed. The temper of the nation was roused
to resent what it reckoned to be mere official complaisance or unworthy indifference Parliament passed
from receiving and reading petitions to investigating
particular cases, and eagerly listened to individual
stories of cruelties, told by the sufferers themselves
at the Bar of the House. One story more than any
other roused horror and anger Early in 1731 Robert

Jenkins, captain of the *Rebecca* trader, had sailed for Jamaica; and near Havana, on his way home with his cargo of sugar, had been boarded by a Spanish guarda-costa. To his assurances that he had nothing but sugar on board, the Spanish officials listened with complete incredulity; searched his ship for logwood or other contraband, but found nothing. Baffled in this direction, they avenged their disappointment on the unfortunate man; strung him up, and cut him down, on his own vessel, three times over; and, as a final outrage, tore off one of his ears, and, contemptuously flinging it to him, bade him take that to his King, as evidence of Spain's views on commercial questions. Then they left him, plundered of his ship's instruments, to work his way home as best he might

Safely. though in this mutilated condition, Jenkins reached England, and laid his ear and himself before the King. Some personal compensation was made to Jenkins himself; no other action at that time was taken. But now, in the midst of the growing excitement, this old story was revived. Parliament turned to Jenkins; ordered him to present himself for examination, and heard his story from his own lips. Allowing for rhetorical or theatrical exaggerations, there is no reason to question the essential accuracy of Jenkins's narrative, although cynical or interested official persons hinted that the pillory was responsible for the absence of the man's ear, and although Burke afterwards called the whole story a 'fable' The nation accepted it as a typical instance of the conduct of Spain, and was driven almost to fury by it 'We have no need of allies,' exclaimed Pulteney, 'the story of Jenkins will raise volunteers.' Parliament took up the question with renewed interest Pulteney, as opposition leader in the

Commons, reviewed the whole course of England's quarrel with Spain ; laid down, one after the other, the various rights which England indisputably had in the New World, and indignantly asked why Spain had been allowed to interfere with every one of them   For years back, he argued, our ships had been seized, our sailors plundered, imprisoned, tortured, enslaved , and no reparation had ever been procurable   He therefore pressed the House to once more categorically assert its privileges in resolutions which could not be mistaken.

Walpole felt considerably embarrassed. He could not call in question the various English rights which Pulteney had laid down ; yet he was unwilling to accept, at this particular moment, the resolutions which vindicated them   He urged the House not yet to be peremptory and explicit, which would make war unavoidable ; but still to be vaguely general, to let ministers continue their negotiations, and, if possible, secure peace   He would not listen to Pulteney's resolutions, and himself proposed in their place an amendment drawn up in quite general terms   Pulteney severely reproached him for this, and bitterly contrasted Cromwell's manner of negotiating and upholding the honour of the country with the action of a Prime Minister who practically cared for nothing but the meaner parts of office, and stood aside in passive indifference while the nation was insulted abroad and mutinous at home   Walpole's tough skin was probably little pricked by Pulteney's angry eloquence ; his majority was still sure, and the Patriots might storm as they pleased

But Carteret, in the Lords, had much better success than Pulteney. The Earl of Cholmondeley, though he was Walpole's own son-in-law, advocated more decisive action than even Pulteney had required   and Carteret went further than Cholmondeley Pulteney had demanded a parliamentary assertion of existing English rights; Carteret went beyond academical discussion, and demanded an effectual securing of them. He had his eye on the heart of the question The real point in dispute was very large and very simple It was not whether Spain had the right to seize English ships found trading in Spanish ports. Spain had that right, just as England might also confiscate Spanish ships in corresponding circumstances. It was not whether Spain might strictly hold down the one South Sea ship to trade of precise limitations. By treaty conditions, Spain fairly had that right. The essential question was very much wider It simply was: Has Spain the right of searching English ships on the high seas? May an English ship, sailing from English possessions in the West Indies home to the Old World, be stopped and boarded by Spanish guarda-costas? The whole English demand was contained in two words: *No search* Here was the essential point of the whole matter, and to this the whole of Carteret's elaborate speech was directly addressed '" No search,"' he said, ' are the words that echo from shore to shore of this island . . . " No search " is a cry that runs from the sailor to the merchant, from the merchant to the parliament, and from parliament it ought to reach the throne'

On this occasion the cry may be presumed to have reached the throne, for the Lords yielded to Carteret's arguments—some even of Walpole's colleagues evidently approving them—and an address was sent up to the King. Yet Walpole managed to get the session finished without definitely committing himself A few slightly vigorous preparations were made, as in the circumstances it was necessary to do something; but the minister's hopes still rested on negotiation and the possibilities of diplomacy. He did, after infinite difficulty, seem to succeed in a minute degree, when a rather vague Convention was agreed to between England and Spain, which arranged that plenipotentiaries should meet at Madrid to attempt to bring matters to a clear understanding. From the various treaties already in existence, these plenipotentiaries were clearly to extract the explicit regulations which limited trade and defined boundaries; they were to settle the sum which Spain should pay to the British merchants for losses already unjustly suffered; and they were—to say nothing whatever about the Right of Search! Such was Walpole's diplomatic success, obtained after infinite difficulty; a vague, conditional agreement, about this and that, in which the one essential point of the whole question was scrupulously avoided. When the thing was announced to parliament and the nation, it was received with unbounded contempt. Chatham, speaking in the House of Lords more than thirty years after, dwelt upon the 'universal discontent' which this miserable Convention excited. The whole question between Spain and England was, indeed, one of those cases where the instinct of the nation was far truer than that of the minister. The nation instinctively felt that it was not a matter for negotiation at all. Carteret saw the same thing. Chatham's speech, delivered long after Carteret's death, gives—if it were needed—direct evidence of this. 'This great man [Carteret, to whose memory Chatham had been paying a tribute] has often observed to me, that in all the negotiations which preceded the Convention, our ministers never found out that there was no ground or subject for any negotiation; that the Spaniards had not a right to search our ships; and

P

when they attempted to regulate that right by treaty,
they were regulating a thing which did not exist.'
Walpole was, in fact, applying the small, peddling
politics which he had known how to use so long for
his own advantage, to a case where not peddling
politics, but clear-sighted patriotic statesmanship
alone would answer.

The paltry Convention arrived in London in the
first weeks of 1739, and on the first of February parliament met. The debate, technically on the Address,
was practically on the Convention. Ministers of course
spoke favourably, though feebly, of their own remarkable piece of work, but the opposition attack was very
keen. The ministry was bitterly referred to as one
which had neither courage to make war nor skill to
make peace. The point of Search not being settled,
what is the use, asked Chesterfield, of these commis-
sioners with their grand name of plenipotentiaries, their
salaries, and their long-winded negotiations? If Spanish
search is to be endured, trade is absolutely ruined.
There will not be an English ship in which Spain will
not declare that contraband goods are carried. They
will find logwood and cocoa, and declare these are contraband; yet logwood and cocoa grow in Jamaica
They will find gold pieces of eight, and declare they
are contraband   Yet are not pieces of eight the current
coin of our own colonies? Carteret spoke severely of
the tame submissions of the ministry, which had almost
invited Spanish insults, and declared that the settlement
of the cardinal point: No search on the high seas:
ought to have been the preliminary to negotiations of
any kind whatever. 'Are plenipotentiaries to determine
whether we shall go to our own colonies safe and return safe? The Cardinal [Fleury] would not suffer a

minister to come into the tenth ante-chamber, that should talk of searching French ships Ask all the young nobility that have travelled : have they not observed that the honour of the English nation hath suffered abroad ? The Court of Spain think you dare not attack them. Show them that you dare, and all is over ' [1]

Though the numerical victory was with the Government, the force of argument was clearly with the opposition. Newcastle and Hervey made a very poor show against Carteret, Chesterfield, and Argyle. But worse parliamentary treatment than this was in store for Walpole, and out of doors the public feeling against him began to run very high   The nation, disgusted at the omission of the main point in dispute, was filled with passion by one of the conditions of the Convention, which agreed that a large sum of money should be paid to Spain for the ships which had been destroyed more than twenty years before by Admiral Byng People asked, with scornful anger, if England was also to pay damages for the destruction of the Spanish Armada. 'The city is in a flame, and almost nobody pleased,' wrote the Earl of Marchmont. 'The prints show Sir Robert's guard in a ridiculous enough light. He is certainly distressed, and with good reason ' [2] The Earl of Stair wrote : ' The whole nation is on our side, and only Sir Robert and his gang on the other .   I hope the time is not far off when his majesty will see clearly that he had no other enemy in this nation so much to be feared as Sir Robert and his gang.' [3] A vivid little piece of evidence from the Magazine in

---

[1] Secker's *Manuscript* ; in *Parliamentary History*, vol. X.   Secker's MS. is the best authority—as far as it goes—for the debates in the Lords.

[2] Marchmont Papers. II 111   March 10. 1739

[3] J M Graham S   II. 217 24

which Samuel Johnson had just begun to toil and drudge for a livelihood, serves to illustrate the universal interest roused by the one question of the day. On one of the February evenings of 1739 London entertained itself with a grand civic masquerade: 'Where, among many humourous and whimsical characters, what seemed most to engage the attention of the company was a Spaniard, very richly dressed, who called himself *Knight of the Ear*; as a badge of which Order he wore on his breast the form of a Star, whose points seemed tinged with blood; on which was painted an Ear, and round it, written in capital letters, the word JENKINS; and across his shoulders hung, instead of a ribband, a large halter, which he held up to several persons disguised like English sailors, who seemed to pay him great reverence; and, falling on their knees before him, with many tokens of fear and submission, suffered him very tamely to rummage their pockets; which when he had done, he very insolently dismissed them with strokes of his halter   Several of the sailors had a bloody ear hanging down from their heads, and on their hats these words: *Ear for Ear*; while on the hats of others was written: *No Search, or No Trade*; with the like sentences.'[1]

The excitement in the nation was reflected in parliament. A week after its meeting, the Duke of Newcastle formally presented to the Lords a copy of the Convention   A Spanish debate of necessity arose, and Carteret took an exceedingly active part in it. Even Government speakers were forced to admit the weight which attached to his views. On this particular occasion he worried the poor Duke of Newcastle in a most effectual way   The Duke presented the Conven-

---

[1] *Gentleman's Magazine* for 1739 p 103.

tion with its separate articles and ratifications. Is there
not another paper? asked Carteret; some protest or
declaration handed in by Spain, the acceptance of which
by England is to be the condition of Spain's observance
of the Convention? How very glad, said Carteret, the
Duke would be to answer such a question, and by his
answer show that while the Government had consulted
for the peace of the nation, it had also remembered its
interest and honour. But ministerialists suggested that
such a request was out of order, and that an informal
question of that kind could not be answered. Where-
upon Carteret again blandly rose: 'My lords, when I
threw out my distant surmises with great simplicity
of heart, I did not wish to do anything formal, or lay
the Duke under any restraint; but thought he would
cheerfully take the hint, and be glad to do so.' Thus
Newcastle was almost forced to rise, and, sadly protesting against the compulsion, he declared that the papers
presented were the only ones which English officials in
Spain had signed. Here was no answer to Carteret at
all. Yes, these are all which *English* ministers have
signed; but is there not something more which Spain
alone signed and handed in? Let us have them all, and
see what private concessions have been made. Otherwise Carteret in his plain way remarked that he would
regard the Convention and its stipulations as 'mere
grimace.' The afflicted Duke rose again; thought he
had answered Carteret; and in his helpless, blundering
fashion declared that if the English officials had signed
no other paper about the Convention, no other paper on
the subject could exist! Carteret quite meekly expressed
his regret that he had not made himself intelligible, and
repeated his question, to which, now, Newcastle rising
once more, had to answer, 'Yes, there is another docu-

ment ' ' I think it very proper,' said Carteret, who had a strong sense of humour, ' to return my acknowledgments to the noble Duke for condescending so readily to answer the doubt I had proposed '

Thus Carteret had extorted from the Government the admission that even the Convention, which parliament and the country found so objectionable, was not all. Behind it, and as the sole condition on which Spain had accepted it, stood a demand on the South Sea Company for immediate payment of a large sum declared to be due to Spain as tax-money on negro slaves ; and if this were not immediately paid, the King of Spain would suspend the Company's Assiento treaty Here was the Convention, with which Government expressed so much curious satisfaction, actually dependent on the result of a private negotiation between the King of Spain and the South Sea Trading Company. We are to force the Company to agree to Spain's demands, or all our negotiating is to be a mere farce, burst out the Duke of Argyle A fresh point was evidently made for the opposition, and the storm steadily gathered force. Petitions against so unsatisfactory a Convention began to pour in ; the London magistrates petitioned ; the Liverpool merchants petitioned ; the West India merchants of London tumultuously thronged about the Houses. The opposition took up the cause of the merchants, and ran the Government very close. Yet so far all the parliamentary proceedings had been little more than preliminary skirmishings ; the real pitched battle began in the House of Lords on March 1, when the Convention itself was formally taken into consideration.

Carteret led the opposition, and gathered into one impressive whole and strikingly drove home an elaborate indictment against the conduct of the Government. He exposed with ease the utter worthlessness of a Convention which obtained neither reparation for the past nor security for the future; severely blamed the Government for leaving plenipotentiaries to argue vital points that admitted no argument, and emphatically declared the proposed agreement destructive and dishonourable to the nation; 'a mortgage of your honour, a surrender of your liberties.' 'I do not often,' he said, ' speak in the learned languages; but I am afraid, my lords, the prophetic phrase which I once heard a most learned lord pronounce, *venit summa dies*, will now be verified' Still, remembering the strong resolutions which the Lords had passed last year—and it was one of Carteret's severest reproaches to the Government that they had done absolutely nothing to give those resolutions any effect—he hoped that he might have a happiness to which he had lately been unaccustomed, and find himself and his views in the majority. Carteret spoke very powerfully, but altogether on the merits of the question, with an entire avoidance of captious or personal attack. With the Duke of Argyle it was otherwise 'It is said in general that the whole debate was an extreme fine one, conducted with great dignity and decency as a national concern, and not personal or ministerial The Duke of Argyle, who spoke for two hours, was the only one who, as I hear, took much freedom with the ministry.'[1] Argyle was indeed very vehement. 'Let who will approve of such a measure, I never will; I will die first ' He was very scornful as well as vehement; and plainly intimated that it was not the ministry but the *Minister* who was responsible for the unsatisfactory state of affairs. Chesterfield also was eloquent against this inglorious Convention, this warlike peace, this perpetual patch-

---

[1] Orlebar to Etough, March 3, 1739. Coxe's *Walpole*, III. 515, 516.

work of a statesman who dealt only with and through the rotten hearts of sycophants and time-servers The very tapestry on the walls, the record of former historic glories, was appealed to; and fervid oratory gloomily hoped that patriotic looms would strike work for the present

The wit and eloquence, as well as the real weight of argument, were conspicuously on the opposition side; yet still the Government majority, though by much smaller numbers than usual,[1] carried the day There was undeniable force in many of the reasons and excuses put forward by the Government—the already heavy debt, the danger from the Pretender; the certainty that France would join Spain These were real arguments of their kind, and on them the Government rested its case; but the broad question, whether the present was not one of those occasions on which all minor hazards must be lightly regarded in the presence of one overwhelming danger, was never faced by Walpole A hand-to-mouth policy, if only a parliamentary majority could be got to sanction it, was all that the Prime Minister had to propose Yet even from the personal point of view, if from no higher, Walpole might have begun to doubt whether his action had been altogether wise The victory which he had just gained in the Lords was not of a very triumphant character; the success which he was about to gain in the Commons was little less than Pyrrhic The Commons took up the Convention a week later than the Lords On the first day of their real proceedings, after two days spent in formal reading of papers, more than a hundred members took their seats before seven o'clock in the morning, and nearly five hundred were present at prayers before ten. The

---

[1] 95 to 74. The Prince of Wales voted with the opposition

Prince of Wales sat in the gallery all day long till midnight, and had his dinner sent to him there, rather than lose anything of the debate Horatio Walpole was the first speaker. Slovenly Horatio did his tedious best to remove what he considered prejudices against the Convention. His general maxims on peace and war were doubtless admirable as sonorous platitudes; the circumstances of Europe might, as he argued, be deplorable enough ; only these were not the questions at issue. 'A piece of waste paper ; that is your Convention,' retorted the opposition Pitt thundered against it Are plenipotentiaries, he asked, to discuss our 'undoubted right by treaties, and from God, and from nature?' 'Is this any longer a nation, or what is an English parliament, if, with more ships in your harbours than in all the navies of Europe, with above two millions of people in your American Colonies, you will bear to hear of the expediency of receiving from Spain an insecure, unsatisfactory, dishonourable Convention? . This Convention, Sir, I think from my soul is nothing but a stipulation for national ignominy, an illusory expedient to baffle the resentment of the nation. . . . The complaints of your despairing merchants, the voice of England has condemned it , be the guilt of it upon the head of the adviser ; God forbid that this Committee should share the guilt by approving it !'

In spite of Pitt's invective, the Committee did share the guilt ; though Walpole's majority, in a House which had once been full of his creatures, had so far dwindled that in a vote of nearly five hundred members he was saved by only twenty-eight The opposition, disappointed, and declaring that the arguments were all on one side and the votes on the other, took the foolishly unpractical step of seceding from the House. Carteret

in vain expressed his disapproval; he could not persuade even Pulteney to oppose such feeble folly. Sir
William Wyndham, in a slightly tragic manner, bade a
final adieu to that parliament, very considerably to the
cynical satisfaction of Walpole; and the ministerialists
were left mainly to themselves. Yet even to the
dullest of their party it could hardly now be doubtful
that war was surely coming. It was now the second
week in May, the Convention which so small a parliamentary majority had approved named May 24 as the
last day on which England would accept the payment
of the small sum with which Spain had reluctantly
agreed to compensate the English merchants. No one,
not even the Government, any longer professed to
believe that Spain would pay the money. Sheer necessity infused a little energy into the proceedings of the
administration. To anticipate the probable action of
France, a subsidy was offered to Denmark, and 6,000
Danish troops were thus gained over to the English
side. Parliament voted unusual supplies and an increase of the forces Carteret earnestly advised an
alliance with Frederick William of Prussia, the most
powerful Protestant ruler on the Continent 'If you
have no hope of Prussia, you will not have a word to
say in Germany; and he may be gained upon right and
good grounds'[1] Carteret's constant and statesmanlike
interest in Prussia and Germany generally has been
signally justified in more modern times, but it is needless to say that his present prudent advice was disregarded.

Thus the days passed on, May 24 among them;
and the Government, asked if Spain had paid the money,
could only answer, No. Once more the Lords had a

---

[1] Secker MS *ut supra*

Spanish debate, the last that was to be necessary. Carteret, of course, took the lead He treated the Convention as a thing which practically no longer existed, and ridiculed the paltry ministerial action which was leaving and allowing the merchant ships themselves to make reprisals on Spanish vessels for the losses which they suffered It was a case, said Carteret, in which the royal navy of Great Britain ought to act Yet the Government still continued its policy of dilatory indefiniteness, and managed to close the session in June without any direct parliamentary condemnation of its conduct. But there was no longer any practical doubt that Spain and England must fight The King was desirous for war; Walpole's own colleagues were by no means unanimous in approval of his peace policy; the feeling of the nation was dead against it. At last, during the summer recess, vigorous preparations began in earnest The English ambassador at Madrid was instructed to require a definite renunciation of the Spanish claim of Right of Search, and to leave the country at once if the reply were not satisfactory. Here at length was definite action; and immediately there was evidence of the spirit of fairness and patriotism which always marked Carteret's conduct in opposition In August 1739 Carteret wrote to the Earl of Marchmont, who, as Lord Polwarth and ambassador at Copenhagen, had been his old friend and fellow-worker in the tangled business of restoring peace to the North of Europe .—

'The ministers are at present, in all appearance, pursuing the sense of the nation, and acting towards the Spaniards as they should have acted long ago. The nation desires no war, but yet will not be contented with such a peace as of late we have had : and if, in

vindication of our honour, and in pursuing the necessary
measures to obtain a good peace, war should break out,
which is most likely, we must repel force by force, from
whatsoever quarter it comes, as well as we can ; and the
showing internal discontents, howsoever founded, at
this time, may precipitate our ruin, but can never have
any tendency to save us   These are my notions ; which
I do not give you as a volunteer ; that would be pre-
sumption ; but I lay them before you, and those friends
you may converse with, because you honour me by asking my opinion   We are all sorry that we cannot make
things better ; for God's sake, do not let us make them
worse, and if the nation is to be undone (which, by
the way, I do not believe it will), let us act so as never
to have reason to reproach ourselves of having done
amiss, though out of zeal and good intentions, in this
critical conjuncture."[1]

England's final demands at Madrid obtained no
satisfaction, and the decisive step was at last taken
A royal manifesto was issued at Kensington, and in
London war between England and Spain was publicly
declared by heralds on November 3, 1739   Parliament met long before its usual time, and the eager
activity of the Lords and Commons reflected the enthusiasm of the people   Carteret, after the Government in
the Lords had done its necessary official speaking, rose
to express the views of the opposition.   Practical
common-sense was as usual at the basis of his policy.
Now you have actually entered upon war, he urged,
let your one consideration be the vigorous conduct of
the war.   Go to the best officers ; select your generals
and admirals, and, having done so, leave their actions
as far as possible to themselves, and let ministers and

---

[1] *Marchmont Papers.* II. 135. 136.

negotiators stand aside.   Do not allow the management
of the war to be as perplexed and timorous as the conduct of the negotiations.   Let the war really be war.
It is evident that among the opposition there was great
fear of a policy of half-measures.   Chesterfield bluntly
expressed this when he said that it would not be a good
omen if those who had been against the war should
be consulted in the conduct of it.   This feeling was,
however, expressed much more plainly in the House
of Commons   There Sir William Wyndham desired to
obtain an agreement that the war should not be ended
till Spain acknowledged the right of British ships to
navigate the American seas   In his plain way, Walpole
declared that he knew Wyndham's speech was levelled
at him, and designed to make him unpopular.   'The
honourable gentleman and his friends have a mind to
take a little diversion, and have singled me out as the
deer for the sport of the day.   But they may find, Sir,
that I am not so easily hunted down as they imagine.
I have lived long enough in the world to know that
the safety of a minister lies in his having the approbation of this House.   Former ministers neglected this,
and therefore they fell   I have always made it my first
study to obtain it, and therefore I hope to stand'
Designed to make him unpopular? sneered Pulteney.   'I
am sorry to say he has very little popularity to lose.'
Pulteney was very severe on Walpole, constantly lashing
the 'right honourable gentleman near me'; for leaders
of Government and of Opposition sat next one another
on the same bench.   Past disasters and inaction were
not forgotten, and mysterious hints of impeachment
were dropped   Walpole might well compare himself
to a baited animal; the political chase had never been
so severe

The war, however, in spite of all these attacks on Walpole and his management, seemed to be beginning successfully. Already, in July, Admiral Vernon had sailed for the West Indies; and when this parliamentary tumult was at its highest had just arrived at Porto Bello. Two days later, on December 3, it surrendered to his attack. An express arrived in London from victorious Vernon with the news in March 1740. The rejoicings were almost inconceivable. Parliament sent congratulatory addresses to the King; Walpole and Newcastle gave grand entertainments in honour of the event; the London Corporation voted the inevitable freedom in the inevitable gold box. Yet even this success was used as a blow against the Government. If Vernon, with only six ships, and no land-force but some two hundred and forty men lent him from Jamaica, had been able to do this, what might he not have done but for a jealous, niggardly Government, which stinted him of ships and deprived him of soldiers? But not the most captious member of opposition could complain of inactivity now. All through the summer months the ports and dockyards were busy; great preparations were on hand to assist Vernon in attacking Cartagena, a more important Spanish town in the New World than Porto Bello itself. In September, Anson sailed with his three ships, to make his memorable voyage round Cape Horn; and in November a large sea and land force left England for Vernon and the West Indies; on board one of the ships of the line being a young surgeon's mate, not yet twenty years old, named Tobias Smollett.

But during all these preparations, two very important events took place on the Continent, which were destined to change the whole complexion of the quarrel. On the last day of May 1740 died Frederick William, second King of Prussia, and Europe knew nothing of the character of his successor ; and on October 20 died the Emperor Charles VI., and the Pragmatic Sanction, which it had been the main business of his life to secure, went to utter ruin, and dragged almost every country of Europe to quarrel and war.

In such threatening European circumstances, the English parliament met again in November 1740. The Lords in opposition were especially energetic from the very beginning of the session. Before the reading of the King's speech was well finished, before the King himself had left the House, the Duke of Argyle was up, and, anticipating the formal harangue of the official ministerialist performer, plunged into an arraignment of the Government Chesterfield, not too well pleased with Carteret's ascendency among the opposition leaders, had recommended this action of Argyle's ; thinking that Carteret, who always represented the more moderate, responsible opposition, would either, by declining to follow Argyle, lose for himself the support of the more advanced party, or, by following Argyle, would seem to be surrendering the foremost place. Chesterfield's somewhat malicious speculations proved fanciful merely Carteret did support Argyle : but he also emphatically kept the lead. Argyle, himself a soldier, confined himself chiefly to the military point of view, and found it an easy task to denounce the conduct of the war from the beginning to the end. One success, not a very overpowering one for all the rejoicings it had caused, there had been ; but no one could fairly give the Government any credit for what Admiral Vernon had done. Argyle beat upon the Government effectively enough on this military side. Carteret also was severe on this matter, but he mainly looked at the subject in

its strict political light   His attack upon the administration, and especially upon Walpole, was very strong
' A minister who has for almost twenty years been demonstrating to the world that he has neither wisdom
nor conduct.   He may have a little low cunning, such
as those have that buy cattle in Smithfield market, or
such as a French valet makes use of for managing an
indulgent master, but the whole tenour of his conduct has shown that he has no true wisdom.   This
our allies know and bemoan ; this our enemies know
and rejoice in '

The attack thus begun was week after week energetically followed up.   The state of the army, the instructions to Vernon in the Caribbean Sea, to Haddock in the
Mediterranean, offered countless opportunities for lively
debate   Such guerilla skirmishing was of the liveliest,
but could not be decisive or thoroughly satisfactory to
either side.   The opposition therefore resolved to put
out all their strength in one grand effort, and to go to
the root of all their complainings—patriotic, some of
them, factious undoubtedly, others—by definitely demanding the resignation of Walpole.   On the same day,
February 13, 1741, this formal attack was made in both
Houses of Parliament.   The House of Lords was crowded
when Carteret rose to deliver his indictment against the
Prime Minister in a long, elaborate speech, worthy of
his unrivalled political knowledge   The whole field of
foreign and domestic politics for a period of nearly
twenty years lay open before him, from the bickerings
between the Emperor Charles and Elizabeth Farnese,
down to the Spanish Convention and the unsatisfactory
management of the war   The endless treatying and
counter-treatying, the imbecile Congresses, the shifting
alliances, the want of anything like a clear and con-

sistent line of action on the part of the Government, offered material which a less able man than Carteret might have turned to good account. The main note of his speech was the one point which is the simple and always consistent explanation of Carteret's chief views on European politics. All through Carteret's lifetime the French had been attempting to aggrandise themselves in Europe at the expense of Germany. Sometimes they had succeeded, as when Fleury had managed to get hold of Lorraine; sometimes they failed, as was once to be very conspicuously the case while Carteret himself was at the head of affairs in England. But always and in all circumstances Carteret's policy was decided and the same. the French must be kept out of Germany. That Walpole's line of action had not clearly kept this policy in view, but that a shilly-shally procedure had made France and Austria our friends and enemies alternately, was Carteret's chief point of reproach.

As usual, Carteret did not treat the question from the personal point of view. 'I am not for appearing in anything peevish or personal,' he expressly said; and, when himself in power, he proved the truth of his assertion by taking the lead in opposing unfair treatment of the fallen minister. But he did not shrink from the political application of his indictment. 'If one physician cannot cure a fever, take another.' 'If people fall asleep on their post, it is mild to say, Pray remove them.' Carteret distinctly declared that if Walpole could be considered competent to extricate the nation from the confusion that existed at home and abroad, he would be willing to let him do it. That could not be, and the inevitable conclusion followed. that the King be advised to remove Sir Robert Walpole from his presence and counsels for ever.

For eleven hours the Lords debated this exciting question, and were very lavish of eager rhetoric. Walpole was very severely handled. 'Except those who depend on him, there are not fifty subjects in the kingdom but most ardently wish to have him removed,' said one peer. 'A saucy master,' who 'hath treated with his usual buffoonery what the nation hath set its heart on,' said another. Argyle was very bitter, and pressed David into the ranks of opposition 'Take away the wicked from before the King,' concluded the too sanguine Duke, 'and his throne shall be established in righteousness' But soon after midnight the Lords decided that this desirable establishment might very well wait. Carteret had been very eloquent, but the time was not yet come 'My Lord Carteret did speak two hours as well as any man in the world could speak, but all in vain,' wrote the Duchess of Marlborough, now very old, but full of patriotism 'One of the finest discourses I ever saw in any language,' the Earl of Stair said of Carteret's speech, though its eloquence had been unavailing. No one, certainly not Carteret himself, expected a numerical parliamentary victory for the opposition Some lively writers even asserted that Carteret had taken up the question unwillingly and was full of vexation and chagrin at the part he played in it One of young Horace Walpole's correspondents ventured to become particular over this view. 'Two minutes after he had made the motion he rubbed his periwig off, and has not ceased biting his nails and scratching his head ever since.'[1] Lively writing of this kind is so very amusing, and it is so agreeable to believe what one would like to believe If Carteret did rub his periwig off, one has an

[1] H. S Conway to Horace Walpole, Feb. 16, 1741.

exact, though a minutely insignificant, biographical fact
As far as other matters are concerned, the lively writer
may be disregarded.

Walpole had thus been successful in the one House,
and he might reckon himself fortunate also in the other.
In the Commons, many members had taken their seats
by six o'clock in the morning; and the debate, which
began before noon, lasted till between three and four
o'clock in the following day. Yet the result was a
foregone conclusion. It was still Walpole's own parliament, and he ran no real risk. He himself treated the
affair in a very confident style, and, in his outspoken
way, declined to listen to any arguments which professed to be based upon patriotism. The whole thing,
he declared, was a mere attempt to get into office, and
the less said of patriotism the better. 'A patriot, Sir!
why, patriots spring up like mushrooms! I could raise
fifty of them within the four and twenty hours. I have
raised many of them in one night. It is but refusing to
gratify an unreasonable or an insolent demand, and up
starts a patriot.' The eloquence of Pulteney and other
opposition leaders was, from the division-list point of
view, wasted; many members declined to vote at all;
and even so important a member of opposition as Chesterfield conceived—though the result showed that he
was wrong—that Walpole had actually been strengthened by his seeming success, and that the opposition
had been broken to pieces. Walpole's levée next
morning was indeed the largest he had ever been
known to hold, and he himself seems to have been
partly thrown off his guard; but essentially his triumph
was superficial only [1]

[1] This once famous debate was the occasion of a very celebrated political
caricature called *the Motion*. The scene is Whitehall and the Trea- 15

Walpole was safe for the time being; but already events were in progress which would add strength to the general outcry against him. The European crash which had been expected to follow the Emperor Charles's death had come without delay　Maria Theresa had instantly been proclaimed successor to her father's Austrian dominions; but in less than two months after the Emperor's death, Frederick of Prussia had invaded Silesia　He declared his willingness to uphold the

Buildings, towards which a coach is being driven at full speed.　Argyle is coachman :—

> ' Who be dat de box do sit on ?
> 'Tis John, the hero of North Briton,
> Who, out of place, does placemen spit on.'

Chesterfield is postilion; Bubb Dodington is a cur between his legs　The passenger is Carteret .—

> ' But pray who in de coaché sit-a ?
> Tis honest Johnny Carteritta,
> Who want in place again to get-a '

The furious pace is threatening to overturn the coach, and Carteret is crying· 'Let me get out!'　Lean Lord Lyttelton is riding behind on a lean hack —

> ' Who s dat who ride astride de poney,
> So long, so lank, so lean and boney ?
> Oh! he be the great orator, Little-Toney! '

Smallbrook, Bishop of Lichfield, bows humbly as they pass

> ' What parson's he dat bow so civil?
> Oh! dat's de bishop who split de devil,
> And made a devil and a half, and half a devil !'

In the foreground, on foot, is Pulteney, leading figures by strings from their noses, and wheeling a barrow full of opposition writings, the *Craftsman, Common Sense,* etc　He is exclaiming. 'Zounds, they are over!'

> ' Close by stands Billy, of all Bob's foes
> The wittiest far in verse and prose .
> How he leads de puppies by de nose'

'Tell me, dear,' writes Horace Walpole from Italy to his friend Conway, 'now, who made the design, and who took the likenesses, they are admirable . the lines are as good as one sees on such occasions.'　The Cartoon is reproduced in T Wright's *Caricature History of the Georges,* p 128　Many editions of it were published, slightly varying in details

Pragmatic Sanction, and in the contest for the Empire to vote for Maria's husband, the Grand Duke Francis; but the condition he required was the cession of Silesia, and Maria would not hear of such a thing. Frederick therefore advanced, first through deluges of rain, then in hard frost, and, finding practically no opposition, was easily making himself master of Silesia. The excitement caused by this in England was very great. The people, who knew nothing of German history, passionately took up Maria's cause. In their eyes, she was an interesting and much injured young Princess; and Frederick was a perfidious robber. George also, though for different reasons, was eager on the same side. He had given his word to Charles, and had signed his Pragmatic Sanction; and George, like his father, was always a man of strict honesty to his promise. Above all, he had his own Hanover to think of; the slightest disturbance in Germany always threw him into a tremor of anxiety. English statesmen, too, and politicians were generally for Maria, though many of them would have been puzzled to say exactly why. But Carteret knew his reasons very well. It was not in opposition to Frederick that Carteret supported the cause of Austria. He was always anxious to induce Maria to come to terms with Frederick, and in little more than a year after this date it was one of the triumphs of his own ministry that he successfully accomplished this. But France was sure to interfere in this internal German question. It was known that France was about to break the Pragmatic Sanction, known, too, that she would not have Maria's husband as Emperor. Support of Maria Theresa was therefore opposition to the designs of France in Germany; and Carteret

On April 19, 1741, the King asked parliament
to assist him in supporting Maria Theresa, and next day
the question was debated. Argyle was cold. Why was
England to stand alone in support of the Pragmatic
Sanction? Chesterfield opposed, with oblique hints at
the King's partiality for his German dominions. But
Carteret approved. 'If this be not done,' he said, 'the
Queen of Hungary will throw herself into the arms of
France . . . This is a case of nobody's seeking; it
arises from the Emperor's death. The King should
hazard all upon it, and we should stand by him . . .
I do not look for popularity; but am now on the
popular side of the question. . . . If the Austrian
dominions are parcelled, France gets enough without
getting an acre of land. We say to France, if you
will keep your treaty, you cannot complain of us;
if you will not, we are safer with open doings'[1]
'The Austrian thunder of my Lord Carteret,' Pitt
some months later in a letter to Chesterfield called
this speech.[2] Neither Pitt nor Carteret knew at the
time that the thunder of artillery had already been
speaking in a far more emphatic manner than the
thunder of eloquence ever could. Ten days before this
debate there had been fought the first pitched battle in
that long war which, with various rests and breathing-
places, really lasted from 1740 to 1762. In drifting,
snowy weather, and confused circumstances on both
sides, the Austrians and Prussians had fallen upon each
other, and Frederick's victory had made the battle of
Mollwitz the signal for a general European war. But
news from the Continent still travelled slowly, and it
was not until April 25 that London heard of the first

---

[1] Secker's Parliamentary MS *ut supra*
[2] Correspondence of the Earl of Chatham. I. 1.

real stroke in the great struggle; on which very day, curiously enough, Parliament voted to Maria Theresa a subsidy of three hundred thousand pounds

But to subsidise the Queen of Hungary was by no means enough for George. Parliament had readily promised him the support he desired, and he hoped, though he was terribly disappointed, to strike decisively into the quarrel at once He hurried over in May 1741 to Hanover, attended by Secretary Harrington, and was as eager as he always was to get to war. He had a respectable army; 6,000 Danes, 6,000 Hessians, were ready for him on subsidy, and his own Hanoverian forces made the total more than 30,000 men Yet to his disgust George found he could do nothing. As a first difficulty, it proved impossible to move the Dutch It took more than two years to persuade these exceedingly heavy allies to stir. But even more perplexing than this was the case of Hanover. In April 1741 Frederick had established a camp of 36,000 men at Gottin, near Magdeburg, ready at once to fall upon Hanover if quarrel should arise between George and himself. So the King of England could not fight because he happened to be also Elector of Hanover He was effectively checkmated; and it was clear that so long as Frederick remained Maria's active enemy, George would simply be unable to act at all. It became therefore his most pressing necessity to remove Frederick from the scene of action. Diplomacy was set to work The English ambassador at Vienna, Sir Thomas Robinson, a heavy, dull man, still vaguely remembered for the terrible parliamentary worryings which later on he suffered from Pitt and Fox, urged and even implored Maria to come to terms with her successful enemy Hyndf… …… …… Perhaps …… Frederick himself in his camp near Mollwitz, and offered English mediation to restore Germanic peace. But the two ambassadors had two very determined young sovereigns to deal with, and the efforts of diplomacy seemed hopelessly vain. Maria would not be moved; and Frederick, far from listening to the arguments of Hyndford, made in June a treaty with the French. The hand of France interfering in Germany was first visible when, after this treaty, the Elector of Bavaria appeared as a candidate for the Empire. This was a second blow to Maria, and in such circumstances Robinson did succeed in persuading her to some faint compliance. In August he hastened to Frederick, who was now at Strehlen, and once more put before him the small concessions which Maria was willing to make. It was quite useless. Frederick, now sure of France, would have his Silesian demands completely satisfied, and would not accept anything less. He continued his own conquests in Silesia, and at the same time two French armies, each of 40,000 men, entered Germany; the one crossing the Upper Rhine, to join the Elector of Bavaria and march towards Vienna, the other over the Lower Rhine, to make for Hanover.

What could George do, either for himself or for Maria? Clearly nothing but negotiate himself out of his difficulties, and continue to urge Maria to do the same. Very contrary to his own wishes, but seeing there was no help for it, he agreed in September to the neutrality of Hanover; and though for a time his importunate attempts to mediate between Austria and Prussia were an utter failure, in that same month success appeared to be at last approaching. Maria had personally appealed to Hungary, and had roused passionate loyalty there. At the same time Frederick, though the French were his allies, was really jealous of their presence in Germany. England seized these two openings as an opportunity for one more diplomatic effort By working on Frederick's jealousy of France, and by pressing upon Maria her need of a short time of respite, the two English ambassadors successfully brought the rivals to an agreement. Thus early in October was made the secret treaty of Kleinschnellendorf, Maria agreeing to cede to Frederick those parts of Silesia which he already held, and Frederick accepting peace, though mock hostilities were for a short time to be continued, to blind and satisfy the French.

While these negotiations were employing George and Harrington at Hanover, a general election had taken place in England. The feeling against Walpole in the country was by this time very strong. Walpole had been for twenty years uninterruptedly in power; every mistake, every failure that had marked the years from 1721 to 1741, was, justly or unjustly, assigned to him. In ecclesiastical affairs he had offended both Churchmen and Dissenters In parliamentary management, his cynical frankness in corruption had often been a little too much for a not very puritanical period. His contemptuous neglect of literature had enrolled all the wits and men of letters against him at a time when political pamphlets and news-letters and satires were read all over the kingdom So early as 1727 Swift wrote of Walpole that 'he has none but beasts and blockheads for his penmen.'[1] But his one unpardonable offence was his conduct in the Spanish war. He had not declared war till resignation of his own power was his only alternative, and when, after Vernon's one success at Porto Bello, the military management sank

[1] Swift

into a dreary round of inaction. failure, and confused
ineffectiveness—the natural result of official incapacity
and of the usual chaotic mismanagement of the English
fighting departments—the angry irritation of the people
instinctively blamed the minister who was known to
have no real heart in the business which he nominally
directed. The fleet in the Mediterranean did absolutely nothing Vernon's expedition against Cartagena,
from which so much had been expected, had gone to
utter ruin and almost disgrace And the country,
which had so eagerly adopted the cause of Maria
Theresa, felt itself further humiliated by the Hanover
neutrality and by the rather unheroic way in which
George's first continental attempt had terminated.
From a general election held in such circumstances,
Walpole could not expect any very great success, and he
seems at this time, very contrary to his usual habit, to
have been full of personal anxieties. His son Horace,
writing in October 1741, says that he who 'was asleep
as soon as his head touched the pillow, for I have
frequently known him snore ere they had drawn his
curtains, now never sleeps above an hour without
waking; and he who at dinner always forgot he was
minister, and was more gay and thoughtless than all his
company, now sits without speaking, and with his eyes
fixed for an hour together. Judge if this is the Sir
Robert you knew '[1]

In October the King and Harrington returned from
Hanover, and early in December the newly elected
parliament met From the very first it was clear that
Walpole was surely falling. Very severe things were
said against his Government. 'I see many motives for
censure, none for approbation, all for distrust,' said

[1] H. Walpole to Mann, Oct. 19, 1741

Chesterfield Instead of an address of thanks, Halifax suggested an address of condolence as more suitable to the occasion 'A thing is said in the speech,' said Carteret, ' which I am sure the King believes,   and yet I would not confirm him in it. He says he has done all he could for the House of Austria. We shall be able to make him change his opinion.' Yet even in the gloomy condition of things Carteret saw what he called some glimmerings of hope ; hope that the King of Prussia might take alarm at the progress of the French ; hope from the King of Sardinia ; hope even from the exceedingly laggard Dutch. Every one of these hopes was in time realised But Carteret, now as always, had strong objections to mere pleasing. flattering words which did not really correspond to the facts of the case ' It is fact we must see,' he declared, and he felt not the slightest disposition to compliment the Government on its military or diplomatic situation. What was the use of words ? ' There were strong words in the last address about the Queen of Hungary ; but they did her no good, and she will not mind these now ' [1]

In the Commons the attack on Walpole was violent and very personal Instead of returning thanks for the conduct of the Spanish war. the opposition indignantly compelled the minister to omit from the address the slightest reference to that imbroglio of mismanagement and disaster. Pulteney made what Horace Walpole is compelled to admit was a fine speech ; but it was also an exceedingly keen personal attack Pulteney even ventured to accuse Walpole not merely of errors or indifference, but actually of treachery and collusion with the enemy Walpole, who had thoroughly re-

covered his health and spirits, spoke for an hour in reply
and self-defence. Yet in spite of all the heat and
rhetoric there was no division. Dividing is not the
way to multiply, said Pulteney with a mild witticism.
But one decision was taken. Walpole challenged Pulteney, who had loaded him with abuse, to name a day
for investigating the charges brought against him, and
declared that he himself would second the proposal.
Pulteney at once accepted, and the great debate was
fixed for January 21, 1742

But before this day could arrive there were repeated
signs that Walpole's fall was close at hand. The meeting of the new parliament was, as usual, followed by
the inevitable debatings over many election petitions;
debates which were always decided as simple questions
of party politics, without any regard to the merits of
each case In one of these divisions Walpole could
only muster a majority of seven. In another, a few
days later, he lost even this scanty support, and the
opposition triumphed by four. Yet 'Sir Robert is in
great spirits and still sanguine,' wrote his son on this
very day. Before Christmas Day Walpole was again
defeated over the once famous Westminster election
petition. 'We sat till half an hour after four,' Horace
wrote to his friend Mann on Christmas Eve, 'the
longest day that ever was known,' says he in those
primitive parliamentary times. 'Sir Robert was as
well as ever, and spoke with as much spirit as ever at
four o'clock. . . . As he came out, Whitehead, the
author of *Manners*, and agent, with one Carey, a surgeon, for the opposition, said, "Damn him, how well he
looks!"' That was a curious old parliamentary scene,
the 'honourable gentleman in the blue ribband,' in the
dark small hours of a December morning defeated yet
unda

master for twenty years ; and beside him an enraged opposition, relieving its feelings in the dialect of the day   These last few weeks of Walpole's political power are the only period in his whole career during which it is possible to feel any personal enthusiasm for him. There is something decidedly attractive in the big, brave way in which he held up against the shoal of his enemies   'He is a brave fellow ; he has more spirit than any man 1 ever knew,' once said brave little George of his useful Prime Minister.

The day for Pulteney's debate came, and the Commons showed the fullest House that had been known for years   Sick and dying men, in flannel, on crutches, were brought down to vote. Walpole's son Robert, Lord Walpole, whose house adjoined the House of Commons, had taken there two or three members who were too ill to go through by Westminster Hall, and meant to pass them in by his own door   The opposition stopped the key-hole with sand   Five hundred and three members voted, and Pulteney was defeated by a majority of three.   Though such a paltry Government victory was really a defeat, Walpole would not resign, but held on, seemingly in the best of spirits, against the advice of his family and private friends. But parliamentary rebuffs continued, and Walpole at last agreed that one more election question should be made the conclusive test   On the first stage of this petition Walpole was defeated by one vote   In the next division, the result was more decisively against him ; and on February 13 he declared, as he left the House, that he would never again sit in it   Next day the King adjourned parliament for a fortnight, and before the Houses met again Walpole had resigned all his employments and had been raised to the peerage as Earl

CHAPTER VII

POWER.

1742-1744.

EVEN before the fall of Walpole, one member of his own
Government had secretly attempted to come to terms
with the opposition. Personal political intrigue was
the one science of which the Duke of Newcastle was
an easy master. 'His name is perfidy,' said Walpole
once. As early as the Porteous affair, Newcastle had
been sniffing about Carteret in an uneasy sort of way,
with a dim, dull foreboding that Carteret would probably soon rise very high indeed ; and when the removal of Walpole became a question of days or hours
only, Newcastle privately sought to negotiate himself
into security with the leading men of the new arrangement. He wrote to Pulteney that he had a royal
message for him, and asked Pulteney to meet him in
strict secrecy. But Pulteney was far too prudent to
enter into underhand communications with a man like
Newcastle. He refused to receive any message by
stealth and in the dark ; Newcastle might come, if he
liked, to Pulteney's own house, by daylight, and in
sight of all his servants At this point Walpole intervened, anxious to do, with the knowledge of his colleagues, what Newcastle had unsuccessfully attempted
by private intrigue. Walpole was with very good

reason alarmed for his own personal safety. Lenity in politics had not yet become a favourite notion; Walpole himself had been a parliamentary prisoner in the Tower. Political excitement was now running higher than at any time since the bursting of the South Sea Bubble, and the cry for an impeachment was very loud and persistent 'Downing Street or the Tower,' was Horace Walpole's lively way of stating the probabilities of the case in the last days of his father's struggle in parliament. In such circumstances, Walpole had the best possible reason for attempting to bargain with his opponents before he positively laid down his power.

Ten days before he resigned, Walpole began his arrangements, and during the fortnight's adjournment he busily continued them. The King knew that the successful opposition was not a united and harmonious party; and he himself, in language suggested by Walpole, said to Pulteney: 'As soon as I found you were at variance among yourselves, I saw that I had *two shops to deal with*, and I rather chose to come to you, because I knew that your aim was only directed against my minister, but I did not know but the Duke of Argyle wanted to be King himself.'[1] The King personally disliked Pulteney; but Walpole succeeded in overcoming that, and so gained his first point. A royal message was entrusted to Newcastle and Lord Chancellor Hardwicke, and Pulteney agreed publicly to receive it; only stipulating that, as Hardwicke was to be with Newcastle, he himself should be accompanied by Carteret. The four accordingly met at Pulteney's house Yet at first the negotiation was quite unsuccessful The royal offer proposed that Pulteney should succeed Walpole

[1] Report of a conversation with Pulteney, Add MSS. 18,915, fol. 28-29.

as Prime Minister This in itself was not likely to be
accepted ; for Pulteney had frequently declared that he
would never again take office.   And even this proposal
was clogged with a condition   The offer was only made
on the understanding that there should be no prosecution of Walpole.   To this Pulteney at once refused to
agree   He was not, he said. bloodthirsty, but it was
beyond his power to bind his party to any such arrangement.   On such terms nothing could be done
Newcastle found himself thirsty, and asked for wine
It was evening, and champagne was brought in ;[1] Newcastle drank to their happier meeting.   Pulteney smi-
lingly said that he would drink to Newcastle in the
words of Shakespeare's Brutus :—

> If we do meet again, why, we shall smile ;
> If not, why then this meeting was well made

Walpole thus failed to secure Pulteney for Premier ;
and it seems probable, though the accounts are confused
and contradictory, that Pulteney desired Carteret to
take the post.   It is probable too that Carteret, while
perfectly willing to serve under Pulteney, considered
his own claims the highest after Pulteney's refusal   It
is not clear whether Walpole objected to this.   He need
not have feared Carteret personally , Carteret was a rare
instance of an eighteenth-century statesman absolutely
free from vindictiveness.   In any case, the offer was
not made   The King, when Pulteney declined the office
for himself, desired that his old friend Sir Spencer
Compton, now Lord Wilmington, might be allowed to
slide into it   To put Wilmington at the head of a
Cabinet which included Carteret and Pulteney was an
arrangement which might have been quoted as a pre-

---

[1] Chaotic Coxe says it was forenoon and negus'

cedent for making Pitt and Fox subordinates of Sir
Thomas Robinson. Pulteney, however, agreed ; saying
to Carteret, who probably did not conceal his dissatisfaction : ' You must be Secretary of State, as the fittest
person to direct foreign affairs.' For himself Pulteney
only required a peerage and a seat in the Cabinet without the seals of any department. On these conditions
an arrangement was accomplished Some of Walpole's
old colleagues, Newcastle, Pelham, Lord Hardwicke, continued to hold their offices , some, like Hervey, were dismissed ; some, like Wilmington and Harrington, changed
their places. The other half of the Government represented the victorious opposition. Sandys, a rather insignificant man, whose ability to spell was considered an
open question, became Chancellor of the Exchequer ;
Carteret's friend Winchelsea took the Admiralty ; Argyle,
with a good deal of angry discontent, the War Office.
Pulteney became an unattached member of the Cabinet.
Carteret himself received the seals which Harrington
resigned, and officially was designated Secretary of State
for the Northern department , but every one understood
that Wilmington was a mere cypher, and that Carteret
was really the Prime Minister The Government was
always spoken of as his.

But before the new arrangements had reached even
this elementary settlement, internal difficulties threatened a troubled career to the new administration The
opposition which overthrew Walpole had itself been a
conglomeration of political parties. Every one of these
thought itself entitled to share the spoils, and every one
of them was discontented when its claims were overlooked. Carteret and Pulteney were the leaders of the
discontented Whigs or Patriots ; yet some of this party,
as Chesterfield, were dissatisfied because they had not

been called to council or offered places. They were offended at the evident superiority of Carteret. The Tories were offended when it became clear that they themselves were to have a very trifling share of influence, and that the Jacobites were to have absolutely none. The Whigs of the Prince of Wales's party were discontented; some, with the places assigned to them; others, like Pitt, Lyttelton, and the Grenvilles, because they had no places at all These parties had all willingly enough united to remove Walpole from power; but as soon as the one object on which they were agreed was attained, they flew asunder again into discordant groups. The rumour that the necessary negotiations had been entrusted to Carteret and Pulteney threw them all into violent agitation. The news that the chief posts in the Government had already been disposed of filled them with impotent passion. They declared that they had been betrayed; and on February 22, the very day of Walpole's resignation, and the day before Carteret received the seals, they assembled in full force to give vent to their indignation At the Fountain, a tavern in the Strand much used for political purposes, between two and three hundred members of both Houses met, and after dinner relieved themselves of much angry eloquence. They invited Carteret and Pulteney to be present. Carteret would not go, saying that he never dined at a tavern; but Pulteney went, only to hear himself abused. Argyle spoke with his usual passion. Using the cant phrase of the day, he declared that the Government should be formed upon a Broad Bottom, and that room must be made for all of them by dismissing every member of Walpole's administration. One enthusiast, who at least ought to have been a very young man, expressed the

same thing with a pleasantly classical flavour, and drank
to cleansing the Augean stable of the dung and grooms.
Argyle sneered at the opposition leaders who had already accepted office; angrily said of Pulteney—who
was exceedingly rich—that a grain of honesty was worth
a cartload of gold; and warmly demanded the prosecution of Walpole. To all this abuse Pulteney replied
with spirit, but with moderation, and the meeting
broke up in an excited and angry condition.

If Walpole wished, as very probably he had intended,
to stir up dissensions in the ranks of his opponents,
he had already very fairly succeeded. Already there
seemed a dangerous possibility that the heterogeneous
forces of opposition would attempt to annihilate one
another. To secure something like an harmonious understanding, a meeting of the chief leaders was held under
the soothing mediatorship of the Prince of Wales. Pulteney quietly declared that the real power of the Government was in the hands of its new members, and that
entirely to get rid of the friends of Walpole was, at that
crisis, simply impossible. Even passionate Argyle seemed
to see the truth and force of this. When the Prince
declared his own satisfaction with the arrangements
which Carteret and Pulteney had made, Argyle, for
all his bitterness, consented to join the Government;
demanding only that for the Tory Sir John Cotton a
place also should be found. An open rupture thus
seemed to have been avoided, and when parliament resumed after its fortnight's adjournment, the late opposition appeared as one united party. But this union was on
the surface only. When the final official arrangements
were announced, it was found that after all there was no
appointment for Cotton. The King had declared that
he was .... 's

family on the throne, and positively declined to accept
the Tory This was too much for Argyle He had
already made no secret of his dissatisfaction with the
Government of which he was himself a member. Glover,
the merchant-poet, known as 'Leonidas' Glover, from
the name of a so-called epic which he had produced at
the age of five-and-twenty, had found Argyle one day
pacing up and down his room and thundering against
Carteret as his enemy.[1]   Argyle now resigned, and
went into bitter opposition.   He even wrote to Orford,
and offered to assist him in demolishing their common
enemy, the new ministry.[2]   Pulteney long afterwards
told Lord Shelburne that it was impossible to understand or describe the confusion that prevailed at that
political crisis ; that he himself lost his head, and was
obliged to go out of town for three or four days to keep
his senses [3]   He returned to London only to hear that
there was already a split in the new Government.

The personal details of the formation of a Government, the rivalries and jealousies, the fightings for stars
and ribbands and places, had never much interest for
Carteret.   Unfortunately, perhaps, for his own political
advantage, he was very contemptuous of all that, and
had his mind set on other things 'In the upper departments of Government he had not his equal,' Pitt said of
Carteret long after Carteret's death.   The destinies of
Europe, the motions of armies, the policy of statesmen,
were Carteret's department , he very willingly let the
provincialisms of politics alone He had come into
power at a very anxious time.   The Treaty of Kleinschnellendorf, by which Maria had freed herself from

[1] Glover's *Memoirs of a Celebrated Literary and Political Character*
[2] Add MSS 9,224, fol 2
[3] Shelburne's *Autobiography* Fitzmaurice's *Shelburne* I 46.

the active opposition of Prussia, had proved a very temporary affair It had removed Frederick from the scene, but it left the French free to act as they pleased While the one French army had, by threatening Hanover, checkmated George and sent him home neutral, the other had pushed on down the Danube, and joined the Elector of Bavaria, who hoped soon to be Emperor They advanced as far as Linz ; it seemed their destination was Vienna itself.   Vienna was in great alarm, but was relieved when, at Linz, its enemies altered their line of march, and turned off direct north to Bohemia. Leaving only a small number of men in the Linz regions to hold their conquests on the Danube, French, Bavarians, and Saxons all made for the North, to meet again at Prag.   And they took Prag ; but there for the time their successes ended   Maria's husband, the Grand Duke Francis, also marched for Bohemia ; and the Austrian general Khevenhuller moved from Vienna to look after the French forces that had been left behind on the Danube.   He recovered Linz itself, retaking it on January 24, 1742, the very day on which the Elector of Bavaria became Emperor Charles VII   But the new Emperor had already appealed for help to Frederick, and Frederick was ready, for he had only granted the Treaty of Kleinschnellendorf on the condition of absolute secrecy, and Austria had paid very temporary regard to this stipulation   Frederick therefore rejoined his allies, and decided, in union with the French and Saxons, to seize Moravia, and if possible sweep down upon Vienna itself.   The plan was no doubt admirable ; yet the Moravian expedition turned out a complete failure. The French and Saxons gave Frederick endless trouble ; the Saxons were very backward and unwilling the French actually left him   Still he pressed on ; but in

such circumstances could not take Brünn, the strong-
hold of Moravia, and soon found himself forced to an
unwilling retreat

It was just when Austrian affairs were in this greatly
improved condition, when the French had turned aside
from Vienna, when Khevenhuller was doing well on the
Danube, when Pandours were entering the Emperor's
own Bavaria, when the Saxons and the French were
deserting Frederick, and when Frederick himself was
about to retreat from Moravia, that the change in the
English Government brought Carteret into power He
was foreign minister; practically he was also Prime
Minister. He was by no means anxious for war, but he
knew his own mind, and was desirous to start his policy
with a clear understanding. In March 1742 he had an
interview with the French ambassador, and while he
frankly told him that England would not consent to the
overthrow of the House of Austria, he desired that the
French Government should also plainly declare its intentions, that, if possible, the two countries might work
together. The ambassador duly reported this to his
master Fleury, and Fleury wrote to Frederick: ' *Votre
majesté aura jugé aisément par tous les discours de my
Lord Carteret, qu'il voudroit se rendre médiateur, et faire
reprendre au roy son maître l'influence qu'il avoit eue
dans toutes les affaires de l'Europe, et je suis bien assuré
que rien n'échappera pas ses lumières* [1] In that opinion
Fleury was perfectly correct; nothing would or did
escape Carteret's ' lights,' and Frederick also was soon
aware of that   It was very early evident that Carteret's
foreign policy was a factor which European Kings
and statesmen would have to consider with respectful
attention

[1] Add MSS 22,542, fol. 51 v° March 29, 1742

Carteret's decisive determination, resting upon un-rivalled political knowledge, was backed up by a warlike King and an eager nation. Half a million was at once voted for the support of Maria Theresa The cause of the House of Austria was recognised as the cause of public good faith and security, and, strangely as such a thing sounds in these later days, as the cause of liberty. When Prince William of Hesse urged upon Carteret that England should take no active part in the continental quarrel, Carteret would not listen for a moment, but declared that it was both the glory and the duty of England to support the Empire against the ambitious interference of France. But Carteret clearly saw that one preliminary step was almost essential. Austria must make peace with Frederick. Carteret had seen this from the first. He had said in Parliament months before that if he had been in power a recon-ciliation between Prussia and Austria would have been his first care Now that power was his, he was true to his old opinion. In his despatches to the ambassadors abroad he never wearied in pressing this view upon them [1] The detachment of Frederick from the alliance with France would, he urged, be a fatal stroke to all the French schemes in Germany. And he was very hopeful of accomplishing it ; for he shrewdly saw that Frederick's most earnest prayer might soon be a prayer for deliverance from his so-called friends. The French were certainly not at all minded to overthrow Austria in order to put Prussia in its place Belleisle and the rather doubtful characters at the French Court, who had entered so eagerly into his scheme for partitioning

[1] The statements made in this chapter regarding Carteret's own opinions and policy, and the quotations from his own language, are almost entirely from his voluminous MS correspondence in the British Museum. It is not desirable to load the page with references in each particular case

Germany and making it little more than a hanger-on of Versailles, had little enthusiasm and less practical help to lavish on an ally, except when it entirely suited their own convenience   Frederick was already feeling this in his unfortunate Moravian expedition , and at the end of April 1742 the Earl of Stair, who had succeeded Argyle at the War Office, and had gone over to the Hague to attempt to rouse the Dutch to something like energy, wrote home to Carteret : ''Tis certain at this time his Prussian majesty is very sick of the French.' So Carteret was hopeful ; the one possible difficulty was his acknowledged inability as yet definitely to answer the question . What is the real character of this new King of Prussia ?   No complete answer was at this time possible for foreign or even for Prussian observers , many of the attempted replies were ludicrous failures.   Horace Walpole with easy infallibility was just laying it down to his friend Mann that Frederick's personal cowardice was a well-established fact.   Carteret's estimate is really true as far as it goes, and is interesting as the admittedly imperfect opinion of one of the keenest political observers in Europe   He writes to the English ambassador, Hyndford, at Berlin : 'From what we know of his [Frederick's] character, the way in which you can hope to make any lasting impression on him is pointing out to him his interest and his danger, rather than that of courtship and exhortation from any other principles   .   Negotiating with him we hold to be extremely dangerous, and your Lordship must have the greatest guard upon yourself in conferring with him '

While Carteret was writing this letter, Frederick was retreating from Moravia   Here was another of what Carteret called Maria's unexpected happy suc-

cesses The King of Prussia, practically abandoned by
his allies, made his way to Bohemia, there to await
Maria's brother, Prince Charles, and his pursuing Austrians.   Yet when Frederick's situation seemed most
unfortunate he had a decided deliverance Prince
Charles entered Bohemia, and on May 17, 1742, fought
the battle known indifferently by the names of Chotu-
sitz and Czaslau.   From the military point of view, the
Austrians might perhaps have been more completely
defeated, but on the political side Frederick might well
be perfectly satisfied.   Maria could no longer refuse to
consider terms of peace.   The English Government received the news of the battle with great concern, and at
once spoke importunately at Vienna   From Frederick
himself there came to the Prussian minister in London
a letter, dated two days after the battle, containing an
offer which was to be communicated to Carteret alone.
The minister would not venture to give to Carteret a
word of it in writing ; 'and was so terrified with being
made responsible with his head for the secret of this
overture, that I could only obtain from him to let me
take down in writing from his mouth the most material
passage.'   This was the passage in which Frederick declared that he could not himself take up arms against
the French, who were nominally at least his allies , but
also asserted his complete willingness to make peace
with Maria, *si on peut porter la reine d'Hongrie à
m'accorder des conditions avantageuses ;*[1] in other
words, if the Queen would sanction the cession of
Silesia.   André, the Prussian ambassador, was ordered
to report Carteret's reply in his very words, and Carteret spoke therefore very cautiously   But he agreed
that Vienna ought to grant Frederick 'advantageous

[1] Carteret to Robinson, May 23, 1742   Add MSS 22,529, fol. 30.

conditions,' and promised that England would continue to press Maria to consent

Reluctantly, but seeing there was no help for it, Maria yielded, and granted the peace which Frederick required. The arrangements were entrusted to the English ambassador, Hyndford, who went to Frederick at Breslau to settle all details with the due formalities. Hyndford was soon successful On June 11 the Treaty of Breslau was signed ; Silesia was ceded to Frederick, and Austria and Prussia were at peace. 'The greatest blow that France has received since the happy accession of the House of Hanover to the crown of Great Britain,' wrote Hyndford gladly to Carteret, two days after the signing ; and Carteret also called it a great and happy event Frederick himself was profuse in compliments to Carteret over the matter ; a work worthy, said Frederick, of Carteret's ministry and of Carteret's own '*grandes lumières*.' In his *Histoire de mon Temps*, Frederick expressly says : '*Le Lord Carteret fut le principal promoteur de cet ouvrage.*' It was indeed a very satisfactory beginning of the minister's power, and it gained him great popularity in England 'Lord Carteret,' wrote one of the permanent Government officials, ' gains great esteem and ground by his resolution and unshaken *fermeté*, and will carry matters, I doubt not, in such a channel that the people will be, as they daily are, more and more pleased.'[1] The Earl of Bentinck wrote from the Hague to his mother, the Countess Dowager of Portland : 'I assure you that if Lord Carteret is the man that advised sending troops into Flanders, it is very much for his honour.

And it was certainly a mighty well-judged

---

[1] Mr Porter to Robinson at Vienna, June 14, 1742. Add MSS. 9,180; fol 113.

thing to show that one is in earnest in the defence of the House of Austria. . . . I heartily wish Lord Carteret good success in all his undertakings. He is in the right way as to foreign affairs. I have seen some of his despatches both in English and in French, and not without admiration as to the principles and sentiments, as well as for the turn and style, but above all for the vigour and spirit, which must save Europe at present.'[1]

Maria's chief enemy was thus removed; and the French and Bavarians, left standing alone against Austria, had meanwhile been faring badly enough. Khevenhuller, since he took Linz, had seized Passau and Munich, and was master of all Bavaria south of the Danube; and the French, who had indeed taken Prag, were now shut up and themselves besieged in it Could not England now, thought Carteret, strike in energetically, and make her second attempt to support the Queen more successful than the first had proved? Carteret, even before these fortunate events, had resolved at least to try Stair, the Commander-in-Chief, held high views of attacking the French frontier towards the Netherlands, of reducing Dunkirk, and even penetrating through an undefended country to Paris Sixteen thousand English troops were to join the Dutch in the Netherlands; George's own Hanoverians were 16,000 more, and 6,000 Hessians were bound to England by subsidy. With Maria's contribution of 14,000 men, the united English and Austrians would number 52,000 in the Lowlands. Reinforced by the promised 20,000 Dutch, the force would be really more than respectable. But the terribly laggard Dutch were the one dark and doubtful spot. Their Government

[1] June 22, 1742 Brit Mus. Egerton MSS., 1,712, fol. 252

had been discussing and protesting and promising for weary months back, and little had come of the almost frantic efforts of diplomacy but endless despatches and infinite futility. Only a few days after he had come into power, Carteret had received from Trevor, the English ambassador at the Hague, the welcome news that Holland had really resolved to be active; but between resolving and carrying out resolutions there was evidently room for much A very few days later Trevor had to write that there was a party in Holland which would take alarm at any proposal that was not as insipid and insignificant as water gruel Now the new, vigorous English Government, resolute to spare no effort, sent over the Earl of Stair as ambassador extraordinary, to see if Holland would not act a little more, and talk a little less. Stair was able to give the Dutch substantial proof of England's earnestness in the cause, for parliament had voted the half-million to Maria on the day on which he left England. And at first it even seemed possible that Stair might be successful.

In England itself the military activity was great A camp was established on Lexden Heath, near Colchester, and frequent reviews were held, to the huge delight of military George and his corpulent son, the Duke of Cumberland; for Cumberland also fancied himself a soldier of genius, and made England pay considerably for that pleasant notion In May the English troops began to embark in the transports at Gravesend; the first instalment of them reached Ostend before that month was over · We send our forces over as fast as possible,' wrote Carteret in June to Stair, ' to be under your command, and our affairs are brought to a much better consistency than I could have hoped for in so short a time. . . . Our measures give satisfaction at home, as all the world now sees that we are no longer to be led by France.'[1] All through the summer the troops continued to cross the sea, and the 22,000 Hanoverians and Hessians were ready to march into Flanders to join them. Surely now the Dutch, seeing 38,000 men in British pay, and Maria's 14,000 ready also to take part, would throw off their heavy sluggishness, and at last co-operate in reality. In spite of all England's efforts, it seemed that after all they would not. In this same month of June Stair had to write to Carteret that not a Dutchman had been in Trevor's house for a month; and the well-meaning, though always slightly impracticable, old soldier—he was now seventy years old—began to ask himself if it was worth while to stay among such a sluggishly ponderous people any longer 'I shall never desire to eat the King's bread when I cannot be useful to his service Whenever that happens, my Lord,' he wrote to Carteret, 'I shall desire to return to my plough, whence your Lordship knows I came unwillingly.'

It was exactly in these very June days, while English statesmen could do little but gaze imploringly with a kind of despairing hope at their exceedingly lethargic allies, that the Treaty of Breslau was successfully accomplished. Even the rather despondent Stair had reckoned that the heavy Dutchmen would stir if only Maria and Frederick could be brought to terms. Here, now, was this actually accomplished; yet the Dutch remained as stolid and immovable as ever. It was exceedingly provoking, for something really important might have marked the next few weeks if there had been anything like cheerful co-operation Maille-

[1] J. M. Graham's *Stair* II 286

bois and his French, who had so long been threatening Hanover, had left Germany altogether when the
new English administration was seen to be in earnest,
and had marched for Dunkirk, anticipating a possible
English attack there. But now, in August, Maillebois
received sudden orders to quit Dunkirk and hasten to
the help of the French besieged in Prag. Carteret
could hardly believe this news when first he heard it.
The departure of the French left the road to Paris
perfectly open—not a French soldier between Paris
and the English army. From another point of view,
however, Carteret strongly disliked this proceeding of
Maillebois, and writing to Hyndford he says that 'it
appears to his majesty to be high time to put an end
to these inroads of the French upon Germany, and to
clear the Empire of those already there.' At the same
time the movement of the French seemed to offer
England a decided military chance. Could not, at the
very least, the Dunkirk question be once for all settled?
Or could not the allied armies give a good account of
Maillebois if he should attempt to return there? George
himself, now that at last there seemed a prospect of
fighting instead of arguing, would go over to put himself at the head of his troops —

> Give us our fiddle ; we ourselves will play,

as the opposition journals unkindly quoted. Carteret
was to accompany the King, who seemed bent upon the
undertaking ; the royal baggage and saddle-horses did
actually get as far as Gravesend ; but they got no
farther It had been intended that Carteret should
take the Hague in his way, and find out once for
all what could or could not be done with the remarkable people there. But in the end it was decided

that Carteret, after visiting the Dutch statesmen, should return to London before the King left England; and it was quite well understood that the King's proposed visit to the Continent would chiefly depend upon the reports which Carteret brought home with him.

Carteret arrived at the Hague on October 5, 1742. All the difficulties which he would meet with from the Dutch official people were represented to him on his arrival; but he replied that the principle to which he had held throughout his whole life was to reject the word 'impossible.'[1] Perhaps, however, he was himself surprised that he actually succeeded with the Dutch He got from them a definite undertaking to join England in paying subsidies to the Queen of Hungary, and a promise that the 20,000 Dutch troops should join the English army with all possible speed At once, after only a week's stay, Carteret hastened to make his way home again, and nearly paid his life for his success After being at sea for five days, he was driven by a violent storm as far north as Hull, with great difficulty the man-of-war on which he sailed succeeded in reaching Yarmouth. From Yarmouth Carteret made his way to London by road; and on the very day of his arrival had an interview with the King at Kensington. Carteret, writes gossiping Horace, 'was near being lost; he told the King that being in a storm, he had thought it safest to put into Yarmouth Roads, at which we laughed, hoh! hoh! hoh !'' being easily amused.[2] Of the minister's serious talk gossiping Horace can give no report; but the day after the interview the royal horses and bag-

---

[1] Adelung, *Pragmatische Staatsgeschichte Europens*, III. a, 294

[2] Duchess of Yarmouth was the English title of one of the King's German women"

gage which had been shipped for Flanders were brought back again to London. There could be no thoughts of a campaign that season; the weather itself was alone sufficient to decide that. The Dutch had at last been secured; but for the present nothing more could be done than to elaborate plans for early and, if possible, decisive action next season. The Austrian general D'Ahremberg came to London to share in the military consultations. He was well received and feasted at many entertainments, which always took the form of suppers; for D'Ahremberg insisted upon dining at eleven o'clock in the morning, an hour or more too early for the English world of fashion. He left London in November, very well satisfied with the newly devised military scheme: the final touches were to be given by himself and Stair in union at the Hague. It had to be confessed that the campaign of 1742 had been lost; but on all sides there was fixed determination to make something of the next one. The troops which had so long idly lingered in Flanders were garrisoned in the Netherland towns for the winter, the English chiefly in the neighbourhood of Ghent; there to wait till the spring of 1743 came round, and military action was again possible. Thus George's second attempt to help Maria Theresa with more than generous money subsidies had practically been as unsuccessful as his first. In the first he had been able to do absolutely nothing; in the second he had actually got his troops upon the ground, but had not been able to use them; in the third he was destined to be successful at last, in a very surprising manner.

The interval between the cantonment of the troops in the Netherlands during the winter months, and the beginning of their march into Germany next year, was occupied in England by a rather stormy session of parliament The discontented members of the late opposition were loudly asserting that Carteret and Pulteney had betrayed them, and were anxious to make Carteret at least feel their resentment. To attack Pulteney was almost superfluous His acceptance of a peerage as Earl of Bath—his Countess was popularly known as the Wife of Bath—had been the signal for the ruin of his reputation Satirists, pamphleteers, epigrammatists exhausted their vocabulary, from the polite sneer down to the vulgarest ribaldry, over an event which Walpole for his own purposes was reckoned to have had a fair share in bringing about [1] His influence even with the Cabinet in which he sat was slight He did not know beforehand of Carteret's important commission to visit the Hague; Newcastle announced it by letter to him, as an event which would probably surprise him. It was Carteret alone, therefore, who had to endure the almost undivided anger of a disappointed and discontented party. They had been attacking him from the very moment when he had formed his Government. In April 1742 Sandys said to Bishop Secker that he could not imagine why they all spoke against

[1] Sir C H Williams's lines are an inoffensive specimen of the general feeling —

> 'Great Earl of Bath, your reign is o'er;
> The Tories trust your word no more,
>   The Whigs no longer fear ye,
> Your gates are seldom now unbarr'd,
> No crowds of coaches fill your yard,
>   And scarce a soul comes near ye. .   .
>
> Expect to see that tribe no more,
> Since all mankind perceives that power
>   Is lodg'd in other hands,
> Sooner to Carteret now they'll go,
> Or even (though that's excessive low)
>   To Wilmington or Sands.'

Carteret, unless it were because he had better abilities
than any of them   Argyle, of course, was one of these
earliest assailants. 'An Emperor may grow weary of
the servility of a senate,' Carteret had once said in parliament   Hardly had Argyle resigned when, with the
irritated pique of a personally disappointed man, he
repeated these words of Carteret's, and bitterly added .
' A minister never will.'   Throughout Carteret's first
session, those who had shared in the work of over-
throwing the old Government, and yet found themselves unimportant and uninfluential under the new,
were fretting with unconcealed bitterness ; in his second
session their angry irritation was naturally increased
There was nothing surprising or, from one point of view,
very important in all this ; the weak point of the
Government was the disunion and discord among its
own members   The old section of the Cabinet, those
who had been the friends and colleagues of Walpole,
could not well agree with the new section who had
driven Walpole from power   The views of the insignificant Wilmington were of no consequence ; no one knew
or cared whether he had any views or not.   But Newcastle and Pelham and Hardwicke were rather the
thwarters than the colleagues of Carteret and the new
element in the Government   The Pelhams especially
were consumed with jealousy at the leading position
which Carteret held. ' My Lord Carteret, who is in the
strictest connection with my brother and I,' Newcastle
had written some six months after the formation of the
new ministry ; but even at that early date there was
hardly more truth than grammar in the sentence   And
their jealousy went on rapidly increasing as every
month showed more clearly that Carteret was the real
master.   To fight against the regular Tory opposition,

reinforced by a number of able Whigs who fancied, or at least pretended to fancy, that they had been wronged and betrayed, and at the same time to hold on his way against the underhand intriguings of insincere colleagues, needed all Carteret's consciousness of ability and high intentions, as well as the courageous buoyancy of disposition which never for a moment forsook him.

Parliament met at the end of November 1742. On the very first day the opposition leaders took up the subject on which they obstinately insisted all through the session. Their order of the day was denunciation of Hanover and all its works. Pitt was chosen as their spokesman. There is no report of what he said on this opening occasion, but he is not likely to have failed in severity. 'Pitt spoke like ten thousand angels,' was the enthusiastic comment of Richard Grenville, afterwards Earl Temple, and the House of Commons on its first day was in an exceedingly animated condition. But the angelic eloquence which transported members with admiration could not perform the altogether prosaic task of gaining their votes; the rhetorical performance was no doubt very fine, but from a ministerial point of view the division-list was far finer. The Lords did not even venture to divide at all; and Carteret was able to congratulate himself on a good beginning. This first night was indeed a fair epitome of the whole session. There was abundance of angry opposition eloquence; abundance of personal abuse and sneering insinuations; but the exciting rhetorical proceedings always closed with the solid victory of the Government. The two chief questions that engaged the Houses are a sufficient illustration. One was the question of the British troops in Flanders. The opposition declared that to keep the troops in garrison there till the next campaign could

begin was what the parliamentary jargon of the day
called a Hanoverian measure, and they insisted that
the men should be disbanded. Murray's eloquence,
supporting the Government, was on this occasion heard
for the first time ; and the defeat of the opposition was
so overwhelming that Carteret gladly reckoned on its
probable good effect abroad   The other question roused
angrier feelings   Was Hanover or was England to pay
for the 16,000 Hanoverian troops which George was
holding under arms ? They had been sent into Flanders
to join the English there ; if they were to be kept
England would inevitably have to pay for them, for the
King's Electoral means were in no way sufficient for such
luxuries. The outcry which the opposition raised was
terrible. Everything, they said, was done for Hanover,
nothing by Hanover. England's interests were invari-
ably sacrificed for the sake of a miserable little German
Electorate   In his slightly elaborate style of fashionable
sarcasm, Chesterfield asserted that the one effectual way
of ruining the Pretender's hopes would be to make him
Elector of Hanover ; for never again would the English people accept a King from that quarter   He even
denounced Hanover and things Hanoverian in a pamphlet which had an unbounded success then, though it
is a weariness to think of now   In the House of Commons the opposition promised themselves a 'glorious
day' over this much-argued question ; and at least
had the day, if they altogether missed the glory   In
the Lords also there was much liveliness. It was hinted
that the Government's resolve to pay the troops was
the decision of Carteret alone. Bath, now in the same
House with Carteret, bluntly contradicted this. 'I am
personally obliged,' said Bath, 'to speak on this subject
by the malice of the world, and the arts of the enemies

of the Government I did approve this measure, and
do approve it. It was not a rash measure of one single
man, but the united opinion of all the administration
who were present.' Carteret's enemies were also disappointed in another direction. They had calculated
that Newcastle would at most give only a silent vote for
the Government policy. But Newcastle spoke decidedly
in support of it Horace Walpole says that Carteret
in his speech was ' under great concern.' There is no
evidence of that in the genuine fragments of the speech
which have survived 'The present question,' Carteret
said, ' is : Will you submit to France or not? I will
always traverse the views of France in place or out of
place; for France will ruin this nation if it can.' The
Government's victory was easy; and the stormy session
ended in April 1743.

And now began in earnest George's third attempt
to check the proceedings of the French in Germany
Although the promise which the Dutch had made to
Carteret had not yet been fulfilled, it was resolved at
the end of 1742 that as soon as the weather allowed
the English troops should leave their garrisons in the
Netherlands, and march into Germany to the support
of the Queen of Hungary. Stair had naturally been
very much vexed at the long inaction In his vexation
he made the singularly inappropriate mistake of fancying that some backwardness on Carteret's part was responsible for the delay. In the last months of 1742
Stair wrote some rather querulous letters to Carteret,
almost upbraiding him with a desertion of the cause
which in opposition he had so strenuously supported.
'I am very sure,' said Stair in one of these letters,
' that you have everything in your power that should
tempt the ambition of a great man.' Carteret good

humouredly enough put him right. He had already
written to Stair in July 1742: 'I am looked upon by
many of my friends and yours as too rash, though I don't
carry my views so far as your Lordship, which may
proceed from my ignorance in military affairs.'[1] Stair
soon found that in reproaching Carteret he had made a
complete mistake, and before the year was over he fully
acknowledged it.—

'I thank your Lordship for the honour of your
private letter of the 22nd of November, O.S, I can
assure your Lordship with great truth that for your own
sake nothing can be a greater pleasure to me than to see
evidently that your Lordship pursues the same system
of foreign affairs which I took to be your system when
your Lordship brought me into his majesty's service. . . .
I am very sure the King, our master, has everything in
his power for the safety and honour of Great Britain,
for the good of Europe, and for his own glory; and
Lord Carteret will with justice be thought the main
spring of moving the great machine'[2]

For indeed there was no backwardness in Carteret
or in the King; but, altogether apart from the slowness
of the Dutch, whose heavy sluggishness has at times
something almost comic about it, there were various
difficulties in the way, the Queen of Hungary herself
being one of the chief of them. Maria was very chivalrous, and high minded, and interesting; but she was
not very practicable to deal with, even when it was her
own interest that was chiefly concerned. Month after
month Carteret had been urging her to gain over the
King of Sardinia and so strengthen herself against
France on the south side of the Alps; yet she would do

[1] J. M Graham's *Stair*, II 287.
[2] Add MSS 6,911; fol 23.

nothing but show what Carteret called an ill-judged in-
flexibility. Her needlessly sharp-tongued way of speaking of the Emperor, the ' so-called Emperor,' the ' pretended head of the Empire,' might, as Carteret said, be
very piquant ; yet its useless acrimony and severity
tended to alienate from her the various members of the
Empire. Her language to George himself, her one firm
ally, was often very bitter and reproachful, little as it
should have been so. All this very considerably increased the otherwise sufficient difficulties of the English
Government Frederick, too, had a word to say He
disliked the entrance of foreign troops into the Empire.
But Carteret replied that his real object was to protect
the Empire and to rid it of the French , and he declined to
allow any foreign power to prescribe the mode of action
which England must adopt. Frederick soon softened
his language, and declared that he would observe an
exact neutrality.

The preliminary difficulties were at length all overcome, and on March 1, 1743, the English troops, after
so many weary months of waiting, began to leave their
headquarters at Ghent, and marched slowly towards
the Rhine. On March 5, in splendid weather, Stair was
at Aix-la-Chapelle, while his men behind him were daily
crossing the Meuse, ' in great health and great spirits,'
he informed Carteret. ' With such troops one might
modestly hope to do anything.' The 16,000 Hanoverians were with them ; Austrian reinforcements
brought the total up to 40,000 men In the rear, and
not yet in actual union with the main body, were 6,000
hired Hessians, and 6,000 extra Hanoverians whom
George himself as Elector contributed George also
was soon in motion, eager to fight. As soon as possible
after the rising of parliament, he and his son Cumber-

land, accompanied by Carteret, left England for the Continent While the King went on at once to Hanover, Carteret remained for a week at the Hague, once more discussing public affairs with the Dutch statesmen, and endeavouring to infuse into their torpid languor something of his own energy.   He found a happy change among them since his last year's visit.   Carteret expressly says that the great parliamentary majorities which had supported the English Government throughout the session had produced an excellent effect in Holland People there had become fully convinced that England was really in earnest ; they adopted the conviction the more easily perhaps now that the enemies of Austria were in a generally unfortunate condition The French had indeed got out of Prag but their interference in Germany had so far come to little more than nothing, while the new Emperor whom they had supported was receiving ruinous blows from Prince Charles and his victorious Austrians.   In these happier circumstances, the Dutch, while Carteret was still at the Hague, at last named the commander for their contribution of 20,000 men Carteret then at once made his way to Hanover.

From Hanover, where he arrived at the end of May, Carteret instructed Stair to get together all his troops, English, Hanoverians, and Hessians, with the least possible loss of time.   Stair had crossed the Rhine near Coblentz in the last days of April, and throughout May was encamped at Hochst, between Frankfort and Mainz, waiting for the Hessians who were following him from the Netherlands.   They had been difficult to get, for they were unwilling to fight against the Emperor, and they never proved of any service to the English in the campaign.   When June came. Stair

waited no longer for them or for the King's own 6,000
Hanoverians, but pushed on, probably himself wishing
to make for Bavaria, and in union with Prince Charles
to clear that neighbourhood of the French. Stair
marched up the Mayn, reaching Aschaffenberg in the
middle of June; but there he halted. On the other
side of the river stood the French general Noailles,
with some 60,000 men; Stair numbered about 43,000,
all told. But Noailles would not be induced to fight.
He hoped to weary out and starve his enemies, and in
that way more effectually beat them. Stair would have
himself attacked Noailles, and so have compelled him
to give battle; but the Austrian general D'Ahremberg
absolutely refused; and thus for days the allied army
lay inactive at Aschaffenberg. It was during this
period of inaction that the King, Cumberland, and
Carteret arrived at headquarters. They found the
army in a very critical condition. Stair and D'Ahremberg were not on cordial terms; the English and
Hanoverian troops did not get on well together. There
were great sufferings among the soldiers, the commis-
sariat department being in a state of very confused
inefficiency. The men were beginning to throw off
discipline; robbing churches, plundering villages; so
that the frightened peasants left their homes, drove
their cattle into the woods, and reduced the supply
department to a worse condition than ever. The efficient force of the army was already lessened by some
5,000 men. But the arrival of the King to some extent
restored matters. Strict orders on matters of discipline
were read at the head of every regiment; George
himself, if always a little ludicrous on the military side,
knew much better how to manage an army than to rule
a kingdom. A letter of Carteret's gives a glimpse of

things at Aschaffenberg in those days of waiting before the battle of Dettingen —

'We have forty or more deserters coming in every day from the French, but they are mostly hussars, Irish and Swiss, very few French, among them some Germans The hussars have picked up some of our people, but the Marshal de Noailles has sent them back with much civility, and we have sent him some of his people, with the same politeness. . . . His majesty is in perfect health and spirits; is always booted, and rides out to several of the most material posts twice a day. The Duke [Cumberland] is very well and very active, and so are the Duke of Marlborough, Lord Albemarle. Lord Bury, and all your Grace's friends. I say nothing of myself, but my son is liked and does his part as a volunteer very well. I make no doubt that all will end with honour and for the good of our country. The Duke D'Ahremberg and Marshal Neipperg are just gone from me (I can write nothing without interruption), so you must forgive any faults I make in writing. They tell me his majesty's orders for the good discipline of the army have had already a very good effect, and that without it we should have been soon in confusion '[1]

After the King had been at Aschaffenberg a week, it was clear that the army could stay there no longer The provision question proved impossible of solution there, and on June 26 George and the generals resolved to fall back down the river to Hanau, where the Mayn takes its direct bend to the left to find its way into the Rhine at Mainz. At Hanau were the magazines, and there too the advancing Hessians had been ordered to wait From Aschaffenberg to Hanau, along the north bank of the river, is some sixteen English miles. Nearly

[1] To Newcastle; Add MSS 22,536 fol 73, 74

midway between the two places, close on the Mayn, was the village of Dettingen, and, just beyond Dettingen, on the other side of the river, another small village, Seligenstadt, destined to be an important little place next day. The line of march was through a cramped valley, from which the army could not possibly turn aside; for their left was bounded by the Mayn, and along the right stretched the woody hills of the Spessart-Wald. The conditions were evidently uncomfortable; but there was no remedy. Very silently, in the early hours of June 27, the allied army began its march. The King was with the English in the rear, for it was reckoned that the enemy's chief attack would be in that quarter. Noailles did indeed seize Aschaffenberg as soon as the English left it, but he had no desire to try any fighting there. He had formed a plan which seemingly could not fail. Observing that the allies meant to withdraw by way of Dettingen, he had, unknown to them, thrown two bridges across the Mayn at Seligenstadt, and sent his nephew, the Duke of Grammont, over with a considerable force to secure the ground in front of the village. Crossing the road of the retreating army, just before they could gain the Dettingen hamlet, a brook came down from the Spessart-Wald to join the river, and so formed a ravine with rough boggy land, difficult for orderly marching. Noailles intended that while the allies were confusedly struggling in this ravine and morass, and while the French batteries, which they could not avoid, were playing upon them from the other side of the river, Grammont should fall upon them in front, and in all human probability end the business. Noailles himself, by seizing Aschaffenberg, had shut out all chance of an escape in the rear, he had his enemy in a trap, and considered the affair as good as ended.

Undisturbed by Noailles, the allies continued their
march, without thought of any danger in store for them
ahead   By eight o'clock in the morning their advanced
parties had reached Dettingen, but not to enter the
village   The unexpected sight of the French and of
the bridges just beyond instantly revealed to them the
real position of affairs, and they galloped back to the
army with the surprising news. The army halted, for
the post of honour now was not the rear but the van,
and George must come to the front. So the English
and Austrians waited, facing the boggy ravine, while
behind it stood Grammont, expecting their approach
with grim satisfaction   The allies had not even two
plans to choose between; they could do nothing but
make a desperate attempt to cut their way straight
through, at whatever cost. Scientific military arrangements in that narrow, cramped ground were next to
impossible. The little that could be done in that
direction was done, and the men were ready to advance;
when suddenly, in the early afternoon, a wild mistake
of the French changed all the chances of the engagement. Grammont, not restraining himself any longer,
broke his uncle's orders, left his own strong Dettingen
position, crossed the ravine, and attacked the enemy in
a position quite as good as his own   For a moment his
mad impetuosity had a touch of success. The allies'
left line broke before the onset of the French cavalry.
But it recovered, and Grammont had no other even
temporary satisfaction to excuse his rash and fatal folly.
From two o'clock till six the battle lasted, and the
French could make no impression anywhere. George
himself led the infantry; his horse ran away with him
early in the action, and during the rest of the fighting he
was on foot   'Don't talk to me of danger; I'll be even

with them.' Before the solid mass of foot-soldiers the French could not stand; they broke and hurriedly retreated The retreat was turned into a flight. Some fled into the woods, many were drowned while trying to cross the river, many were cut down before they could reach the two bridges. The English were left in undisturbed possession of the field; and their little King, full of martial enthusiasm, remained on the ground till ten o'clock at night, contentedly dining there on a cold shoulder of mutton

Carteret, as a civilian, had no personal share in the battle. He sat all through the hours of the engagement in his coach close to the field of action, and witnessed one of the ludicrous episodes of the day when the Archbishop of Mayence came up to his carriage window, and, in the height of the action, cried out to Carteret: '*Milord, je proteste contre toute violence*'[1] That same night, from the Dettingen cottage which he shared with the Austrian marshal Neipperg, Carteret wrote home to Newcastle a short and hurried despatch announcing the victory The graces of style of the polite letter-writer were, in such very confused circumstances, hardly to be looked for; and Carteret's letter, though it did all that was necessary in the way of accurate information, was in style abrupt and awkward enough. Small wits at home made very merry over what they reckoned as its defects. Lord Shelburne, surely with some exaggeration, notices it as a remarkable fact that neither Pitt nor Carteret could write an ordinary letter well. But no one was more willing to recognise the imperfections of this jerky, bulletin-like little missive than Carteret himself What is unfortunately the one anecdote of Carteret in Boswell's book

[1] Add MSS 11 262 fol 13

tells how he exclaimed after writing his despatch:
'Here is a letter expressed in terms not good enough
for a tallow-chandler to have used' Literary defects,
however, counted for little in consideration of the news
which the letter brought.   The nation went wild with
joy over its remarkable victory; illuminating the streets,
lighting bonfires, firing guns   'My Lord,' writes Horace
Walpole of his father, ' has been drinking the healths
of Lord Stair and Lord Carteret; he says, since it is
well done, he does not care by whom it was done. . .
The mob are wild, and cry, Long live King George, and
the Duke of Cumberland, and Lord Stair, and Lord
Carteret, and General Clayton that's dead!'   More lasting than the noisy enthusiasm of the people was Handel's
thanksgiving music ; whose *Dettingen Te Deum* is pretty
much all that is left of this once so famous victory.

The allied army without loss of time safely made its
way to its magazines at Hanau, where it was joined by
the Hessians and the extra Hanoverians.   Jealousies
and recriminations between the English troops and their
foreign allies were not few, and Stair in disgust resigned and returned 'to his plough'   Many communications and negotiations with the French commander
Noailles thus fell necessarily into Carteret's hands,
and a jealous opposition at home asked . Is Carteret
the new Commander-in-Chief, then? thinking there was
considerable sprightliness in the question   The 'three
Johns,' Argyle, Stair, and Carteret, offered a chance to
some rather indifferent verse-monger :—

> John, Duke of Argyle we admired for a while,
>   Whose titles fell short of his merit ,
> His loss to repair, we took John, Earl of Stair,
>   Who, like him, had both virtue and merit

Now he too is gone.   Ah! what's to be done?
  Such losses how can we supply?
But let's not repine, on the banks of the Rhine
  There's a third John his fortune will try

By the Patriots' vagary, he was made Secretary,
  By himself he's Prime Minister made;
And now to crown all, he's become General,
  Though he ne'er was bred up to the trade

But Carteret had more serious arrangements than
temporary military ones to make   The newly elected
Emperor was now left without allies; the French, who
had set him up, were beaten and already making their
way out of the Empire.   It was pressingly essential for
this puppet-Emperor to secure his speedy peace with
England.   He had been trying this by help of Prince
William of Hesse, all through the year 1742   Between
Carteret and the Prince there had been a copious correspondence; more or less beseeching on the Prince's part,
who dwelt earnestly on the admirable qualities of the
Emperor, and begged English official commiseration for
a sovereign in difficulties   But Carteret was always
politely firm; dead against an admirable Emperor who
was closely bound to the French, whose proposed plans
of arrangement were mere 'visionary and impracticable
schemes,' made, too, as the English Government discovered, in private concert with France   As nothing
came of his very self-interested appeals, the Emperor
next year went further   In June 1743, while George
and Carteret were still at Hanover making ready to join
the army, Prince William of Hesse arrived there with a
letter from the head of the Empire.   The Emperor
offered to accept any terms of peace which England
could procure him from Vienna, if only they were com-
patible with his honour and dignity.   The appealing

vagueness of this letter was replied to by Carteret with
no lack of clearness He reported home to Newcastle:—

'When I had read it, I told him [Prince William]
plainly, that the King would never advise the Queen of
Hungary to make the least cession of any part of her
dominions to the Emperor ; and that no peace could be
made between the Emperor and the Queen of Hungary
without his Imperial Majesty's giving up all claims and
pretensions to the Queen of Hungary's entire dominions,
that if his Imperial Majesty would immediately and
publicly detach himself from France, we would endeavour to do him the most good we could, provided it
was not at the expense of the Queen of Hungary, who
would not so much as sacrifice a village to him.   . The
Prince of Hesse then asked me whether the King would
propose a cessation of arms between the Emperor and the
Queen of Hungary I answered him, No , that the
Queen of Hungary and her auxiliaries would push to
the utmost all their advantages , that if we run risks,
and fought battles and succeeded, we would make the
most of them , but yet we would rather avoid those
extremities , therefore I could answer for nothing but
the security of his Imperial Majesty's person and liberty
at Frankfort, when once he shall get there ; but if he
should be intercepted in his journey thither by the
Austrians, we could not be blamed   . The Prince of
Hesse did not talk to me upon any other subject, and I
did not give him any encouragement so to do, but am
to see him to-morrow, when we shall talk upon divers
other things He only told me *en passant*, that we had
found the true way to deal with the Court of Berlin, and
that the King of Prussia would observe an exact neutrality I told him that we had no arts, but proceeded,
with relation to his Prussian majesty, as we would

towards all other German powers, with civility, courage, and truth ; that the King and his ministers knew no other politics   I left him to dress to go and dine with the King.'

This was three weeks before the battle of Dettingen. Carteret clearly let the Emperor understand that England would be no party to patching up a separate peace between himself and Maria Theresa so long as he clung to his alliance with the French.   This decision would not, as the Prince said to Carteret, be *fort consolant* to the Emperor ; but Carteret was firm, and nothing more could be got from him   Diplomacy now yielded to arms ; and if there was little consolation to an unfortunate Emperor in the limited promises of statesmanship, there was less by far in a surprising battle of Dettingen. Negotiations after that decisive event became therefore more active than ever   The Emperor had safely reached Frankfort ; the English headquarters were at Hanau, where George remained for two months after the battle.   Once more Prince William of Hesse appeared on the scene   Carteret received him with the sincere wish to secure a definite and friendly understanding.   'Britannic Majesty is not himself very forward ; but Carteret, I rather judge, had taken up the notion , and on his Majesty's and Carteret's part, there is actually the wish and attempt to pacificate the Reich ; to do something tolerable for the poor Kaiser '[1]   On one preliminary condition, however, Carteret was decisively insistent.   The Emperor must altogether and at once cut himself loose from the French.   Charles was eager to recover his Bavaria from Maria ; eager also for money to tide him over his present ruinous circumstances   What might be done in these directions Carteret prudently declined to say ; Prince William

' Carl' *F* · · *G* · XIV C ﹐ V.

could extract from him nothing but the promise that England would give all possible help to the Emperor as soon as he sincerely joined the allies in driving the French out of Germany. With this reply Prince William returned on July 7, 1743, from Hanau to Frankfort. The two or three days immediately following produced several vague, general propositions from the Prince, which Carteret politely refused to entertain; till the Emperor, considering that the French were already in full retreat, and knowing that his own circumstances could by delay become only worse instead of better, resolved to accept Carteret's preliminary. Precisely one week after the Prince had taken Carteret's reply to Frankfort, he informed Carteret that the Emperor agreed, that he would renounce all his pretensions to Austrian dominions, and entirely quit the French alliance. One week had brought matters so far. Frederick of Prussia approved, he wrote from Berlin to Carteret, expressing his great esteem, and signing himself *votre très-affectionné ami, Fédéric.* Carteret himself, though not forgetful of the obstinacy of Maria Theresa, was fully hopeful of success. 'All Europe sees what a great scene this is, what a glorious figure his majesty makes,' he wrote to Newcastle. 'France has not been for a century under so great difficulties as at present, and if the Emperor, the Empire, and the States-General will heartily join with his majesty, the Queen of Hungary, and the King of Sardinia, there is all the probability and, I will venture to say, as much certainty as human affairs will admit of, to trust that, by the blessing of God, a safe, lasting, and general peace may be procured, not impossible in this very campaign.'

Such were the plans and hopes of Emperors, Kings, and statesmen; all of them unfortunately forgetting

that in a high official position in Whitehall sat a
ridiculous Duke of Newcastle On July 15 the Prince
went to Carteret, confident of getting the official signatures which would finish the affair, but found himself
quite disappointed.   There was money involved in the
treaty ; a monthly subsidy to be paid to the Emperor
till his present very broken circumstances could be
somewhat retrieved   George and Carteret had both to
tell the anxious Prince that ministers in London must
first be consulted before they could put their hands to
that; that fifteen days must pass before a messenger
could go and come.   All Carteret's hopes and wishes
were for the acceptance of the treaty ; he urged it
upon his colleagues in London as the essential preliminary to the union of all Germany against the
French   It was in vain.   Why not make peace with
France, and leave Germany alone altogether ? asked
the ministers in England, and refused to have anything
to do with the proposed arrangement.   On August 1,
1743, this reply reached Hanau, and Carteret had to
let Prince William know that for the present the only
result was failure.   A ridiculous Duke of Newcastle
had ruined the far-seeing plans of the statesman whose
mastery of foreign affairs was known in every capital in
Europe.   A ridiculous Duke, who believed that Hanover was north of England, and probably thought that
Dettingen was on the top of Cape Breton (which in
later years he was so refreshed to discover was an
island), had interfered with the statesmanship of the
one English minister to whom the intricacies of German
politics were no insoluble mystery   The peddling
pedanticism of the most imbecile even of political
Dukes, for whom politics ranged from potwallopers to
Knights of the Garter and back again had its way;

and Carteret's high schemes for the pacification of the
Empire and the defeat of French plans in Germany
were forced to yield before the ignorant insularities of
the Cockpit at Whitehall There was, in addition, personal abuse and misconception of himself involved in
this failure—if Carteret had not been too proud to
think or complain of that.   The Emperor, Prince
William of Hesse, Frederick of Prussia, all reckoned
that the fault was Carteret's alone.   Brochures were
printed on the Continent dwelling painfully on the
mystery and iniquity of the affair; Prince William
himself sent to the Hessian minister at the Hague a
long indictment of Carteret and his treachery. 'Prince
William's accusation of Lord Carteret makes a great
noise here, and will, I hope, be duly refuted in England,'
wrote Mr. Trevor, English minister at the Hague.[1]
The Kings and kinglets of the Continent, imperfectly acquainted with the beautiful working of English party
politics, could not understand how it was that when
the English King and the English chief minister professed to desire a certain political action they should
yet be unable to realise their desires   Prince William
professed to believe that Carteret had never consulted
the Regency in England at all, and that his account of
the failure of the scheme was sheer falsehood   Even
Frederick the Great, it is regretfully surmised,[2] felt
convinced that it was all Carteret's trickery and
treachery   Carteret bore it all, as well as the still
more ignorant abuse which was awaiting him in
England, in a very proud, uncomplaining way ; conscious
how unjust it was, but having already lived in the
thick of politics for thirty-two years. 'Carteret, for

[1] Sept 15, 1744.
[2] By Carlyle, the only historian who has thought it worth while to

this Hanau business, had clangours enough to undergo, poor man, from Germans and from English; which was wholly unjust His trade, say the English—(or used to say, till they forgot their considerable Carteret altogether)—was that of rising in the world by feeding the mad German humours of little George; a miserable trade! Yes, my friends;—but it was not quite Carteret's, if you will please to examine!'[1]

Carteret's high plan of reconciling the Emperor and Maria Theresa, and of so uniting all Germany against the French, thus went to ruin, and no more negotiating at Hanau was possible. In these circumstances the English camp there was struck, and at the end of August the King and Carteret arrived at Worms For there was still one more diplomatic effort to make, hardly of an easier, though of a much more modest kind than the Hanau one Since all Germany could not be got to work unitedly against the French, it remained to bind together as closely as possible such anti-French powers as there were. Outside England, which always furnished the necessary supplies, Maria Theresa's chief ally was the King of Sardinia. While Germany had been busy with Silesian wars, sieges of Prag, battles of Dettingen, there had been much intricate and heavy fighting on the south side of the Alps; France and Spain together doing all the hurt they could to Austria in her Italian possessions. In this southern business Maria Theresa's chief support was Charles

---

understand and appreciate Carteret, a great distinction for Carteret Carlyle regrets that on this matter of the Hanau Treaty Frederick took up such a misconception of Carteret *Frederick*, Book XIV Chap V. According to the *Marchmont Papers*, however, Andrié, Prussian Minister to England, was convinced, by Carteret himself, how the truth really lay, and wrote to Frederick accordingly *Marchmont Papers*, I. 48.

[1] Carlyle's *Frederick*, Book XIV Chap V

Emanuel, King of Sardinia; but for him this alliance was rapidly losing all its charm. The original agreement between the two sovereigns was of a very vague character, and left Charles Emanuel at full liberty to side with the Bourbons if Austria failed to satisfy his requirements. To get rid of this provisional state of things, and definitely bind the King and the Queen together, had been one of Carteret's earliest desires. In May 1742, three months after he had come into power, he urged this policy on the Vienna Court. To Austrian affairs in Italy the Sardinian King's friendship was clearly indispensable; while on the other hand Charles Emanuel stood in danger of possible Bourbon resentment, and was being tempted by actual Bourbon offers. Carteret earnestly pressed Maria Theresa to secure him at once by yielding him the moderate terms he required, and promised that the English King would cheerfully send a fleet to the Mediterranean, even alone, if the Dutch refused to join. Robinson, however, found it very hard work at Vienna. The Court was suspicious of England, and angry that English fighting help was so very slow in coming; though what could George in his then checkmated condition do? Austria also was just about to make her cession of Silesia to Frederick, and gloomily asked if her next proceeding was to be a cession to Sardinia. Better yield a trifle of Lombardy than lose all you have in Italy, was Carteret's reply; and Maria Theresa reluctantly found herself compelled to agree. Her promise was given, and Charles Emanuel honestly and successfully fought for his ally; but was gradually worked into an irritated, threatening condition as the time passed by, and there came no sign that the promise was meant to be kept. Carteret was very anxious, he feared that Sardinia, treated with

this shabby ingratitude, must yield to Bourbon temptations. To Carteret's relief, Sardinia appealed to
George, and offered to leave the decision of the case
with England If George refused, Charles Emanuel
would at once go over to France ; but he expressed full
confidence in English intervention Carteret was much
relieved. 'I own,' he wrote from Hanover in the
weeks before the battle of Dettingen, 'I was very
anxious about it. from several intelligences that I had ;
but I think this letter under his own hand, at this time,
and in so explicit a manner, may set us at rest if we
make a good use of it, which shall not be neglected.
And hereafter, when these things may become public,
several ingenious persons at home, who say our
measures have been mad, will see that one of the
prudentest and wisest Princes in Europe has not
thought so, and will risk his whole upon them.'[1]

'Which shall not be neglected,' wrote Carteret ; nor
did he neglect it. Austria, of course, was difficult to
manage ; the square mileage of Robinson's despatches
was largely increased by this business But Austria, if
only in self-protection, had to agree; and the Treaty
of Worms, signed on September 13, 1743, definitely
secured Sardinia to the right side. George undertook
to keep a strong squadron in the Mediterranean as long
as it might be needed there, and to pay a large yearly
subsidy to Charles Emanuel; Maria Theresa unreservedly
promised him the small portions of territory which he
required ; and he, in return for all this, rejected all
Bourbon temptations and ranged his 45,000 men on the
side of Austria. Thus, if there should be another campaign, Carteret had secured one important preparation
for it ; 45,000 men fighting *for* instead of *against* made

[1] Carteret to Newcastle, June 6, 1743 Add MSS. 22,536. fol 59, 60.

a weighty difference of 90,000 men. With this Treaty of Worms Newcastle and the Regency at home did not interfere. They approved of it and ratified it; for which complaisance Carteret was no doubt grimly grateful to them

The differences between Carteret and the Pelhams on questions of foreign politics were not a cause but only a symptom of the dissatisfaction which had from the very first existed between the two sections of the Cabinet The want of cordiality between Walpole's old colleagues and Walpole's old opponents became mere jealous disgust on the part of Newcastle, Pelham, and Hardwicke, when they discovered that Carteret, nominally Secretary of State, was practically himself the Government They were Carteret's colleagues; that did not hinder them from working and conspiring against him To weaken Carteret's influence, to get rid of him altogether from the Government which he led in spite of them, became the supreme object of these very feeble political personages, who fancied that the Government of England was by nature their monopoly, and that men of genius had nothing whatever to do with it. A special incident about this time happened to help them. A few days after the battle of Dettingen, Wilmington, Prime Minister and prime mediocrity, had died Carteret hoped that Bath might succeed him; the Pelhams wished and hoped otherwise Bath had declined to make any application for the post before it was actually vacant, but Henry Pelham, urged on by Orford, showed no such delicacy; perhaps with excusable inability to discover any difference between Wilmington alive and Wilmington dead Bath, too, applied when Wilmington was no longer even a political cypher, and his letter was sent to Carteret at Hanover. Each

applicant felt considerable difficulties in his way, and
neither could make sure of success. Bath was unpopular with the King, unpopular everywhere. 'My Lady
Townshend said an admirable thing the other day,'
writes Horace Walpole. 'He [Bath] was complaining
much of a pain in his side. "Oh!" said she, "that can't
be; you have no *side*;"' such the brilliancy of political
ladies. Pelham, on the other hand, knew that Carteret's wish in this matter was against him, and began
to think it hopeless to struggle against Carteret's desire,
or perhaps even to be afraid of success gained in
such circumstances. The much robuster Orford had
to encourage his friend If the King should after all
prefer Pelham, Carteret, wrote Orford, would never
break with Pelham for that. 'But *manet altâ mente
repostum*,' added the old minister, warningly, remembering what had been his own conduct in regard to all
political appointments, and thinking that Carteret in
that department was such another as himself No
better proof of the contrary could have been desired
than Carteret's letter announcing that the King's choice
had fallen on Pelham. Carteret wrote from Mainz, to
which town the King and he had now got on their road
homewards to England, and after stating frankly that
he himself would have preferred the appointment of
Bath, and that he had placed that proposal before the
King, he continued —

'You see I state the affair very truly and naturally
to you, and what could anybody, in my circumstances,
do otherwise? If I had not stood by Lord Bath, who
can ever value my friendship? And you must have
despised me. However, as the affair is decided in your
favour by his majesty, I wish you joy of it, and I will
endeavour to support you as much as I can, having

really a most cordial affection for your brother and you, which nothing can dissolve but yourselves; which I don't apprehend will be the case. I have no jealousies of either of you, and I believe that you love me; but if you will have jealousies of me without foundation, it will disgust me to such a degree, that I shall not be able to bear it; and as I mean to cement a union with you, I speak thus frankly. His majesty certainly makes a very great figure, and the reputation of our country is at the highest pitch; and it would be a deplorable fatality if disputes at home should spoil all the great work.'[1]

This was certainly a straightforward letter; Newcastle himself, in a private note to Lord Chancellor Hardwicke, confessed that it was a manly one. To Newcastle also, on the same date, Carteret wrote a kindly note, in reply to the fussy querulousness of the Duke, who fancied himself neglected if every mail did not bring from Carteret confidential letters as well as official despatches. Carteret did his best to soothe him. The business connected with the army and with the negotiations had been great, the King had been ill; Carteret himself had been 'so ill, that I thought I should not be able to hold out' The interesting part of the letter is its close:—

'As to complaints upon want of concert, while the King is on this side the water, and at the head of an army, I don't look upon them as serious; and therefore, though my friends tell me so, I shall not force the nature of things But, as I have courage enough, God be thanked, to risk, in a good cause, my natural life, I am much less solicitous about my political life, which is all my enemies can take from me; and if they do, it

---

[1] Carteret to Pelham, August 27, 1743. Coxe's *Pelham*, I 85, 86.

will be the first instance in which they hurt me ; though
I must own that my friends have been near ruining me
at various times ; of which I shall take care for the
future, being past fifty-three ' [1]

Pelham thus became nominal Prime Minister ; much
to the satisfaction of Orford and the angry disgust of
Bath. But Pelham at once found his position a very
difficult one. His main desire was to free himself from
Carteret ; and then, by reconstructing the Government,
to revert as far as possible to the old lines of Walpole's
policy. He had no intention whatever of accepting
Carteret's frank proposals for harmonious co-operation.
Consequently a struggle between Carteret and Pelham
was inevitable. 'If you offer any schemes without a
concert with him,' wrote Orford to Pelham, ' that will
be jealousy with a witness ; and that, he has told you,
he will not bear.' But that is just what the Pelhams
were resolved to do. Newcastle, never so much in his
element as when plotting against a colleague, was already
busily scheming with Orford how to drive Carteret from
the Government. In the same letter in which he ac-
knowledges that Carteret had written to him in an
' open, friendly manner,' the Duke speculates what he
and his brother shall do with him when he returns
Newcastle even drew up in writing a memorial against
Carteret and his policy, practically asking for his dismissal ; and it required Pelham's stronger sense and
caution to persuade his brother not to present this
paper to the King For Pelham and Orford clearly
saw that Carteret's chief support was his great personal
and political influence with the King ; any crude attempt
to injure him in that quarter would only be likely to
irritate George, and to do Carteret more good than

---

[1] Coxe's *Pelham*, I 87, 88

harm. To get rid of Carteret by personal complaints
to the King, and by argumentative expostulations on
the minister's influence or policy, seemed simply hopeless. The slower but probably sure way of success
remained · by promises, intrigues, and plots, to weaken
their own colleague's position in parliament, and so
make his long continuance in power impracticable To
gain over every discontented Whig, and rally them all
against the man who was a truer Whig than any of
them, was Orford's reiterated advice to Pelham. This,
backed by the anti-Hanoverian cursing and groaning of
the Tories and Jacobites, and by endless repetition of the
miserable falsehood that Carteret's foreign policy rested
on his desire to gain the King's personal favour, might
be expected to do what was wanted without very much
loss of time.

While these underground arrangements were busily
proceeding, Carteret was on his way home, taking the
Hague on his route, and coming to the conclusion that
Dutch ability to give good help against the French was
not nearly so much wanting as Dutch will. On November
26, 1743, George and the Duke of Cumberland arrived
in London, Carteret following them a day later; and
with the grand ball which in the next week took place
at St James's in honour of the King's birthday (where
the Duke, fairly recovered from his Dettingen wound,
danced with much devotion, and indeed was reckoned
not to limp nearly so much as Colley Cibber's birthday
verses), the new London political season fairly began.
A most confused season it seemed likely to be. ' All is
distraction,' wrote Horace Walpole . ' no union in the
Court, no certainty about the House of Commons: Lord
Carteret making no friends, the King making enemies:
Mr Pelham in vain courting Pitt, etc ; Pulteney unre-

solved. How will it end?' It began with a Babel of
parliamentary abuse directed against Carteret Jacobites, Tories, discontented Whigs, hopelessly discordant
on almost every other matter, on this displayed an easy
unanimity Chesterfield had the first opportunity. He
chose to represent the royal speech which on December 1
opened the session as particularly the speech of 'the
minister,' and as a sign of a disunited Cabinet ; an unfortunate charge, for the document was the composition
of Lord Chancellor Hardwicke.[1] The main drift of
Chesterfield's speech, that England should leave Germany absolutely alone and confine herself to her war
against Spain, was, as an abstract proposition, perfectly
reasonable ; as a contribution to the practical politics
of the day it was useless , for England could only leave
Germany severely alone if France would do the same ;
which evidently France would not. Hanover, of course,
under veiled insinuations, was not forgotten by Chesterfield ; few political speeches of those days are free from
that most wearisome of topics Hanover and abuse of
Carteret, that practically was Chesterfield's speech ;
though for formality's sake he insisted that the Lords
should inquire particularly into every step of the war
and the negotiations, 'the Green Bag itself upon your
table,' a parliamentary proceeding of frightful solemnity.
Carteret's reply was triumphant. ' Easy and animated,'
Walpole's panegyrist Coxe calls it ; Yorke notes that
Carteret ' spoke with great confidence and spirit, and
was reckoned to get the better of Lord Chesterfield '
He had, indeed, an accomplished success to point to.

---

[1] Hardwicke's son, the Hon. Philip Yorke, expressly says so Yorke,
who often attended the debates in the Lords, and was himself an M P ,'
kept a MS parliamentary journal from Dec 1743 to April 1745 It is printed
in Vol. XIII. of the *Parliamentary History*, and is, while it lasts, the best
authority

It was his fixed policy to check the French and their designs on Germany, and there was not now a French soldier in the Empire   As the first work of his ministry, Maria Theresa had been reconciled with Frederick, and that first great success had been followed up by the actual co-operation of the Dutch with England, by the decisive defeat of France in Germany, and by the successful agreement between Austria and Sardinia.   Continue vigorously what has so successfully been begun, was the urgent drift of Carteret's speech : while from the personal point of view he would, he said himself, be the very first to press for a minute inquiry into all that had occurred.   No second speaker ventured to carry on the attack which Chesterfield had opened, and the honours of the debate distinctly remained with Carteret

The discussion on this same occasion in the House of Commons was not limited to a parliamentary duel. Pelham, the leader of the House, was not present; his seat had been vacated by his new official appointment, and he had not yet been re-elected.   But Dodington and Lyttelton and Grenville were there to attack Carteret ; Winnington, Fox, and Sandys to defend him , the two sides striving with each other to endless lengths on the battle of Dettingen, the Treaty of Worms, and above all on Hanover   What Dodington or Sandys had to say on these most exciting topics is now indifferent to every one; but Pitt also was there, and especially concerned himself with Carteret.   This occasion practically opened Pitt's period of violent invective against Carteret; a period which lasted till Pitt himself got into office, when his tone changed.   In his violent way Pitt now styled Carteret 'an execrable, a sole minister, who had renounced the British nation, and seemed to have drunk of the potion described in poetic fictions, which

made men forget their country.'[1]   Carteret did not fail
to find defenders against this excited rhetoric. 'His
integrity and love to his country,' said the Chancellor
of the Exchequer, 'were equal to his abilities, which
were acknowledged by the whole world'   Pitt's unpar-
liamentary violence could not pass without rebuke, but
he did not allow himself to be checked, and soon ex-
ceeded the abusiveness of this first outburst. It was all
in the game of party politics: Pitt himself had not yet
held any responsible office; his eloquence was impas-
sioned and reckless, and he himself was reckless and im-
passioned in the use of it   Fox always spoke to the
question, Pitt to the passions, said Horace Walpole.
Pitt's political career, from its commencement onwards
till the outbreak of the Seven Years' War, has nothing
specially noticeable about it, unless heated party spirit
and passionate eloquence are so ; though after that date
it was noteworthy as few others are. Till the year
1756 Pitt was a free lance, fighting for his own hand ;
and he never used his chartered liberty more extravagantly than in the session which followed the battle of
Dettingen   What Yorke said of his conduct in one of
these debates does equally well for his tactics in them
all : 'Mr Pitt spoke rather to raise the passions than
convince the judgments of his hearers, which he is too
apt to do, though in that way I never heard anybody
finer.' Pitt found his second opportunity when parliament debated if England should keep the Hanoverian
troops in its pay for the campaign of 1744   The opposition insisted that England should not, and repeated
various vague, unauthenticated rumours of disagreements between the English and Hanoverian soldiers.
on the truth or falsehood of which the opposition and

[1] Yorke's Parliamentary MS

the military members wrangled at great length   Officers
who had been in the camp and at the battle contradicted
the vague stories which had been so eagerly credited for
party reasons; and the proposal to dismiss 22,000 men
in the middle of a war was too absurd to be successful.
But it served Pitt's turn well enough. 'His Majesty,'
said he, ' yet stands on the firm ground of his people's
affections, though on the brink of a precipice; it is the
duty of parliament to snatch him from the gulf where
an infamous minister has placed him, and not throw
paltry flowers on the edge of it, to conceal the danger.
It may be a rough, but it is a friendly hand which is
stretched out to remove him.'   To call Carteret an
' infamous minister' was not sufficiently abusive for
Pitt; he became so violent and personal that it was
necessary to call him to order.   He continued his
charges with but little abatement, and ended by rhetorically declaring that the ' great person' (the parliamentary expression for the small person who was King)
was hemmed in by German officers and by one English
minister without an English heart.

The same question was brought before the House of
Lords by Sandwich, whose speech had Pitt's bitterness
without the ability. His motion ventured to assert
that faithful Englishmen at home, and the English
forces abroad, were filled with heart-burnings and
jealousies at the conduct and favoured treatment of
their Hanoverian allies   Sandwich wearisomely reca-
pitulated the well-worn charges: how a considerable
body of Hanoverian troops had refused to obey Stair's
orders during the battle, how a Hanoverian officer had
refused to obey him after it; and so on through all the
wearisome catalogue, every item of accusation being
absurdly untrue, with the exception of one small inci-

dent which had resulted simply from a misunderstanding and had been explained entirely to Stair's satisfaction. Carteret, not wishing to let the debate continue,
as it had begun, on a false issue, rose at once and
plainly declared that the stories and rumours which had
been repeated by Sandwich were false. In spite of this,
Chesterfield continued the tale which Sandwich had
begun, and lamented that the joy with which the army
had received its victory had been damped by the discontents and jealousies which had followed it. Yorke
has unkindly but particularly preserved one of Chesterfield's sentences. 'My lords,' said he, speaking of the
English soldiers, 'the triumphal laurels yet green upon
their brows were soon overshadowed by the gloomy
cypress.' Chesterfield passed from these distressing
botanical details to dwell on what he reckoned military defects during and after the battle; a quite
fair subject for opposition attack, but not one which in
any way touched Carteret personally, who was not a
soldier. and had no responsibility for military arrangements. Perhaps for that very reason, Carteret's reply,
which had mainly to concern itself with a defence of
the operations of the campaign, was not reckoned to be
one of his finest performances, but rhetorical rather and
exaggerated; but when Carteret left the military side
for his own sure ground of statesmanship he was himself again 'The finest stroke in his speech was his
appeal, not to the people of England who had reaped
the benefit of the King's wise counsels and vigorous
measures, but to those who had received detriment
from them—France and Spain; that thought he worked
up like an orator.'[1] But France and Spain would not
listen

<hr>

Yorke's Parliamentary MS

U

These first two debates were closely followed by many others which were little more than variations on the same theme. Sandwich on one of these occasions declared that he would bring this subject of Hanover before the House of Lords in as many different shapes as Proteus could assume ; and that is really what the opposition did   It was in vain for the Government to defeat its enemies and fancy the thing was ended ; the discomfited opposition easily wriggled out of the Government's grasp, and instantly appeared again in an irritating novelty of form.   And the opposition could not, in any of its Protean disguises, refrain from attacking Carteret.   When the House of Commons had decided that the Hanoverian troops should be continued in British pay, the faction of defeated discontent ventured to demand that England should not continue the war unless she was immediately joined by the Dutch.   Pitt was not very zealous to push opposition so far as this, though he supported the proposal in a half-hearted way ; but he was far from being half-hearted in the language of his personal attack.   He styled Carteret a 'desperate rhodomontading minister,' and solemnly asserted that for the last six months the little finger of one man had lain more heavily upon the nation than the loins of an administration which had existed for twenty years.   Bubb Dodington, whose name is synonymous with political infamy, declared that Carteret was endeavouring to make himself despotic with the King, and the King despotic with the country.   The opposition was easily delivered to defeat and ridicule over its senseless proposal to make English action dependent on what it might please the Dutch to do ; but still the infatuated attacks were continued.   Pitt declined to aid the more headlong spirits who wished, by refusing supplies for the British troops in Flanders, to make a campaign in 1744 impossible; but he amply made up for this reticence by his violence against the renewed English payment of the Hanoverian soldiers The opposition had made artful use of this unpopular proposal, and knew that everything Hanoverian excited passionate feeling in the country. Carteret had already received a threatening letter from 'Wat Tyler,' to tell him that three hundred men had sworn to tear him limb from limb if he should propose to continue the Hanoverian troops in British pay. With one exception, the ministry wavered, frightened by the noisy outcry; but the exception was an important one, for it was Carteret himself. All but Carteret despaired of success. The others would have dropped the measure; but that was not Carteret's way. He received, too, effective aid from one who for twenty years back had met him with nothing but opposition. Orford, who had now little more than a year to live, left his retreat at Houghton, and warmly urged his friends in London to assist the Government on this point It was not from any love to Carteret; but rather from statesmanlike feeling and personal regard for the King whom he had served so long. His help was undoubtedly effective; his son, Horace, in his exaggerating way, writes that but for Lord Orford the Hanoverian troops would have been lost. Horace himself spoke in favour of the Government, and gained much approval for his elegant eloquence. But the dainty phrases of this amateur dabbler in politics were followed by work of a much rougher kind One member openly attacked the King by name, and threw the House into such confusion that it was compared to nothing better than a tumultuous Polish Diet. Pitt spoke to the passions; above all, to the personal passions He very adroitly flattered the

Pelhams, whom it pleased him to call the 'amiable' part of the administration; against the odious part he exhausted abusive invective. Carteret was the 'Hanover troop minister, a flagitious task-master'; the 16,000 Hanoverian soldiers were his placemen and the only party he had. Pitt wished that Carteret sat in the House of Commons, that he might give him more of his angry eloquence 'But I have done; if he were present, I would say ten times more.'[1] On the second day of the debate, Pitt abandoned the vocabulary of insult for a picturesque despair; and said, as if he really believed it, that to pay the Hanoverian soldiers would be to erect a triumphal arch to Hanover over the military honour and independence of Great Britain. But common-sense got the better of party passion. To dismiss 22,000 men without knowing how to replace them was too absurd; to have refused from Hanover a benefit which would have been gladly accepted from any other quarter would have been the triumph of pettish senselessness The Government majority was large; yet Proteus only took another shape.

But in the midst of all this angry rhetoric, there came an alarm which for the moment quieted party faction While Chesterfield was sneeringly lamenting that the Crown of three Kingdoms was shrivelled beneath an Electoral cap, and, in his exquisitely refined way, was declaring that Carteret, by laying the Treaty of Worms before parliament, had at last 'voided his worms';[2] while Pitt was violently perorating on the minister's 'audacious hand,' and dimly hinting at an impeachment; and while Carteret, fearlessly defending

---

[1] H. Walpole to Mann, Jan. 24, 1744.

[2] This is in Yorke's *Journal*, but the Parliamentary History is too polite to publish it It is in Add MSS 9,198 fol 66 v°

his own policy, was asserting that discontents had been roused by wicked and groundless misrepresentations, news came to London that France and the Young Pretender together were about to attempt a descent on the English coast.

Not very much in the military way had been done after the battle of Dettingen Louis XV., his enterprises having so thoroughly failed, withdrew his troops from Germany, and in little more than a month after the battle was applying to the Diet at Frankfort for a restoration of peace. The Queen of Hungary's response was very high and scornful. Compensation for her lost Silesia was with her a fixed idea ; why should not the compensation come from France, if it were impossible to get it from other quarters? While George was resting at Hanau, and Carteret was planning treaties for Newcastle to ruin, the King and the minister were visited by Maria's brother-in-law Prince Charles and the Austrian General Khevenhuller, full of schemes and proposals for following up the victory and invading France itself. In August 1743 it was rumoured everywhere in London that at a grand Hanau entertainment, at which Prince Charles was present, Carteret had proposed as a toast, *Dunkirk, Lorraine, and Alsace.* But nothing came of all these hopes and plans, that year. The English army went into winter quarters in the Netherlands ; and though Prince Charles tried in various places to make his way across the frontier into Alsace, he never could He too went home in October 1743, and nothing remained settled but that the fighting must begin again next season.

France, seeing the haughty way in which her proposals had been rejected, quite gave up the peace view, and made great preparations for the new campaign.

The French plans seemed especially to threaten the frontier towards the Netherlands; and Carteret, who had lost no courage under the unscrupulous attacks of political enemies, remained true to his undeviating line of foreign policy. On December 30 he wrote to the English minister at the Hague :—

'The first plan of France was, under pretence of sustaining the Elector of Bavaria, to ruin the House of Austria. To come at that, they were willing to forfeit their faith and reputation They have received a check in that design, have squandered immense sums ineffectually, and lost whole armies in the prosecution of it. These disappointments they impute to his majesty and the States, and there is no doubt but they meditate the severest revenge, and will not fail to take it, if we have not, under the blessing of God, recourse to the forces He has given us for our security, and for reducing that ambitious power within its true bounds.'

Carteret therefore urged Holland, for its own sake, to put an end to parsimony and pusillanimity, and to join heartily with England in a determination to convince France 'that we are not to be terrified into any base submission to her will, but that, as our only object is a fair and honourable peace, we are not afraid of contending for it by a just and vigorous war.'

So far, neither France nor England had been a principal in this war. England was only the ally of Austria, France, the ally of Bavaria. But the whole tendency of things had necessarily been drawing the two powers into direct personal antagonism; and the action of France in the first weeks of 1744 was the prelude to the open declaration of war. In January, George was informed that the Old Pretender's son had left Rome for Paris, under pretence of sharing in a hunting-party It was known that France had been equipping a fleet at Brest; it was rumoured that the Young Pretender was about to join it The excitement in London was considerable; the ministry met frequently; officers everywhere were ordered to their posts. In February the Brest squadron sailed; some twenty men-of-war, followed soon by four others They entered the Channel on February 14, and reached Dungeness early in March, anchoring there while Comte de Saxe was busily putting 15,000 men on board transports at Dunkirk. Timid persons feared the French might quickly push up the river as the Dutch had done in 1667, and march direct on London But Admiral Norris, with a larger fleet than the French one, sailed round the South Foreland to meet them. On March 5 Norris, off Folkestone, was in sight of the enemy at Dungeness; the Kentish cliffs were crowded with gazing watchers eager to see the engagement. Fortunately or otherwise, they were disappointed. That same evening a storm began, raging all through the night; and the planned invasion was ruined without any fighting whatever. The French fleet was driven from its Dungeness anchorage, leaving anchors and cables behind it; Saxe's transports never ventured out of Dunkirk roads.

Declaration of war by France against England soon followed this abortive attempt; the French manifesto being characterised by Carteret as ' an insolent and impudent production, which contains, with regard to the views and conduct of France, a barefaced mockery and imposition upon the common-sense of mankind, and, with regard to those of his majesty, is full of misrepresentations and falsehoods.' England replied with a counter-declaration. Stair, forgetting old grievances, had already left his ' plough,' and, with much royal apprecia-

tion of his loyalty, had become Commander of the troops
at home. The English army in Flanders was recruited ;
the Dutch troops, due by treaty to England in case
of an invasion, began to arrive in the river   George
sacrificed his usual visit to Hanover ; the parliament
did what was necessary in the way of supplies ; and Carteret, who was suffering from the universal malady of
eighteenth-century statesmen, had lost nothing of his
cheerfulness through illness.   'I have neither speech
nor motion,' he wrote to Lord Chancellor Hardwicke
on the day after the English declaration of war, 'leaving
what I had with Lord Bath.   My gout is not gone off,
but I am in good spirits.'[1]

'I am in good spirits.' This was only another way
of saying : 'I am Lord Carteret.'   But Carteret's good
spirits did not rest upon a false feeling of security, or
upon any ignorance of the circumstances which were
personally threatening him   Carteret knew perfectly
well that his position as a minister was at this time pre-
carious. The imperfect cohesion of the mixed Government which had succeeded Walpole's had been a cause
of difficulty and weakness from the very first ; in 1744
the split had become too wide to be bridged over
While England and France were declaring war against
each other, the members of the English Cabinet were
declaring war among themselves. Newcastle, one of
whose detestable peculiarities was to treat all political
differences from the personal point of view (declining
private intercourse even with his brother when they
were not wholly agreed on political action), could not at
this time meet Carteret at dinner. The Duke D'Ahremberg was in London in March ; but Carteret could not
go to the entertainments which the Pelhams gave him.

[1] Harris' *Hardwicke*, II. 65.   April 12, 1744.

It was impossible to be blind to the real meaning of all this. Government on such conditions could not last. Carteret, who had a way of putting his meaning into words too plain to be mistaken, told the brothers that they might take the Government themselves if they pleased ; but that if they either could not or would not, he himself would take it. 'There is anarchy,' he said to them, 'in Holland, and anarchy at home. The first may be removed by a Stadt-holder ; but to remove the latter things must be brought to an immediate decision ' A letter from Newcastle to Hardwicke shows how plainly Carteret spoke, and how irreconcilable the difference was :—

'I had a very extraordinary conversation with my Lord Carteret, going with him yesterday to Kensington ; which, with the late incidents that have passed between us, produced a more extraordinary declaration from him to my brother and me last night. He said, that if my Lord Harrington had not been gone, he intended to have spoke very fully to us ; that he would do it when your Lordship, Lord Harrington, and we should be together ; that things could not remain as they were ; that they must be brought to some precision ; he would not be brought down to be overruled and outvoted upon every point by four to one ; if we would take the Government upon us, we might , but if we could not or would not undertake it, there must be some direction, and he would do it. Much was said upon what had passed last year, upon the probability of the King's going abroad, etc. Everything passed coolly and civilly, but pretty resolutely, upon both sides. At last he seemed to return to his usual profession and submission.

'Upon this, my brother and I thought it absolutely necessary that we should immediately determine

amongst ourselves what party to take ; and he has
therefore desired me to see your Lordship, and talk it
over with you in the course of this day. We both look
upon it, that either my Lord Carteret will go out (which
I hardly think is his scheme, or at least his inclination),
or that he will be uncontrollable master My brother
supposes that, in that case, he means that we should go
out. I rather think he may still flatter himself that
(after having had this offer made to us, and our having
declined to take the Government upon ourselves) we
shall be contented to act a subordinate part. Upon the
whole, I think the event must be, that we must either
take upon us the Government, or go out.'[1]

Not to 'go out,' if in any way he could possibly
stay in, was the one principle to which Newcastle was
constant throughout his long parliamentary career.
From this point, therefore, his vague jealousy and dislike of Carteret changed into a firm determination to
get rid of him. Newcastle's letters to Hardwicke,
without whom he could do nothing but bribe and be
ridiculous, are full of it. It was his element ; he could
feel that he was in reality engaged in politics when he
was intriguing against a colleague He had intrigued
against Walpole ; he had attempted to intrigue with
Pulteney ; he was now intriguing against Carteret, in
the coming years he was to intrigue against Pitt and
Fox Craggs once said that a Secretary of State might
be honest for a fortnight, but could not possibly continue such conduct for a month. Newcastle never tried
it even for the fortnight

The plot against Carteret was to succeed, but only
after long and difficult operations The outbreak of
the war with France was itself slightly in Carteret's

[1] June 6, 1744

favour. There were onlookers who reckoned that his knowledge of foreign affairs would make his continuance in power necessary, and that the Pelhams would have to yield to his superiority. His position was strengthened by the failure of the French invasion, and by the expectation of a successful campaign. But this expectation went all to ruin. It had been first intended that the King himself should go to Flanders; but Newcastle and his party declared that if that were so they would all resign, and the plan had to be abandoned.[1] The English commander was therefore Marshal Wade; with him was the Austrian D'Ahremberg; both of them terribly incompetent persons, especially when a Marshal Saxe was opposed to them. Whilst Wade looked on, his army doing literally nothing, Louis the Well-beloved and his generals were proceeding much as they pleased in the Netherlands, town after town yielding easily to their success. The only check which somewhat interrupted the victorious progress of France came from quite a different quarter. Prince Charles, Maria Theresa's brother-in-law, had been unable last year to invade France after Dettingen; but in this new campaign he was trying it again, and on the last day of June 1744 actually succeeded in crossing the Rhine into Alsace. Louis at once ended his ornamental patronage of his army in Flanders: left to Saxe the easy task of looking after Wade; and himself hastened to Metz, to terrify adoring France by his illness there, and to adopt the religious view till his recovery was complete. Could not old Wade in this altered state of things now do something? There were difficulties; he and D'Ahremberg were not on the best of terms; the Dutch were as usual demonstrating their indisputable pre-eminence

---

[1] Historical MSS. Commission. Report III 278.

in phlegmatic sluggishness; the French were perhaps somewhat superior in numbers. But Wade himself was probably the chief difficulty of all. He was suspected of leaning to the Pelham side of the administration, and of showing no great anxiety to carry out the instructions which he received from Carteret; while in military matters he was quite incompetent. 'He is old and quite broke,' wrote the Earl of Bentinck from the Hague; 'so that when he has been four hours a-horseback, he wants two days to recover the fatigue.'[1] Wade might have been a match for Sir John Cope; opposed to Saxe he was merely a comic figure. He did, indeed, with his Austrian and Dutch allies, continue to hold war councils that came to no decision, and to make confused military movements that resulted in no action; more than that he did not do. When the campaign closed, the English and their allies had done absolutely nothing; they had simply stood by to see the French win. 'The ever-memorable campaign of 1744 is now closed in Flanders,' wrote Trevor from the Hague in October. 'What posterity or the parliament will say of it, the Lord knows'

Thus the expectation that Carteret's position at home would be strengthened by a successful campaign abroad was completely falsified. The only thing worth calling a success in the whole continental struggle was the defeat of Frederick of Prussia's first expedition in the second Silesian war; and in that success England had no share. Frederick, clearly seeing that in Maria's haughty humour he was by no means yet secure in his hold on Silesia, had again allied himself with France, and in August, greatly to the disturbance of the English King, had struck into the quarrel once more 'I wish

---

[1] Brit Mus Egerton MSS 1,713, fol 61 v°.

he was Cham of Tartary!' said passionate little George
once to Chesterfield of his incomprehensible cousin.
This sudden diversion compelled Prince Charles to withdraw from Alsace, and Frederick, beginning brilliantly,
took Prag; but there all his success ended. The Austrians, trusting to weather and famine to do their
business, would not fight him; and Frederick, baffled,
could do nothing but retreat to Silesia, while his garrison
withdrew from the one place that he had captured
This, a success for the cause which England was supporting, was not a success of which England in any
direct way could adopt the credit; and, even if it had
been so, it would have come too late to affect appreci-
ably the course of ministerial dissensions in London.
The date of Carteret's fall was coincident with that
of Frederick's failure.

By the summer months of 1744 it had become clear
that the Government as it stood could not expect to
meet the new session of parliament. There was now
hardly even the pretence of union between the new
and the old elements in the ministry which Carteret
directed. The political intriguing of the Pelhams had
easily reinforced itself by the deliberate employment of
unbounded public misrepresentation. Everything that
had failed at home or abroad was laid to the charge of
Carteret. It was Carteret's fault that Prussia had once
more struck into the war, Carteret's fault that Wade
was old and imbecile, and the Dutch the heaviest and
slowest mortals in Europe. The old falsehoods were
eagerly brought out once again, and Carteret was
accused of grasping at despotism, and of prolonging the
war for the ends of his own selfish ambition Carteret,
on his side, imprudently perhaps but very naturally,
did not care to conceal his contempt for Newcastle,

and made no mock professions of confidence in other
colleagues who were almost ostentatiously conspiring
against him. Carteret knew that the Pelhams were toiling
and plotting to remove him; but he was not disheartened,
and not at all inclined to yield without a struggle. He
had the King strongly on his side; and this more than
anything vexed the souls of his rivals; for never had
George's disgust with them been so angrily evident as
now   The King did not attempt to conceal it; his personal friend, Lord Waldegrave, says that his countenance
could not dissemble. Newcastle bitterly complains of
the King's manner, looks, and harsh expressions; it
added to the Duke's anguish that he received this treatment in the presence of Carteret himself. He tells his
brother that they and their friends must compel the
King to choose between Carteret and themselves, or
Newcastle must despairingly resign. 'If nothing of the
kind can be agreed upon, I must, and am determined to
let the King know, that my having had the misfortune
to differ in some points from Lord Carteret had, I found,
made me so disagreeable to his majesty, that, out of
duty to him and regard to myself, I must desire his
leave to resign his employment; for, indeed, no man can
bear long what I go through every day, in our joint
audiences in the closet '[1]

Pelham was not much happier   He replies to his
brother next day: 'I was at Court to-day, and designed
to have gone in to the King, after the drawing-room was
over, but as Lord Carteret went in, and as I saw
nothing particular in his majesty's countenance to make
me over-forward, I chose to put it off till to-morrow.'
'To-morrow' was doubtless just as unpleasant as 'to-
day' could have been. Disagreeable incidents, as

---

[1] Newcastle to Pelham, August 25, 1744.

Newcastle mildly termed them, occurred daily; much to the intriguer's distress, who was alarmed at the King's contemptuous indifference George was simply slighting him; and it was dangerous to let the King adopt the notion that from the Pelhams there was nothing to be hoped and nothing to be feared. The brothers, therefore, having failed so far in all their attempts, now turned to more decisive measures They appealed to the leading Whigs in opposition, to Pitt, Chesterfield, Lyttelton, and the others, to join them; and these, after very slight delay, unreservedly agreed. Then the final step was taken. Hardwicke, at Newcastle's request, drew up a long Memorial, denouncing Carteret's conduct and policy. The Pelham party resolved to present this document to the King, and to give him the option between Carteret's dismissal and their own resignations

On November 1, 1744, Newcastle handed the Memorial to the King. In little more than an hour George returned it to Newcastle House. He was not disposed to yield. On November 3, Carteret and Newcastle were with the King together, and Carteret after the audience was for five minutes alone with George. Newcastle concluded that in this private interview the King told Carteret of the Pelhams' accusations and demands, ' probably with assurances of his support, and recommending management and some compliance to Lord Granville [1] I conclude this day the scheme of conduct will be settled between the King and Lord Granville, which will, I believe, be what I always foresaw : a seeming acquiescence, depending upon Lord

---

[1] By the death of his mother, Carteret became Earl Granville on October 18, 1744 Till the close of this chapter, it will be more convenient to continue to speak of him as Lord Carteret.

Granville's *savoir* to defeat it afterwards, and draw us
on. This is what I most dread; and I own I think
nothing will prevent it but a concert *entamé*, in a proper
manner, directly with Lord Chesterfield.'[1] Pelham and
Hardwicke asked audiences to enforce their written
arguments, but were received with unconcealed ill-
humour. To Hardwicke the King expressed his great
regard for Carteret, and declared . ' You would persuade
me to abandon my allies; that shall never be the
obloquy of my reign, as it was of Queen Anne's; I will
suffer any extremities rather than consent.' George
was no more inclined to abandon his minister than to
abandon his allies Carteret had served him well;
ingratitude was not among the King s many faults and
failings. Both he and the Prince of Wales made every
effort to spoil the Pelhams' plot. The Prince had
already tried to mediate between the rival ministers;
but that was plainly hopeless. He then attempted to
gain over to Carteret's side the leading Whigs in opposition. Here again he failed, for the Pelhams had been
before him. Yet Carteret still continued minister; and
Newcastle, slipping away from the bold words of the
Memorial, became once more all timid anxiety. He
began to speculate. Might not Carteret still remain
in the Government, but in a less commanding position?
Without a glimpse of insight into his colleague's character, Newcastle was inclining to fear that Carteret, if
dismissed, would throw himself into violent opposition;
and with equal obtuseness he suggested that Carteret
might be induced to remain in the ministry if he were
made Lord President, and had the offer of the Garter
But in that case, what would the Walpole section say?
and without them Newcastle had sadly to confess that

[1] Newcastle to Hardwicke , Nov 3, 1744

he and his personal friends could not carry on the Government even if it were put into their hands.

It was to the head of the Walpole party that the King, as a last resource, turned. He summoned Orford from Houghton to London. Orford, reluctantly obeying, arrived only a few days before parliament was to meet, and very unwillingly gave his opinion. It was not in favour of Carteret. Shortly after Carteret's Government had been formed, Orford, referring to a coach accident at Richmond which had been amusing the political world, said to Carteret in the hearing of the King and Newcastle. 'My Lord, whenever the Duke is near overturning you, you have nothing to do but to send to me, and I will save you.' The promise was very badly kept, though Carteret doubtless felt little surprise at that. Carteret now could do no more. Parliamentary influence and envious personal passions were united against him, and the King, with great reluctance and ill-humour, agreed that he should resign. On November 24 the Pelhams triumphed, and Carteret ceased to be Secretary of State.

'Who would not laugh at a world where so ridiculous a creature as the Duke of Newcastle can overturn ministries!' Horace Walpole may laugh ; serious onlookers are likely to consider contemptuous disgust the more appropriate feeling. The history of the rise and fall of ministers ought to be the favourite reading of the cynical ; and their favourite episode ought to be the triumph of Newcastle over Carteret. Corruption, treachery, and imbecility triumphed over patriotism and genius. The thing was so false and shameless that it has extorted angry protests from observers who are in no danger of being styled sentimentalists. 'It is difficult to .. him "Carteret" made the victim of so contemptible an intrigue, without feeling some motions of sympathy and indignation.'[1]　The fawning falseness of the Duke of Newcastle is the fitting centre of one of the most disgraceful episodes in the history of political intrigue.

[1] William Godwin's *Life of Pitt*, 34, 35

CHAPTER VIII.

GRANVILLE AND THE PELHAMS.

1744–1754

RATHER more than a month before his fall, Lord Carteret had become Earl Granville. His mother, Countess of Granville in her own right, died on October 18, 1744; her son succeeded her in the title

When the session opened on November 27, the parliamentary scene was very chaotic So difficult had been the Pelhams' task, that Granville had been removed only three days before, and in that short interval the brothers had already discovered that the fall of their rival was by no means the end of their troubles and dangers. 'The King,' Horace Walpole reported to his Florence friend, 'has declared that my Lord Granville has his opinion and affection; the Prince warmly and openly espouses him. Judge how agreeably the two brothers will enjoy their ministry ! To-morrow the parliament meets: all is suspense ! Everybody will be staring at each other !' A first difficulty embarrassed the Pelhams when they attempted to satisfy the heterogeneous mass of politicians who had helped them to get rid of Granville The discontented Whigs, represented by Chesterfield, had joined in the intrigue ; and Pitt, whose early political career is not at all edifying, had concurred. Tories also had been of the number, and all looked for

their reward With a kind of timid hopefulness the
brothers therefore thought to strengthen themselves
against Granville, of whom they still stood in great
fear, by forming a mixed Government chosen from each
of the political parties; a Government which the cant
phrase of the day denominated Broad Bottom The
arrangement was not altogether easy. The Whigs
grumbled that there should be any Tories at all; the
Tories grumbled that they themselves were so few
But a second difficulty hampered the negotiations still
more. The King was full of passionate resentment at
the way in which the Pelhams and their friends had
treated him; and he was especially angry with Newcastle, whom he truly enough styled a jealous puppy,
unfit to be leading minister. He showed his irritated
annoyance by violent opposition to many of the intended
changes When Chesterfield was proposed to him as
Lord-Lieutenant of Ireland, the King burst out, ' He
shall have nothing I command you to trouble me no
more with such nonsense. Although I have been forced
to part with those I liked, I will never be induced to
take those who are disagreeable to me.' Royally angry
as he was, George in this instance had to yield, and
Chesterfield, commissioned with an embassy to the Hague
before going to Dublin, received a parting audience of
less than one minute But as for Pitt, who had excelled all in the unrestrained bitterness of party violence,
the King declined altogether; and Pitt's claim for the
present was not pushed. So troublesome were these
various disputes and differences that it was close upon
Christmas before the ministerial changes were completed.
Henry Pelham was Prime Minister, Newcastle, probably
still believing that Hanover was in Scotland, became on
this occasion Secretary for the South where there was

a fresh geographical field to conquer Harrington took
the Northern department, as it was desirable that at
least one of the Foreign Secretaries should know something about foreign affairs.   Hardwicke remained Lord
Chancellor ; Chesterfield went to Ireland ; other places
were filled by Bedford, Grafton, Gower, and Henry
Fox.

The Duke of Newcastle, who had thus had his way
and set himself with appalling self-satisfaction to the
considerable task of governing England, is the most curiously ridiculous being who ever took a leading part in
English political affairs Merely to set eyes upon the man,
to hear him talk, to see him move, gave one an irresistible
sense of the ridiculous He never walked, but shuffled
along with a hasty trot, in a constantly confused and
bustling hurry. His talk was a bubbling stammer which
added the most ludicrous emphasis to the chaotic medley
of his private conversation. His public speaking was
equally absurd He could not reason ; he rambled in-
conclusively through all the intricacies of his subject,
perpetually contradicting himself, yet quite unconscious
of his own imbecility. Hervey says that those for whom
he spoke generally wished that he had been silent, and
those who listened wished so always. The fussy, untidy
hurry that marked his talk was equally conspicuous in
his way of doing business The town said of him that
he lost half an hour every morning, and ran about all
the rest of the day unsuccessfully trying to overtake it.
He was full of agitated eagerness to plunge into political
business of all kinds, and when he had got it he did
not know how to do it Meddling with everything, he
fretted and tormented himself about everything. His
jealous imagination perpetually fancied and brooded
over slights which had absolutely no existence, and then

he became peevish and miserable and quarrelsome. As
suddenly he would be all emotional and maudlin friendliness again, and flatter while he feared In a letter of
his own in which he rather curiously says, 'I am not
vain of my abilities,' he remarks of himself. 'My temper
is such that I am often uneasy and peevish, and perhaps
what may be called wrong-headed, to my best friends,
but that always goes down with the sun, and passes off
as if nothing had happened.'[1] It is true he was not
naturally a bad-tempered man, and he profusely prac-
tised the easy virtue of being abundantly good-natured
whenever he had his own way.

Newcastle's foolishness was only equalled by his
falseness. It was part of the fidgety hurry of his
character that with flurried effusiveness he scattered
promises right and left ; and he never kept any of them.
But more serious than the falseness of hastily stuttered
assurances was his persistent and invincible treachery
to his own political colleagues. His word, spoken or
written, could never be believed. Walpole said that his
name was Perfidy, and Pitt plainly called him 'a very
great liar.' His life was one long intrigue ; and falseness to every one who met him on the political road was
the sole principle to which he was unswervingly consistent The history of his political treachery is the
story of his political life His boldness in underhand
intrigue was in singular contrast with his excessive
political and personal timidity. The Duchess of Yarmouth once told him that he had been brought up in
the fear of God and of his brother When Chesterfield
introduced his bill for the amendment of the Calendar,
Newcastle was much alarmed at such daring reform
He did not like new-fangled things, he said, and im-

[1] Brit Mus Add. MSS 9.175 fol. 77-79. Oct 14 1739

plored Chesterfield to leave it alone. He was afraid to
sleep in a bedroom by himself, and would rather have a
footman lying on a pallet beside him than be solitary
for the night. He looked ready to drop with fear on
his first interview with George II., for he had once
offended the Prince of Wales, who now was King ; the
passionate little Prince had fiercely trodden on his toe
and had roared. ' You rascal, I will find you ! ' The
town, to whom the ludicrous Duke was a perpetual fund
of amusement, declared that while the rebels were
marching south in 1745, Newcastle tremblingly shut
himself up in his room for a whole day, reflecting
whether he had not better declare for the Pretender
He was never out of England till he was about sixty,
and then was much distressed at the thought of the
Channel crossing Once when attending the King to
Hanover he would only venture over in a yacht that
had recently weathered a heavy storm But his timidity
took its most amusing form in his apprehensive anxiety
for his health. Even those who flattered him made a
jest of his frightened precautions and his troops of
physicians and apothecaries. A guest at Claremont
once felt somewhat unwell after eating a few mushrooms. Newcastle immediately ordered that all the
mushroom-beds at Claremont should be destroyed He
passed his life in the constant fear of catching cold
Often in the heat of summer, says Waldegrave, ' the
debates in the House of Lords would stand still, till
some window were shut, in consequence of the Duke's
orders The peers would all be melting in sweat, that
the Duke might not catch cold.' He coddled himself
everywhere and in everything When he had conquered his fear of the Channel so far as to attend the
King to Hanover, he pestered those who were to be his

hosts on the route with the most elaborate directions
for his domestic security. While he was Secretary of
State and leader of the Government in the House of
Lords, he found time to write in his own hand letters of
most minute instruction on this absorbing topic The
curious can still consult his manuscripts. He bids the
English minister at the Hague taste wines for him ; buy
a carriage for him, and be sure that the seats are
quilted ; actually sends him patterns of cloth for the
lining, and implores him to look anxiously to the linch-
pins and have plenty of spare tackle lest anything should
break He does not leave all this to servants or secretaries, or to the female portion of his household, but
does it all at vast length with his own ministerial hand
Above all he never forgets the airing of the beds. 'I
beg that they may be lain in every night for a month,'
he writes once when announcing an approaching visit
to the Hague. 'Pray let the beds be laid (*sic*) in from
the time you receive this letter,' he says on another
occasion. To get his feet wet, or even cold, was mar-
tyrdom to him In the Abbey, at the funeral of George
II , the Duke of Cumberland suddenly felt himself
weighed down from behind It was Newcastle, who
had stepped upon his train to avoid the chilliness of the
marble floor Horace Walpole saw Newcastle, then
actually Prime Minister himself, at a ball in 1759, and
wrote to Montagu .—

'He went into the hazard-room, and wriggled, and
shuffled, and lisped, and winked, and spied . Nobody
went near him , he tried to flatter people that were too
busy to mind him ; in short, he was quite disconcerted ;
his treachery used to be so sheathed in folly that he
was never out of countenance , but it is plain he grows
old To finish his confusion and anxiety, George Selwyn,

Brand, and I went and stood near him, and in half whispers, that he might hear, said, " Lord ! how he is broke ! how old he looks! ' Then I said, "This room feels very cold : I believe there never is a fire in it " Presently afterwards I said, "Well, I'll not stay here ; this room has been washed to-day " In short, I believe we made him take a double dose of Gascoigne's powder when he went home '

The dreary tract of history presided over by this ridiculous yet cunningly treacherous being did not open very brilliantly for the new ministry. The King made no attempt to conceal his displeasure, and treated his advisers very badly In little more than a month after Granville's fall, Newcastle was speculating on the probable date of his own dismissal ; and Hardwicke, when in an audience he begged the King for support and confidence, could not for some time obtain a word in reply The royal favour was reserved entirely for Granville and his friends. And public affairs did not go well It was professedly on account of his foreign policy that the Pelhams had conspired against Granville, yet the first act of the reconstituted ministry declared that there would be no alteration in foreign measures The cry was soon raised that though ministers had turned Granville out they were simply continuing Granville's policy, and Newcastle recognised the truth and the danger of the accusation when he wrote to his brother : ' We must not, because we *seem* to be in, forget all we said to keep Lord Granville out ' When on February 5, 1745, the Government proposed that the English troops in Flanders should be continued during that year, their adversaries declared that this was merely an old measure from a new ministry ; but Pelham found an enthusiastic supporter in Pitt He was very ill, came down to the

House with the mien and apparatus of an invalid;[1] some even thought he could not live long, and in his speech he spoke of himself as a dying man   But he used abundant gesture and rhetoric, and his eloquence bore down all opposition   He professed to believe that the whole question in 1745 differed from the question as it stood the year before; for Granville had fallen, and all romantic attempts to assist Austria in the recovery of what Pitt called the *avulsa membra Imperii* had fallen with him.   In other words, Pitt in his rhetorical way accused Granville of having directed his foreign policy towards the recovery of Silesia for Maria Theresa; a ridiculously untrue accusation against the chief agent in obtaining the Treaty of Breslau.   'The object now is,' said Pitt, ' to enable ourselves, by a close connection with Holland, to hold out equitable terms of peace both to friends and foes, without prosecuting the war a moment longer than is necessary to acquire a valid security for our own rights and those of our allies, as established by public treaties'   What else at any time had been Granville's object?   But the necessities of party politics are stern.

Pitt did not fail to flavour his compliments to Pelham with invective of the usual style against Granville.   The policy sanctioned by the 'rash hand of a daring minister ' was reproachfully contrasted with the moderate and healing measures of the new patriotic administration   A brightening dawn of national salvation had at last met Pitt's patriotically straining eyes, and he would follow it as far as it would lead him.   It first of all led him into a position where a statesman with the most rudimentary respect for consistency might have felt very uncomfortable   On no subject had Pitt so lavished his scornful rhetoric as on the connection between England and

[1] Yorke's Parliamentary Journal

Hanover, and nothing had more scandalised his eloquent
patriotism than the English payment of Hanoverian
soldiers. How bitterly he had upbraided Granville for
this, and how his prophetic soul had been vexed by
visions of the degradation of England before a petty
Teutonic province! Yet now, when the Pelhams, fearful
of seeming to continue everything which Granville had
done, with dull timidity proposed a juggle by which
England, while appearing no longer to pay these troops,
should really continue to do so, Pitt at once supported
them with strong approval. An annual subsidy of
300,000*l.* had been voted to Maria Theresa since the
beginning of the war. Pelham now proposed that the
Queen should receive 500,000*l.*, and it was perfectly well
understood that with the difference she was to support
the Hanoverian troops which the English Government
thereupon magnanimously resigned. Nobody was deceived; England was simply paying with the left hand
instead of with the right. Ministers of course descanted,
with all the solemnity of augurs, on the paternal regard
of his majesty and the benevolent royal desire to put an
end to jealousies and heart-burnings. Augurs have to
talk like that. But Pitt also, who was free from any official
obligation, eulogised the wisdom and goodness of the
Prince who had so graciously condescended to accept
what was a mere sham and subterfuge; and, when he
was attacked for his shameless inconsistency, he could
only fall back on the pleasant and convenient desire
that all that had previously passed on this question
might be buried in oblivion. The equivocal arrangement proposed by the Government was agreed to,
but it was easy for Granville's friends to make some
very telling observations. The Pelham section of the
administration had only last year strongly approved of

paying the Hanoverians, yet now they were making a virtue of seeming to dismiss them, the Pitt section had seemed to consider the very personal existence of these men on the face of the earth as a national grievance; yet now they were voting English money to support them. The whole transaction placed the ministry in so bad a light that it was reckoned that Granville, if he had chosen to show any resentment, could have taken almost any revenge he pleased

Granville did not interpose, and the Pelhams passed through the rest of the parliamentary session with but little trouble. But the King's displeasure with them was not lessened, and the events of the year 1745 were not of a kind to strengthen their Government Foreign affairs had at first seemed in a hopeful way, Frederick's failure in Bohemia had raised Austrian expectations; and, on January 20, the death of the Emperor Charles VII. broke the union between France and Bavaria. The new Bavarian Elector came to terms with Maria Theresa, and sanguine observers hoped that this fortunate peace might be the forerunner of a general one. Far from it. The war still went on in its double fashion; England against France in the Netherlands, Frederick against Austria in Germany, rather like two separate wars than the co-operation of allies And England was fortunate nowhere. The Duke of Cumberland had gone to the Hague in high spirits, to put himself at the head of the allied army, but Saxe beat him at Fontenoy, and town after town fell into the hands of the French Austria fared just as badly. In battle after battle Frederick was victorious; and one week before the close of the year Maria Theresa was compelled to yield, and to confirm to Prussia the cession of Silesia.

This state of things was sufficiently disgusting to

George, and he reckoned his ministers mainly responsible for his misfortunes. The grand improvement in home and foreign affairs which was to result from the dismissal of Granville had certainly nowhere appeared. The King accused Newcastle of having cheated and deceived him, and threw the Duke into deep distress When parliament ended in May 1745, Newcastle and his allies told George that if he persisted in using them so badly they could not face another session But George took no notice, and went off to Hanover with Harrington, whom he did not yet hate more than all the other ministers together. When the King returned, his ill-humour increased. In September 1745 Newcastle wrote to the Duke of Richmond that the administration had no power ; that the King would hardly vouchsafe to them a word on business, that he used bad language to them in their private interviews, telling Pelham further that he was incapable and a mere looker-on at other men's policy, and roundly calling his advisers ' pitiful fellows.'[1] While the Government was in this wretched situation at home, the French were making unchecked progress in the Netherlands, and urgent appeals for assistance were coming from the Dutch Granville counselled firmness and vigour ; but the Pelhams did little or nothing. They even ventured to choose this period of irritation for a deliberate demand which the King felt intolerable They required that Pitt should be made Secretary at War. The King at first absolutely declined, Pitt, he said, might have any office but that. When the ministers continued their importunities, George bitterly complained that his action was being forced, and he lamented to Lord Bath that he

[1] Historical MSS Commission, Report I 115 MSS of the Duke of Richmond

was not a King but a prisoner   On Bath s advice he
positively refused that special appointment for Pitt, and
Bath admitted to Harrington that the advice was his.
'They who dictate in private should be employed in
public,' dryly replied the Secretary , and though Pitt
gave up his claim, and the Government acquiesced in
the refusal, the Pelhams resolved to give the King a
lesson which he would hardly be likely to forget

On January 17, 1746, Charles Stuart had defeated General Hawley at Falkirk   It was while a
serious rebellion was still successfully fighting against
the sovereign that the responsible ministers of the crown
resolved to resign   There was no question of principle
at issue , while English troops were fighting a Pretender
the Pelhams threw up the Government as a mere speculation in personal and party tactics   They seem to have
persuaded themselves, with good enough reason, that
the King was anxious to get rid of them as soon as
public affairs would allow   They resolved to anticipate
him. Sacrificing every feeling of responsibility and
patriotism to their jealousy of a dreaded rival and to
their determination to let the King feel that they themselves were indispensable, they produced a political crisis
in the midst of a military rebellion   On February 10
their scheme, well calculated with ingenious selfishness,
was started by the resignation of Lord Harrington   He
angered George by the rough indecency of his behaviour.
Instead of returning the purse and seals into the King's
hands, he flung them down on the table and declared
he could no longer serve with honour [1]   Newcastle, who
resigned the same day, managed better with his master.
He himself wrote that in their interview the King was
'very civil, kind enough, and we parted very good

[1] Lord Marchmont's Diary   *Marchmont Papers*, I 182.

friends.' The Government had now lost both its Foreign
Secretaries. Instantly the seals of both departments
were sent to Granville : the one for himself, the other
for whomever he might select   On the very next
day, Granville attended at Court as minister, and despatched a circular to the ministers abroad, informing
them that the King 'has been pleased to appoint me to
resume the place of principal Secretary of State, and
to execute the business of both offices for the present '
Bath was made First Lord of the Treasury ; Granville
and Bath together were to rearrange the dilapidated
administration.

So far well ; but on this same day of Granville's
appointment, Pelham, whom Granville had no wish to
remove from the ministry, also resigned, and was followed
by many other members of the Government   It was
announced that other important resignations would take
place next day   The ingenious scheme of the Pelhams
was thus evident at once.   In order to distress the
King, and to make the formation of a new ministry
impossible, they had induced every important member
of the existing administration, and many who were the
very reverse of important, to follow them into retirement   The success of such well-laid plans could hardly
in any case have been long delayed, though authorities variously estimate the amount of support on which
Granville might have fairly counted. On one event,
however, Granville can hardly have reckoned   On
February 12, Lord Bath, in a fit of frightened irreso-
lution, resigned the office which he had only accepted
the day before.   He had taken Lord Carlisle with
him to Court, to present him as one of the new ministers ; but instead of introducing him to the King, Bath
himself went in about for a private audience, resigned

his own seals, and then 'sneaked down the back-stair, leaving Lord Carlisle kicking his heels at the fire in the outer room'[1] Thus the difficult attempt which, by the King's desire, Granville was making, was practically ruined a few hours after its commencement Horace Walpole gives a lively account of the conclusion of the affair. Lord Bath, says Walpole, in a letter very weak on the grammatical side,

'Went to the King, and told him that he had tried the House of Commons, and found it would not do. Bounce! went all the project into shivers, like the vessels in Ben Jonson's *Alchymist*, when they are on the brink of the philosopher's stone. The poor King, who, from being fatigued with the Duke of Newcastle, and sick of Pelham's timidity and compromises, had given in to this mad hurly-burly of alterations, was confounded with having floundered to no purpose, and to find himself more than ever in the power of men he hated, shut himself up in his closet, and refused to admit any more of the people who were pouring in upon him with white sticks, and golden keys, and commissions, etc. At last he sent for Winnington, and told him he was the only honest man about him, and should have the honour of a reconciliation, and sent him to Mr. Pelham, to desire they would all return to their employments'[2]

It was on February 14, two days after Bath's resignation, that the King was forced to this determination, and on that same day Granville resigned, and Newcastle and Harrington resumed their places Lord Marchmont saw Granville come out from his parting audience with the King. 'He met the Duke of Newcastle going

[1] *Marchmont Papers*, I. 174.
[2] H Walpole to Mann· Feb 14 1746.

in ; and they made each other a dry bow, and passed
on.' That was a curious little scene, full of the sarcasm
of politics The imbecile Duke had once more defeated
the man of genius. It is not probable that on this
particular occasion Granville expected anything else.
In obedience to the King, he had cheerfully made the
attempt ; but he seems to have done it against his own
judgment, and he certainly did not deceive himself
with expectations of success He did not think it
necessary to inform the ambassador at Florence of
his appointment ; before a courier could get there, he
said, he should be out of power again. On a later
occasion he distinctly declared that he was forced into
the thing by Lord Bath,[1] whose own conduct on the
occasion fully justified the nickname of 'weathercock'
Pulteney But it is not necessary to exaggerate the
effect which Bath's fright and betrayal produced on
the new arrangements. It only hastened what could
not in any case have been long in coming Against
the overwhelming parliamentary influence of the Pelhams it was impossible to stand ; and the brothers
knew that they had resigned only to be recalled
They perhaps were not even much surprised that the
summons came to them so very quickly Bath had
been First Lord of the Treasury for one day ; Granville had been Secretary of State for less than four.

To small wits this curious political episode was a
godsend and source of mild rapture Gentle dulness
feared to walk the streets by night, lest it should be
seized by the press-gang and forced into the Cabinet.
In a moment of inspiration it was discovered that the
friends of Granville were Granvillains. Other brillian-
cies, hardly inferior to these, dazzled the political world.

1 Walpole to Mann, June 18, 1746

Y

But the King was not among the laughers. Granville himself took the thing in the most good-humoured way; but George was full of anger and vexation. He asked Bath to write a full account of the way in which his ministers had treated him. 'Rub it in their noses,' he said royally, 'and if it be possible make them ashamed.' To the Duke of Newcastle he called Harrington a rascal; to Harrington he called the Duke a fool. He treated Harrington with special incivility, and never forgot his grudge against him; for he had been the first minister to resign. Four years later, when there was a question of some official appointment for Harrington, the King flew into a rage. 'He said the generalship of marines was to be the reward of everybody who flew in his face: that that was the case of that old rascal Stair that my Lord Harrington should have his ears cut off. . . . At last he said, "He deserves to be hanged; and I am ready to tell him so." '[1] Pelham, not so hardened to abuse as his brother, was soon again threatening resignation. He told the King he would rather Granville should have his place than keep it himself. The retort was obvious. 'You make it impossible for him to have it, and then want me to give it to him.' Gossip of the town did indeed soon point to Granville as destined speedily to be minister again; but the King had received his lesson, and did not forget it. Ministers are the King in this country, he had once said to Lord Chancellor Hardwicke; and he now yielded with angry disgust. 'Go back?—yes, but not without conditions!' Harrington had insisted when the Pelhams resumed their places after Granville's four days. One of the conditions concerned Pitt, and the sure sign of the King's surrender was the admission of Pitt to office   Tears were seen in his eyes when Pitt first appeared in the drawing-room to kiss hands.[1]

For two years more after this short ministerial crisis the war in the Netherlands dragged drearily on under the dull direction of the Pelhams   It was one long story of mismanagement and failure.   During the Scotch rebellion, English help was withdrawn from the Austrians in Flanders, and the French were left to do as they pleased.   Their successes were numerous : nearly all the Austrian Netherlands fell into their hands.   Yet they began to think of peace.   They had lost their Bavarian alliance . they had lost Prussia when Frederick had made peace with Maria Theresa ; they lost active help from Spain by the death of the Spanish King in the summer of 1746.   In these circumstances, a Congress, as futile as those at Cambrai and Soissons, was opened at Breda in September, and sat wearily there till March 1747, when it broke up, having done nothing   The war, with its long list of losses and defeats, continued.   The Pelhams were not happier in their management of their own domestic concerns   Party politics were in a more or less confused condition, and party feeling was running high.   It was in this year 1746 that Gibbon, a schoolboy of nine years old, was in his own words 'reviled and buffeted' because his ancestors had been Tories   The ministers themselves were quarrelling with one another.   Harrington, the one Secretary, very naturally wished to put an end to the war ; Newcastle, the other, terribly anxious to gain the King's personal favour, desired that the wretched military business should continue.   The dispute was only closed by the dismissal of Harrington with a heavy pension ; though in official language he

resigned on account of his age and infirmities. Being
old and infirm, he was naturally made Lord-Lieutenant
of Ireland. On October 29, the day after Harrington's resignation, Chesterfield took the vacant place;
anxiously pressed to accept by Newcastle, who feared
that if he refused the King would again send for Granville Chesterfield accepted, hardly, as he said, knowing
whether he was on his head or his heels; and the
chaotic condition of the ministry became every month
more evident Chesterfield's conversations with Lord
Marchmont give a most curious picture of the way in
which the so-called Government of England conducted
the nation's affairs. The King hated all his advisers;
but, unable to get rid of them, left them to do as they
pleased, bitterly saying that he was not competent to
assist them in cases of difficulty. 'No real business was
done,' said Chesterfield to Marchmont; 'there was no
plan, and, in differences of opinion, the King bid them
do what they thought fit, and continued very indolent,
saying that it signified nothing, as his son, for whom he
did not care a louse, was to succeed him, and would
live long enough to ruin us all; so that there was no
Government at all.' In October 1747 Chesterfield told
Marchmont that he did not know where the Government lived. There was no Government; they met, and
talked, and then said, Lord! it is late, when shall we
meet to talk over this again? In that same month, the
differences between Newcastle and his brother were so
extreme that they could not speak to each other
without falling into a passion, and actually declined to
meet The leader in the House of Commons would not
see the leader in the House of Lords Pelham and
Chesterfield were anxious for peace; Newcastle, not
understanding what he was talking about, urged the

continuance of the war. Before the year was out Chesterfield, disgusted with his personal situation, and declaring that what might become of the other ministers was no business of his, resolved to resign. He did so in February 1748; 'on account of the ill state of his health,' wrote Newcastle with unblushing officialism. The Secretaryships were once more shuffled. Newcastle returned to his old Northern Department, the Duke of Bedford became Secretary for the South.

Chesterfield on resigning had left behind him a protest against the prolongation of the war. But already the war was practically over. The King's speech at the opening of the session in November 1747 had announced, without open sarcasm, the meeting of one more European Congress. This Congress duly commenced to assemble at Aix-la-Chapelle in March 1748, Lord Sandwich being the chief English representative. On the last day of April, England, France, and Holland, finding it impossible to overcome the vexatious delays of Austria and Spain, privately signed preliminaries of peace on their own account, leaving the others to agree at their leisure. Fighting therefore ceased; and on October 18 the definite Treaty of Aix-la-Chapelle was signed by all parties. Thus at length the unfortunate war was over; yet the peace created no enthusiasm, and even little approval, in England. It was evident from the first that the so-called peace was only a temporary arrangement which practically concluded nothing. England had been at war with France and Spain; this fantastic settlement left the leading questions of dispute between the three countries still undecided. The very question which had been the original cause of the war, the Spanish claim of Right of Search, was not even mentioned in the treaty, and while England acquired Cape Breton, nothing was done towards defining an intelligible boundary-line between the English and French possessions in North America. The treaty or armistice of Aix-la-Chapelle left all this in the vague, and was little more than the commencement of a truce which managed to last for eight years.

The political history of England during the two or three years which immediately followed the peace is of the very slightest interest. It is hardly to be called political history at all. Parliament was tranquil and doing nothing; in the session of 1750 the fullest House and largest division were on a disputed turnpike bill. A little languid agitation accompanied the patronage which it pleased the Prince of Wales to give to such mediocre opposition as there was, a Princely patronage from which Granville held quite aloof. Otherwise, the political world found its sole excitement in the personal squabbling of Newcastle with members of his own Government, and in the shifting schemes and combinations with which he was perpetually busied. Having already disgusted and alienated Harrington and Chesterfield, Newcastle was now elaborating a quarrel with the Duke of Bedford. As the Pelham Government originally stood, Bedford had been at the head of the Admiralty. When he was promoted to the Secretaryship of State, his influence secured the Admiralty appointment for his friend Sandwich. The intimacy between Sandwich and Bedford annoyed Newcastle, and the very friendly intercourse of the King's favourite son Cumberland with the Bedford party roused all the Prime Minister's jealous alarm and treacherous timidity. In his usual way he began to scheme for Bedford's removal. He was so frightened and so willing to humiliate himself when-

ever he seemed to see the slightest menace to his own
personal power, that he even attempted to win over
Granville to his side, and in June 1749 offered him the
Lord-Lieutenancy of Ireland; but Granville refused
Having failed here, and finding no success in his schemes
for dismissing his colleague, Newcastle was soon going
through his favourite performance and threatening to
resign The ministers unkindly told him that he might
do as he pleased Of course he did not resign; and in
April 1750, overcoming his dread of the Channel for
the second time in his life, he accompanied the King to
Hanover. From the Hague he poured out his distresses
to his brother :—

'I think it a little hard that the Duke of Cumberland and the Princess Amelia should use me so cruelly
as they have done : excommunicate me from all society,
set a kind of brand or mark upon me and all who think
with me; and set up a new, unknown, factious young
party [Sandwich and Bedford] to rival me, and nose me
everywhere This goes to my heart I am sensible, if
I could have submitted and cringed to such usage, the
public appearances would have been better, and perhaps
some secret stabs have been avoided ; but I was too
proud and too innocent to do it'[1]

How could proud innocence endure the stabbing
and the branding and the nosing any longer? Newcastle accordingly now began to lose and bewilder
himself in a confused medley of ridiculous or impossible
plans. If Bedford could not be got out of the way,
Newcastle would himself cease to be Secretary of State,
and become Lord President Could not Sir Thomas
Robinson, or even Chesterfield, once more take the
seals? Hardwicke immediately informed the Duke that

the ministry would not accept Robinson, and the King
would not accept Chesterfield. Then Newcastle blandly
suggested Granville, and with amusing superciliousness
assured Pelham that Granville would make a very good
Secretary, and would be the greatest conceivable assistance to them in their management of foreign affairs.
Newcastle even professed to be no longer afraid of
Granville. 'My Lord Granville is no more the terrible
man ; *non eadem est ætas, non mens*.' When Pelham,
who probably knew better, replied that if Granville
were made Secretary of State he would himself resign,
Newcastle immediately declared that Granville was of
course out of the question 'I *opiniâtre* nothing,' he
wrote in his terrible jargon to Hardwicke. 'Lord
Granville is dropped ; I will never mention him more'[1]
So schemes were sketched only to vanish, and in
November, when the King and Newcastle returned,
things were in a more confused condition than ever
They rapidly became worse. When Pelham at last
ventured to propose to the King the removal of Bedford,
the King absolutely refused. Newcastle was in despair.
He would resign, and Granville might form a new ministry. He quarrelled afresh with his brother, and they
refused to meet except on public affairs. The confusion,
the faction, the endless intriguing were so bewildering
that even sneering and cynical onlookers of the
Horace Walpole stamp confessed themselves sick of
the contemptible scene.

The political imbroglio seemed almost at its worst,
when an unexpected event came to the assistance of
the Pelhams On March 31, 1751, the Prince of Wales
died. The Leicester House opposition, of which party
Bolingbroke was the only member much above medio-

---

[1] Add MSS 9,224, fol. 80 81

crity, was thus broken up, and the Pelhams were corre-
spondingly relieved. They now felt strong enough to
have their own way about Bedford, in spite of the
King's refusal to dismiss him. By dismissing Sandwich,
who owed his place to Bedford, they would make it
impossible for Bedford himself to keep office. In June
Sandwich was removed, and Bedford resigned next
day. Two or three days later a more startling announcement was made. Pelham had repeatedly and
positively declared, in public and in private, that he
would never again serve as a colleague with Granville.
Yet on June 17 Granville became Lord President of
the Council in the Government of the Pelhams Probably each side felt its need of the other. Newcastle
during his residence at Hanover had never been weary
of urging upon his brother how useful Granville would
be to'them in their foreign politics, and how dangerous
opposition might become if Granville should choose to
put himself at the head of it. Granville, on his side,
had learnt from personal experience that it was impossible for any statesman to hold power if opposed by
the Pelhams' parliamentary influence. After all that
had passed during so many years a perfect reconciliation
was hardly to be hoped for; but a common understanding was arranged in a very informal way. Granville and Pelham met privately at the house of a friend;
one of the two, it is impossible now to say which,
arriving there in a mysteriously muffled-up condition,
unrecognisable to any one. They talked to each other
with considerable reserve. But their host was determined that the negotiation should not fail At the
right moment he produced, with perfect success, a good
supper and good wine. The preliminary coolness soon
passed away, and next day it was known to all the

world that union was restored between them.[1] But the agreement was one of convenience and toleration far more than of eager co-operation Granville told the Pelhams that he would work harmoniously with them, and he kept his word On the day before he accepted office he wrote to Newcastle :—

'Your Grace may depend on my cordial attachment, which I shall explain further when I see you. I am glad that Mr. Pelham has told you that he will support your measures *jointly*; which is all I can desire, dreading nothing so much as disputes, which I will never occasion or promote'

But Granville's personal opinion of the Pelhams of course remained what it had always been , and the Pelhams feared Granville hardly less as a friend than as an enemy Observers thought that they had good ground for fear, and that Granville would soon be master again in fact if not in name 'Lord Granville,' wrote Horace Walpole on the day after the appointment. 'is actually Lord President, and, by all outward and visible signs, something more , in short, if he don't overshoot himself', the Pelhams have ; the King's favour to him is visible, and so much credited that all the incense is offered to him ' Writing from memory many years later, the same observer reports that when Granville was wished joy on the reconciliation he replied: '"I am the King's President ; I know nothing of the Pelhams ; I have nothing to do with them " The very day he kissed hands, he told Lord D——, one of the dirtiest of their creatures, "Well, my lord, here is the common enemy returned "'[2] The anecdote may be

---

[1] Mr Nugent, afterwards Earl Nugent, at whose house Granville and Pelham met, told the particulars as above to the House of Commons in 1784 *Parliamentary History*, XXIV 634

[2] *Last Ten Years of George the Second*. I 171.

true or false ; less likely perhaps to be false than true
Henry Pelham at least would have believed it. He had
yielded to the King and to his brother, and had consented
to Granville's return, though people found it difficult
honourably to reconcile Pelham's acquiescence with his
often-repeated statements on the subject ; but he was at
least unfailingly consistent in his suspicion and dread
of Granville. More than a year after Granville had
joined the ministry, Pelham was convinced that he was
only lying by, waiting his opportunity which was sure
to come. In September 1752 Pelham wrote to his
brother :—

'I have no reserve with regard to Lord Granville
I am resolved to live well with him, which I can easily
do if we have no public meetings ; for he takes care we
shall have no private ones. My opinion of him is the
same it always was ; he hurries forward all these German affairs, because he thinks he shows his parts and
pleases the King ; in both which I think he is mistaken [1]
But believe me, he lies by, he has as much vanity and
ambition as he ever had, and he sees the King's personal
inclination to his ministers is as it was ; he hopes therefore in all these contradictory circumstances that something may fall out, and then he is sure to succeed ; in
which I believe he is in the right . . . Notwithstanding
this, when we meet at the Regency Council, we laugh.
and are as good friends as can be.' [2]

Pelham's fears and suspicions were groundless.
Three years of unbroken quiet passed by, and party
politics seemed no longer to be in existence. It was
then not Granville but Pelham himself who, in a quite
inevitable way, opened the gates of strife again.

---

[1] In both which the mistake was Pelham's own.
[2] Coxe Pelham ii 152

CHAPTER IX

LAST YEARS.

1754–1763.

GRANVILLE lived nearly twelve years after becoming President of the Council, and held that office uninterruptedly till the day of his death. But his active political career was practically over. He continued to take a keen interest in political affairs; and in the exciting domestic and foreign questions which filled the closing years of the reign of George II. he was always ready with witty speech and experienced counsel. But in the strife of parties he declined now to play any other part than that of adviser and mediator. He held a dignified office. while Secretaries came and went, he continued to be the King's President; his personal position was influential; his advice carried with it the weight of the statesman who had been engaged in public affairs from the time when he had left the University. From the vulgar self-seeking of politics he had always been free; and now, when years were coming upon him and health was failing, its legitimate ambitions had no overpowering attraction for him Twice again he was asked to take the highest place, and become Prime Minister of England, but each time he refused. Political fate had not always used him too kindly; he had been thwarted and baulked by some of the most insignificant beings who ever brought politics down to their own low level   But he now contested it with them no longer, 'resigned, in a big contemptuous way, to have had his really considerable career closed upon him by the smallest of mankind;'[1] and when the blundering incapacity of Newcastle put revenge within easy reach, Granville refused to take it

The three years' political quiet ended when Pelham unexpectedly died on March 6, 1754   'I shall now have no more peace,' said the King ; and he spoke the exact truth.   For more than three years the political world at home was a chaotic scene, where ministers and ministries rose and fell as faction and intrigue demanded   And when the miserable exhibition was over and a strong Government held undisputed power, England was engaged in a war which was not concluded when the King died.   The strictly political history of the last six years of the reign of George II is concerned almost exclusively with these two series of events.   They were unconnected at first, but soon ran into each other, so that the settlement of what was originally a mere vulgar rivalry in corrupt personal politics had an important influence upon a war which affected three continents.

It was easy to find a successor to Pelham's office. For a moment, Newcastle had gone into transports of grief for his brother's death, and with his customary effusiveness had declared that he would give up everything, and have nothing more to do with public affairs.   But of course he soon recovered, and, being evidently born to govern England, appointed himself Prime Minister in his brother's place   But he could not also appoint himself leader in the House of Commons ; and as all the

[1] Coxb : *P . L . ' R . . \ VIII. Chap III

prominent members of the Government were now in the
House of Lords there was no one to whom, as a matter
of course, the leadership of the Commons seemed to
belong   Political gossip was soon busy with many
names.   Chesterfield, contemplating the confusion from
his comparative retirement, in his usual religious way
thanked God that he was now nothing but a bystander,
and found cynical amusement in watching the mysterious
looks and important shrugs of the small blockheads of
politics, whose mystic solemnity on such occasions is
sometimes seriously taken by simple persons   When
all the irresponsible gossiping was over, it was found
that practically there was only one man of leading
ability in the House to whom the vacant post could be
offered   Murray, the Attorney-General, capable of holding any position, found no attraction in politics, and reserved himself for the highest seats of his own profession.
Pitt, Paymaster of the Forces, had little influence in the
House where he had sat for nearly twenty years   He
had confined his intimacy to a small knot of personal
relatives, keeping himself apart from the mass of members in a hardly disguised scornful isolation.   He was
also angrily hated by the King, and to Pitt, with his
overwhelming reverence for the royal office even in the
person of George II., this seemed a calamity against
which it was useless to strive   It is humiliating to read
the words written at this time by the man who, three
years later, was himself the real ruler of England:—

' All ardour for public business is really extinguished
in my mind, and I am totally deprived of all consideration by which alone I could have been of any use
The weight of irremovable royal displeasure is a load
too great to move under ; it has sunk and broke me   I
succumb, and wish for nothing but a decent and inno-

cent retreat, wherein I may no longer, by continuing
in the public stream of promotion, for ever stick fast
aground, and afford to the world the ridiculous spectacle
of being passed by every boat that navigates the same
river.'[1]

Murray and Pitt being thus out of the question,
Newcastle's choice seemed almost necessarily confined
to Henry Fox, the Secretary at War. Strictly speaking,
Fox had no more genuine political ambition than Murray,
or at least he soon renounced whatever real political
aspirations may once have attracted him. But he did
care very much for what could be made out of politics,
and was miserably willing to drop all aims at a distinguished career and to do dirty work in the dregs of
parliamentary life simply for the money which his
degradation gained him. For no higher object, he was
content to earn the sneers of his contemporaries and
the vexed scorn of posterity. Granville in vain urged
him the other way. Fox had not yet, however, fallen
so low as this; and though he showed an excessive
eagerness to seize Pelham's vacant place, his conduct in
the negotiations that followed contrasts very favourably
with the proceedings of Newcastle. Pelham had died
at six o'clock in the morning. Before eight Fox was at
the Marquis of Hartington's, starting the necessary
arrangements. At first they seemed to go successfully
enough. Fox himself was to be leader of the House of
Commons and Secretary of State. He announced it to
a friend, with candid self-criticism :—

'Know then the Duke of Newcastle goes to the
head of the Treasury, and I am to be Secretary of
State, of course Cabinet Councillor, and at the head of
the House of Commons. . . . Now what do you think

of this new Secretary of State? Why, that he is got
into the place in England that he is most unfit for. So
he thinks, I can assure you.'[1]

Newcastle, though he reserved to himself the actual
disposal of the money spent in parliamentary corruption—the secret-service money, as official pleasantness
politely called it—promised that Fox should always know
how the gifts of a grateful minister had been distributed.
But the Duke, who watched over the bribery department with a timid and jealous exclusiveness, soon began
to fear that he had offered the new Secretary too much
He was anxious to take back his word, yet he could
not deny the agreement which he had made with Lord
Hartington, the manager of the negotiations With
characteristic deception, Newcastle devised a subterfuge which allowed him to slink out of his difficulty.
He might, he said in his sleek way, have used words
which meant what Hartington and Fox had understood
them to mean; but certainly he himself had never
understood them so; he had been thrown into such
anxiety and affliction and grief by his brother's death
that his memory was all upset; but he had never intended that Fox should have anything to do with secret
money or patronage. Fox, reasonably enough asking
how he was to manage the House of Commons if he
did not know who was bribed and who not, declined to
accept the leadership on these niggardly terms, and
resigned the seals on March 14, the day after he had
received them. Newcastle then tried a most ludicrous
experiment. As he could not get a man of ability to
accept office on the mere footing of a clerk, he resolved
to appoint a so-called minister who would do what he

---

[1] Fox to Lord Digby March 12, 1754 *Eighth Report* of the Hist.
MSS. Commission, p 220

was told and ask no questions. He selected Sir Thomas
Robinson, the rather dull Vienna diplomatist of the
Silesian war times ; a man who knew nothing whatever
about parliamentary affairs Robinson was actually
made Secretary of State, and set at the head of the House
of Commons. The dual leadership was indeed most
curious. The head of the Government in the House of
Lords was little better than an idiot ; the leader in the
House of Commons did not know the elementary language of parliamentary life, and as a speaker was so
ludiciously absurd that his best friends could not keep
serious faces while they listened to him

The opportunity was too tempting to be lost by Pitt
and Fox. Pitt, slighted by Newcastle and neglected by
the Court, could not be enthusiastic in support of the
Government of which he was an inferior member ; Fox
had just been refused a distinguished office because he
would not accept it on ignominious conditions The two
subordinates, therefore, lately not on very good terms
with each other, began to draw together. When
Parliament met in November 1754, Pitt and Fox made
Robinson's life a misery to him Pitt did not spare even
Murray and Newcastle himself ; Fox actively assisted
Robinson in making himself ridiculous. Robinson
pathetically declared that he had not desired the high
office which he held. Pitt coolly replied that if any one
else had wished it, Robinson would not have had it.
Steady party men voted with the Government, but
laughed while they did so. Far less than all this was
enough to frighten Newcastle, and he was perplexed
between dread of dismissing the two rebels and dread
of keeping them. He ended by adopting the less
dangerous plan of attempting to divide them A negotiation, managed by the King's personal friend Lord

Waldegrave, was opened with Fox: and in the spring
of 1755 Fox consented to enter the Cabinet and serve
under Robinson without attacking him. Granville, to
whom personally it was a question of no moment, had
judged Fox's interest and conduct in politics by his
own high standard, and had predicted his certain promotion. 'I must tell you,' wrote Fox to his wife at the
end of 1754, 'a compliment of Lord Granville's imagination, and whether I tell you because it is pretty,
or because it flatters me, or both, you may judge. I
was not present "They must," says he, "gain Fox.
They must not think it keeps him under in the House
of Commons They cannot keep him under. Mix
liquors together, and the spirit will be uppermost." '[1]
Granville could not have predicted that Fox would
soon be willing to sink to the very bottom

Though the alliance between Pitt and Fox was thus
broken, the domestic dispute was still far from settled,
and at this point it became entangled in the difficulties
and dangers from abroad. The long truce gained by
the treaty of Aix-la-Chapelle was nearly over; the
final stage of the war was threateningly near. The
first signs of trouble came from North America. Between the English and the French Colonies in America
there was no fixed and indisputable line of division.
The French ventured to insist that the English colonists
should confine themselves to the ground East of the
Alleghanies, between the mountains and the sea. What
was West of the Alleghanies the French, with magnificent effrontery, claimed as their own: and Canada
they already had. Confused conditions and conflicting
demands resulted in colonial war, and it was soon clear
that the war could not be limited to the colonies In
1754 George Washington. making his first historical

Quoted in Trevelyan *Early Life of C. J. Fox* p 19 n.

appearance, was defeated by the French ; in the spring
of 1755 the English Government was sending out troops
to North America.   The French did the same , and war
between France and England, though as yet not formally
declared, had practically begun.   Its opening event
was not an omen of its close   On July 9. 1755, the
English General Braddock was surprised and defeated
by the united French and Indians at Fort Duquesne
When the war ended there was no Fort Duquesne any
longer   Its name had been changed to Pittsburg.

In spite of the troubled condition of public affairs,
the King refused to forego his yearly visit to Hanover
In his absence, important questions came before the
ministers who formed the Regency.   One of the most
pressing of these referred to the relations between
England and France.   One English fleet had already
been sent to America.   In July 1755 another was ready,
but the ministry, in the awkward state of affairs, with
war still undeclared, were much perplexed in drawing
up the instructions which were to guide the admiral.
When Sir Edward Hawke sailed with his fleet, what
was he to do with it ?   The Duke of Cumberland was
for acting as if the country was formally at war.   Lord
Chancellor Hardwicke wished for time and recommended caution.   Newcastle was delightfully ridiculous   He ' gave his opinion that Hawke should take a
turn in the Channel to exercise the fleet, without having
any instructions whatever '[1]   Imbecility of this description was the Prime Minister's contribution to the
government of the country.   Granville first was of
opinion that the English fleet should act hostilely, but
only against French men-of-war   ' Lord Granville,'
Fox told Dodington, ' was absolutely against meddling

Lord Waldegrave   Memoirs p. 17

with trade—he called it vexing your neighbours for a little muck.'[1]   Granville's view seems to have been adopted; but when the news of Braddock's disaster reached England things were recognised as serious beyond anticipation, and Granville's counsel adapted itself to the graver circumstances   'The Duke of Newcastle in Council,' says Lord Shelburne, 'proposed seizing the French men-of-war.   Lord Granville laughed at that, and was the cause of seizing the merchant-men upon the principle of common sense—if you hit, hit hard; which measure, suggested by Lord Granville, who could not be considered as more than a looker-on in Council, saved us from ruin.'[2]   Orders were sent to Hawke accordingly, who seized everything he could lay hands on; yet France did not declare war.

While his ministers were thinking of France, George was thinking of Hanover.   For the protection of his inestimable possession he had been, and still was, paying subsidies on all hands, offering money for men wherever a continental ruler would deal with him   It was an annoying circumstance that at the very moment when these expensive arrangements might have been of some practical use the date of the termination of some of them fell due.   George saw no remedy but to make new ones.   At Hanover he therefore occupied himself with this congenial business.   His treaties with Saxony and Bavaria were expiring; he entered upon new agreements with Hesse and even with Russia.   The Hessian treaty was actually concluded, and the King indifferently sent it over to England to be ratified as a matter of course.   This seemingly innocent performance had a most startling consequence.   It drove the

---

[1] Dodington's *Diary*, July 21, 1755

[2] Lord Shelburne's *Autobiography.* Fitzmaurice's *Shelburne,* 1 79.

excitable political world into a crisis which lasted for nearly two years. The scenes played on the stage of English politics between 1755 and 1757 were more like the sudden changes of farce or pantomime than the sober proceedings of sane politicians and statesmen They began when the Chancellor of the Exchequer, Legge, urged, it is said, by Pitt, refused to sign the Treasury warrants for the Hessian subsidy Newcastle immediately was filled with terrified astonishment. He hastened to Pitt, and with fawning flattery and maudlin fulsomeness tried to secure his assistance. Pitt clearly let Newcastle understand that he would accept nothing less than the Secretaryship of State, with a Secretary's full powers, and that he would not support the Russian subsidy, or a political system founded on subsidies Newcastle was greatly distressed, but not yet sufficiently intimidated to yield to Pitt's requirements In his alarm he had already appealed to Granville As soon as rumours of the opposition to the subsidies had begun to spread, Granville had said to Newcastle: ' You will now be served yourself as you and your brother served me Your colleagues will not abuse you themselves, but will sit still and rather encourage the abuse than defend you.'[1] When Legge's terrible refusal had scared Newcastle out of the little sense he possessed, he offered to yield his place that Granville might take it ; but Granville, outwardly laughing, said with bitter contempt that he was not fit to be First Minister, and refused. Having thus failed to throw his own responsibility upon Granville, and having failed to induce Pitt to manage his affairs in the House of Commons, Newcastle was compelled to turn once more to Fox. Granville, though he did not know what Fox thought on the subsidy question, mentioned his name to the King, and undertook the negotiation between Fox and Newcastle. The two met, Fox declaring to the Duke that this was the last time he would ever meet him to see if they could agree. Granville first proposed that Fox should be Chancellor of the Exchequer. Newcastle, terribly jealous always when the control of money was in question, replied that if that were so Fox and he would not agree for a fortnight. At last Granville arranged that Fox should become Secretary of State and leader of the House of Commons. It was much against Newcastle's inclination, but he could not help himself The Lower House could not go on in a state of anarchy, and except Fox there was no one who was willing to accept the management on Newcastle's terms. Robinson was easily got rid of. much to his own relief, being let down softly with the assistance of an Irish pension, and a cypher, as witty persons thought, was thus turned into figures In November 1755 the House met under its new leader.

A week after the meeting of parliament Pitt and Legge were dismissed. Pitt, though a member of the Government. had distinguished himself in the debate on the address by a very eloquent attack on Newcastle and Fox In a still remembered sentence, he compared the union between Fox and Newcastle to the junction of the Rhone and Saône at Lyon. Fox after the debate asked Pitt whether the Rhone stood for himself or for Granville Pitt rather enigmatically replied: 'You are Granville;' a statement very wide of the mark. Pitt's rhetorical triumph was great; but he could make no impression upon the position of the Government. When parliament approved the continental treaties which the King had made, Pitt continued to protest, -

and, resuming the old Hanoverian abuse which he had dropped while in ministerial favour, he asserted that England was on the way to bankruptcy for the sake of Hanover, a place too insignificant to be marked on the map of Europe. Why, he asked, should England, like Prometheus, be chained with fetters to that barren rock? Pitt took little by his oratory, and the end of the session silenced his parliamentary eloquence; but the eloquence of facts was about to pronounce against the Prime Minister even more emphatically than Pitt himself England declared war against France on May 17, 1756. The spring had been an anxious one, passed apprehensively in the vague terrors of a dreaded invasion. As usual, England was quite unprepared for war. She was so deficient in men for her own protection that she was forced to send for the Hanoverian and Hessian troops, due by treaty if necessary for self-defence; while in the Mediterranean, Gibraltar and Minorca were in a very neglected condition France took quick advantage of English remissness. In April a fleet sailed from Toulon and made for Minorca The French landed at Port Mahon; and for a month such garrison as there was resisted them as well as it could, till Admiral Byng (son of the Byng who had destroyed the Spanish fleet at Messina) came up with his fleet and attacked the French cruising off the island That same night, May 20, having done nothing effectual against the enemy, Byng made off for Gibraltar, and left the garrison unhelped Still for more than a month it held out; but before the end of June could resist no longer, and the war opened for England with the loss of Minorca.

The indignation caused by this unhappy news was very great, and Newcastle was soon in the midst of

another political crisis.   Parliament had ended in June
1756, while the Minorca question was still nominally
undecided.   The place of Lord Chief Justice, the object
of Murray's ambition, was already vacant, and Newcastle's parliamentary difficulties began afresh when
Murray, in spite of almost boundless bribes, refused to
sit another session in the House of Commons.   He
would be Lord Chief Justice or nothing ; the Crown, he
said, could not give him an equivalent for the post he
desired.   A still more severe blow from the House of
Commons came from Fox.   The new Secretary of State
had held his office for less than eight months, but he
had already begun to find little satisfaction in it.   Newcastle treated him badly ; the King, pleased at first, had
become cold and dissatisfied.   ' His majesty,' wrote Fox
at the close of the session, ' is, from being excessively
pleased, become discontent with me, and cold, not to
say very cold, to me.'[1]   To stand up in the House of
Commons single-handed against Pitt, and defend the
so-called policy and apologise for the blunders of a
minister who treated him rather as an enemy than a
colleague, was not work for which Fox felt inclined ;
and in October he informed Newcastle that he intended
to resign.   Once more Granville was called in to
arrange things for Fox, though Granville did not
altogether approve of the resignation.   On October 15
he took to the King a letter from Fox.   He had behaved
to Newcastle, Fox wrote, as well as he was able, yet he
was not supported ; his credit in the House of Commons
was accordingly diminished, and he could not carry on
the business any longer.   Newcastle was negotiating
with Pitt, let Pitt become Secretary of State, and Fox

[1] Fox to Sir C. H. Williams, May 29, 1756   Add. MSS. 9,196, fol.
109.

would willingly make room for him   With this letter
Granville went to the King   The account of the interview must be given by Horace Walpole .—

'When Granville arrived with this letter at Kensington, he said, "I suppose your majesty knows what
I am bringing." "Yes," replied the King, "and I
dare say you disapproved and dissuaded it " "Yes,
indeed, Sir,' said he (as he repeated the dialogue himself to Fox. "And why did you say so ?" asked Fox.
"Oh !" said he, shuffling it off with a laugh, "you know
one must, one must").[1] The King, whom Newcastle
had just left, seemed much irritated against Fox, talked
of his ingratitude and ambition, quoted the friends of
Fox that he had preferred   . and when he had
vented his anger against Fox, he abruptly asked Lord
Granville : "Would you advise me to take Pitt ?"
"Sir," said he, "you must take somebody." "What !"
cried the King, "would you bear Pitt over you ?"
"While I am your majesty's President," replied the
Earl, "nobody will be over me." The King then abused
Lord Temple much , and at last broke forth the secret
of his heart. "I am sure," said he, "*Pitt will not do
my business.*" "You know," said Lord Granville to
Fox, "what *my business* meant :—Hanover." The
supposition did honour to Pitt—but it seems the King
did not know him.'[2]

Granville reported the result of the interview to
Newcastle as well as to Fox. 'Lord Granville told
me,' wrote Newcastle to his monitor Hardwicke, ' that

[1] There was no dissimulation on Granville's part. He did not approve
of Fox's resignation. See Newcastle's letter, p. 346, where Granville says
that he will ' *still* endeavour to make him [Fox] alter his mind ,' and also
his conversation with Fox after the resignation was accomplished.

[2] Horace Walpole's *Last Ten Years of the Reign of George II.*, II.
89, 90.

he found the King was so angry with Fox that he had rather have anybody than him. The King underlined the paper, in Lord Granville's presence, to show him what part he was offended at The King told Granville that he had done too much for Fox . . . and then ordered my Lord Granville to tell Fox that he was much offended at this step, and that he would have him appeal to his own conscience whether he had done right in these circumstances My Lord Granville told me he should carry the answer immediately, that he should not repeat the strong things which the King said, that he would do no hurt, that he would still endeavour to make him alter his mind, if it was only for one session. But this makes it absolutely necessary not to lose a moment in applying to Mr. Pitt.'[1]

Fox could not alter his mind On October 18 he had his parting audience with the King, who was calm and serious, said Fox, full of anger, but determined not to show it. From the King Fox went to Granville, and received a rebuke which he had probably not expected. He was beginning the catalogue of his complaints with an affected declaration that he had no ambition and, after all, did not very much care, when Granville, ' that shrewd jolly man,' as Horace Walpole calls him, interrupted these fluent professions of indifference. 'Fox,' said Granville, 'I don't love to have you say things that will not be believed If you was of my age [Granville was now sixty-six], very well, I have put on my night-cap; there is no more day-light for me— but you *should* be ambitious. I want to instil a noble ambition into you; to make you knock the heads of the Kings of Europe together, and jumble something

[1] Newcastle to Hardwicke, Oct. 15, 1756 Harris' *Hardwicke*, III. 73, 74

out of it that may be of service to this country '[1] But
to appeals of this kind Fox was deaf.

Newcastle was indeed in a distressing case Murray
had left him, Fox had left him, and now that these two
were gone there was not a man in the House of Commons who had courage to look Pitt in the face. In his
fright and anxiety for self-preservation, Newcastle had
already recognised the necessity of securing Pitt He
had been scheming for this even before Fox's resignation ; he became painfully eager for it when it was clear
that Fox would certainly go. But when he sounded
Pitt he got a blank refusal. As Granville had answered
Newcastle's proposals with the bitter retort that he was
not competent to be First Minister, so now Pitt severely
replied that he could never presume to be the associate
of so experienced a statesman as Newcastle. Pitt was
resolved to join no ministry of which Newcastle was
the head. Newcastle began to think that it was a very
wicked world It is amusing to listen to the querulous
asseverations which he lavished on Hardwicke, protesting his own innocence so often that at last he came to
believe it, and full of an open-eyed astonishment that
the political world could venture to exist in a manner
which was unsatisfactory to him. He felt himself the
cruelly treated centre of a deeply tragic performance.
' A consciousness of my own innocence, and an indifference as to my own situation may, and I hope in God
will, support me against all the wickedness and ingratitude which I meet with. . . . My dearest, dearest
lord, you know, you see, how cruelly I am treated, and
indeed persecuted by all those who now surround the
King.'[2] It does not seem to have occurred to him

[1] H Walpole's *Last Ten Years*, II 88.
[2] Newcastle to Hardwicke, Oct and Nov 1756 Harris' *Hardwicke*,
III. 8(-·

that, as he and his management were an unrelieved
failure, his straightforward course was to resign
Straightforward things never did occur to him.   Rather
than resign, he was willing, since all his other attempts
had failed, to humiliate himself once more before the
dreaded Granville   When Pitt refused assistance,
Newcastle hastened to Granville, and implored him to
exchange places with him and become Prime Minister.
Granville, old, and in poor health, knew far better than
to quit his dignified position and spoil the last few
years of his life for the personal convenience of the
Duke of Newcastle   'I thought,' he said in his homely
style, 'I had cured you of such offers last year.   I will
be hanged a little before I take your place, rather than
a little after' [1]   If Granville had cared, which he never
did, for personal revenge, he might have had his feelings
of triumph   The false and foolish politician, who had
intrigued against him and driven him from power, had
now a second time gone down on his knees to him,
begging him to take the highest post, and had been
twice refused   Newcastle could do no more.   Deserted
by Fox, scorned by Pitt, contemptuously let alone by
Granville, he could cling to power no longer.   On
November 11 he unwillingly resigned

All necessary arrangements had already been made.
The King had first desired that Pitt and Fox should
sink past differences and join in one administration.
But Pitt refused to act with Fox.   The Duke of Devonshire, to whom the King then appealed, attempted a
reconciliation, but found Pitt inflexible   The King
complained bitterly of what he called the insolent way
in which Pitt treated him, and lamented, as he well
might, the miserable condition of public affairs.   But

[1] *Last Ten Years.* II 87 88

the distressing confusion only made Pitt's assistance more than ever desirable, and one last effort was made to obtain it   It was resolved to draw up in writing a scheme of administration and policy, and to ask Pitt to accept that scheme and join the Government of the Duke of Devonshire, if, after all, he refused, a Government must then be formed without him. On November 2, Granville, who had himself composed the document, presented it to the King   It was a short paper, but 'replete with good sense;'[1] and the offers which it made were such that Pitt could not with any show of reason refuse them   He agreed, therefore, to become Secretary of State in the Government of which the Duke of Devonshire was the nominal head.

Innocent onlookers might have supposed that now, at the end of 1756, the long political crisis was at last over   Cynics with a turn for prophecy might have safely asserted that the real crisis was only just beginning   When Parliament met in December, the House of Lords, against the opinion of Pitt's brother-in-law, Temple, thanked the King for the presence of his Electoral troops from Hanover   Pitt in the height of the invasion panic had opposed the demand for these troops, and the address of the House of Commons offered no congratulations on the subject   The King, encouraged by the action of the Lords, insisted that the Commons should take back their address and insert a corresponding paragraph   Pitt, who did not go through the formalities of accepting office till December 4, two days after the meeting of parliament, at once let it be understood that he would not accept the seals if the King attempted anything of the kind   At this point Granville struck into the dispute, and persuaded

---

[1] Duke of Bedford to his Duchess, Nov. 2, 1756   Lord J Russell's *Bedford Corr* p cl c   II 208

the King to give way. Even before this the King had
shown his dissatisfaction. The royal speech was Pitt's
work, and George disliked it. In private conversation
he did not care to conceal his sentiments An adventurous printer had published a spurious speech, and was
to be punished for so great a breach of privilege The
King, when he heard of it, hoped that the punishment
would be of the very slightest description, for he had
read both speeches, and said that, as far as he understood either of them, he liked the forged one better
than his own. In addition to this discontent on public grounds, the King soon conceived a personal irritation against Pitt and Temple. They did not manage
their official intercourse with him in the prompt business manner which he liked, and wearied him with
rhetoric and long speeches. Pitt, indeed, had few
opportunities of personally offending, for gout kept him
much away from Court and Council. When he did
appear in the Cabinet, his haughty mind, harassed by a
sick body, produced such wild and impracticable
schemes that Granville, who thoroughly recognised
Pitt's powers, said once after a Council-meeting: 'Pitt
used to call me madman, but I never was half so mad
as he is.' Little, however, as he saw of the Secretary,
George in the early spring of 1757 had had quite enough
of him, while he found Temple positively unbearable.
A disagreeable fellow, the King called Temple ; pert and
insolent when he attempted to argue, and exceedingly
troublesome when he meant to be civil. In his exaggerating way, the King was soon declaring that he was
in the hands of scoundrels, and would endure their
insolence no longer These royal phrases were more
than mere irritated rhetoric. Early in April 1757
the King ordered Pitt to resign

For eleven weeks England was without a settled Government   Before actually dismissing Pitt, the King in his angry distress had sounded Newcastle.   The Duke was eager enough to return to power, but he was terribly afraid of the political difficulties of the time, and he dreaded the resentment of Pitt.   He was so irresolute and changeable that the King's patience was completely exhausted, and he turned to Fox.   But the plan which Fox drew up came to nothing, and when Pitt was dismissed there was no one ready to succeed him.   Whilst freedoms and gold boxes innumerable were being lavished on the fallen Secretary, the sovereign was in a deplorable condition, and statesmen were busily devising fantastic combinations which fell to pieces before they could be completed.   Newcastle attempted to gain over Pitt, and Pitt contemptuously refused to have anything to do with him.   The Duke solemnly declared that he would never again dream of Pitt as a colleague ; and a few days afterwards was importuning him more than ever   Pitt, swallowing his contempt, this time agreed.   The King then reappeared on the scene, and, having given Newcastle permission to treat with Pitt, refused the plan which the two had drawn up.   Newcastle testily retorted that now he would not act at all without Pitt ; the King sulked, and declared that he was very badly used.   So the confused scene changed to worse confusion every day.   At last a little light seemed to break when Waldegrave, the King's personal friend, undertook, though reluctantly, the formation of a Government.   He made some progress, although Fox, who was to be a leading member, did not seem very confident of success   But Granville encouraged them :—

'However we were somewhat animated by Lord

Granville, who assured us, in his lively manner, that we could not fail of success. That the whole force of Government was now firmly united ; Army, Navy, Treasury, Church, and all their subordinate branches That though volunteers did not come in so fast as had been expected, we had the whole summer before us to raise recruits · and though of late years ,ministers did not think themselves safe without a majority in the House of Commons of 150 or 200, he remembered the time when twenty or thirty were thought more than sufficient '[1]

This arrangement under Fox and Waldegrave might possibly have worked ; Newcastle evidently feared that it would. A Government concerning which his opinion had not been asked, and from which he was himself excluded, was on the point of completion. If intrigue could do anything, Newcastle was resolved that such a settlement should go no further Remembering his successful tactics of more than ten years ago, he secretly worked upon Lord Holderness, the cypher Secretary of State, and persuaded him to resign. The King too remembered what had followed Harrington's retirement ; and though he accepted Holderness's resignation with angry dignity, he declined to enter upon a hopeless contest. Other resignations would be sure to follow, he dispiritedly complained ; almost everybody was abandoning him *O Richard, O mon Roi !* He refused to put Waldegrave and Fox, who were trying to serve him, to any further useless trouble, and agreed to accept any arrangement which Newcastle and his 'footmen' could make with Pitt. Each side having been convinced of its need of the other, an accommodation was not difficult To Newcastle, with the title of

---

[1] Lord Waldegrave's *Memoirs*, p. 122.

Prime Minister, Pitt very willingly left the whole department of patronage and corruption; while Pitt himself, at the end of June, received back the seals as Secretary of State, and with them the practical direction of the policy of the Government

The story of the Seven Years' War belongs, as far as English political history is concerned, to the life of Pitt. Party politics seemed to have fallen dead Parliament met to vote subsidies to Frederick and to sanction the requirements of Pitt, otherwise it had nothing to find fault with, and nothing to do. Everything was managed by seven or eight of the leading members of the administration, who formed a small governing body which Granville called the *Conciliabulum*. In this little council, Pitt and Hardwicke, Granville and Newcastle, met on friendly terms; always meaning to agree, wrote their Secretary at War, who was not one of the privileged number, or, if they differed, differing amicably 'I never,' writes War Secretary Lord Barrington, 'remember the country so much united in its politics, or in such good humour with its ministers. . The Duke of Newcastle, Lord President, Lord Hardwicke, Lord Mansfield, the two Secretaries of State, and Lord Anson form what Lord Granville calls the *Conciliabulum* They meet continually, and their opinion is the advice given to the King. They always mean to agree, and if they differ, they differ amicably. I am convinced at present there is not a man among them who wishes ill to the others, and who is not persuaded that any rupture, or even ill-will, would be a misfortune to himself'[1] Lord Shelburne's testimony on this point is indisputable. 'I have heard Lord Chatham say,' Shelburne writes,

[1] Barrington to Sir Andrew Mitchell, Dec 11 1757 Add MSS 6831, fol. 11-11

'they were the most agreeable conversations he ever experienced'·—

'The war produced a strong Council and a strong Government. The Cabinet Council was composed of the Duke of Newcastle, Mr. Pitt, Secretary of State, Lord Keeper Henley, Lord Hardwicke, Lord Mansfield, Lord Granville, Lord Holdernesse, Lord Anson, and Lord Ligonier. There were no party politics, and consequently no difference of opinion. I have heard Lord Chatham say they were the most agreeable conversations he ever experienced The Duke of Newcastle, a very good-humoured man, was abundantly content with the whole patronage being left to him .   Lord Hardwicke

. was kept in order by Lord Granville's wit, who took advantage of the meeting of the balance ·of all parties to pay off old scores, and to return all that he owed to the Pelhams and the Yorkes He had a rooted aversion to Lord Hardwicke and to all his family, I don't precisely know for what reason, but he got the secret of cowing Lord Hardwicke, whose pretensions to classical learning gave Lord Granville, who really was a very fine classical scholar, a great opportunity To this was added his knowledge of civil law, in which Lord Hardwicke was deficient, and, above all, his wit; but whatever way he got the key, he used it on all occasions unmercifully. In one of the short-lived administrations at the commencement of the war, Lord Granville, who had generally dined, turned round to say, 'I am thinking that all over Europe they are waiting our determination and canvassing our characters The Duke of Newcastle they'll say, is a man of great fortune, who has spent a great deal of it in support of the present family. Fox, they'll say, is an impudent fellow who has fought his way here through the House of Commons; as for me, they know me throughout Europe, they know my talents and my character; but I am thinking they will all be asking, *Qui est ce diable de Chancelier?* How came he here?"[1]

The nation was as singularly harmonious as the Cabinet, proud of the victories which were being won in three continents, and of the great minister who inspired them. So the last three years of George II's reign passed away in political quiet and satisfaction. But with the death of the old King, whose sad ministerial troubles had ended so happily after all, there came a very great change An uneducated, inexperienced, narrow-minded young Prince succeeded to the throne, and the policy of his mother and her favourite was not the policy of Pitt. Their first anxious determination was to get rid of the minister, then second, to end the war In order that a German Princess might see carried out in England the political principles which were the pride of the most absurdly insignificant German Courts, Pitt himself was to be dismissed, and his great work was to be hacked and botched by an almost unknown Scotch peer of the Court groom species, distinguished for nothing but his fine legs and his turn for the amateur stage. Bute, indeed, looked terribly wise, and had a great deal of pompous mystery about him; he liked to be in solemn solitariness, and when he was minister always went down the back stairs at Court. He had as much classical learning as he could pick out of a French translation, and he knew what history could be learned from tragedies. But there he stopped On the side of public affairs, his sole qualification for attempting to direct political events that concerned three continents

[1] Fitzmaurice's *Shelburne*, I. 85–87

was the fact that he had lived for many years in the Hebrides.

Bute's proceedings were not long delayed. In March 1761, having removed from the Government men whose opinions were likely to be in the way, and having filled their places with others who could be trusted to do precisely what the new King and Court desired them to do, Bute made himself Secretary of State   Pitt still remained, holding his post with great loyalty, though the designs of the Court against him were only too clear   He was even perfectly willing to make peace with France if he could obtain duly satisfactory terms. France in her very low condition desired nothing better than to be out of the war altogether, and especially to settle her English quarrel, which lay quite apart from the main continental question.   In the same month in which Bute introduced himself into the Government, the Duc de Choiseul attempted negotiations with Pitt. On April 5 Granville wrote to Pitt :—

'Lord Granville presents his compliments to Mr. Pitt, and thanks him for the communication of his answer to the Duc de Choiseul, together with the draught of the memorial '

Then Granville continues in the first person :—

' Neither of these draughts can, in my judgment, be mended ; and when this great affair comes out into the world, every person of candour will agree to impute the happy setting out of this great affair, as well as the success of it, which God grant, to the right author ; whose spirit, and perseverance, and judgment, under some discouragements, to my own knowledge have produced this salutary work   Ever yours,

'GRANVILLE.'[1]

Chatham Correspondence, II. (111.)

Early in June an English agent arrived at Paris. and a French one came to London, to conduct the negotiations. Pitt's terms were very high. Fresh victories were still improving his position, and he was not inclined to yield a single advantage which he had gained He had taken Belleisle and made new conquests in the East and West Indies while the peace negotiations were in progress; and on any concession to France in the Canada and Newfoundland region he was inexorable. ' Not the breadth of a blanket,' he privately said, when De Choiseul urged some small footing for the French fishermen in Newfoundland waters Yet still there seemed some probability that France would accept the English conditions. The offers of France were undoubtedly large. The Duke of Bedford, who was soon to take a not very creditable part in the final arrangements, says that in July Granville considered the agreement which the French seemed willing to make more advantageous to England than any ever concluded with France since the time of Henry V.[1] But Pitt was already seriously suspicious that there was something hidden behind Choiseul's proposals On July 15, France dragged Spain into the negotiations, suggesting that King Carlos might mediate between France and England Pitt indignantly refused to allow Spain any voice in the question. The meetings of the *Conciliabulum* became very animated. Horace Walpole reports one in August, when Pitt produced, at the request of the Council, a draught of the final concessions which could be offered to France. The ministers thought the document drawn rather too much in the style of an ultimatum; Granville thought its fine phrases too rhetorical for a paper on business of state ' Lord Granville took the draught, and applauded it

---

[1] Lord John Russell's *Bedford Correspondence* III 26

exceedingly, said it deserved to be inserted in the *Acta Regia*; but for his part he did not love fine letters on business' With humorous and good-natured exaggeration Granville added that he thought in negotiations bad Latin was better than good. This not very severe criticism produced an excited outburst from Pitt. Not an iota of his letter should be altered, he said. Bussy, the French negotiator, had had some communications with Granville 'I understand from Bussy'—began Granville, when Pitt interrupted: 'From Bussy? nor you, nor any of you shall treat with Bussy · nobody shall but myself'[1] But at the next meeting Pitt was more moderate, and admitted some small modifications. The negotiations, however, such as they were, came soon to an abrupt close. On August 15, 1761, there was signed between France and Spain a Family Compact, which plainly meant that Spain would join France in the war against England Pitt received early and secret information Clearly understanding the meaning of the news, and seeing that Spain was only awaiting a favourable opportunity for declaring war, Pitt resolved to forestall her in that. On September 18 he informed the Council of this private Bourbon alliance, and proposed immediate war with Spain. Granville desired time to consider so important a step A second meeting was held, from which Granville was absent, and at which no resolution was taken On October 2 the Council held a third and very important meeting. Pitt spoke with strong feeling, and said that if his advice were rejected he would not sit in that Council again Lord after Lord delivered his opinion (except Pitt himself there was not a Commoner in the Cabinet), Granville, Devonshire, Hardwicke, Newcastle, Anson, Ligonier, Mansfield, Bute,

[1] H Walpole's *Memoirs of George III* [68 69

and not one of them supported Pitt's proposal. Except
for his brother-in-law Temple, Pitt stood absolutely
alone   He virtually resigned.   It fell to Granville, as
President of the Council, to speak in the name of the
Cabinet on this occasion.   The very imperfect accounts
that remain give curiously discrepant reports of the
language which Granville is said to have employed.
But even without other direct evidence which fortunately
exists on this matter, no one well acquainted with
Granville's career and character could believe that
he spoke the words which are put into his mouth by
the enemies of Pitt   If this account[1] were to be believed, Granville addressed Pitt in a very contemptuous
manner .—

   'I find,' says this report, ' that the gentleman is
determined to leave us, nor can I say that I am sorry
for it, for otherwise he would have compelled us to
leave him ; but if he be resolved to assume the right
of advising his majesty, and directing the operations
of the war, for what purpose are we called to Council?
When he talks of being responsible to the people, he
talks the language of the House of Commons, and forgets that at this board he is only responsible to the King.
However. although he may possibly have convinced
himself of his infallibility, it remains that we also should
be equally convinced, before we resign our understand-
ings to his direction, or join with him in the measure
which he proposes.'

   'I am sorry old Carteret should have ended so !'
laments Carlyle   It is very certain that old Carteret

---

[1] It originally appeared in the *Annual Register* for 1761, pp 43, 44, and
was adopted by the Rev Francis Thackeray in his distressing *Life of Pitt.*
Unfortunately, Carlyle followed Thackeray in this instance (*Frederick,* Book
XX. Chap X), and so has given currency to what might otherwise have
been contemptuously rejected

did not at all end so. Instead of scornfully sneering at
Pitt's infallibility and openly exulting over his departure
from the ministry, Granville expressed in the most emphatic way his admiration for Pitt and his regret for his
resignation. The various historical chroniclers admit
that there is this other version, but apart from this
the whole point is cleared up in the simplest and most
satisfactory of ways. Granville himself repeatedly
denied that he had ever used the language which this
forged speech ascribed to him, and a contradiction and
explanation appeared in print in 1763, a few months
after Granville's death. Almon, the bookseller, a great
admirer of Pitt, wrote in 1763 a 'Review of Lord
Bute's Administration,' and its first pages, printed before
Bute actually resigned, tell the story of this spurious
speech :—

'After Mr Pitt and Lord Temple had taken their
leaves of the third and last Council summoned to deliberate on the conduct of Spain, the late Earl Granville, then
Lord President, rose up to speak. Upon this occasion those ministerial tools [supporters of Bute] already
refuted, framed a speech out of their own heads, and
printed it as the genuine one of Lord Granville's. The
world read this invented speech no doubt with astonishment; but his lordship, in order to do justice to himself,
several times declared that there was not even *one* word
of truth in that spurious production: that so far from
its containing *any* of *his* sentiments, it was just the contrary; for at that time he expressed (in his own nervous
and manly eloquence) his very high opinion of Mr. Pitt's
wisdom, penetration, abilities, honour, and integrity,
and in a very particular and most emphatical manner
spoke of the innumerable and almost insurmountable
difficulties which Mr Pitt and Lord Temple had had

to struggle with ' [1] These words precisely correspond with those used by Granville in his letter to Pitt already quoted. Internal evidence would of itself have been sufficient. Granville did not at the very end of his life lose the courtesy and high spirit which had distinguished him from the beginning.

Pitt resigned office on October 5 Within three months his policy was clearly justified by the English declaration of war against Spain. Granville, in a divided Cabinet, was one of the advocates for war The English successes in 1762 were very brilliant, but of no personal service to Bute, for they were rightly ascribed to the preparations and policy of Pitt. They were rather an embarrassment to the unpopular Secretary of State; for they did not increase the chances of a speedy peace, and Bute was bent on ending the struggle. He managed to make a considerable advance towards his object when he appointed himself Premier in May. Newcastle, persistently slighted by Bute and the young King, resigned in disgust, and Bute appropriated the highest place. He used his greater power to press the policy which he had been attempting to carry out even while Pitt was still in the Cabinet. From the party of the Whigs he had gained over, among others, the Duke of Bedford. To him Bute entrusted the negotiations with France, and in November preliminaries were signed Bedford's own eagerness for peace was so great that he was willing to agree to worse terms than even Bute himself. Bedford regretted the English victories of 1761; he desired to abandon Frederick entirely, he would have let Spain recover Havana for nothing The chief matter for wonder is that the peace, in the hands of a negotiator of this stamp, was so very advantageous as

[1] Almon's *Review of Lord Bute's Administration* pp 7 8

it really was. Its treatment of Frederick was by no
means chivalrous; its absurd disregard of valuable conquests which England was making while the negotiations
were still in progress was inexcusably careless, but
otherwise it was a peace extremely favourable to England, though some concessions were admitted which
Pitt would have refused. Pitt would have done his
best to utterly ruin France as a commercial and naval
power. The actual settlement made by Bute was probably wiser in policy; though Bute's action rested on
vindictive hatred of the great statesman and on a
shameful want of patriotic feeling. The peace in itself
was nationally advantageous, but personally disgraceful
to the minister who negotiated it

But Bute's eagerness for peace was not shared by the
country, which was proud of what it had done, and
ashamed of deserting Frederick. Pitt's popularity, lost
for a moment when, on his resignation, his wife became
Baroness Chatham and he himself accepted a pension,
had almost instantly returned, while Bute was the most
unpopular man in the kingdom   If then the Court
party hoped to consummate its policy by obtaining
parliamentary approval of the peace, parliament must
in some way be prevented from reflecting what was
evidently the feeling of the nation.   To assist him in
this degrading jobbery, Bute found a willing tool in
Fox, whose passion for money-making had already sunk
him very low in his office of Paymaster.   Bribed by a
seat in the Cabinet, and the promise of a peerage, Fox
undertook to secure a majority for the peace. When
parliament met in November 1762 it was evident that
he had kept his word. In the Lords, Bute was in no
danger; in the Commons, Fox's bribes had carried all
before them   The only opposition worth speaking of

came from Pitt, who, though very ill and permitted to sit during the greater part of his speech, opposed the peace in a harangue of three hours and a half. A majority of five to one approved the negotiations, and the Court triumphed.

Meanwhile Granville was dying For the last three or four years he had been slowly but visibly declining Yet his spirits remained unbroken, and his interest in men and affairs undiminished. 'Lord Granville,' wrote his friend, Lord Hyde, to Sir Andrew Mitchell at Berlin, 'is much as he was as to spirits and dignity, at least to us, who see him daily and partially Perhaps you would perceive that time had made its impression and lessened both We often talk you over and wish for the stories we are to have when you return.'[1] This was eighteen months before Granville's death ; he and Hyde never had Mitchell's stories of the war and Fred erick In May 1762 Horace Walpole told Mann that Granville was much broken. In December Chesterfield at Bath heard that Granville was dying. 'When he dies,' wrote Chesterfield, 'the ablest head in England dies too, take it for all in all.' Granville was by this time so far gone that his best friends could not desire the lengthening of his life. 'He was almost bent double, worn to a skeleton, quite lost the use of his legs, and spent the best part of the day in dozing'[2] But he gave a most characteristic illustration of the old Car teret high spirit, culture, and patriotism when he was actually on his death-bed Robert Wood, author of an Essay on *The Original Genius of Homer*, which inter ested Goethe in his younger days, was Under Secretary of State in the closing period of the Seven Years' War,

---

[1] Bisset's *Memoirs of Sir A. Mitchell*, I. 156 June 27, 1761.
[2] Add. MSS. 30,999 fol. 16

and frequently had interviews on business with Granville. The occasions were few, says Wood, on which Granville, after giving his commands on state affairs, did not turn the conversation to Greece and Homer. A few days before Granville died, Wood was ordered to wait upon him with the preliminary articles of the Peace of Paris. 'I found him,' writes Wood in the Introduction to his Essay, 'so languid that I proposed postponing my business for another time; but he insisted that I should stay, saying it could not prolong his life to neglect his duty; and repeating the following passage out of Sarpedon's speech, he dwelled with particular emphasis on the third line, which recalled to his mind the distinguished part he had taken in public affairs:—

Ὦ πέπον, εἰ μὲν γὰρ πόλεμον περὶ τόνδε φυγόντες
αἰεὶ δὴ μέλλοιμεν ἀγήρω τ' ἀθανάτω τε
ἔσσεσθ', οὔτε κεν αὐτὸς ἐνὶ πρώτοισι μαχοίμην
οὔτε κέ σε στέλλοιμι μάχην ἐς κυδιάνειραν·
νῦν δ' (ἔμπης γὰρ κῆρες ἐφεστᾶσιν θανάτοιο
μυρίαι, ἃς οὐκ ἔστι φυγεῖν βροτὸν οὐδ' ὑπαλύξαι)
ἴομεν [1]

'His lordship repeated the last word several times with a calm and determined resignation; and after a serious pause of some minutes, he desired to hear the treaty read, to which he listened with great attention, and recovered spirits enough to declare the approbation of a dying statesman (I use his own words) "on the most glorious war and most honourable peace this nation ever saw" [2]

This was the last scene. Granville, aged seventy-

---

[1] *Iliad* XII 322-328
[2] Wood's *Essay*, p 5 n (Ed 1824). Matthew Arnold, *On Translating Homer*, p 18, quotes this last episode in Granville's life as 'exhibiting the English aristocracy at its very height of culture, lofty spirit and greatness.'

three, died on January 2, 1763. 'He died at Bath. previous to which he was delirious, and imagined himself in the other world, where, meeting an old Clerk of the House of Commons, he gave him an account of all that had happened in the interval between their deaths with infinite wit, accuracy, and humour, insomuch that it was a pity it was not taken down.'[1] He was buried among his ancestors in Westminster Abbey One may regret the loss of the last flashes of Granville's wit and humour; but his quotation of Sarpedon's words to Glaucus formed a more fitting close to his life than the wittiest of parliamentary gossip 'For if, escaping the present combat, we might be for ever undecaying and immortal, neither would I myself fight among the foremost nor would I urge you on to the glorious battle , but now—for a thousand fates of death stand close to us always, and no mortal can escape or evade them— let us go.'

[1] Lord Shelburne's *Autobiography* Granville did not die at Bath, but at his own house in Arlington Street.

CHAPTER X

PRIVATE LIFE; PERSONAL CHARACTERISTICS.

In the midst of the busy excitement of the life of a political leader, one of Carteret's frequent phrases was · 'I love my fireside.' When he became practically Prime Minister, Carteret had refused to attend the great political gathering at the Fountain on the plea that he never dined at a tavern. His private life was an exceedingly happy one, and, in spite of the coarse license which much of the political criticism of his day allowed itself, the most unscrupulous enemy found it impossible to employ against Carteret the satirical abuse or malicious libelling to which the notorious lives of too many eighteenth-century politicians so easily exposed them. Swift, who had no foible of unduly flattering the great, in 1724 dedicated a poem to Carteret as 'Manly Virtue' personified. Carteret had married almost immediately after leaving the University, and Swift humorously apologises for the fact that 'during the prime of youth, spirits, and vigour, he has in a most exemplary manner led a regular domestic life; discovers a great esteem and friendship and love for his lady, as well as true affection for his children.' His house was exceedingly hospitable; his family was numerous, and their alliances splendid and prosperous. Speaking once in one of the innumerable debates on the Hanoverian troops, Carteret said:—

'I hope it cannot be suspected of me that I prefer any interest to that of my native country, in which I hazard too much not to wish its prosperity; for I am allied, my lords, to most of the principal houses in the kingdom, and can number a very great part of this august assembly among my relations'

Swift, writing on the occasion of the marriage of one of Carteret's daughters, said that he thought Carteret the happiest man in all circumstances of life that he had ever known: and Pelham held that if Carteret could make as good foreign alliances for his country as he had made domestic settlements for his family, he would be the ablest minister that England had ever had

The head of the Carteret family till Carteret himself was fifty-four years old was his mother, Grace, Viscountess Carteret and Countess Granville. She was the youngest daughter of Sir John Granville, Earl of Bath. Her husband George, Baron Carteret, died in 1695, and she survived him for half a century, but did not marry again She lived to be ninety, dying on the same day (October 18, 1744) as old Sarah of Marlborough She seems to have had much force and decisiveness of character, and a frank, even sharp plain-spokenness which keenly sensitive persons found rather trying It was perhaps from her that Carteret inherited the homely directness and idiomatic force which marked his private conversation and were not excluded from his stately parliamentary eloquence. Swift would not like Countess Granville the less for the plainness of her speech: and she shared the intimacy with the Dean, which it seemed a law of nature that every member of Carteret's household should enjoy. From Hawnes, Carteret's seat in Bedfordshire she wrote to Swift in the early years of her son's opposition to Walpole :—

'DEAR SIR,—I have received the honour of your commands, and shall obey them, for I am very proud of your remembrance I do not know we ever quarrelled ; but if we did, I am as good a Christian as you are,—in perfect charity with you. My son, my daughter, and all our olive-branches salute you most tenderly . . . . Will you never come into England, and make Hawnes your road ? You will find nothing here to offend you, for I am a hermit and live in my chimney-corner, and have no ambition but that you will believe

    'I am the charming Dean's

      'Most obedient, humble servant,

                'GRANVILLE.' [1]

Though the old Countess here calls herself a hermit of the chimney-corner, she and her somewhat imperious ways were well known in London society ten years after the date of this letter. She lived to see her son practically Prime Minister of England ; and her proud satisfaction induced good-humoured observers to speak of her by the nickname of the Queen-Mother. By less lenient persons, who dwelt more on the sharpness of her tongue and manners, she was familiarly alluded to as the ' Dragon' ; and pleasant if exaggerated stories of the vehement impetuosity of old Countess Granville's eloquence amused gossipers in a sufficiently innocent manner. One harmlessly heightened specimen will be enough. In 1743, when the Countess was eighty-nine years old, Mrs. Elizabeth Montagu wrote to the Duchess of Portland :—

'All the gifts of tongues bestowed on mankind are

    ' ⸺ XVIII ⸺

retired to Mr Finch's, in Savile Row ; the general voice lives there in the person of the Countess of Granville. I went there with Mrs Meadows on Sunday. . . I wish your Grace had been present ; we had many good scenes, but the scene of tenderness and sorrow was the best of all ; she sighed, and tossed, and thumped, and talked, and blamed, and praised, and hoped, and used the greatest variety of expression, and suffered the greatest change of temper that ever poor soul did ; most pathetically did she break out, giving an account of Lady Carteret's death. "Poor dear Lady Carteret got her death going abroad with a cold ; for if poor dear Lady Carteret had a fault—not that I know that poor dear Lady Carteret had a fault—nay, I believe that poor dear Lady Carteret had not a fault—but, if she had a fault it was that she loved to dress and go out too well—you know poor dear Lady Carteret did love to dress and go out ; and then, you know, she never spared herself ; she would talk, always talk—but it was to be so ; it was ordained that she should die abroad." All this . . . . and much more . . . . did she utter in a breath. . . . I shall resume the thread of her discourse next winter, for I daresay it will run on as long as the fatal sisters spin the thread of her life. She asked after your Grace, and gave a very cordial and friendly hum and thump of satisfaction upon hearing you was well. The old woman showed a love for Miss Carteret, which makes me think she has more goodness than people suspect her of.'[1]

Indeed, there was a very great deal of goodness and family affection in the old Countess In 1743, while Carteret was with the King in Germany and the battle of Dettingen was at hand, she wrote :—

[1] *Letters of Mrs Elizabeth Montagu*, II. 252 255.

BB

'My Dear Son,—You are infinitely kind and good to me in making me easy about Lady Carteret, whose illness has lain very heavy upon my spirits I hope she will have no relapse, and that we may have all a happy meeting in October. I am glad to hear you design to take your son under your protection, that I may also see him. I am in great hopes he will turn out a man of business, for there is nothing I detest so much as an idle fellow . The Duchess of Marlborough has been lately told that there has been a duel between you and a foreign minister, which report does not affect me in the least, though I can't help mentioning it. Fanny [Carteret's youngest daughter] presents her most humble duty to you; she writes a long letter to her mama . . . . I beseech God to bless and preserve you in good health, and give you success in all your undertakings for the honour and glory of your King and country

'I am, my dearest son, with gratitude and tenderness,

'Entirely yours,

'GRANVILLE'[1]

The Lady Carteret referred to in these letters was Carteret's first wife, Frances, only daughter of Sir Robert Worsley and of Frances, daughter of the first Lord Weymouth She was descended, on her mother's side, from the Earl of Essex, Queen Elizabeth's unfavoured favourite. Her mother, Lady Worsley, whom we have already seen as the intimate friend of Swift, had been, as Horace Walpole says, 'a beauty and friend of Pope', and as the living lustre of Lady Carteret's eyes obtained Swift's metrical celebration, so a verse of Pope's commemorates that of Lady Worsley's.[2]

---

[1] Brit Mus Add MSS 32,116, fol. 402. June 5, 1743.

[2] See Pop . . . .

Frances, the daughter, was born in 1694, and in 1710, before she was seventeen, she married Carteret at Long-leat. Like her mother, she was exceedingly beautiful, and was one of the most brilliant figures at the Courts of the first and second Georges. Mrs. Delany, who by birth was one of the Granville family, and rather vaguely speaks of Lord and Lady Carteret's children as her 'cousins,' gives repeated proof of Lady Carteret's supremacy among the beauties of the London world Swift said that when she was in Ireland she was handsomer than all the young beauties at the Castle Court taken together; and even when she was no longer young, and was surrounded by her own beautiful married daughters, the verdict of observers was at times inclined to be: *O matre pulchra filia pulchrior.* She was very musical, too, having a fine voice which she had taken great pains to cultivate, and delighting in the operas, oratorios, and concerts which London enjoyed in the days of Handel. She seems to have had a kindliness of disposition and an easy agreeableness of manner which were very attractive. The old Countess Granville, not the readiest person to please or to be pleased, said that Lady Carteret was as good as an angel to her She had not been many weeks in Dublin before Dr William King, the aged Archbishop of Dublin, was with friendly familiarity spoken of as her lover. Swift was always her attached friend.

Lord and Lady Carteret were happy in seeing their children brilliantly established in life. Their eldest daughter, Lady Grace Carteret, whose beauty as a child was much rhymed about while Carteret was in Ireland, married the third Earl of Dysart, and was the mother of the fourth and fifth Earls. Louisa, the second daughter, married Viscount Weymouth and became

mistress of Longleat. Lady Louisa Carteret seems to
have had a large share of the good humour and complaisance of mind and manner that characterised her
father and mother The third daughter, Georgiana
Carolina, was first married to the Hon. John Spencer,
brother of Charles Duke of Marlborough, and grandson
of the Dowager Duchess 'Daughters are no burden
to my Lord Carteret,' wrote Lord Berkeley of Stratton
on the occasion of this marriage. 'It is not the only
instance of his good luck' Carteret was certainly well
satisfied with the marriages of his daughters, the more
so because they were marriages of affection, for neither
Lord nor Lady Carteret forced the inclinations of their
children. 'Choose a gentlewoman and please yourself,'
was the advice which Carteret once long afterwards
gave to one of his grandsons ; and he followed the same
principle in the case of his own daughters The principle worked well Replying in 1735 to congratulations
from Swift, Carteret wrote: 'If alliances and the
thoughts of prosperity can bind a man to the interests
of his country, I am certainly bound to stand by
liberty' 'Our cousins are now growing the most considerable people in the kingdom,' wrote Mrs Delany
on the occasion of the marriage of the third daughter
By her second marriage, the Hon Mrs Spencer became
Countess Cowper.

The marriages of her three eldest daughters took
place during the lifetime of Lady Carteret. In 1743,
when Carteret was at the height of his power, Lady
Carteret accompanied him in his journey with the King
and the Duke of Cumberland to Hanover. There she
was taken ill ; and George, who was about to leave for
headquarters to fight his battle of Dettingen, offered
that Carteret should not accompany him to the army,

but should remain behind at Hanover. Lady Carteret
begged that she might not interrupt Carteret's service
to the King, and indeed she did not seem to be in any
special danger. But she died in June, soon after the
King and Carteret had left for Aschaffenberg. From that
little town, on the day on which he received the news,
Carteret wrote to his late wife's confidential attendant .—

'You may easily judge how much I suffer for my
irreparable loss, and I should be distracted if I did not
know that you had been with her, and that she has
been affectionately taken care of by you. If she has
left you any directions for me, I beg I may know
them and I shall punctually and exactly obey them   I
entreat you not to leave Hanover till I return, for I
can't be easy without talking to you. I approve of
depositing the dear remains in a vault in a church
till further orders, in such a coffin as is fit for her
quality, and strong to bear carriage. It is a terrible
thing to be forced to write upon such subjects, but
I trust nobody but you, and that there may be no mistake I would not write by anybody but myself for
more sureness . . . . I will keep up my spirits as well
as I can under this great misfortune   I have not
written to my family   I have not seen my son since I
knew this fatal news, which was but this morning.'[1]
Lady Carteret's body was brought over to England in
November 1743 in the ship in which Carteret himself
returned ; and though then Carteret outwardly appeared
in good spirits, those who knew him thought they were
assumed and outward only. Lady Carteret left behind
her one unmarried daughter, Lady Frances Carteret,
who in 1748 became Marchioness of Tweeddale. Like
all her sisters, Lady Frances was very musical, and like

[1] Brit. Mus. Add. MSS. 32,416 fol. 410. June 13–24 1743.

her father she was an accomplished linguist. Three
months after her marriage Horace Walpole met her,
and said that she was ' infinitely good-humoured and
good company, and sang a thousand French songs
mighty prettily.' In 1749 the Earl of Morton wrote of
her to Andrew Mitchell, afterwards the well-known
ambassador to Frederick the Great: 'I saw your
Marquis and his lady at Yester It is a noble house,
and the lady seems mightily pleased with it and with
the country. She is very merry and easy, and sang
Greek, French, and Scotch songs to me '[1] Mrs. Delany
thought there was more sentiment in the Marchioness
of Tweeddale than in any other member of the family,
and her own directions for her funeral do not contra-
dict this view She long survived her husband, and
ordered that she should be buried as near him as
possible, wearing her wedding-ring, and with her husband's letters to her in her coffin.

In April 1744 Carteret astonished the London world
by a second marriage Gossip had been associating
his name with a relative of his own, the Honourable
Elizabeth Granville, daughter of Pope's friend Lord
Lansdowne. Daisy, as her friends called her, was one
of the maids of honour, celebrated for her beauty, and
very affectionately treated by Carteret and all his family.
Some of them indeed thought that Carteret's kindness
to her was excessive, and that he made too great a
' fuss' with Daisy. But there was nothing more than
kindness in it. Speculating gossipers, as well as the
worlds of fashion and of politics, experienced the bewildering pleasure of a total surprise when it was
suddenly announced that the leading English minister
was to marry the leading English beauty of the day,

[1] Bisset's *Mitchell*, I 13 *n*

Lady Sophia Fermor, daughter of Lord and Lady Pomfret.

Lady Pomfret, who, as Boswell could not help coming from Scotland, could not help being the grand-daughter of Judge Jeffreys (though on her mother's side she traced her descent from Edward I), was one of those well-meaning but fussy, meddlesome, and terribly inconsequential women of whom it is impossible for posterity to see anything but the slightly ridiculous side. She had been Lady of the Bedchamber to Queen Caroline ; and leaving Court in 1737, on the death of the Queen, went abroad with her husband and family, arriving at last at Florence towards the close of 1739. There the Pomfrets hired a vast palace and gardens that had belonged to the Medici, and held weekly gatherings much frequented by English and Italian society. The English ambassador, Sir Horace Mann, Lady Mary Montagu, Horace Walpole, Lord Lincoln with his governor, Pope's friend Spence, and many others were among their guests. Lady Pomfret, a well-educated woman, but with a fatal turn for amateurish pedantry, dabbled in literature, translated Froissart ; is said to have written a life of Vandyke, of which fortunately nothing is known ; and corresponded profusely with the Countess of Hertford, mingling gossip on books, antiquities, art, and Italian sight-seeing with very bad verses of the descriptive kind. Horace Walpole, who had certain private reasons of his own for a grudge against her, takes specially malicious delight in dwelling on the ridiculous side of Lady Pomfret. He makes her responsible for sayings as solemnly absurd as if they had been the Duke of Newcastle's. He writes once to his friend Mann in November 1741 : —

'Lady Townshend told me an admirable history. It

is of our friend, Lady Pomfret   Somebody that belonged
to the Prince of Wales said, they were going to *Court*;
it was objected that they ought to say, going to Carlton
House, that the only *Court* is where the King resides
Lady Pomfret with her paltry air of significant learning
and absurdity, said, "Oh Lord! is there no *Court* in
England but the King's?   Sure there are many more!
There is the *Court* of Chancery, the *Court* of Exchequer,
the *Court* of King's Bench, etc "   Don't you love her?'

Horace Walpole did not love her; but it is tolerably
clear that he loved one of her daughters as much as an
amateur dilettante and fashionable fribble could   He
had a portrait of Lady Sophia as Juno in his miscellaneous toyshop at Strawberry Hill. 'Harry, you must
come and be in love with Lady Sophia Fermor; all the
world is or should be,' he wrote to his friend Conway
in October 1741, when he and the Pomfrets had come
back by different routes to London   All the world
included himself; and the pains he takes to be elabo-
rately sarcastic at Lady Pomfret's expense admit of a
very simple explanation.   Lady Pomfret had practically
warned him off.   She by no means intended the first
English beauty of the day to entangle herself with the
youngest son of a mere country squire.   Suitors far
more eligible than Horace Walpole could not be wanting; one, whose success would not have displeased
Lady Pomfret, had already been fluttering around
Lady Sophia on the Continent, sharing the sight-seeing
and Italian entertainments of which she was the beautiful centre   This was Lord Lincoln, nephew of the
ridiculous Duke of Newcastle.   Lincoln seems to have
been decidedly serious in his attentions, but Newcastle
could interfere with as meddlesome effectiveness in love
as in politics   He insisted, for prudential family reasons,

that Lincoln should marry Pelham's eldest daughter. Lincoln sighed as a lover, and obeyed as a nephew

The Pomfrets returned to England in October 1741, and Lady Sophia at once became the reigning beauty in London as she had been the recognised queen at Florence People did not wonder; for, as Lady Mary Montagu, who knew her well, said, Lady Sophia Fermor's beauty was her least merit She was as famous at the Court of George II as her accidentally better remembered relative, the Arabella Fermor of the *Rape of the Lock*, had been at Queen Anne's 'Handsomer than all,' she was, says Horace Walpole, at a famous London ball in 1741; 'but a little out of humour at the scarcity of minuets; however, as usual, she danced more than anybody, and, as usual too, took out what men she liked or thought the best dancers'[1] Those who knew her felt no surprise at her successes. 'I am very well acquainted with Lady Sophia Fermor,' wrote Lady Mary Montagu in 1744, 'having lived two months in the same house with her I shall never be surprised at her conquests.' But there was some surprise when the effectual conquest proved to be that of the leading English minister. The story of this episode in Carteret's life must not be told by any other than Horace Walpole; but allowance must constantly be made for his

---

[1] This was a ball at Sir Thomas Robinson's, not the Sir Thomas of Vienna and diplomacy, but another, eccentric man: 'a tall uncouth man, and his stature was often rendered still more remarkable by his hunting-dress, a postilion's cap, a tight green jacket, and buckskin breeches He was liable to sudden whims, and once set off on a sudden in his hunting-suit to visit his sister, who was married and settled at Paris He arrived while there was a large company at dinner The servant announced *M Robinson*, and he came in, to the great amusement of the guests. Among others, a French abbé thrice lifted his fork to his mouth and thrice laid it down, with an eager stare of surprise Unable to restrain his curiosity any longer, he burst out with, "Excuse me, Sir, are you the famous *Robinson Crusoe* so remarkable in history?"' *Walpole*, II 139 [?]

general affectation and exaggeration, his delight in assisting Lady Pomfret to make herself ridiculous, and his thinly concealed pique that Lady Sophia Fermor was quite out of his own reach. Walpole kept his friend Mann at Florence fully informed of the doings of the London world :—

'Who do you think is going to marry Lady Sophia Fermor?—Only my Lord Carteret!—this very week!—a drawing-room conquest. Do but imagine how many passions will be gratified in that family! Her own ambition, vanity, and resentment—love she never had any,[1] the politics, management, and pedantry of the mother, who will think to govern her son-in-law out of Froissart. Figure the instructions she will give her daughter! Lincoln is quite indifferent, and laughs. My Lord Chesterfield says, "It is only another of Carteret's vigorous measures." I am really glad of it, for her beauty and cleverness did deserve a better fate than she was on the point of having determined for her for ever. How graceful, how charming, and how haughtily condescending she will be! How, if Lincoln should ever hint past history, she will

> Stare upon the strange man's face
> As one she ne'er had known'

This letter was written near the end of March 1744; but the wedding was slightly delayed by Lady Sophia's illness. Scarlet fever attacked her, and for four-and-twenty hours she was in serious danger. On Carteret's side, sympathetic anxiety brought on a fit of the gout.

'My Lord Carteret's wedding has been deferred on Lady Sophia's falling dangerously ill of a scarlet fever; but they say it is to be next Saturday. She is to have

---

[1] Because she did not love *me*, Horace means.

sixteen hundred pounds a year jointure, four hundred pounds pin-money, and two thousand of jewels Carteret says he does not intend to marry the mother and the whole family. What do you think my Lady intends?'

On the evening of April 14, 1744, the marriage took place at Lord Pomfret's house. Carteret's mother, the very old Countess Granville, was invited, but did not go ; his own daughters he purposely did not invite, fearing, says Mrs Delany, that it might affect them too much, 'and he has indeed,' she adds, 'acted with a tenderness towards them that I did not imagine had been in his nature.' Horace Walpole prattles on .—

'The chief entertainment has been the nuptials of our great Quixote and the fair Sophia. On the point of matrimony she fell ill of a scarlet fever, and was given over, while he had the gout, but heroically sent her word that if she was well he *would* be so They corresponded every day, and he used to plague the Cabinet Councils with reading her letters to them. Last night they were married, and as all he does must have a particular air in it, they supped at Lord Pomfret's At twelve, Lady Granville, his mother, and all his family went to bed, but the porter : then my Lord went home, and waited for her in the lodge ; she came alone in a hackney-chair, met him in the hall, and was led up the back-stairs.'

Walpole's circumstantial account has the disadvantage of being inaccurate ; Lord and Lady Carteret returned to their home together, in the usual way of reasonable beings ; but it would have been less piquant to say so in a letter intended to supply gossip to Lady Sophia's friends and admirers in Florence. The Florentines were delighted at the English beauty's success,

and with enthusiastic daring rushed into Latin hexa-
meters and Italian Cantatas in celebration of the marriage of the English minister and the 'Farmoria virgo.'
London congratulations and festivities over the affair
were also very numerous :—

'There is to be a great ball to-morrow at the
Duchess of Richmond's for my Lady Carteret. the
Prince is to be there. Carteret's court pay her the
highest honours, which she receives with the highest
state. I have seen her but once, and found her just
what I expected, *très-grande dame*; full of herself, and
yet not with an air of happiness. She looks ill and is
grown lean, but is still the finest figure in the world.
The mother is not so exalted as I expected ; I fancy
Carteret has kept his resolution, and does not marry
her too. . . .

'I will not fail to make your compliments to the
Pomfrets and Carterets ; I see them seldom, but I am in
favour ; so I conclude, for my Lady Pomfret told me
the other night that I said better things than anybody.
I was with them at a subscription ball at Ranelagh last
week, which my Lady Carteret thought proper to look
upon as given to her, and thanked the gentlemen, who
were not quite so well-pleased at her condescending
to take it to herself My Lord stayed with her there till
four in the morning. They are all fondness—walk together and stop every five steps to kiss . . The ball
was on an excessively hot night ; yet she was dressed in
a magnificent brocade, because it was new that morning
for the inauguration day I did the honours of all her
dress : "How charming your ladyship's cross is ! I am
sure the design was your own !"—"No, indeed, my
Lord sent it me just as it is "—"How fine your ear-rings
are !"—"Oh ! but they are very heavy.' Then as much

to the mother.   Do you wonder I say better things than
anybody ? . . .

'I met my Lady Carteret the other day at Knapton's,
and desired leave to stay while she sat for her picture   She is drawn crowned with corn, like the Goddess
of Plenty, and a mild dove in her arms, like Mrs
Venus. . . .

'You would be diverted with the grandeur of our
old Florence beauty, Lady Carteret   She dresses more
extravagantly, and grows more short-sighted every day;
she can't walk a step without leaning on one of her
ancient daughters-in-law.   Lord Tweeddale and Lord
Bathurst are her constant gentleman-ushers   She has
not quite digested her resentment to Lincoln yet. . . .
Here is a good epigram that has been made on her:—

> Her beauty, like the Scripture feast,
>   To which the invited never came
> Deprived of its intended guest,
>   Was given to the old and lame. .   .

'My lady is in the honeymoon of her grandeur   She
lives in public places, whither she is escorted by the old
beaux of her husband's court; fair white-wigged old
gallants, the Duke of Bolton, Lord Tweeddale, Lord
Bathurst, and Charles Fielding ; and she all over knots,
and small hoods, and ribbons   Her brother told me
the other night, "Indeed, I think my thister doesth
countenanth Ranelagh too mutch!"   They call my Lord
Pomfret King Stanislaus, the Queen's father'

So far Horace Walpole's superficial and exaggerated
gossip.   One slight reference to the marriage is from
Carteret himself.   He wrote to his friend Tyrawley, the
English ambassador to Russia —

'I thank you for your particular kind letter on my

marriage   My lady will always be glad of the offers you make   Our friendship has been long, my dear lord, and shall remain as long as I live.

'Now for a joke, was it not a bold thing in me to marry so young and so fine a woman as Lady Sophia Fermor?   But it turns out well, with all the *laudades* imaginable   *Adios, tu atento y seguro servidor hasta la muerte,*

'CARTERET.' [1]

Tyrawley replied :—

'In answer to your joke, I always took you for a bold man   My Lady Carteret is certainly what your lordship says.   I used to see her sometimes at the Duchess of Richmond's, and I thought her in person, understanding, behaviour, and in all respects, by much the finest young lady in England.   I must now quote two or three lines on this subject, out of a letter I lately received from Madame de Wendt, from Hanover :— *" Que pensez-vous, milord, de notre cher Milord Carteret, qui s'est consolé si tôt avec une jeune femme de la perte de notre bonne Miladi?   Ne justifie-t-il pas bien ce qu'a dit quelqu'un que c'est un objet vivant qui console d'un mort ? "'* [2]

Granville's fall from power did not affect the brilliancy of his new Countess or the great popularity of her weekly receptions.   This vexed the soul of the Pelhams.   The ridiculous Duke had already this year behaved with excessive absurdity over another famous marriage that had followed a month after Carteret's. As the Duke of Richmond refused to listen to Henry Fox's proposal of marriage with Lady Caroline Lennox, Fox and Lady Caroline settled matters for themselves by a private wedding.   To Newcastle's fussy meddle-

---

[1] Add MSS 23,631 , fol 33.   August 28, 1744.
[2] Add. MSS 23,631 : fol 82

someness this rather innocent performance seemed on a level with important business of state When Carteret was going through the rooms one day at Kensington, soon after the news of this wedding had spread, he was summoned up to Newcastle to talk of a 'most unfortunate affair,' a matter greatly affecting the Duke, who would not make any secret of it from Carteret. 'I thought,' said Carteret, 'that our fleet was beaten, or that Mons had been betrayed to the French. At last it came out that Harry Fox was married, which I knew before. This man, who is Secretary of State, cannot be consoled because two people, to neither of whom he is any relation, were married without their parents' consent!' All the town was soon laughing at Newcastle and his 'most unfortunate affair.' The Duke also made himself ridiculous over Countess Granville's dangerous entertainments, and even complained to Orford that Horace Walpole frequented them; but Orford only laughed at him and his timid absurdity :—

'The great present disturbance in politics is my Lady Granville's assembly; which I do assure you distresses the Pelhams infinitely more than a mysterious meeting of the States would, and far more than the abrupt breaking up of the Diet at Grodno. She had begun to keep Tuesdays before her lord resigned, which now she continues with greater zeal. His house is very fine, she very handsome, her lord very agreeable and extraordinary; and yet the Duke of Newcastle wonders that people will go thither. He mentioned to my father my going there, who laughed at him. . . You can't imagine how my Lady Granville shines in doing honours, you know she is made for it My lord has new furnished his mother's apartment for her, and has given her a magnificent set of dressing plate;

he is very fond of her, and she as fond of his being so.'

One last quotation from Walpole closes the story of this too brief happiness :—

'Before I talk of any public news, I must tell you what you will be very sorry for—Lady Granville is dead. She had a fever for six weeks before her lying-in, and could never get it off. Last Saturday they called in another physician, Dr. Oliver : on Monday he pronounced her out of danger. About seven in the evening, as Lady Pomfret and Lady Charlotte [1] were sitting by her, the first notice they had of her immediate danger was her sighing and saying, " I feel death come very fast upon me'" She repeated the same words frequently—remained perfectly in her senses and calm, and died about eleven at night. Her mother and sister sat by her till she was cold It is very shocking for anybody so young, so handsome, so arrived at the height of happiness, so sensible of it, and on whom all the joy and grandeur of her family depended, to be so quickly snatched away ! '

Countess Granville died on October 7, 1745 Her only child, Sophia, became in 1765 the wife of Lord Shelburne, first Marquis of Lansdowne.

The town, in its gossiping way, was soon busying itself with rumours of a possible third marriage of Lord Granville. The town was quite wrong in that. For the last seventeen years of his life Granville was a widower When his little daughter Sophia was ten years old, he took her home from the care of Lady Pomfret; and he had a son of his first marriage surviving to succeed him in the title His two eldest sons had

---

[1] Lady Charlotte Fermor, Countess Granville's sister. She was governess to the children of George III and died at St James's in 1813, aged 88.

died in infancy, the third, Robert, in striking contrast with the brilliancy of the other members of his family, made no figure in the world, and has left no memory behind him. He succeeded to the earldom on his father's death in 1763, and himself died, unmarried, in 1776, when the title of Granville became extinct.

As a parliamentary orator Granville, by common consent, stood in the very highest rank. He had the physical advantage of a fine person, graceful manners, and a very handsome countenance. He was of 'commanding beauty,' says Lord Shelburne; and Horace Walpole uses the same expression —

> Commanding beauty, smoothed by cheerful grace,
> Sat on the open features of his face.

Swift speaks of his 'most comely and graceful person,' and chose as the motto of a welcoming poem, when Carteret was expected in Ireland as Lord-Lieutenant, Virgil's line :—

> *Gratior et pulchro veniens in corpore virtus*

But his oratory could easily have dispensed with these not unwelcome physical enhancements. He shone in all styles as a speaker. His reputation in the grand style of eloquence was very great. Demosthenes had been his special study. He was also as effective in argumentative as in declamatory speech. No orator's fine phrases or rhetorical ingenuity could hide from him the real point of any question at issue. Chesterfield was not inclined to be too lenient a critic of Granville; yet Chesterfield says of him: 'He was one of the best speakers in the House of Lords, both in the declamatory and the argumentative way. He had a wonderful quickness and precision in seizing the stress of a ques-

tion, which no art, no sophistry, could disguise to him.'
Granville's really wonderful political knowledge would
have enabled him, even if he had possessed no extraordinary rhetorical gifts, to be a political speaker
always worth listening to Even very ordinary persons
can generally speak fairly well on subjects with which
they are thoroughly acquainted But Carteret was not
an ordinary person, and his almost boundless information was displayed in parliamentary discussion with all
the charm of a rich and cultured eloquence which
flowed, thought Walpole, 'from a source of wit, grandeur, and knowledge' It was rich in historical allusion,
and often very pleasantly flavoured by Carteret's easy
familiarity with the classics Lord Shelburne, who,
however, had never himself heard Granville, thought
that his oratory was suited rather for the Senate than
for the people. If it had been otherwise, it would have
been eloquence out of place ; for what other audience
than the Senate had an English statesman in the reign
of George II.? But while Granville's eloquence was
doubtless usually cast in the grand style which was
familiar to the House of Cowper and Bolingbroke
and Mansfield, he could, when occasion required, speak
in the plainest language of idiomatic homeliness and
matter-of-fact unconventionality A militia bill which
he opposed he called ' impracticable nonsense,' and ' a
shoeing-horn to faction.' When in 1732 the House of
Lords was engaged with Bentley and his academical
quarrels, Carteret called some of the articles which
Trinity College brought against the Master ' the dis-
tempered frenzies of cloistered zealots '[1] He was also
especially well-known for the idiomatic directness of his
language in private conversation Before the outbreak

[1] Monk *Bentley*, p. 706.

of the Seven Years' War, he opposed any interference with French trading-vessels, and called it 'vexing your neighbours for a little muck.' The smaller European Princes, whose assistance could only be had after much haggling and cheapening of bargains, were in Carteret's language 'Shopkeeper Kings.' When the war with France began badly, and Newcastle with scared timidity begged Granville to become Prime Minister, he replied : 'I will be hanged a little before I take your place, rather than a little after.' In a letter to Swift he speaks of an insignificant legal functionary as a ' machine in a furred gown ' He was asked once who wrote the King's speech in a certain year It was the Lord Chancellor Hardwicke. ' Do you not see,' said Granville, ' the blunt pen of the old Attorney ? ' He was probably speaking of the undisguised inconsistency of politicians in and out of place, when he said to the King that no two things were so different as a cat in a hole and a cat out of a hole

In private life Carteret's wit and conversational powers, his humour and his good humour, made him very attractive He was a great talker, with a very extensive range of subjects. He had the Englishman's rarest gift, the art of conversation. But his table-talk has all vanished. Horace Walpole might have preserved much of it, but amusing letters are so much more easily filled with ball-room gossip or with George Selwyn's dreary fantasticalities on coffins and corpses. Carteret's talk was not of the Selwyn type It was not of that rather wearisome verbal cleverness which finds a sure perpetuation in jest-books and anecdote corners. Carteret could talk epigrammatically enough when he chose Steele and Addison, he said, were excellent companions for a young man in the beginning,

the other towards the close; for by the time that Steele
had drunk himself down, Addison had drunk himself
up But Carteret's mind was too rich and full to be
ever on the strain to say something striking which
might be quoted in the clubs and coffee-houses as Lord
Carteret's last good thing He was, says Lord Shelburne,
overflowing with wit, but 'not so much a *diseur de bons
mots*, like Lord Chesterfield, as a man of comprehensive
ready wit, which at once saw to the bottom, and whose
imagination never failed him.   He said that such a
man was a stupid man, but an admirable hearer He
said his house was the neutral port of the Finches,
who carried on the conversation by each of them addressing him and never each other. He said when all
his other stories failed him, Ireland was a constant
resource During his stay there as Lord-Lieutenant,
there was no end of the ridicule with which it supplied
him'

Carteret's good-humour was not less attractive than
his conversation He was never 'as disagreeable as the
occasion would permit.' His wit, frankness, and hospitality, and the accomplishments and attractions of his
family, made his house very popular, and he never
allowed political differences to interfere with the intercourse of social life. His refined simplicity hated flattery;
his open frankness and easy familiarity removed all
coldness from his aristocratic breeding. Plain and
simple in his manner, Lord Shelburne found him on
the one occasion on which he saw him; and Carteret
liked his friends to be plain and simple with him. When
he was Lord-Lieutenant of Ireland he delighted to visit
men of wit and learning on the most homely terms,
and was disappointed when his unexpected arrival was
received with ceremonious apologies for omissions and

defects. Dr. Delany especially pleased him by the easy unembarrassment with which he welcomed him when Carteret once unexpectedly called upon the Doctor, and said he was come to dine :—

'Others,' said Carteret to Delany, 'whom I have tried the same experiment on, have met me in as much confusion as if I came to arrest them for high treason, nay, they would not give me a moment of their conversation, which, and not their dinner, I sought; but hurry from me, and then, if I had any appetite, deprive me of it by their fulsome apologies for defects. This is like a story I heard the Dean [Swift] tell of a lady who had given him an invitation to dinner. As she heard he was not easily pleased, she had taken a month to provide for it. When the time came, every delicacy which could be purchased the lady had prepared, even to profusion, which you know Swift hated. However, the Dean was scarce seated, when she began to make a ceremonious harangue, in which she told him that she was sincerely sorry she had not a more tolerable dinner, since she was apprehensive there was not anything there fit for him to eat; in short that it was a bad dinner. [*Here Swift swore as only an eighteenth-century clergyman could, and asked*] Why did you not get a better? Sure you had time enough! But since you say it is so bad, I'll e'en go home and eat a herring. Accordingly he departed.'[1]

Carteret carried his good-humour into public life. He took success and defeat with the same good natured cheerfulness, and was quite indifferent to personal abuse. Lord Hervey has preserved a characteristic instance of the unruffled and even amused complacency with which

[1] Mrs Pilkington's *Memoirs*, III 67-70. Not a good authority; but the above is in accordance with the character of both Carteret and Swift.

Carteret listened to the unjust reproaches of disappointed politicians On one occasion during the long opposition to Walpole, the minister's Tory enemies in the House of Lords thought that Carteret had been too moderate, and one of them, in Hervey's hearing, said to him with the due spicing of profanity which gives so fine a flavour to much of the genuine old Tory dialect of the day: '" By——, Carteret, I know not what you mean by this; but whatever you mean, I believe after this you will not find it very easy to get any party or any set of men to trust you again I am sure I will not, and where you will find fools that will, I don't know. . . . By ——, Carteret, we all know you." . . . Lord Carteret turned to us who were sitting by him and said, with a cheerful unconcern, not at all affected or put on, but quite natural, " Poor Aylesford is really angry."' And Lord Mansfield told Marchmont that throughout the long intrigue which drove Carteret from power in 1744 Carteret's behaviour had been admirable; that he had never once lost his temper This fineness of temper is the more noticeable because Carteret was politically ambitious, and made no pharisaical attempt to deny that on repeated occasions Walpole and the Pelhams had used him badly It would have been easy to have been good-humouredly careless if Carteret had been sick of power or pining for retreat But in 1744 Carteret was in the full vigour of his activity, and an anecdote which must refer to the time when he was made Lord President of the Council shows that many years later, when his health was already breaking, it was not because he was indifferent to power that he bore no vindictiveness Carteret was cheerful and unresentful though he felt wounded. He had given to a friend a copy of the polyglot Bible, and his friend had rebound it in a sumptuous manner Carteret saw the book in its adorned condition, and said, ' You have done with it as the King has done with me . he made me fine and he laid me by.'

No man was more fiercely attacked with personalities than Carteret, but he never returned the abuse, and kept no vindictiveness ' He was neither ill-natured nor vindictive,' says Chesterfield, rather superfluously. He had frequent opportunities of revenging himself upon the Pelhams, but he only laughed at them instead [1] A smaller man than Carteret would have remembered with bitterness the outrageous personal attacks, the lavish insolence, and the cruelly unjust rhetorical vituperation with which Pitt, in the stormy days of his political irresponsibility, had not been too proud to assist the commonplace Pelhams and Harringtons and Hardwickes in their intrigues against the colleague whom they envied and feared But Carteret forgot all that; and it was perhaps not without some well-justified feelings of remorse that, long after Carteret's death, the Earl of Chatham spoke of him in the House of Lords as ' this great man,' and added . ' I feel a pride in declaring that to his patronage, to his friendship and instruction I owe whatever I am ' [2] Carteret had been most unfairly and most unjustly treated by Walpole; yet when Walpole had fallen and the triumphant majority of his enemies were using means fair and unfair to prove him guilty of illegal practices, it was Carteret who opposed an unjust bill

---

[1] But first to Carteret fain you'd sing ,
   Indeed he's nearest to the King,
     Yet careless how you use him .
   Give him, I beg, no labour'd lays,
   He will not promise if you praise,
     And laugh if you abuse him '—*Political Ballad of* 1742.

[2] *Parliamentary History* XVI 1 097 Nov 22 1770

which the Commons had passed against the late minister, and led the Lords in rejecting it. And Carteret was as faithful to his friends as he was placable to his enemies. When his early patron, Sunderland, died in 1722, it was rumoured that the French Regent Orleans had in conversation accused Sunderland of intriguing with the Jacobites. Carteret, whose health had suffered through Sunderland's death, wrote to his friend Schaub at Paris, asking for an explanation of this very ridiculous charge. In a letter which was not meant for show, for it was marked, 'very secret; burn this,' Carteret said. 'I will sooner die than give up my friend's character, which I will contend for to the hazard of everything.'[1]

Beyond his humour and his good-humour, Carteret had in public life high spirit and infinite courage. He was not a degenerate descendant of the Sir Philip Carterets and the Sir Richard Grenvilles. 'The Granville blood has too much fire in it to bear stewing!' wrote his daughter, Countess Cowper, once after a visit to an unwholesomely heated house. Carteret's brilliant boldness was naturally the characteristic which most impressed the average observer in his own day, for it made him stand out in strong relief from the plodding commonplace of Walpoles, Pelhams, Hardwickes, and Harringtons. But his daring and spirit were not at all what they have too often been misrepresented to be. By bitter political opponents in the later years of his own life, and often by more modern writers who, if they had taken the trouble to look at what Carteret himself has written, could hardly have made the mistake. Carteret has been confidently described as a man of erratic, dashing, foolishly daring audacity. In the dimly veiled nomenclature of the political pamphlets of

---

[1] Brit. Mus. Sloane MSS. 4,204, fol. 67, 68.

the time, while Newcastle is Bubble-Boy and Walpole
is Bob Bronze. Carteret, John Bull's steward, is Jack
Headlong.   But Carteret's fearlessness in politics rested
on his unrivalled political knowledge, and was altogether
different from the wild daring of the adventurer who
is bold only because he is ignorant.   Carteret always
knew what he wanted, and was perfectly content to
take the every-day method of obtaining it; but if every-
day methods failed, he was not afraid to meet unusual
difficulties with unusual spirit   When in his northern
negotiations as English mediator he accepted, on his own
responsibility, Prussian and Danish treaties with Sweden
which the Prussian and Danish ministers were afraid to
put their hands to, he was undoubtedly bold, but he
was not rash.   He did it only after the most patient
painstaking and long continued laborious endeavour;
and he expressly said that he disliked the bold strokes
which, however, he was not afraid to make   Bold
action which is the result of mature consideration and
perfect acquaintance with the facts of a case has no
connection with impetuous recklessness.   When in the
continental war Carteret proposed schemes which the
other ministers rejected as wildly daring, it was because
long study and varied experience had made him a
master of European politics, while his colleagues knew
little more than the rudiments of the science.   But
misrepresentation is the easiest of all political arts, and
nothing was simpler than to assert over and over again
that Carteret's plans were all mere audacity and foolish
daring.   This has become the stale commonplace of
every political reference that may occasionally be made
to him; till it is almost as tiresome to be told that
Carteret was reckless as it is to be told that Hooker
was judicious   At the same time, it is a little curious

and not quite easily reconcilable with this facile criticism
to note that a special characteristic of this reckless
statesman was his extraordinary devotion to work, and
his patient persistence in all the business that came
before him.   He was always willing to take pains   'I
have a working brain,' he once wrote from Stockholm
in the thick of the diplomatic stupidities which wearisomely interrupted his complicated negotiations.   When
he went to Holland in 1742 to try to rouse the phlegmatic Dutch from their lethargy, he told the functionaries who represented to him all the difficulties which he
would encounter, that he held the principle that nothing
in the world was impossible, and that his own experience
had taught him that persevering steadfastness in this
principle was the way to success.   This is hardly the
note of recklessness

Persistent misrepresentation was one of the difficulties which Carteret, like other statesmen, had to struggle
against; but he does not seem personally to have cared
much about it   While he undoubtedly had political
ambition, he was quite careless about political popularity in his own day.   His political ambition was of
the kind which he had vainly endeavoured to instill into
Henry Fox.   The vulgar and merely insular ambitions
of politics had no attraction for him, and many of the
checks which he met with in his career were due to
his contemptuous neglect of the usual political methods
of his day.   Winnington once found Carteret reading
Demosthenes, and told him he was working for his own
ruin   The *Court Almanack*, said Winnington, was the
book which Carteret should have been studying   Indifferent to popularity, he was careless of the usual
means of gaining it.   It is easy to sympathise with and
appreciate his conduct in this matter; but from the

point of view of his own political aims, his scornful
carelessness was often injudicious and certainly injurious
to him. It greatly weakened his power in parliament.
It was very natural that a man of genius should slight
and despise Newcastle; but Newcastle was a great
parliamentary force, and Carteret treated him with
neglectful contempt How much more prudent to have
managed Newcastle as Pitt managed him afterwards,
keeping the real mastery in his own hands, while allowing the Duke to revel in his own congenial department!
It might have been more difficult for Carteret than for
Pitt to do this; but it was Carteret's own maxim that
nothing was impossible. Newcastle in his unmeaning
way said that Carteret was a man who never doubted.
He never doubted that Newcastle was a fool; and imprudently he did not care to conceal what he thought.
Small personal neglects irritated colleagues who were
already sufficiently inclined to be jealous; and Carteret's
carelessness of everything but the strictly political side
of politics did not attract to his support the rather
numerous parliamentary persons for whom politics were
chiefly a matter of social self-interest. Regardless of
ceremonial decorations himself, he cared nothing who
had this Garter or that green ribband. His contemptuous indifference weakened him, for it drove important
nobodies to other ministers who would condescend to
listen to them; and Newcastle, whose element this
thoroughly was, unfortunately was not Carteret's friend.

The whole herd of preferment hunters found it useless to apply to Carteret He simply took no notice
of them. Two instances illustrate his not unnatural
but fatally imprudent indifference In September 1742
the Duchess of Portland writes to Mrs. Delany's sister,
Anne Granville

'I went the Sunday before I came out of town to the Arch-Dragon [Countess Granville, Carteret's mother] by appointment, to know of her whether the report of our friend's promotion was to be depended on ; and after flattering her pretty sufficiently she told me she knew nothing of the matter, that she believed there was nothing in it, and that her son was never interested in anybody's business, his whole mind being taken up in doing good to the nation, and till the French was drove out of Germany, and Prague was taken, he could not think of such a bagatelle as that ' [1] Carteret was perfectly impartial in his indifference ; for the preferment desired on this occasion was for a relation of his own.

Horace Walpole is the chronicler of the second instance. When Granville became President of the Council in 1751, Lord Chief Justice Willes was congratulated on the return of his friend to Court Willes replied :—

'He my friend ? He is nobody's friend. I will give you a proof Sir Robert Walpole had promised me to make my friend Clive one of the King's Council, but too late! I asked him to request it of Mr Pelham, who promised but did not perform. When Lord Granville was in the height of his power, I one day said to him, My Lord, you are going to the King ; do ask him to make poor Clive one of his Council. He replied, What is it to me who is a judge or who a bishop? It is my business to make Kings and Emperors, and to maintain the balance of Europe. Willes replied, Then they who want to be bishops and judges will apply to those who will submit to make it their business ' [2]

Carteret even damaged his own private circumstances by his too contemptuous neglect of his own

[1] Mrs Delany, *Autobiography and Correspondence*, II 195.
[2] H. Walpole's *Last Ten Years of George II*, I 146, 147

personal advantage   Scornful of money in public life, he was carelessly indifferent to it in private.   Shelburne gives a curious and perhaps somewhat exaggerated illustration of Carteret's blameworthy imprudence :—

'Both he [Carteret] and Sir Robert Walpole were above money, particularly the former.   Lord Carteret was more careless than extravagant   When his daughter Lady Georgiana was going to be married to Mr. Spencer, much against the inclination of Sarah, Duchess of Marlborough—with whom he had been in great favour, but had lost it on some political account—he suffered the day to be fixed for signing the settlements and solemnising the marriage without any thought how he was to pay her fortune.   His family, knowing that he had not the money, was under vast uneasiness as the day approached, and as far as they could venture, reminded him of it, to no purpose, till the very day before, Sir Robert Worsley, Lady Carteret's father, came to him, and, speaking of the marriage, said he hoped he was prepared with Lady Georgiana's fortune, because he knew the Duchess of Marlborough's violence and her aversion to the marriage.   He said undoubtedly that it could not be supposed that he was unprepared. "Because if you are," says Sir Robert Worsley, "I have 5,000*l.* at my bankers, with which I can accommodate you"   He said, "Can you really?   If so, I shall be much obliged to you, for, to say the truth, I have not a hundred pounds towards it."   At one time he had an execution in his house, brought by a coal-merchant to whom he owed two thousand pounds   His coach, etc , was stopped   As soon as it was taken off, he saw a man in the hall whose face he did not recollect.   It was the merchant   He went up to him made a very

gracious bow, and the man served him to the day of
his death'

While Carteret, regardless of party or private considerations, was thinking of the politics of Europe, the
Pelhams were thinking of the politics of the Cockpit
The Pelhams were wise from their own small point of
view, while Carteret's conduct was doubly imprudent,
for his strength in the House of Commons was small,
apart from the assistance which the Pelhams might be
willing to give him.   For, over and above the weakness
which he might have avoided if he had condescended
to the usual arts of parliamentary management, if, as
Winnington said, he had studied parliament more and
Demosthenes less, Carteret had in the course of his long
career disadvantages in parliament for which he was in
no way personally responsible   He had never sat in
the House of Commons, and in the reign of George II.
the House of Lords was no longer the clearly superior
House, as it had been when Carteret first entered parliament   He had also suffered serious losses near the
beginning of his public life by the deaths of his
two friends Stanhope and Sunderland, his introducers
to active political work   These losses left Carteret, a
young man of thirty, with very little but his own genius
to help him, exposed to the jealous political enmity of
the masterful minister who kept himself at the head of
English affairs for twenty years   There is no need to
seek for or to invent explanations of Walpole's lifelong
opposition to Carteret   Friends and enemies alike
recognised that Carteret was a man of indisputable
genius, of very great political ability, and of high-spirited
independence and individuality.   That was quite enough
to make it impossible that he and Walpole should long
act together   Careless and indifferent about most things

else, Walpole was terribly in earnest whenever it was a question of his own undivided personal power. It is not surprising that a man who quarrelled about political influence with a respectable mediocrity like Townshend found it absolutely necessary to free himself from colleagues like Pulteney and Carteret. The striking thing, in itself a very strong proof of the force of Carteret's character and of his pre-eminence in politics, is the fact that for nearly half of Walpole's long rule, from 1721 to 1730, Carteret was actually a member of Walpole's Cabinet. Walpole could only get rid of Carteret after an unremitting struggle of nearly ten years.

Parliamentary disadvantages continued to accompany Carteret when he himself succeeded to Walpole's power. It was a time of general war, which had been commenced and, as far as England's part in it was concerned, hopelessly mismanaged before Carteret became minister; and, though he did all that one man could do, he was thwarted by jealous colleagues who shared neither his genius nor his knowledge His ministry was divided and a compromise, the Whig party was in antagonistic sections. Absorbed by the war, involved in foreign negotiations, much absent from England, Carteret left the management of home and domestic affairs too much to ministers who were delighted to plot against him undisturbed by his presence. He was practically Prime Minister and Foreign Minister; it was not only natural but essential that during his most anxious period of power he should be mainly occupied with foreign affairs. Unfortunately this allowed to treacherous colleagues almost unrestricted scope for intrigue and easy opportunity for unbounded public misrepresentation. Carteret was prolonging the war for the sake of his own ambition, for the sake of

Hanover; to gain the personal favour of the King; for a hundred other reasons as perfectly false as these. When one considers the small hold which Carteret had on parliamentary support, the jealous intrigues of his colleagues from the very beginning of his career, his own careless neglect which naturally offended the self-esteem of persons in important situations, and his complete indifference to personal popularity, it is not strange that the shoal of his enemies—his political enemies, for he had no private ones—at times triumphed over him, and made his political career a somewhat chequered one

But Carteret had other resources than politics Unlike Walpole, who, his son Horace says, 'loved not reading nor writing,' Carteret was a highly educated scholar and an instructed lover of literature. On the political side his knowledge was very great and undisputed. He was intimately acquainted with the public law of Europe and the internal laws of the various European countries. The intricacies of the constitution of the Empire were no mystery to him His knowledge of European history was equally profound, extending even to obscure points usually left with cheerfulness to the monopoly of the professional historian. Harte, author of the life of Gustavus Adolphus, wrote in his preface, after Carteret's death: 'It was my good fortune or prudence to keep the main body of my army (or in other words my matters of fact) safe and entire The late Earl of Granville was pleased to declare himself of this opinion; especially when he found that I had made Chemnitius one of my principal guides; for his Lordship was apprehensive I might not have seen that valuable and authentic book, which is extremely scarce. I thought myself happy to have contented his Lordship even in the lowest degree; for he understood the German and Swedish histories to the highest perfection.' On the more strictly literary side Carteret had an extraordinary acquaintance with languages, literatures, and philosophy It was of no consequence to him in what language the foreign ministers might choose to send their despatches, or in what language he himself might reply to them As Horace Walpole called him 'master of all modern politics,' so Chesterfield called him 'master of all the modern languages' French or Italian, Spanish or Portuguese, German or Swedish; it was indifferent to him which he wrote and which he spoke He even turned his attention to the Sclavonian languages and literatures. With the classical languages he also had an easy familiarity. Swift, whom Carteret himself once silenced with a quotation from Virgil, with grave irony says of him that he had a 'fatal turn of mind toward heathenish and outlandish books and languages . . It is known, and can be proved upon him, that Greek and Latin books might be found every day in his dressing-room, if it were carefully searched. . . I am likewise assured that he has been taken in the very fact of reading the said books, even in the midst of a session, to the great neglect of public affairs. . . . I have it from good hands, that when his Excellency is at dinner with one or two scholars at his elbows, he grows a most insupportable and unintelligible companion to all the fine gentlemen round the table. . . I am credibly informed he will, as I have already hinted, in the middle of a session quote passages out of Plato and Pindar at his own table to some book-learned companion, without blushing, even when persons of great stations are by.'[1]

Carteret's reputation as a Greek scholar was espe-

[1] Swift Works VII 285-301

cially high He had taken his love of Greek with him
from Oxford to Denmark and to Ireland, and he kept it
throughout his life, quoting Homer on his death-bed
He wrote of his son to Swift: 'I tell him, study Greek,
καὶ οὐδὲν οὐδέποτε ταπεινὸν ἐνθυμηθήσῃ οὔτε ἄγαν ἐπι-
θυμήσεις τινός. He knows how to construe this, and I
have the satisfaction to believe he will fall into the
sentiment, and then, if he makes no figure, he will yet
be a happy man'[1] Homer and Demosthenes were
Carteret's two favourite Greek authors An *Enquiry
into the Life and Writings of Homer*, which appeared in
London in 1735 was assumed, though incorrectly, to
be his. In 1732 he encouraged his friend Bentley to
undertake an edition of Homer which Bentley had
meditated six years before. Carteret personally assisted
by borrowing for Bentley all the manuscripts which he
was able to procure, some of them from his old Christ
Church friend, Mr Harley, now second Earl of Oxford
Carteret wrote to Oxford in August 1732 :—

'Having heard that your lordship has several curious
manuscripts of Homer, I take the liberty to acquaint
you that Dr Bentley has lately revised the whole works
of Homer, which are now ready for the press, with his
notes, some of which I have seen, and are very curious;
and he desires leave to collate your manuscripts upon
some suspected verses in our present editions If your
lordship will be pleased to let the Doctor have the manuscripts for a short time for that purpose, I shall be
obliged to you I have set the Doctor at work, and
would be glad to procure such assistance as he desires,
that he may have no excuse not to proceed If your
lordship has no objection to this request, you will let
him have the manuscripts to be perused at Cambridge,

[1] Swift, *Works*, XIX 50 March 24, 1737

upon his application to you. I desire the honour of an answer, that I may acquaint the Doctor with it. As you are a known encourager of learning, and learned yourself, I hope this request will not be disagreeable to you'

And again in March 1733 :—

'I thank your lordship for your great goodness in sending me the eleven manuscripts of Homer and relating to him, and for your permitting me to send them to Dr. Bentley. I shall take his receipt for you, and I am persuaded he will take great care of them ; they shall be returned to your lordship with thanks and honourable mention of you.'[1]

Of Carteret and Bentley—whose Homer was never published—there is a curious anecdote :—

'Dr. Bentley, when he came to town, was accustomed, in his visits to Lord Carteret, sometimes to spend the evenings with his lordship. One day old Lady Granville reproached her son with keeping the country clergyman who was with him the night before till he was intoxicated Lord Carteret denied the charge ; upon which the lady replied that the clergyman could not have sung in so ridiculous a manner unless he had been in liquor The truth of the case was, that the singing thus mistaken by her ladyship was Dr. Bentley's endeavour to instruct and entertain his noble friend by reciting Terence according to the true cantilenga of the ancients.'[2]

Of a less-known scholar than Bentley, Dr. John Taylor, commonly called Demosthenes Taylor, Carteret was the special patron. Taylor—who is vaguely remembered as 'the most silent man, the merest statue of a man,' whom Johnson ever met, the man who, dining once in Johnson's company, distinguished himself by

uttering in the course of the dinner the one word
' Richard '—produced an edition of Demosthenes ; and
Carteret, who had specially studied that author and had
much of him by heart, helped Taylor in his work with
books and abundant counsel   Taylor was particularly
sorry that he could not use for his book some of the
manuscripts in the Royal Library at Vienna.   Carteret
applied to Maria Theresa, for whom he had done so
much, and got Taylor what he wanted.   He gave Taylor
other practical help.   In 1757 he secured for him the
Residentiaryship of St. Paul's.   When Carteret asked
the King for this, George demurred.   He had never, he
said, heard of Taylor, the preferment was a valuable
one, and should be given to a scholar of reputation.
With quiet quickness Carteret replied that Taylor's
scholarship was famous throughout Germany.   There
was no need to say more to George II

Taylor was entrusted by Carteret with the education
of his grandsons, Lord Weymouth and the Hon. Henry
Frederick Thynne.   Carteret himself laid down the
plan and methods of their education, with complete
remembrance, says Taylor, of the answer of the old
Greek, who, when asked what he desired his children to be taught, replied, ταῦτ', εἶπεν, οἷς καὶ ἄνδρες
γενόμενοι χρήσονται.

Demosthenes was the subject of a German letter
written by Carteret to a clerical friend of literary tastes.
That an English politician of the nineteenth century
should write to his friends in German would call for no
special notice ; but in 1736 things were different   The
King of England was a German, but German was an
unknown language to his English subjects   Carteret
was the only Englishman who could speak German with
the King , it may safely be stated that no leading

Enghsh statesman except Carteret could have read six consecutive words of German. A German letter of Carteret's may therefore be quoted, if for no other reason than that Carteret was the only prominent Enghsh politician who could have written one. In 1736, and in the orthography of the day, Carteret wrote to the Rev. Mr. Wetstem, rector of Helmingham, Ipswich :—

'LIEBER VON HELMINGHAM,—Die schöne ubersetzung von Griechischer beredsamkeit, so er mir geschict hat, erfordert von mir alle ersinnliche erkentlichkeit. Ich sehe mit verwunderung der Alten spur, und dass Teutsch so von Ihrem feder fliesset, der weitlaufigen und gewaltigen Griechischen Schriebart sehr nahe kommt. Es ist gewiss dass der Redner hat nicht so viel verlohren als in der Francosischen ubersetzung Tourreil war ein gelehrter und geschichter man. Er verstunde, wie seine anmerkungen bezeugen, dess Redners innerste meinung, aber die Francosische sprache ist allzu schwach und unterliegt, wan Demostenis wichtige und strahlende gedancken mit durchdringender macht fortkommen solten. Ich sehe und fuhle dass ihr Teutsch ist fahig, das alte Griechische feuer anzuzunden, welches in die andern ubersetzungen so Ich gesehen habe ist gantz ausgeloscht Ich wunsche ihnen alles gluck in dieser ehrlichen bemuhung, und bitte erlaubniss meinen brief mit einer Schweitzerischen wahrsagung zu enden, welche Ich in Schweitzerischen gedicten gelesen habe—

> Die Tugend wird du selber geben
> Was gutes Ich du wunschen kan

'Ich verbleibe, Ihr Eyfriger Schuler und Diener,
'CARTERET.' [1]

[1] Brit Mus Add MSS. 32415 fol 341 April 14 1736

However much engrossed he might be in public affairs, Carteret always had time for the claims of learning and literature :—

> Who that can hear him, and on business, speak,
> Would dream he lunch'd with Bentley upon Greek,
> And will to-night with Hutcheson regale on
> The feast of Reason in the tough To Kalon ?[1]

In the midst of his Swedish negotiations he visited Upsala University, and delighted in the society of its learned men   They also were delighted with him, and Carteret kept up pleasant relations with them and their University in later years.   While harassed in Dublin by the unhappy coinage scheme, he took considerable trouble to find out the moral philosopher Hutcheson, whose anonymously published *Inquiry into the Original of our Ideas of Beauty and Virtue* had interested him. Carteret astonished Hutcheson by his acquaintance with philosophical thought as much as he delighted him by the intimacy of his friendship.   Indeed, to have anything like a tincture of scholarship or literature was sufficient to gain Carteret's favour   Many a struggling writer received from him not merely empty and easy patronage, but effective help   His treatment of an obscure writer, one Cleland, son of the Colonel Cleland who sat for the Will Honeycomb of the *Spectator*, is thoroughly characteristic of Carteret   Cleland. not the most respectable of characters, found himself in trouble before the Privy Council for the nature of one of his publications   He pleaded poverty, and the truth of his plea was painfully evident.   Carteret, when Cleland promised never again to have anything to do with literary ventures of that doubtful kind, obtained him a pension

---

[1] Lord Lytton's *St. Stephen's*

of a hundred a year; on which the unfortunate man afterwards mainly lived, doing miscellaneous writing, and faithfully keeping his promise.

The names of many of those who in their day were grateful for Carteret's assistance have long since been forgotten by posterity. The glimpses to be obtained of Carteret's connection with literary names not likely to pass into such rapid oblivion are tantalisingly superficial. There is no positive evidence that Carteret knew Voltaire; but it is probable that they had met, for Voltaire was in England from May 1726 till the early months of 1729, and Carteret was in London every year of his Irish Lord-Lieutenancy. Swift also was in London in 1726 and 1727; and it is not likely that Swift would have left Voltaire and Carteret unknown to each other. Voltaire got his *Henriade* printed in London in a very cheerful pecuniary manner, and sent an early copy of it to Carteret in Dublin. 'I sent the other day a cargo of French dulness to my Lord-Lieutenant,' Voltaire wrote to Swift in 1727. No doubt he knew the man to whom he sent his superlative epic. With the early work of another young author Carteret was also acquainted. In 1761, Gibbon, then aged twenty-four, published his French *Essai sur l'Etude de la Littérature*. Mallet wrote to Gibbon in June 1761. 'I found Lord Granville reading you, after ten at night. His single approbation, which he assures you of, will go for more than that of a hundred other readers.' Addison was another of Carteret's friends, though Carteret was not yet thirty when in 1719 Addison died. From Stockholm, Carteret wrote home to Craggs in December of that year. 'I had so true a friendship for Mr Addison, and shall always retain so great respect for his memory, that I shall do my best to procure subscriptions for his Works, not only from Her Majesty and the Prince, but from the most distinguished persons in Sweden.' Gay, too, had pleasant intercourse with Carteret The *Beggar's Opera* had been produced in 1728 in London, and Carteret and Swift had enjoyed it in Dublin. 'We have your opera for sixpence,' Swift wrote to Gay, 'and we are as full of it *pro modulo nostro* as London can be, continually acting, and house crammed, and the Lord-Lieutenant several times there laughing his heart out.'[1] When Carteret's Lord-Lieutenancy was over, he became personally acquainted with Gay. From Amesbury, the seat of the Duke and Duchess of Queensberry, Gay wrote to Swift:—

'Lord Carteret was here yesterday, in his return from the Isle of Wight, where he had been a-shooting, and left seven pheasants with us He went this morning to the Bath, to Lady Carteret, who is perfectly recovered He talked of you three hours last night, and told me that you talk of me. I mean, that you are prodigiously in his favour, as he says . . . . He seemed to take to me, which may proceed from your recommendation, though, indeed, there is another reason for it, for he is now out of employment, and my friends have been generally of that sort, for I take to them, as being naturally inclined to those who can do no mischief.'[2]

Pope also was remembered in the conversations between Carteret and Swift in Dublin No details remain of the intimacy between Carteret and Pope; foolish anecdote poorly fills up the blank by trying to believe that they once passed a whole evening to-

[1] Elwin's *Pope*, VII. 125. March 28, 1723.
[2] Swift. *Works* XVII. 315. 316. Nov 7 1730

gether in debating whether one should say Cicero or
Kikero :—

> To sound or sink in *Cano*, O or A,
> Or give up Cicero to C or K [1]

But Carteret's greatest friend was Swift himself.
Their early intimacy and the renewal of their friendship
in Ireland have already been sufficiently dwelt upon
They never saw each other again after Carteret left
Dublin in 1730, for Swift, though invitations from the
Carterets were not wanting, never revisited England
after the death of Stella The friendship thenceforth
was continued by correspondence, of which the existing
printed part is probably only a very meagre portion.
In 1734 Carteret wrote to Swift :—

'I had the honour of your letter, which gave me a
considerable pleasure to see that I am not so much out
of your thoughts, but that you can take notice of events
that happen in my family I need not say that these
alliances [the marriages of his daughters] are very
agreeable to me, but that they are so to my friends
adds much to the satisfaction I receive from them
They certainly enable me to contract my desires, which
is no inconsiderable step towards being happy As
to other things, I go on as well as I can ; and now
and then observe that I have more friends now than I
had when I was in a situation to do them service This
may be a delusion; however, it is a pleasing one. And
I have more reason to believe a man, now I can do him
no good, than I had when I could do him favours,
which the greatest philosophers are sometimes tempted
to solicit their friends about   Lady Worsley. my
wife, and daughters, to whom I have shown your letter,

not forgetting my mother, present their humble service to you. And I desire to recommend the whole family, as well as myself, to the continuance of your favour.'[1]

Again in 1735 —

'I thank you for taking notice of the prosperous events that have happened to my family. If alliance and the thoughts of prosperity can bind a man to the interest of his country, I am certainly bound to stand by liberty; and when you see me forgetful of that, may you treat me like Traulus and Pistorides.[2] I am impatient for four volumes, said to be your works, for which my wife and I have subscribed; and we expected a dozen of copies from Mr. Tickell last packet. I intend these works shall be the first foundation of the libraries of my three grandsons. In the meantime they will be studied by my son and sons-in-law. . . . Sir, that you may enjoy the continuance of all happiness is my wish; as for futurity, I know your name will be remembered, when the names of Kings, Lord-Lieutenants, Archbishops, and parliament politicians will be forgotten; at last, you yourself must fall into oblivion, which may happen in less than a thousand years, though the term may be uncertain, and will depend on the progress that barbarity and ignorance may make, notwithstanding the sedulous endeavours to the contrary of the great prelates in this and succeeding ages My wife, my mother, my mother-in-law, my etc , etc., etc. all join with me in good wishes to you.'[3]

Once more, two years later:—

' Your late Lord-Lieutenant [Duke of Dorset] told

---

[1] Swift, *Works*, XVIII. 208, 209. April 13, 1734
[2] Lord Allen and Rich Tighe, whom Swift had satirised while Carteret was Lord-Lieutenant.
[3] Swift, *Works*, XVII. 277-279 March 6, 1735

me, some time ago, he thought he was not in your favour. I told him I was of that opinion, and showed him the article of your letter relating to himself. I believe I did wrong; not that you care a farthing for Princes or ministers, but because it was vanity in me to produce your acknowledgments to me for providing for people of learning, some of which I had the honour to promote at your desire, for which I still think myself obliged to you. And I have not heard that since they have disturbed the peace of the kingdom, or been Jacobites, in disgrace to you and me.

'I desire you will make my sincere respects acceptable to Mr Delany. He sent me potted woodcocks in perfection, which Lady Granville, my wife and children, have eat; though I have not yet answered his letter My Lady Granville, reading your postscript, bids me tell you that she will send you a present; and if she knew what you liked, she would do it forthwith. Let me know, and it shall be done, that the first of the family may no longer be postponed by you to the third place. My wife and Lady Worsley desire their respects should be mentioned to you rhetorically; but as I am a plain peer, I shall say nothing but that

'I am, for ever, Sir,

'Your most humble and obedient servant,

'CARTERET'[1]

It is hardly possible that a really satisfactory life of Carteret should ever now be written. It is more than a hundred and twenty years since he died, after an active political life that extended over more than half a century; but he found no Boswell among his own contemporaries, and, with a really curious indifference to the brilliancy of his political career and to the charm of

[1] Swift Works XIX 50 51. March 21 17

his personal gifts and character, posterity has been content to drop him from its memory. Not quite so entirely, indeed, as it has dropped its unrememberable Hardwickes and Harringtons, in an uneasy sort of way posterity sometimes vaguely wonders why it does not know more of Carteret. But this merely nominal and unintelligent remembrance has itself been a misfortune. For if the man of genius was not to be remembered with true and full knowledge, it was a double wrong that an unintelligible and impossible figure should be set up to play fantastic tricks in the records of English history, and that this should gravely be declared to be the figure of Lord Carteret. For the Lord Carteret of the English historian is a fantastic impossibility. At once a great statesman and a mere bombastic fanatic ; a great genius and an insincere trifler ; an unrivalled scholar and a frivolous *farceur* and consumer of Burgundy ; a despiser of stars and places and money, and a selfish place-hunter, content that the country should go to ruin if only he might cling to office. That figure is in a word incredible and impossible. It may not now, after so long a lapse of time, be possible to substitute a completely satisfactory portrait in place of the absurdly exaggerated and distorted one. But at least it is possible to look without prejudice at the not inconsiderable body of first-hand evidence which remains, and to refuse credence to most of the facile and self-contradicting criticism of the many writers who, after all, on this subject are not many voices, but only many echoes. Carteret suffered enough from self-interested misrepresentation during his own lifetime. No one can have any interest in misknowing him now ; no one now can find any profit or satisfaction in blaming or praising him unduly. Posterity's sole interest in him, if it has any

interest at all, is simply to know what his career and
character really were; to extricate them from the
chaotic contradictions of political partisanship, as well as
from the easy negligence and echoing repetitions of
writers who would not knowingly misrepresent, but who
have not cared to examine at first-hand for themselves.
Let it be granted that Carteret had faults and committed
mistakes; he paid dearly enough for them in his own
lifetime, and they were hardly of the kind to merit the
reproof of posterity He made the mistake of despising
political jobbery, of refusing to flatter influential imbecility, of scornfully neglecting the greedy crowd of
place-hunters and pensioners and fawning flatterers,
who thronged a corrupt Court and revelled in a corrupt
society Carteret neglected all that; and in the days of
George II. it was impossible to neglect it with impunity.
He paid for it in his own lifetime by seeing power fall
to those who would take the mean and customary ways
of obtaining it It is a pity that he should continue to
pay for it still. The motto of the noble house of which
Carteret was the most distinguished member must itself
appeal to the inquirer who ventures to examine Carteret's career for himself; for his examination will not
have led him far before he discovers that to know what
can be known and to tell what can be told of such
a statesman and genius as Carteret is indeed *Loyal
Devoir*.

INDEX.

———•>•———

PRINTED BY
SPOTTISWOODE AND CO. NEW-STREET SQUARE
LONDON

1926

Lightning Source UK Ltd.
Milton Keynes UK
UKOW05f1808021115

261951UK00004B/229/P